THE AMERICAN CONVENTION ON HUMAN RIGHTS

THE AMERICAN CONVENTION ON HUMAN RIGHTS

Crucial Rights and Their Theory and Practice

Cecilia MEDINA

2nd edition

intersentia
Cambridge – Antwerp – Portland

Intersentia Ltd
Sheraton House | Castle Park
Cambridge | CB3 0AX | United Kingdom
Tel.: +44 1223 370 170 | Fax: +44 1223 370 169
Email: mail@intersentia.co.uk
www.intersentia.com | www.intersentia.co.uk

Distribution for the UK and Ireland:
NBN International
Airport Business Centre, 10 Thornbury Road
Plymouth, PL6 7 PP
United Kingdom
Tel.: +44 1752 202 301 | Fax: +44 1752 202 331
Email: orders@nbninternational.com

Distribution for Europe and all other countries:
Intersentia Publishing nv
Groenstraat 31
2640 Mortsel
Belgium
Tel.: +32 3 680 15 50 | Fax: +32 3 658 71 21
Email: mail@intersentia.be

Distribution for the USA and Canada:
International Specialized Book Services
920 NE 58th Ave. Suite 300
Portland, OR 97213
USA
Tel.: +1 800 944 6190 (toll free) | Fax: +1 503 280 8832
Email: info@isbs.com

The American Convention on Human Rights (2nd edition). Crucial Rights and Their Theory and Practice

ISBN 978-1-78068-321-8
D/2016/7949/7
NUR 820

British Library Cataloguing in Publication Data. A catalogue record for this book is available from the British Library.

To Pablo, Amalia Matilde, Anaïs and Max,
and to the memory of Jerónimo

PREFACE

The first English edition of this book on the American Convention on Human Rights advanced the idea that a second edition would show the Court on its way towards maturity. This is indeed the case; the Court has developed greatly and its case law has been affirmed in many respects. In addition, my idea when I started to work on the case law of the Court was that the egregious violations of human rights seen in the first cases would dwindle to give way to new case law addressing problems of democratic societies. In that prediction, I was wrong. I did not take sufficient account of the delay the Inter-American Commission on Human Rights had in processing cases and of the fact that a systematic effort would be made to attempt to clear the significant backlog. From 2004 to 2014 – the period of case law covered in this edition – the Commission has sent a considerable number of cases to the Court concerning facts that occurred in the 1980s and 1990s, many of them massacres or disappearances. This means that systematic and gross violations have been a significant part of the Court's work despite the change in political and social circumstances in the region.

This second edition is not merely an update on the jurisprudence. As I mentioned in the first edition, I suspended my writing when I was elected to the Court, as I believed my approach to the analyses of the Convention and the Court's jurisprudence would probably be changed by this experience. The knowledge I acquired in the law of the different States under the jurisdiction of the Court, the many social and cultural problems on the continent, and my experience of the different approaches that were necessary to build a good relationship with the States while at the same time maintaining independence, needed some time to sink in. Only after it had settled in did a review of what I wrote in the first edition seem sensible. I believe I was right about this. Certain subjects began to emerge as being more significant than before and so they had to be explored and developed further. Moreover, there is a further reason why merely updating the first edition would not have been adequate. In this regional system for the protection of human rights, political factors are always present. When I look back to the State Parties as they were at the beginning of my term and later at the end of it, I cannot ignore the major changes they underwent. The Court grew at that time and this must be taken into account. The first edition shows the Court handling cases during periods of non-democratic States or States that had recently been able to do away with dictatorships. The jurisprudence of that time reflects this and it is with that perspective in mind that the judgments should be read: a Court struggling to make of the American Convention an instrument that would start improving the human rights situation of those living in the American continent in hostile environments. However, from 2004 to 2014 the Court adjudicated for States already in the process of accustoming themselves to international human rights law and international supervision. This period also saw an increasing number of cases reaching the Court whose legal nature reflects the problems of States already embarking on the process towards democracy. They deal not only with deprivation of lives, or torture, or arbitrary deprivation of life during dictatorships, but also with *inter alia* freedom of speech, structural discrimination, and the lack of proper protection for women's human rights and for persons due to their sexual orientation. Cases involving alleged violations of torture or ill-treatment and of personal freedom continue to come in, but not in the framework of a situation of generalized gross, systematic violations; instead, they mainly arise from remaining practices of badly trained police forces and judiciary.

My experience in the Court as a judge from 2004 to 2009 reaffirmed my belief that the American Convention, although written along the same lines as the European Convention, does not completely resemble it: the reality of life on the American continent shows through in many provisions. Europe and its Council of Ministers belonged to a group of States that were determined to eradicate Nazism from their lands and promote respect for human rights. Latin America wrote the American Convention, I believe, with the hope that if they wrote the words and placed them in a treaty, there would be a chance for human rights to become important and respected at some future point in time. There is an old saying from colonial times that guided the Spanish conquistadors when carrying out the king's orders: one respects the order but does not comply with it (*se acata, pero no se cumple*). This position, much attenuated, still remains today. There was a glimpse of this when the Inter-American Commission on Human Rights (the Commission or IACHR) was created in 1959. A resolution of a Meeting of Ministers of Foreign Affairs established the Commission; however, the Meeting had in principle no power to create organs of the Organization of American States (OAS), a problem they circumvented by deciding the organ would be a *sui generis* entity. Some countries opposed this initiative because "to create an organ to promote the rights before respect of these rights became a precise and clear obligation" would be illogical.[1] Among the defenders of the setting up of this organ was the delegate of Venezuela. He did not resort to legal or technical arguments but to what he thought was the appropriate approach, asserting that, leaving legality aside, "there is [in America] a democratic surge which must be put to use to strengthen everything that serves the purpose of

1 The most coherent opposition came from the delegate from Uruguay, quoted in C. Medina, *The Battle of Human Rights. Gross, Systematic Violations and the Inter-American System*, Martinus Nijhoff Publishers, Dordrecht/Boston/London, 1988, pp. 67–68.

making human rights to be respected". The Honduran delegate added his vote "because it means a voice of encouragement to American democracy".[2] This has been the spirit of the system.

The fact of life that a written legal provision would not necessarily be complied with and that there would probably be obstacles placed in the way of victims wishing to avail themselves of the system made the drafters of the Convention take some precautions to limit that possibility, and it is these precautions that made the American Convention unique. The Commission and the Court, making use of their powers to interpret the Convention and to decide on their Rules of Procedure, developed the sometimes scant provisions in the Convention with regard to the functions of both organs. They aimed at making the Convention adequate for the sorts of cases that they would have to deal with, while also taking into account the volatile political situation in many countries. One precaution is the admittance of an *actio popularis* to start cases before the Commission. It was expected that disappeared individuals, those subject to prolonged arbitrary detention, or those subject to severe physical or psychological ill-treatment could not or would not start a case before the system against the State that was subjecting him or her to those severe violations. Thus, the way out was that the individual complaint could be started by the victim, a third person, a group of persons, or any non-governmental entity legally recognized in one or more Member States of the OAS,[3] with or without the victim's knowledge or consent. In its Rules of Procedure, the Commission stated that it "may also, *motu proprio*, initiate the processing of a petition which, in its view, meets the necessary requirements".[4] In the Rules of Procedure of the Court, there is the possibility of ending a case through friendly settlement, acquiescence of the responding State to a complaint, or discontinuance as a result of the petitioner's decision to withdraw his or her complaint. In spite of the clear intention of the parties to the case in all three of these situations, a provision in the Rules gives the Court the power to decide to continue the case "bearing in mind its responsibility to protect human rights".[5] There is thus the possibility of going beyond the will of the parties when the Court feels that it has not considered the protection of human rights properly. The Court will not allow any arrangement between the alleged victim and the State that could be detrimental to the scope and content of all human rights for all those under the umbrella of the inter-American system. In this sense, the Court sees its role as going beyond that of a judge deciding individual cases: it is the custodian of the public order created by the system.

As one can observe, the Commission and the Court take on a very important role in looking after individuals who certainly appear to be in a weak position

2 *Ibidem.*
3 American Convention, article 44.
4 IACtHR, Rules of Procedure 2009, Article 24.
5 IACtHR, Rules of Procedure 2009, Article 64.

with respect to the States. This attitude shows that the Court has felt the need – due to the frequent periods of dictatorships or authoritarian regimes that have plagued the continent – "to apply the Convention as creatively as possible to counter the authoritarian tendency of those who have ruled the continent and the tendency of society towards the maintenance of privileges that lead to discrimination".[6] Regardless of the continent's peculiarities, the conduct of the Court is common among international supervisory organs. There are strong reasons in the field of international human rights law to support it. Human rights treaties give the judges or other international decision-makers ample room to exercise their functions creatively. The Convention is formulated in terms of principles and general norms, which require further development in the face of new situations; the evolution of society will also require new interpretations from the Court; in this sense, interpretation is dynamic. The fact that interpretation must be *pro persona* also allows the Court to spread its wings, as it were, to make human rights available to everybody and to define the mechanism by which it operates in a manner that will help all.

The organization of this book has not been easy. The rights examined are closely interlinked. Life and integrity are sometimes analyzed together by the Court; the right to personal liberty, as set forth in the American Convention, contains aspects related to integrity and to due process; due process and the right to judicial remedy are so entwined that the Court has almost never separated them in a judgment. Furthermore, the phenomenon of disappearances touches all these rights – and this is reflected in each chapter – but yet it has an individual identity that I thought should be addressed in a chapter of its own. I hope the reader will not be confused by this new approach. In addition, as I find the social, cultural and economic situation an important element in the study of human rights, a few pages are dedicated to very briefly examining this subject.

---

6 See C. Medina Quiroga, "The Role of International Tribunals: Law-making or creative interpretation?" in Dinah Shelton (ed), *The Oxford Handbook of International Human Rights Law*, Oxford University Press, 2013, pp. 649–669.

ACKNOWLEDGMENTS

A book necessarily requires the participation of several actors, and this book is no exception. The first actor I want to thank is the University Diego Portales, which took me under its wings when I left the University of Chile. I deeply appreciate the possibility of having an academic bond at this stage of my career with a university whose work I have admired for a long time. This is not the first time that this university has welcomed me, as it also sheltered me when I returned from exile. For all this, I am grateful.

I have always had a close connection with several students and, in general, with young lawyers whom I have met during my academic life. I do not think I could have finished this book without the help and the encouragement of four of these brilliant young people who took time aside from their heavy schedules to read various versions of this book. My deepest gratitude to Claudia Sarmiento and Valeska David, outstanding former students of mine, for reading several chapters and giving me valuable comments that I have incorporated into my writing. Also, my deepest gratitude to two wonderful officers of the Inter-American Court of Human Rights with whom I worked with much pleasure for six years in my time as a judge of that tribunal, Oscar Parra and Romina Sijniensky; their comments have also constituted an improvement for my work.

I received many valuable comments from my husband, Waldo Fortin. I am grateful for these but also for his patience during the long time it took to produce this publication.

I want to thank Pascual Cortés, a former assistant at the Law School of the University of Chile, who helped me with the research of the Court's case law and did a remarkable job. He also had an important role in devising the book's thematic index.

My daughter Caroline helped me with all technical details and did the table of cases. I am very grateful for this work that takes time and precision.

A special mention to Ann-Christin Maak and Rebecca Pound, who made the process of editing so pleasant for me, and to Intersentia, which made this book possible.

CONTENTS

TABLE OF CASES

CHAPTER 1
THE COURT AND ITS CIRCUMSTANCES

1. INTRODUCTION

1. The purpose of this chapter is varied. First, I wish to offer the reader a comprehensive overview of the political and social context in which the Inter-American Court of Human Rights carries out its activities. Although human rights are universal, every region finds ways to adjust this universality as far as protection systems are concerned. In order to fulfil their role as comptrollers of States' compliance with the obligations emerging from the respective treaties, these systems need to be able to deal with different realities in the States and the culture in which the people are immersed at a given time. Second, once the Court is set within its context, this chapter will deal with several issues that form part of the basis of the Court's work which are applied to all types of cases and rights.

2. SOCIAL AND POLITICAL LANDSCAPE

2. A salient feature of Latin America in the time the system was set up was a clear inclination from the States not to comply with international legal norms. These norms had been subscribed to and ratified in the spirit of being nominally "in the club" of those States who respect and are concerned with international human rights rather than with the aim of actually applying them. The adoption of the American Declaration of the Rights and Duties of Man (American Declaration) passed almost unnoticed for 11 years.[1] In 1959, the Inter-American Commission on Human Rights[2] (IACHR or Commission) was created. Some delegates rejected the idea of a Commission since there was no Convention that would set forth State obligations in the matter of human rights. However, the majority thought that legal and technical arguments did not justify rejecting this idea. Latin America was undergoing "a democratic surge" that had to be

1 The American Declaration of the Rights and Duties of Man was adopted by the Ninth International Conference of American States, Bogotá, Colombia, 1948. Text available at: www.oas.org.

2 For a comprehensive analysis of the history of the Commission, see C. Medina Quiroga, *The Battle of Human Rights. Gross, Systematic Violations and the Inter-American System*, Martinus Nijhoff Publishers, Dordrecht/Boston/London, 1988.

put to use in order to advance the protection of human rights; furthermore, there was the conviction that to take this step would send a strong message of encouragement to Latin American democracy.[3] While 1948 was a year of rhetoric and Utopia, and 1959 saw the first attempt to make this true, 1969 was the year in which a number of these aspirations took form. The American Convention on Human Rights (ACHR, American Convention or Convention)[4] was the result of a long and arduous struggle aimed at introducing in society a democratic and more just way of life. The American Convention came to life on a continent with significant economic and social disparities, rigid class distinctions, illiteracy, and lack of health assistance for the poor, to name a few of its miseries. These flagrant violations of the essential principle of non-discrimination and of economic, social and cultural rights – in 1969 not yet widely known legal concepts but very much present in the daily lives of the poor – were not the only ones. There was in terms of civil and political rights a pervasive and perverse recurrence of dictatorships with their usual sequel of assassinations, torture and whichever other means were deemed necessary to prevent any sort of opposition to the powers they held.

The Convention created the Inter-American Court of Human Rights (IACtHR or Court)[5] in what can be seen as a strong response to dictatorships and the appalling situation of human rights in many of the Organization of American States (OAS) Member States. The Court did not start its functions in a vacuum; on the contrary, its efforts were to follow and improve the path initiated by the Commission from 1960 on, inspired mainly in the democratic ideals to which people aspired.[6] The Court could not ignore the Commission's historical imprint where the political factor played a very important role. It was imperative for the Court to find a way to deal with illegal actions, those not only incompatible with the Convention to which States were party but also with the standards set by the Commission in its application of the American Declaration and the domestic criminal laws of the States themselves. On a continent where

3 See Fifth Meeting of Consultation of Ministers of Foreign Affairs, Santiago, Chile, 1959. Full text of the Meeting Foreign Affairs, *Final act* (OEA/Ser.C/II.5). Actas y Documentos (OEA/Ser.F/III.5, Spanish), pp. 227 and 229.

4 The American Convention was signed in San Jose, Costa Rica, on November 22, 1969, during the Inter-American Specialized Conference on Human Rights. Currently, it has been ratified or acceded to by Argentina, Barbados, Bolivia, Brazil, Chile, Colombia, Costa Rica, Dominica, Ecuador, El Salvador, Granada, Guatemala, Haiti, Honduras, Jamaica, Mexico, Nicaragua, Panama, Paraguay, Peru, the Dominican Republic, Suriname and Uruguay. On September 10, 2012, Venezuela denounced the Convention which had been ratified in 1977. This denunciation took effect one year later, on September 10, 2013. As a result, any alleged violation of human rights taking place in Venezuela after this date may not be examined by the Inter-American Court. However, Venezuela remains bound by the OAS Charter and the American Declaration of the Rights and Duties of Man, which allows the Commission to continue monitoring the human rights situation in Venezuela.

5 ACHR, Articles 52 and following.

6 Fifth Meeting of Consultation, *supra* n. 3, pp. 225–229.

the application of the Declaration by the Commission had done so much, the existence of a Court was an important factor in improving the struggle against egregious human rights violations that affected thousands and thousands of individuals. The Court, without ignoring its legal framework, has applied the law in an innovative way to deal with instances mostly of gross systematic violations. In this, it has been a pioneer.

3. Much of what the reader will see in this book is a result of the context in which the Court has worked. Disappearances, for example, gave rise to the concept that family members of the disappeared become victims in the case. The situation of indigenous peoples prompted the Court to revisit the idea of the right to property and its association with the cultures of these peoples. The appalling treatment of children developed the concept of the right to life, to include therein health and educational issues. It is difficult then to find areas of human rights handled by the Court that have not been influenced by the social, economic and political circumstances of the region. By this, I do not mean to say that there has been an undue pressure on the Court, but that the Court has developed its case law with a view to finding the most appropriate solutions to the ailments of the people on the continent.

3. GENERAL LEGAL FRAMEWORK

4. The Court has jurisdiction to supervise States' compliance with obligations emanating from various sources. The first is the American Convention on Human Rights, which created the Court itself. Other treaties explicitly conferring jurisdiction to the Court are the Additional Protocol to the American Convention on Human Rights in the Area of Economic, Social and Cultural Rights (Protocol of San Salvador)[7] and the Inter-American Convention on Forced Disappearances of Persons (Disappearance Convention).[8] Other treaties still did not explicitly confer jurisdiction to the Court, but the Court has interpreted certain provisions as granting it that jurisdiction. These are the Inter-American Convention to Prevent and Punish Torture (the Torture Convention)[9] and the

7 The Protocol of San Salvador was adopted at San Salvador, El Salvador, on November 17, 1988 and entered into force on November 16, 1999. Article 19(6) confers jurisdiction on the Court with respect to the right to organize trade unions (Article 8) and the right to education (Article 13). Text of the Protocol available at: www.oas.org/en/iachr/mandate/basic_documents.asp.

8 The Disappearance Convention was adopted in Bélem do Pará on June 9, 1994 and entered into force on March 28, 1996. Jurisdiction was granted to the Court in Article XIII. Text available at: www.oas.org/en/iachr/mandate/basic_documents.asp.

9 The Torture Convention was adopted in Cartagena de Indias, Colombia on December 9, 1985 and entered into force on February 28, 1987. Text available at: www.oas.org/en/iachr/mandate/basic_documents.asp. According to the Court, Article 8 gives the Court jurisdiction.

Inter-American Convention on the Prevention, Punishment and Eradication of Violence against Women (Convention of Bélem do Pará).[10]

5. Aside from these treaties, the Court operates under the premise that, since human rights are universal, it is possible to construe a *corpus juris* with other treaties and jurisprudence from other supervisory organs to interpret and apply the Convention. A typical *corpus juris* applied by the Court, for example, is composed of the international norms and jurisprudence relating to the rights of the child. The Court lacks jurisdiction over these treaties, but they serve to illuminate the scope of rights set forth in the Convention. In addition, the Court often makes use of other international instruments, which are not *per se* enforceable by any supervisory organ, but which serve to expand the conventional norms, which usually are of a very general character. In this sense, the Court often refers to declarations or rules, usually adopted within the framework of the UN, although not coming from the General Assembly, such as the various rules dealing with the protection of persons under detention. Again, the Court will not find that there has been a violation of the rules themselves but will understand that these or other rules contribute to explaining the scope and content of the rights in the Convention and being guided by them will be possible to find a violation of the Convention. Through the judgments of the Court, these instruments start to be treated as a legal norm. Various chapters of this book will provide examples of *corpus juris* and also of so-called soft law.

6. The idea of the unity of international human rights has also been used in the way the Court complements international human rights law with international humanitarian law. The Court has said: "all persons, during internal or international armed conflict, are protected by the provisions of international human rights law, such as the American Convention, and by the specific provisions of international humanitarian law". There is nothing to prevent the "convergence and application of the provisions of international human rights law embodied in the American Convention and other international treaties" and the Court has applied this criterion in several cases – such as the cases of Molina Theissen,[11] Bámaca Velásquez[12] and the Massacre of Mapiripán.[13] In addition, the Court has ordered provisional measures in the light of a situation of extreme gravity and urgency in the context of an armed conflict, as it did, for example,

10 The Bélem do Pará Convention was adopted in Bélem do Pará, Brazil, on June 9, 1994 and entered into force on March 9, 1995. Court jurisdiction emerges from Article 12. Text available at: www.oas.org/en/iachr/mandate/basic_documents.asp.

11 *Case of Molina Theissen v. Guatemala*, judgment on reparations, paras. 15 and 41 and judgment on merits, para. 40 and third and fourth operative paragraphs.

12 *Case of Bámaca Velásquez v. Guatemala*, judgment on reparations, para. 85; and judgment on merits, paras. 143, 174, 207, 213 and 214.

13 *Case of the Massacre of Mapiripán v. Colombia*, para. 114.

in the Matter of the Pueblo Indigena de Kankuamo.[14] In short, for the Court, "international human rights law is fully in force during internal or international armed conflicts".[15]

7. This chapter will concentrate on the American Convention, which sets the obligations of the States, compatible restrictions on rights, and suspension of obligations. The Torture Convention, the Disappearance Convention and the Bélem do Pará Convention will be examined in relation to particular aspects of the American Convention in the relevant chapters.

4. THE AMERICAN CONVENTION ON HUMAN RIGHTS

8. The American Convention on Human Rights was the culmination of a process that began in 1948 with the OAS's passage of the American Declaration. The Convention is the framework within which States and international organs can operate to realize the purposes for which the treaty was adopted.

4.1. THE HOLDERS OF HUMAN RIGHTS

9. The Convention grants human rights only to human beings, and does not extend that protection to legal persons. In several cases regarding the right to property of indigenous communities, the Court has acknowledged that Article 21 protects private property of individuals as well as the communal property of these communities. Moreover, the Court accepts the possibility of respecting not only this form of property but also the way of life and culture of these peoples. Such interpretation, however, brings up the problem of rights holders who are not individual persons but a collective group of people acting as such. The Court has not quite clarified the matter. In the case of Mayagna (Sumo) Awas Tingni Community, it stated that "article 21 of the Convention protects the right to property in a sense which includes, among others, the rights of *members* of the indigenous communities within the framework of communal property".[16] In that case, Judge García Ramírez, based on some international instruments concerning the indigenous peoples,[17] explained that:

---

14 Order of the Inter-American Court of Human Rights of July 5, 2004, eleventh paragraph of the considerations.

15 *Case of the Serrano Cruz sisters v. El Salvador*, paras. 112 and 113.

16 See *Case of the Mayagna (Sumo) Awas Tingni Community v. Nicaragua*, paras. 149–150 (emphasis added).

17 Geneva Convention No. 169 Concerning Indigenous and Tribal Peoples in Independent Countries (ILO, 1989) and Draft Declaration on Discrimination against Indigenous Peoples,

> In the final analysis, the individual rights of indigenous persons and the collective rights of their peoples fit into the regime created by the more general instruments on human rights that apply to all persons, as illustrated by the texts of the more specific instruments for which there exists an ever broader and more robust consensus...[18]

He expanded his reasoning in the case of Plan de Sánchez Massacre, where, mindful of Article 1(2), he held that "[t]he collective rights of the community are not blended with those of its members, and the individual rights of the members are not absorbed or subsumed in the former". Each "category" retains its own entity and autonomy.[19]

10. In the case of Moiwana v. Suriname,[20] the Court decided, "the Moiwana *community members* may be considered the legitimate owners of their traditional lands".[21] In Moiwana, in his concurring vote to the judgment of the Court, Judge Cançado Trindade also expressed conformity with the Court's decision that "the petitioners are the *titulaires* of the rights set forth in the Convention". He added that to deprive them of the faculty to submit their own pleadings would in fact constitute an "undue restriction [... of] their condition as subjects of the International Law of Human Rights. Beyond that, there remains the question of the evolving condition of peoples themselves as subjects of international law".[22]

Following Moiwana, the Court – referring only to Paraguay – found that:

> For Paraguayan legislation, the indigenous Community has ceased to be a factual reality to become an entity with full rights, not restricted to the rights of the members as individuals, but rather encompassing those of the Community itself, with its own singularity. Legal status, in turn, is a legal mechanism that grants them the necessary status to enjoy certain basic rights, such as communal property, and to demand their protection when they are abridged.[23]

---

prepared by the United Nations Economic and Social Council's Sub-Commission on Prevention of Discrimination and Protection of Minorities (E/CN.4/Sub.2/1994/2/Add.1, April 20, 1994).

18 *Case of Mayagna (Sumo) Awas Tingni Community v. Nicaragua*, vote of Judge García Ramírez, para. 6.

19 *Case of Plan de Sánchez Massacre v. Guatemala*, concurring vote of Judge García Ramírez, paras. 4–5.

20 See T.M. Antkowiak, "Rights, resources, and rhetoric: indigenous peoples and the Inter-American Court" (2014) 35 *U. Pa. J. Int'l L.* 113–87, Seattle University School of Law Legal Paper Series, electronic copy available at: http://ssrn.com/abstract=2390405.

21 *Case of Moiwana v. Suriname*, para. 134 (emphasis added).

22 *Case of Moiwana v. Suriname*, concurring vote of Judge Cançado Trindade, para. 12. For general studies, cf. e.g. P. Thornberry, *Indigenous Peoples and Human Rights*, Manchester University Press, Manchester, 2002, pp. 1–429; S. James Anaya, *Indigenous Peoples in International Law*, 2nd. ed., Oxford University Press, Oxford, 2004, pp. 3–291; J. Castellino and N. Walsh (eds.), *International Law and Indigenous Peoples*, Martinus Nijhoff, Leiden, 2005, pp. 89–116 and 249–267.

23 *Case of Yakye Axa Indigenous Community v. Paraguay*, para. 83.

In the case of Xámok Kásek, Judge Vío Grossi took a slightly different position. In his vote, he advanced the idea that international law now allows for a broader understanding of Article 1(2) that "would also include the collectivities or communities, such as the indigenous peoples, to the extent that at least some of these rights extend to these entities. Rights that, consequently, the members may only enjoy and exercise through the collectivity and because they form part of it, which, all things considered, would imply that such rights are not merely of an individual nature".[24]

11. I believe the Court has not taken the line suggested by the dissenting opinion of Judge Vio Grossi of giving a wide interpretation to Article 1(2). What the Court has said, in my understanding, is that the right to use and enjoy the communal land belongs to the members of the community, who are entitled to a system of their own to organize their land. Since the Court has found that the Convention protects the right to a collective property it is then for the State to take the legal or other measures necessary to allow the indigenous peoples the enjoyment of this right. One of them could be the recognition of an indigenous people as a legal person. This would allow them to exercise the attributes of their collective property safeguarded by national law. So far, from what the Court has said in the judgments mentioned, one could conclude that in those cases where indigenous people have been recognized as a people at the domestic level, it is the collectivity that has the right to use and enjoy the communal land. The members of the community are entitled to a system of their own to organize their land. This will take the form of a legal person. The recognition of personhood will make the exercise of the right operational and the State will be bound to recognize it. Some of the cases conclude by declaring the obligation of the State to grant legal personality to the indigenous community in order to end the precariousness of their enjoyment. The failure to do so will constitute a violation of Article 3.[25] In other cases where the legal recognition of these peoples is lacking, such as Moiwana, the Court has only found that the member of the community is the holder of the right to collective property and refrained from exploring the issue of legal personality. In short, the jurisprudence has not yet dealt in depth with this issue.[26] Currently there is a request by Panama for an

24 *Case of Xákmok Kásek Indigenous Community v. Paraguay*, concurring vote of Judge Vío Rossi, para. 26. This quotation requires an explanation. The version in Spanish is found in paragraph 26 of the vote. There is one English version where the quotation, with difficult wording, can be found in paragraph 24. There is another version in English of the whole judgment, different from the previous one, on the webpage of the Court, where the quotation can be found at paragraph 26. Finally there is a quotation, on the webpage of the Court, of the separate vote of Judge Vío Grossi, similar to the first one, but in paragraph 25. The quotation used here is the one of the complete judgment as it appears now in the page of the Court.

25 On Article 3, see further Chapter 2.

26 This is just a brief glimpse of a difficult subject. For a wider treatment of the Court's jurisprudence with regard to indigenous peoples see O. Ruiz Chiriboga, "The right to cultural

Advisory Opinion of the Court regarding the issue of who the holders of human rights are. With this Opinion, there will be an opportunity for the Court to study the matter further.[27]

4.2. THE SUPERVISORY ORGANS

12. The system's supervisory organs are the Inter-American Commission on Human Rights created in 1959 during the Fifth Meeting of Consultation of Ministers of Foreign Affairs[28] and the Inter-American Court of Human Rights. According to the Convention itself and the OAS Charter,[29] the Statute of the Inter-American Commission passed by the General Assembly of the OAS[30] and its own Rules of Procedure,[31] the Commission has several functions. The most important are: (i) promoting human rights in all OAS Member States; (ii) examining the general situation of human rights in those countries; and (iii) examining individual communications submitted against OAS Member States whether parties or not parties to the Convention.[32] For that latter function, and with regard to OAS Member States who are not party to the Convention, the Commission operates under the OAS Charter and under its statute, and the human rights it safeguards are the ones addressed in the American Declaration. With regard to States party to the Convention, the Commission gets its authority directly from the American Convention itself. This allows the cases examined by the Commission to be sent to the Court, whether by the Commission itself

---

identity of indigenous peoples and national minorities: a look from the Inter-American System" (2006) *Sur: International Journal on Human Rights*, issue 5, English edition, pp. 43–70, available at: www.surjournal.org. See also T.M. Antkowiak, *supra* n. 20.

27 See www.corteidh.or.cr/solicitudoc/solicitud_14_11_14_esp.pdf.

28 Resolution VIII of the Fifth Meeting of Consultation of Ministers of Foreign Affairs, note 3.

29 The OAS Charter was adopted during the Ninth International Conference of the American States, held in Bogotá, Colombia, 1948. As of December of 2001, the Charter had been modified by the following instruments: the reform protocol of the Charter of the Organization of American States known as the "Protocol of Buenos Aires", signed on February 27, 1967, during the Third Special Inter-American Conference; the reform protocol of the Charter of the Organization of American States known as the "Protocol of Cartagena de Indias", passed on December 5, 1985, during the 14th Special Period of Sessions of the General Assembly; the reform protocol to the Charter of the Organization of American States known as the "Washington Protocol", approved on December 14, 1992, during the 16th Special Period of Sessions of the General Assembly; and finally, the reform protocol of the Charter of the Organization of American States known as the "Protocol of Managua", adopted on June 10, 1993, in the 19th Special Period of Sessions of the General Assembly.

30 The current Statute of the Inter-American Commission was passed during the Ninth Regular General Assembly of the OAS, held in La Paz, Bolivia, on October 21–23, 1979.

31 The current Rules of Procedure of the Inter-American Commission were approved by that body on its 137th Regular Period of Sessions, held from October 28 to November 13, 2009, and modified on September 2, 2011 and in its 147th Regular Period of Sessions, held on March 8–22, 2013, entry into force on August 1, 2013.

32 IACHR Statute, Articles 18–20.

or by a State Party, as long as the processing of the case before the Commission has concluded and the State against which the case is brought recognizes or has recognized the Court's jurisdiction.[33]

13. The case law of the Inter-American Court emerges from hearings and rulings on these individual cases. Without prejudice to this contentious jurisdiction, the Court also has an advisory jurisdiction that allows it to interpret the provisions of the American Convention or "other treaties"[34] on human rights protection in the States of the Americas at the request of an OAS Member State or an organ thereof.[35] Although in these cases the Court produces an Advisory Opinion that is not binding on the States, it constitutes an authorized interpretation of the provisions of the Convention that the Court itself, as well as the Commission, use as a basis for future interpretations.

4.3. PROTECTED RIGHTS

14. The American Convention sets forth civil and political rights, found in Articles 3–25. The Convention's catalogue of civil and political rights differs in some aspects from the ones in other general human rights treaties. As the Convention is one of the most recent general treaties on human rights, the drafters were not only able to use the textual models of the International Covenant on Civil and Political Rights (ICCPR)[36] and the European Convention but were also able to examine the practice of the European system, which began in 1953. In addition, the rights are drafted in such a way that from time to time they allow for the traditions and idiosyncrasies of OAS Member States to be seen. As said before, this book will examine some selected rights in detail later on.

15. After dealing with civil and political rights in Articles 3–25, Article 26 refers to economic, social and cultural rights. Although these are just as much rights as civil and political rights, the fact that they have not been cataloged[37] has

---

33 ACHR, Articles 51 and 62. Regarding the procedural aspects of the inter-American system, see J.M. Pasqualucci, *The Practice and Procedure of the Inter-American Court of Human Rights*, Cambridge University Press, Cambridge, 2003.

34 ACHR, Article 64.

35 *OC-1/82, para.* 52.

36 International Covenant on Civil and Political Rights (ICCPR), adopted and opened for signature, ratification and accession by General Assembly Resolution 2200A (XXI) of December 16, 1966. Entry into force March 23, 1976.

37 Article 26 makes reference to the rights "implicit in the economic, social, educational, scientific, and cultural standards set forth in the Charter of the Organization of American States as amended by the Protocol of Buenos Aires". Today they correspond to the standards on "Integral Development" in the rewritten text of the OAS charter and changes introduced by the Protocols of Cartagena de Indias, Washington, and Managua, making reference to achieving compliance through progressive development.

required an effort of interpretation by the Court.[38] There is also no clarity with regard to the obligations that these rights impose upon the States. Article 1 of the Convention, applicable in principle to all the rights therein, directs States to "undertake to respect the rights and freedoms recognized herein and to ensure to all persons subject to their jurisdiction the free and full exercise of those rights and freedoms". Article 26, in its turn, requires States "to adopt measures, both internally and through international cooperation, especially those of an economic and technical nature, with a view to achieving progressively the full realization of the rights".[39] To confuse the matter further, there is the Protocol of San Salvador adopted specially to deal with economic, social and cultural rights.[40] The Protocol contains some of these rights and defines State obligations with regard to them in a way that suggests, in principle, an approach that is different and not as effective as the approach used with civil and political rights.[41]

16. Nevertheless, there is no doubt that in applying the civil and political rights found in the Convention, the system's supervisory organs can and should consider their economic, social and cultural aspects. The United Nations Human Rights Committee has taken this route. Some examples demonstrate the broad scope that civil and political rights can have if applied in this way. In its 1982 General Comment on the right to life, the Committee was critical of restrictive interpretations of this right, noting that in taking positive measures to guarantee it, the State must, among other things, take all possible measures to decrease infant mortality rates.[42] In General Comment No. 25 on Article 25, entitled "The right to participate in public affairs, voting rights and the right of

---

38 See UN Committee on Economic, Social and Cultural Rights General Comment No. 16 (2005): Substantive issues arising in the implementation of the International Covenant on Economic, Social and Cultural Rights. The equal right of men and women to the enjoyment of all economic, social and cultural rights (Article 3 of the International Covenant on Economic, Social and Cultural Rights). O. Parra, "Justiciabilidad de los Derechos Económicos, Sociales y Culturales ante el sistema interamericano", Comisión Nacional de los Derechos Humanos, November 2011, Mexico. O. Ruiz Chiriboga, "Ignoring the Protocol of San Salvador? Not the Best Solution (Non) Justiciability of Economic, Social and Culture Rights in the Inter-American System", available at: http://ssrn.com/abstract=1940559. T.M. Antkowiak, *supra* n. 20. See also T. Melish, *Protecting Economic, Social and Cultural Rights in the Inter-American Human Rights System*, Orville H. Schell Jr. Center for International Human Rights, Yale Law School and Centro de Derechos Económicos y Sociales, Ecuador, 2002, available at: www.law.yale.edu/documents/pdf/Intellectual_Life/MANUAL_OAS_INGLES.pdf.

39 On progressiveness, see CESCR General Comment No. 3, 1990, *The nature of States parties' obligations*, particularly paras. 2–9.

40 Text of the Protocol available at: www.oas.org/en/iachr/mandate/basic_documents.asp.

41 Protocol of San Salvador, Articles 1 and 19. Article 19(6) allows for the submission of individual communications before the Commission and for the possibility of the intervention of the Court only with regard to the right to education and union rights as autonomous claims.

42 HRC, General Comment No. 6, Article 6 (16th period of sessions), April 30, 1982, para. 5.

equal access to public service", it held that "[f]reedom of expression, assembly and association are essential conditions for the effective exercise of the right to vote and must be fully protected. Positive measures should be taken to overcome specific difficulties, such as illiteracy, language barriers, poverty, or impediments to freedom of movement which prevent persons entitled to vote from exercising their rights effectively".[43] It has also taken this route in its Concluding Observations to States Parties on the reports they submit. For example, the Committee stated in Canada's final observations concerning the right to life that it "is concerned that homelessness has led to serious health problems and even to death. The Committee recommends that the State party take positive measures required by article 6 to address this serious problem."[44] As can be seen, the combination of the obligation to guarantee and the prohibition of discrimination allows civil and political rights a broadness that helps to diminish the artificial breach between them and economic, social, and cultural rights.

17. At the outset, the Inter-American Court did not have much opportunity to deal with Article 26. In the case of Five Pensioners on social security issues, the Court decided that the case did not lend itself to an application of Article 26. It decided that this right should be measured in function of the growing coverage of economic, social and cultural rights in general, and of the right to social security and to a pension in particular, of the entire population. It was necessary to bear in mind the imperatives of social equity, and not take a decision in respect of the circumstances of a very limited group of pensioners, who did not necessarily represent the prevailing situation.[45]

18. In later cases, the Court has given a clear indication that it will have jurisdiction with respect to certain social rights matters that can be subsumed under the rights to life and to personal integrity.[46] The Court ascribed responsibility to the State for the violation of the rights to life and personal integrity of Ximenes Lopes, who had been mistreated and had died in a mental institution. The Court found "that the States must regulate and supervise all activities related to the health care given to the individuals under the jurisdiction thereof, as a special duty to protect life and personal integrity, regardless of the public or private nature of the entity giving such health care".[47] Brazil had failed

---

43 HRC, General Comment No. 25, Article 25 (57th period of sessions), July 12, 1996, para. 12.

44 HRC, *Concluding Observations of the Human Rights Committee, Canada* (65th period of sessions), April 7, 1999, para. 12.

45 *Case of the Five Pensioners v. Peru*, para. 147.

46 On this, see Chapter 2.

47 *Case of Ximenes Lopes v. Brazil*, para. 89.

to regulate and supervise the activities in the clinic where the victim was, so it had incurred international responsibility.[48]

In the Albán Cornejo case, dealing with a death in a private clinic, the Court makes an explicit connection between the right to life and the right to health. It finds that the rights to life and humane treatment are directly and immediately linked to human health care and refers to the Protocol of San Salvador that defines the right to health "as the enjoyment of the highest level of physical, mental and social well-being".[49] Again, as in Ximenes Lopes, the State had incurred responsibility by the omission of the duty to supervise the rendering of the public service to protect the right to life.[50]

The case of Acevedo Buendía *et al.* dealt with social security rights. There, the representatives of the victims invoked Article 26 and the State objected to the Court's jurisdiction. The reason given was that "such right [to social security] is not enshrined by the American Convention and it is not even one of the two rights (right to organize trade union and right to education) that would be actionable before the Inter-American system, in accordance with the provisions of Article 19(6) of the Protocol of San Salvador".[51] The Court rejected that contention since the Convention gives the Court full jurisdiction over all rights contained therein.[52] Referring to its competence on Article 26, it remarked that civil and political rights had social and economic aspects in them over which the Court should have control, quoting in this regard the Airey case in Europe.[53] However, it refers to its jurisdiction as limited to the progressive development of the rights.[54] The examination did not go further because this case was "not centered on some measure adopted by the State that hindered the progressive realization of the right to pension" but on the "State's non-compliance with the payment ordered by the domestic courts". Consequently, the violations found were those of Article 25 and 21 of the Convention.[55] In a concurring opinion, Judge García Ramírez admitted that before this judgment the Court's treatment of social, economic and cultural rights had been very limited and that in this judgment this had improved when reaffirming its competence – which should now be well-established – to rule on possible failures to comply with Article 26 of the American Convention. Accordingly, the Inter-American Court "understands that the observance of Article 26 may be claimed and required". The Court

48 *Ibidem*, paras. 87 and 90. The Court quotes a similar European judgment: European Court of Human Rights, *Case of Storck v. Germany*, Application No. 61603/00, judgment of June 16, 2005, p. 103.

49 *Case of Albán Cornejo et al. v. Ecuador*, para. 117.

50 *Ibidem*, para. 119.

51 *Case of Acevedo Buendía et al. v. Peru*, para. 12.

52 *Ibidem*, paras. 16 and 17.

53 *Ibidem*, para. 74. See European Court of Human Rights, *Case of Airey v. Ireland*, judgment of October 9, 1979, Series A, No. 32, para. 26.

54 *Ibidem*, paras. 75–76.

55 *Ibidem*, para 106.

would have to assess the two dimensions of the facts. The first dimension alludes to "the observation of the progressive development, which makes the best effort to achieve it" and the second to "the denial of the regression, which is contrary to the principles and the *corpus juris* of the human rights and that it also must be assessed by the corresponding venues".[56]

19. The case of Furlán and family does not pronounce on Article 26, but there is an interesting concurring opinion of Judge Macaulay forcefully arguing that the Court should have found a violation of Article 26. Furlán was a 14-year-old child that entered an abandoned military property where he had a serious accident that left him with grave injuries and disability. The accident took place when he tried to hang from a 40–50-kilogram crossbeam on one of the pieces of equipment, which fell on his head. After being in a deep coma for over a year he was discharged to receive out-patient care with difficulties in his speech and in the use of his upper and lower limbs. After two attempted suicides, the family claimed damages from the State, which were not processed by the courts as there was a suspension, "for a period of 120 days, of law suits and administrative claims against the National Government and Public Sector entities".[57] The Court found violations of Article 8 on due process, *inter alia* because of a delay of over ten years for the trial and its execution.

Judge Macaulay stated her opinion "about the possibility of resolving a part of the controversy from a perspective regarding the direct justiciability of economic, social and cultural rights under the scope of article 26 of the American Convention".[58] She starts by invoking the Court's Advisory Opinion on the American Declaration,[59] which contains and defines the basic human rights set forth in the OAS Charter. That leads her to affirm: "The Charter of the Organization cannot be interpreted nor applied in human rights matters without integrating its standards with the corresponding provisions in the Declaration".[60] She recalls that the American Declaration contains both a right to health and a right to social security.[61] She continues by pointing out that "the Court has specified various aspects of the notions of progressive realization and non-regression in social rights matters". Moreover, the Court has pointed out that, "besides regulating the progressive development of these rights, a systematic interpretation of the American Convention requires an understanding that the obligations of respect and guarantee are applied also to economic, social, and cultural rights".[62] An interesting turn in her analysis is that she places the focus not on the progressive

56 *Ibidem*, concurring vote of Judge García Ramírez, para. 21.
57 *Case of Furlán and family v. Argentina*, para. 79.
58 *Ibidem*, concurring opinion of Judge Macaulay, para. 1.
59 Advisory Opinion OC-10/89 of July 14, 1989, Series A No. 10, para. 39.
60 *Case of Furlán and family v. Argentina*, concurring opinion of Judge Macaulay, para. 3.
61 *Ibidem*, para. 4.
62 *Ibidem*, para. 5.

or regressive realization of the rights but on the duty to guarantee them and the interpretation for the latter. There, she uses the *pro persona* principle of interpretation and Article 29 of the Convention, quoting the Court's opinion that the American Convention cannot be interpreted in a way that "restricts the enjoyment or the exercise of the rights recognized in other conventions to which the States are parties".[63] With regard to the sources that should be employed, such as the Protocol of San Salvador and the International Covenant on Economic, Social and Cultural Rights (ICESCR), Judge Macaulay argues that the Protocol "did not establish any provision aimed at limiting the scope of the American Convention". Furthermore, the Protocol's Article 4 sets forth clearly that "a right which is recognized or in effect in a State by reason of internal law or by virtue of international instruments, may not be restricted or curtailed on the pretext that the Protocol afore-mentioned does not recognize the right or recognizes it to a lesser degree". Her last reason to dismiss the idea that the Protocol may limit the Convention is that it "would lead to the absurd consideration that the American Convention can have some effects among the Participating States of the San Salvador Protocol while having another effect for the States that are not parties to the said Protocol".[64]

20. From this examination, one could arrive at certain conclusions in terms of the Court's position with respect to Article 26. Article 26 may be invoked before the Court, which has jurisdiction to examine it, limited to deciding on progress or on regression. Clearly, this subject will not come before the Court so easily within these constraints. What the Court has done, specifically regarding the right to health, is to subsume the facts in the rights to life and to personal integrity. Former Judge Macaulay's position advances this by changing the focus from progression or regression to the obligation to ensure rights that are already set forth in the domestic jurisdiction. This seems to be a good approach because it might give a possibility to join Article 26 with Article 1, giving thus more relevance to the former.

21. The academic debate over the justiciability of economic, social and cultural rights is far from over.[65] Nor is it over within the Court itself. There is no firm ground to assert the justiciability of all these rights and there has been no Court position on what these rights should be.

---

63 *Ibidem*, para. 7.

64 *Ibidem*, para. 8.

65 See O. Ruiz Chiriboga, "Ignoring the Protocol of San Salvador?", *supra* n. 38. There he discusses the various positions academics have taken regarding the jurisdiction of the Court over these rights. The article also contains an extensive bibliography on the subject.

4.4. STATE OBLIGATIONS

22. State obligations form a very important part of the Convention. Their interpretation can render the Convention extremely useful or almost useless. The Court has given the utmost care to this task and it is here where one sees in full force the creative interpretation of the Court to address the significant faults of States regarding human rights. Accordingly, States' obligations will occupy an important part of this book.

The drafts that gave rise to the Convention included the obligation for States to respect and guarantee the human rights of persons "subject to *their territory* and jurisdiction."[66] However, on approval of the Convention, reference was made only to jurisdiction. Therefore, it is important to have a clear guideline to decide when a State has jurisdiction outside of its borders.

The Inter-American Commission ruled admissible a case containing sixty similar petitions regarding the military action carried out by the United States in Panama in December 1989 in order to arrest Manuel Noriega.[67] It also ruled admissible a case on the United States' bombardment in Grenada that destroyed Richmond Hill Insane Asylum, causing the death of 16 persons there.[68] The Commission, however, did not explicitly state the legal grounds on which it had based its ruling of admissibility, without treading into the legal concept of jurisdiction of a State when violations occur outside its territorial jurisdiction.[69]

Other international bodies have taken dissimilar positions on this subject. The Human Rights Committee decided long ago that a State's consulate decision not to grant or renew a passport was an action carried out within the jurisdiction of that State.[70] The European Court of Human Rights found that a bombing carried out by some European States on the territory of another State was not

---

66 *Inter-American Yearbook on Human Rights 1968*, General Secretariat of the Organization of American States, Washington DC, 1973, pp. 236–418.

67 IACHR, *Case 10.573*, report dated October 14, 1993, published in IACHR *Annual Report 1993*. The United States argued that the Commission did not have jurisdiction because it was an "advisory organ" without authority to rule on cases and that it could only review allegations of violations with reference to the American Declaration, "which is an agreed statement of non-binding general human rights principles" (para. 21). There is no published history on the final result of this case.

68 IACHR, *Case 9.213*, report on admissibility, published in IACHR, *Annual Report 1986–1987*. This case concluded with a friendly settlement and the Commission did not give arguments on the problem of jurisdiction.

69 In Europe, in the *Bankovic case* against a number of States parties to NATO, the petitioners had argued that a country that enters the air space of another State and bombs that State begins at that moment to exercise "jurisdiction" as regards its responsibility for the human rights violations presumably committed. The European Court did not agree.

70 UN HRC, *Sophie Vidal Martins v. Uruguay*, Communication No. R.13/57, March 23, 1982, para. 7.

under the jurisdiction of the former States, preferring a notion of an "essentially territorial" jurisdiction.[71]

One of the consequences of the rise of international human rights law as a branch of international public law has been the difficulty in establishing proper concepts to define the relationships between States and relationships between States and individuals, which are radically different. Possibly the term "jurisdiction" should be revised in the future in order to adjust it to new circumstances that affect and violate human rights.

23. In principle, the obligations established in the Convention apply equally to all States Parties. However, Article 28 of the Convention establishes that: "Where a State Party is constituted as a federal state, the national government of such State Party shall implement all the provisions of the Convention *over whose subject matter it exercises legislative and judicial jurisdiction*".[72] Undoubtedly these words seem less categorical than, for example, Article 50 of the ICCPR, which establishes that its provisions "shall extend to all parts of federal States without any limitations or exceptions."

The final draft of Article 28 originated with the initiative of the United States, which was trying to keep the Convention from causing a centralization of power in the federal government and away from the States forming the federation.[73] The original draft of the project ordered federal States to take the measures necessary to make the provisions of the Convention effective in all States, provinces, or federal departments, along with other territories under their jurisdiction.[74] From a legal point of view, however, the inclusion of the phrase emphasized in paragraph 1 does not succeed in liberating the federal State of its responsibility for violations of the Convention committed by states in the federation. Paragraph 2 requires them to take immediate measures in order for the corresponding authorities to make the provisions necessary for compliance with the Convention with regard to all individuals under the jurisdiction of the State in question.

---

71 European Court of Human Rights, *Bankovic et al. v. Belgium, The Czech Republic, Denmark, France, Germany, Greece, Hungary, Iceland, Italy, Luxembourg, The Netherlands, Norway, Poland, Portugal, Spain, Turkey and The United Kingdom*, decision on admissibility of December 12, 2001, para. 62. The Maastricht Principles on Extraterritorial Obligations of States in the Area of Economic, Social and Cultural Rights (2012) establish principles which, in my view, are the most appropriate to express standing international law. Although it refers only to economic, social and political rights, its Article 5 does not exclude its application to civil and political rights, given the indivisibility and interdependence of all rights. I am thankful to Valeska David for pointing this out to me.

72 Article 28(1). Emphasis added.

73 *Report of the United States Delegation to the Inter-American Conference on Protection of Human Rights*, reproduced in T. Buergenthal and R. Norris (eds.), *Human Rights. The Inter-American System*, Booklet 15, Oceana Publications, Dobbs Ferry, New York, 1984, p. 64.

74 Inter-American Specialized Conference on Human Rights, San José, Costa Rica, November 7–22, 1969, *Minutes and Documents*, General Secretariat, OAS, Washington DC, 1979, p. 24.

Curiously but fortunately, the rule is different when a new State is created. Paragraph 3 of Article 28 requires States that agree to integrate into a federation or other kind of association to ensure the pact governing the community itself incorporates the provisions of the Convention. Thus, the Convention may continue to be effective in the new State created including every part thereof.[75]

24. The Court has referred to the federal clause on some occasions, first in its Advisory Opinion 16, where it said "international provisions that concern the protection of human rights in the American States [...] must be respected by the American States parties to the respective conventions, regardless of whether they have a federal or a unitary structure."[76] The Court has ruled similarly in provisional measures ordered against Brazil.[77] Again in Garibaldi it stated:

> The Court considers that States Parties must guarantee and ensure respect for all the rights embodied in the American Convention to all persons subject to their jurisdiction, without any limitation or exception based on their internal structure. The legal system and practices of the entities that form a Federal State party to the Convention must conform thereto.[78]

4.5. OBLIGATIONS TO RESPECT AND TO ENSURE[79]

25. Article 1 of the Convention establishes two important obligations for States Parties: the obligations to *respect* human rights and to *ensure* their full and free exercise.[80] These obligations are immediately internationally applicable and

---

75 See T. Buergenthal, "The Inter-American System for the Protection of Human Rights", in *Inter-American Juridical Yearbook 1981*, Washington DC, 1992, pp. 80–120 (83–85) and D. Fox, "The American Convention on Human Rights and Prospects for United States Ratification" (1973) 3 *Human Rights* 243–281 (254–260).

76 Advisory Opinion *OC-16/99*, Series A No. 16 para 140.

77 "Brazil is a federal State, and [...] the Urso Branco Prison is located in one of its federative units; however, this does not exempt the State from complying with its protection obligations. [...] The State must organize its internal structures and adopt all necessary measures, in accordance with its political and administrative structure, to comply with these provisional measures." *Matter of the Urso Branco Prison, provisional measures with regard to Brazil*, Order of the Inter-American Court of Human Rights of May 2, 2008, fourteenth considering paragraph.

78 *Case of Garibaldi v. Brazil*, para. 146, quoting the *Escher case*, para. 219.

79 There have been attempts to classify the obligations of the States in order to make them more explicit. The United Nations, for example, speaks of the obligations to respect, protect and fulfil. I will not follow that classification. I will try to explain what the two obligations in the American Convention mean for the practice of the Court's case law, because I think that will reflect a clearer picture for readers.

80 Article 1(1) set forth: "The States Parties to this Convention undertake to respect the rights and freedoms recognized herein and to ensure to all persons subject to their jurisdiction the free and full exercise of those rights and freedoms, without any discrimination for reasons

bind the State with regard to all individuals subject to its jurisdiction, without discrimination.[81] The obligations found in Article 1 refer without distinction to all rights in the Convention. The obligation to respect requires that the State and its agents do not violate the human rights established in the Convention. It is thus an obligation to refrain or to abstain from interfering with the right. In this sense, the Court asserted in its Advisory Opinion 6 that:

> The protection of human rights, particularly the civil and political rights set forth in the Convention, is in effect based on the affirmation of the existence of certain inviolable attributes of the individual that cannot be legitimately restricted through the exercise of governmental power. There are individual domains that are beyond the reach of the State or to which the State has but limited access. Thus, the protection of human rights must necessarily comprise the concept of the restriction of the exercise of state power.[82]

The Court has held the same position in all its case law.

26. In contrast, the obligation to ensure requires the State to take the necessary actions to guarantee that all individuals subject to the State's jurisdiction are able to exercise their rights. The Inter-American Court of Human Rights exhaustively analyzed the content of that obligation in the case of Velásquez Rodríguez, which examined a disappearance in Honduras. In its judgment, the Court found the following:

> The second obligation of the States Parties is to "ensure" the free and full exercise of the rights recognized by the Convention to every person subject to its jurisdiction. This obligation implies the duty of States Parties to organize the governmental apparatus and, in general, all the structures through which public power is exercised so that they are capable of juridically ensuring the free and full enjoyment of human rights. As a consequence of this obligation, States must prevent, investigate and punish any violation of the rights recognized by the Convention and, moreover, if possible attempt to restore the right violated and provide compensation as warranted for damages resulting from the human rights violation.[83]

This State action must not be simply formal. Regarding this, the Court added that "[t]he obligation to ensure [...] is not fulfilled by the existence of a legal system designed to make it possible to comply with this obligation – it also

---

of race, color, sex, language, religion, political or other opinion, national or social origin, economic status, birth, or any other social condition."

81 In all Latin American States, provisions in treaties that have been ratified by the States or to which the States have acceded form part of the national legal order.

82 IACtHR, *The word "laws" in article 30 of the American Convention on Human Rights*, Advisory Opinion *OC-6/86* of May 9, 1986, Series A No. 6, para 21.

83 *Case of Velásquez Rodríguez v. Honduras*, para. 166.

requires the government to conduct itself so as to effectively ensure the free and full exercise of human rights."[84]

27. In issues of human rights then the State cannot limit itself to avoiding conduct that violates those rights. Rather, it must also take the positive actions that may be necessary to make it possible for individuals subject to its jurisdiction to be able to exercise and enjoy their human rights. Positive actions require a variety of steps destined to obtain a variety of results. Societies are not composed of individuals who are equal, be it because of their race, sex, physical capabilities, social or economic conditions. If States must respect and ensure the full and free *exercise* of their rights to all, it follows that the State will have to take different measures to satisfy them all. The need to differentiate between groups in different situations will require the adoption of different measures, maybe temporarily or perhaps permanently as, for example, for people with disabilities. The Court was clear on this in the case of the Pueblo Bello Massacre. There, it affirmed:

> Thus, when interpreting and applying the Convention, the Court must pay attention to the special needs for protection of the individual, the ultimate beneficiary of the provisions of the respective treaty. Owing to the nature *erga omnes* of the State's treaty-based protection obligations, their scope cannot be determined on the basis of a vision that focuses on the sovereign will of the States and merely on the effects of inter-State relations. These obligations devolve upon all subjects of international law and presumptions of non-compliance must be determined in function of the need for protection in each particular case.[85]

28. For methodological reasons I will describe the obligation to ensure as constituting a cycle that repeats itself. There will first be the need to prevent violations. If the violation has been committed, the State will have to react to the violation in certain ways. Subsequently, it will have to make reparation to the victim of the violation. Finally, it will have to examine why the violation occurred in order to adjust the preventive measures for the future, usually through guarantees of non-repetition. The prevention for the future will again constitute the prevention mentioned at the beginning. This notion of a cycle will allow a State to comply fully with its obligations. It is not easy to distinguish each part of this cycle; sometimes it will not even be possible to do it: what constitutes prevention of certain possible violations will be at the same time a reaction to violations already committed.

---

84 *Ibidem*, para. 167.

85 *Case of the Massacre of Pueblo Bello v. Colombia*, para. 117.

4.5.1. *Prevention*

29. To prevent violations being committed and to allow everybody to exercise their human rights freely and fully, the State's first obligation is to make sure international laws have an effect within their jurisdiction. It falls to the State and not to international law to decide on the most appropriate method of complying with this, whether through the incorporation of those laws directly or through the establishment of domestic laws reproducing them. In any case, once the international treaty is in force for the State, it must adjust all its domestic law to conform to it.

Ensuring that individuals are able to use and enjoy their human rights is primarily the responsibility of States, as they are in the best position to ensure this on an everyday and immediate basis; international supervision always comes late and generally *ex post*. The obligation exists even when in certain legal systems the entry into force of the treaties may have the effect of striking down domestic laws that are contrary to international ones. Prevention requires the State to make a careful review of its domestic legislation for the purpose of eliminating discrepancies that may exist between domestic legislation and international law – that is, it must go through a process of adjusting domestic law to the Convention. It should be noted that the scope and content of human rights can be broadened by law, while its restrictions, as indicated in Article 30 of the Convention and the case law of the Inter-American Court, cannot go beyond those specifically provided for in the Convention and then only by means of a law in the formal and material sense.[86] The State's task is to facilitate the exercise of human rights and it does not do so by leaving its fate only up to judicial interpretation, even when it can be maintained that tribunals themselves are obliged to attempt an interpretation of domestic law affecting human rights that is in harmony with the State's international obligations in this area.

30. To prevent violations, the State must also establish adequate and effective remedies that individuals can exercise to claim against violations of their human rights. The standards for remedies that are "adequate and effective" are the result of extensive international case law. The Inter-American Court developed the meaning of those two words in two cases against Honduras on the obligation of those who turn to the inter-American system to exhaust domestic remedies before doing so. *Adequate* means "that the remedies' function within the domestic legal system is suitable for addressing the infringement of a legal right." *Effective* means "capable of producing the result for which it was designed".[87] The term "effective" does not imply that every remedy sought must necessarily be granted; it means that there is at least a

---

86 *OC-10/89*, para. 17.

87 *Case of Velásquez Rodríguez*, para. 64, and *Case of Godínez Cruz*, para. 67; both v. Honduras.

serious possibility that the remedy will be granted.[88] The Court found in a 2001 ruling that:

> The nonexistence of an effective recourse against the violation of rights recognized under the Convention constitutes a transgression of the Convention by the State party in which the situation in question is taking place. In this sense, it should be highlighted that in order for the remedy to exist, it is not enough for it to be provided for in the Constitution or the law, or for it to be formally admissible. Rather, it must be truly suitable for establishing whether a human rights violation has taken place and providing the necessary remedy.[89]

The Court has pronounced on the effectiveness of a remedy on many occasions, but not always in precisely the same terms. In the case of the Massacre of Mapiripán,[90] the Court links the definition of effective remedies with the way the trial has developed at the domestic level, and states:

> When it assesses the effectiveness of domestic remedies sought under national administrative-law jurisdiction, the court must establish whether the decisions taken by the latter have in fact contributed to ending impunity, to insuring non-recidivism of injurious acts, and to guaranteeing free and full exercise of the rights protected by the Convention.

In Chocrón Chocrón, the Court explained that it had to "observe whether the decisions made in it have made an effective contribution to ending a situation that violated rights, by ensuring the non-repetition of the harmful actions and guaranteeing the free and full exercise of the rights protected by the Convention".[91] In the case of Cepeda Vargas, the Court again linked the defects of the trial and the application of Article 8 with the concept of effective remedies. It states that the remedies were not effective "to ensure access to justice, to investigate and eventually punish all those who participated in committing the violations, including the possible participation of paramilitaries, and to provide integral reparation for the consequences of the violations."[92]

An apparent inconsistency exists here that will be addressed again when dealing with Articles 8 and 25 of the Convention.

31. The existence of remedies is not enough to exhaust the State's obligation, as it must also establish the conditions necessary for the exercise of the rights. For example, in order to guarantee due process, the State must – among other things

88 *Case of Velásquez Rodríguez*, paras. 67–68 and *Case of Godínez Cruz*, paras. 70–71; both v. Honduras. Also see *OC-9/87*, para. 24.

89 *Case of the Mayagna (Sumo) Awas Tingni Community v. Nicaragua*, para. 113. In the same sense see: *Case of Ivcher Bronstein v. Peru*, para. 136; *Case of Cantoral Benavides v. Peru*, para. 164, and *Case of Durand and Ugarte v. Peru*, para. 102.

90 *Case of the Massacre of Mapiripán v. Colombia*, para. 210.

91 *Case of Chocrón Chocrón v. Venezuela*, para. 128.

92 *Case of Cepeda Vargas v. Colombia*, para. 167.

– issue procedural rules, allocate funds for the creation of the court system, ensure the existence of law schools for training attorneys, and provide free legal aid to those lacking resources, when necessary.

32. This obligation (to create the conditions for the effective exercise of rights) also implies the need to remove obstacles even when those obstacles arise not from domestic law but from social structure and culture. The State therefore must promote human rights in the understanding that this means educating the domestic community about them. In addition, it must launch campaigns to create the conditions to allow the exercise of human rights and to ensure they are respected by everyone – including all State agents, who must be instructed on their international obligations and trained to be able to fulfil them. This aspect of the obligation is particularly applicable when there are groups whose human rights are constantly violated for cultural reasons. Consider, for example, the principle of non-discrimination based on sex. Although each action that violates this principle can be brought before the courts, with the corresponding possibility that it will eventually be redressed, the establishment of remedies does not exhaust the State's obligation when a violation is massive and systemic. Limiting action to merely addressing each violation – which to start with involves time and money, as well as evidence requirements that are sometimes impossible to meet – would constitute an injustice and failure to comply with international obligations. It would be equivalent to placing this group affected by constant violations in the situation of never having direct enjoyment of its rights except by turning to the courts. In cases such as these, therefore, the State must make a careful review of the way in which society functions and design policies that result in achieving the goal of making the enjoyment and exercise of human rights effective for all individuals.

As can be seen, the specification of the first aspect of the obligation to ensure has broad scope, stretching from the promotion of rights and the removal of government or non-government obstacles, to special measures for groups that are at a disadvantage in relation to the rest of the community.[93]

33. A full sense of what prevention demands from states can be found in the case of Cotton Field, which handled the situation of three victims in Ciudad Juárez in Mexico. The Court distinguished in that judgment two "crucial" moments where prevention failed in the case. The first was after the kidnapping of the three victims and before the discovery of their bodies; the second, prior to the disappearance of the victims.[94] Concerning the first moment, the State was

93 On this point, see T. Buergenthal, "To Respect and to Ensure: State Obligations and Permissible Derogations", in L. Henkin (ed.), *The International Bill of Rights. The Covenant on Civil and Political Rights*, Columbia University Press, New York, 1981, pp. 72 and 77–78.

94 *Case of González et al. ("Cotton Field") v. Mexico*, para. 281.

aware that this type of kidnapping of young women carried a real and imminent danger of them being tortured and killed. Consequently, prevention of violations of personal integrity and life should have been carried out with strict adherence to due diligence.[95]

With regard to the second moment, the Court remarked that there was no violation of Articles 4 and 5. It reasoned that the State obligation to guarantee "does not imply its unlimited responsibility for any act or deed of private individuals, because its obligation to adopt measures of prevention and protection for private individuals in their relations with each other is conditional on its awareness of a situation of real and imminent danger for a specific individual or group of individuals and the reasonable possibility of preventing or avoiding that danger."[96] However, it stated that "the Court can only note that the absence of a general policy which could have been initiated at least in 1998 – when the Comisión Nacional de Derechos Humanos (CNDH) warned of the pattern of violence against women in Ciudad Juárez – is a failure of the State to comply in general with its obligation of prevention".[97] With this decision, there may be the possibility of advancing along the road to better and prompter prevention by at least warning the State that it is infringing the Convention. It is difficult to imagine the Court going further. This would imply exercising jurisdiction in cases where massive or systematic violations occur without specifying anything more than a group of indeterminate individuals and, moreover, attributing responsibility to the States for omitting actions to prevent without there being a clear and imminent risk to specific individuals.[98]

4.5.2. The State's Reaction to a Violation

34. In its first judgment, the Court resolved that States, as a consequence of their obligation to ensure human rights, "must prevent, investigate and punish any violation of the rights recognized by the Convention."[99] Although the Court formulated this as a rule, the wideness of this resolution has to be understood with regard to the type of violation being examined in Velásquez, the forced disappearance of the victim. It is true that if a violation is perpetrated and the action constitutes a criminal offense in the national legal order, this reaction would be the proper one. The commission of a criminal offense will require a judicial trial and all the agents that are involved in it – police, State medical experts or others – must exercise their functions according to the law or be held responsible. The international standard will be set according to Article 8 of the Convention as interpreted by the Court. Nevertheless, the reaction must

95 *Ibidem*, para. 283.
96 *Ibidem*, para. 280.
97 *Ibidem*, para. 282.
98 In this same sense, see *Case of Véliz Franco et al. v. Guatemala*, paras. 137–139.
99 See *Case of Velásquez Rodríguez v. Honduras*, para. 166.

be different in other forms of violations. If the violation originates in a law that is incompatible with the Convention, the reaction should take the form of a derogation or amendment of the law. If the violation has been committed by a national court that did not act according to international standards, the State's reaction will probably have to be to order the State to initiate a new trial.

In cases where investigation of facts is necessary, States must comply with a series of conditions imposed by the Court. The investigation, trial and punishment must naturally be undertaken "in a serious manner and not as a mere formality preordained to be ineffective."[100] The examination of Article 8 of the Convention will show that basic principles exist for ensuring due process. Among them should be highlighted the existence of an independent and impartial organ with enough authority to carry out an efficient investigation, within a reasonable period of time.[101] These guarantees are established for actions carried out by judicial organs. However, it is clear that the need for serious investigation prior to the judicial proceeding requires guarantees of independence and impartiality to extend to the non-judicial organs that carry out the initial investigative work. This will ensure effectiveness, for example in the determination of the circumstances surrounding a death at the hands of third parties to decide whether there is a basis for the State to exercise its punitive authority.[102]

All this raises the interesting question of how this stand can be reconciled with the discretion generally granted to prosecutors to decide whether to proceed to a criminal trial. The Court has not ruled on this point. If the violation amounts to certain criminal offenses, such as deprivation of life, the obligation to investigate is not a discretionary act of the States. I would suggest that in the case of the taking of a life, for example, a right that cannot be suspended even under martial law, this discretion to prosecute must be reduced to a minimum and can only be exercised to dismiss the possibility of bringing charges against someone who, based on the investigation, is not clearly involved in the facts. There would be no discretion to decide not to investigate the facts at all. However, the Court has not ever referred to the issue.

35. The judgment handed down in the case of Garrido and Baigorria clearly established that "Argentina has a legal obligation to investigate the facts leading to the disappearance [...] and to bring to trial and punish the authors, accomplices, accessories after the fact, and all those who may have played some role in the events that transpired".[103] The case of Garrido and Baigorria clarifies that the

---

100 *Ibidem*, para. 177.

101 *Case of Myrna Mack Chang v. Guatemala*, concurring opinion of Judge Sergio García Ramírez, para. 35.

102 The matter will be examined in Chapter 6.

103 *Case of Garrido and Baigorria v. Argentina*, judgment on reparations, para. 74. Paragraph 73 of the same judgment cites settled case law on these obligations.

obligation to investigate is different from the obligation to provide reparations. The victim of a human rights violation can decline the indemnity due and the State will not have to pay it. If the person in question pardons the perpetrator of the violation, this does not exempt the State from its obligation to investigate, prosecute and punish that perpetrator except for in the case of crimes prosecuted only at the request of an individual.[104] The Court's ruling implies that the State must take *ex officio* action to investigate, try and punish perpetrators of an act of this nature. The obligation is a "legal duty" that must be fulfilled "regardless of what agent is eventually found responsible for the violation. Where the acts of private parties that violate the Convention are not seriously investigated, those parties are aided in a sense by the government, thereby making the State responsible on the international plane".[105] Therefore, the obligation must be fulfilled consistently, unavoidably and without discrimination.

4.5.3. Obligations Arising from Noncompliance[106]

36. According to international law, reflected in the Draft Articles on Responsibility of States for Internationally Wrongful Acts,[107] a State incurs several obligations because of the commission of an internationally wrongful act. The first obligation is to cease the violation if it is continuing. A second obligation is to offer appropriate assurances and guarantees of non-repetition, if circumstances so require.[108] As to the reparations, the third obligation, they "shall take the form of restitution, compensation and satisfaction, either singly or in combination, in accordance with the provisions of this chapter".[109] Restitution means "to re-establish the situation which existed before the wrongful act was committed".[110] Satisfaction is indeterminate in the Draft Articles. As examples, they mention an acknowledgment of responsibility, an expression of regret or other appropriate modality.[111]

Article 63 of the American Convention sets forth the consequences for a State that has violated a human right. The provision directs the Court, when finding a violation has been committed, "to rule that the injured party be ensured the

---

104 *Ibidem*, para. 72.

105 *Case of Velásquez Rodríguez v. Honduras*, para. 177. In this sense, see *Case of Myrna Mack v. Guatemala*, para. 156.

106 The subject deserves a book not a few pages. The Court has done a vast amount of work on what the Court calls in general reparations.

107 International Law Commission, *Draft Articles on Responsibility of States for Internationally Wrongful Acts*, November 2001, Supplement No. 10 (A/56/10), chap. IV.E.1 (Draft Articles on Responsibility), available at: legal.un.org/ilc/texts/instruments/english/draft articles/9_6_2001.pdf.

108 *Ibidem*, Article 30.

109 *Ibidem*, Article 34.

110 *Ibidem*, Article 35.

111 *Ibidem*, Article 37.

enjoyment" of the rights violated and, if appropriate, "that the consequences of the measure or situation that constituted the breach of such right or freedom be remedied and that fair compensation be paid to the injured party".

37. In reparations, as restitution is extremely rare in international human rights law, compensation is usual and satisfaction takes many varied forms.[112] In terms of compensation, the Court usually assesses loss of earnings as well as expenses incurred because of the violations, for example funerary costs and others, all of which constitute the pecuniary damages. According to the Court, "[n]on-pecuniary damage can include the suffering and hardship caused to the direct victims and to their next of kin, the harm of objects of value that are very significant to the individual, and also changes, of a non-pecuniary nature, in the living conditions of the victims".[113] An examination of the case law of the Court will find that it does not require evidence for non-pecuniary damages.[114] The Court increases the amount of this compensation depending on the type of the violation and the conduct of the State when perpetrating it. Satisfying the victim of a violation of human rights committed with clear malice by a State agent will require greater reparations than when the violation is the result of an oversight, as the resulting lack of safety and fear is greater in the former case. In fact, in the judgment on the Humberto Sánchez case, the Court found that due to "the grave circumstances in this case", one of which was the prevailing impunity attributable to the State, it must order the payment, in equity, of compensation for non-pecuniary damages.[115] In its considerations for establishing reparations in the case of Myrna Mack Chang, the Court took into account the poor handling of the judicial proceedings, their lateness, and the obstructions that prevented punishment for all those responsible of the actions. All these factors had caused the relatives of the victims "feelings of insecurity, defenselessness, and anguish."[116] As can be seen, in both cases the Court took the gravity of the conduct of the State into account when establishing this type of compensation.

38. Many measures of satisfaction resemble the examples of the Draft Articles on State Responsibility, such as "performing acts or implementing projects with public recognition or repercussion, such as broadcasting a message that officially

112 On reparations in the inter-American system, see T.M. Antkowiak, "Remedial Approaches to Human Rights Violations: The Inter-American Court of Human Rights and Beyond" (2008) 46 *Colum. J. Transnat'l L.* 351, 386–391 and *An emerging mandate for International Courts: victim centered remedies and restorative justice*, Seattle University School of Law Legal Paper Series No. 11–18, available at: http://ssrn.com/abstract=1919084.

113 *Case of the Massacre of Plan de Sánchez v. Guatemala*, judgment on reparations, para. 80.

114 *Case of Bámaca Velásquez v. Guatemala*, judgment on reparations, para. 62; *Case of Trujillo Oroza v. Bolivia*, judgment on reparations, para. 85; and *Case of Juan Humberto Sánchez v. Honduras*, para. 175.

115 *Case of Juan Humberto Sánchez v. Honduras*, paras. 172 and 176.

116 *Case of Myrna Mack Chang v. Guatemala*, para. 271.

condemns the human rights violations in question and makes a commitment to efforts designed to ensure that they do not happen again. Such acts have the effect of restoring the memory of the victims, acknowledging their dignity, and consoling their next of kin".[117] In addition, the obligation to investigate the circumstances of the violation and act upon it by punishing the guilty author serves the purpose of satisfaction for the victims.[118] The Court orders measures to rehabilitate the victims through medical and psychological assistance,[119] or study scholarships for children of victims,[120] which may also be deemed as satisfaction in a broad sense.

39. Orders to educate public employees and even society in cases where the social culture is discriminatory,[121] those to train judges and other actors of the judicial process in international human rights standards or those related to the creation of state organs to perform health or educational activities are properly guarantees of non-repetition. In the Contreras *et al.* case the Court ordered the State to

> [e]nsure that the different bodies of the justice system involved in the case have the human, financial, logistic, scientific and other resources necessary to perform their tasks adequately, independently and impartially, and adopt the necessary measures to guarantee that judicial, prosecutorial and investigative officials and other agents of justice have an adequate security and protection system, which takes into account the circumstances of the cases for which they are responsible and the place where they work, and allows them to perform their functions with due diligence, and to protect witnesses, victims and next of kin.

40. The Court usually does not separate the obligations to make reparation and to ensure non-repetition. Reparations are meant for the victim; non-repetition is directed toward the future and individuals other than the victim. The Court's work in this field has been ground breaking. Probably an inducing factor has been the sort of violations experienced by the population over which the Court has jurisdiction. There is a significant number of individuals who have been subject on and off to dictatorships. In addition, there is still a

---

117 *Massacre of Plan de Sánchez v. Guatemala*, para. 80.

118 *Case of the Serrano sisters v. El Salvador*, paras. 64–65; *Case of Gómez Lund et al. v. Brazil*, para. 180.

119 *Case of Cantoral Benavides v. Peru*, judgment on reparations, para. 99.8; *Case of Durand and Ugarte v. Peru*, judgment on reparations, para. 45.3; *Case of Rosendo Cantú et al. v. Mexico*, paras. 252–253, 295.19 and 21; *Case of Fernández Ortega et al. v. Mexico*, paras. 251–252, 277–278, 308.17, 18 and 24.

120 *Case of Rosendo Cantú v. Mexico*, para. 295.20.

121 *Case of Gelman v. Uruguay*, paras. 276–278; *Case of Vélez Loor v. Panama, para.* 272; *Case of Gomes Lund et al. v. Brazil (Guerrilha do Araguaia)*, para. 283; *Case of Ibsen Cárdenas and Ibsen Peña v. Bolivia*, para. 258; *Case of Contreras et al. v. El Salvador*, paras. 186 and 213.8; and *Case of Cotton Field v. Mexico*, paras. 541 and 602.23.

significant number of people living in a world of extreme discrimination – caused, among other things, by poverty, race and sexual orientation. This population has borne and still bears cruel and inhuman conditions and does not receive much attention from the States that exercise jurisdiction over them. What the Court does, actually, is order the States – through reparations and guarantees of non-repetition – to comply with all their obligations under the Convention, a treaty that they are bound to respect by their own free will. Reparations and guarantees of non-repetition relate to the facts of the case, the violations found and the damage proven: the Court "must respect all these factors to ensure that its ruling is appropriate and in keeping with the law".[122] In this respect, it would be advisable for the Court to start differentiating the measures consistently. If judgments are examined, one finds that rehabilitation, for example, is sometimes under satisfaction,[123] and other times under "other measures", satisfaction referring only to the publication of the judgment in a national newspaper.[124]

The lack of consistency is repeated with other forms of reparation as well.

4.6. OBLIGATION TO COOPERATE

41. In addition to the obligations examined in the preceding sections, States have a third obligation: the obligation to cooperate with the international organs monitoring them. This obligation derives generally from their status as parties to the treaty and from the existence of a principle of international law that requires States to comply with treaties in good faith. This obligation appears specifically in the American Convention. Article 41(d) of the Convention grants the Inter-American Commission on Human Rights the authority to ask OAS Member States to submit reports on the measures taken on the subject of human rights. In addition, Article 48, which regulates the processing of individual communications before the Commission, establishes that the State *shall* send the information requested by the Commission within a reasonable period of time and that, in the event that the Commission should decide to carry out an investigation, "the States concerned *shall* furnish to it [...] all necessary facilities".[125]

The obligation to cooperate is thus clear and includes providing information that is timely, pertinent, and truthful with regard to the general situation of

[122] IACtHR, *Case of Fernández Ortega v. Mexico*, para. 85. See also *Case of Ticona Estrada et al. v. Bolivia*, para. 362, and *Case of the Dos Erres Massacre v. Guatemala*, para. 227.

[123] See the *Case of Rochac Hernández et al. v. El Salvador.*

[124] See the *Case of Tarazona Arrieta v. Peru.*

[125] The apparent mandatory character of "shall" has not been interpreted as such by the Commission. I do not think the reason is a legal one. The Commission apparently believes that if it were to attempt using it that way, it would only be faced with a blunt negative reaction of many States in the system. Nevertheless, the text says otherwise.

human rights in the State or with regard to a fact that the international body is weighing. On this subject, the consistent position of oversight organs has been that the States are in a unique position to provide them with the information necessary for evaluating whether States are complying with or violating international law.[126]

42. As a consequence of this position, the Inter-American Commission has adopted a provision in Article 39 of its Rules of Procedure according to which:

> The facts alleged in the petition, the pertinent parts of which have been transmitted to the State in question, shall be presumed to be true if the State has not provided responsive information during the period set by the Commission under the provisions of Article 38 of these Rules of Procedure, as long as other evidence does not lead to a different conclusion.

The Inter-American Court supported this position by establishing that "the silence of the accused or elusive or ambiguous answers on its part may be interpreted as an acknowledgment of the truth of the facts set forth in the application, so long as it is not contradicted by the record or is not compelled as a matter of law."[127] It has also repeatedly indicated that the State:

> cannot rely on the plaintiff's inability to present evidence in the proceedings since, in such cases, it is the State that controls the means to clarify the facts that have occurred in its jurisdiction and, therefore, in practice, it is necessary to rely on the cooperation of the State itself in order to obtain the required evidence.[128]

Although the statement was made with regard to cases of disappearance, it is valid for all those cases in which the State is in possession of the evidence of a violation of any human right.

4.7. OBLIGATION TO CONTROL CONVENTIONALITY

43. Through the development of the obligation to control conventionality, the Court has placed on national judges a special responsibility. In the case of Almonacid it considered that when a State is a party to a treaty, its judges are particularly bound to compliance. In a novel formulation, it wrote:

> This forces [judges] to see that all the effects of the provisions embodied in the Convention are not adversely affected by the enforcement of laws which are contrary to its purpose and that have not had any legal effects since their inception.

---

126 See, for example, HRC, *Santullo v. Uruguay*, Communication 9/1977, ruling of October 26, 1979, paras. 7 and 10 and *García Lanza, Weismann de Lanza and Lanza Perdomo v. Uruguay*, Communication 8/1977, ruling of April 3, 1980, para. 15.

127 *Case of Velásquez Rodríguez v. Honduras*, para. 138.

128 *Case of Bámaca Velásquez v. Guatemala*, para. 152.

> In other words, the Judiciary must exercise a sort of "conventionality control" between the domestic legal provisions which are applied to specific cases and the American Convention on Human Rights. To perform this task, the Judiciary has to take into account not only the treaty, but also the interpretation thereof made by the Inter-American Court, which is the ultimate interpreter of the American Convention.[129]

This is the "*conventionality control*".[130] Judge García Ramírez seems to be the first to mention it, in his concurring vote in the case of Tibi. There, he compares the domestic control of constitutionality carried out mainly by constitutional courts or other equivalent organs, with a control of conventionality that falls within the powers of the Court. The Inter-American Court analyzes "the acts that are brought before it in connection with the legal standards, principles, and values of the treaties on which it bases its adjudicatory jurisdiction". He explains that in the logic of the system

> there lies the idea that the rulings of the Court must be reflected, in the manner and according to the terms set forth in domestic law – as the bridge between the international and the national systems – in domestic legislation, in domestic jurisdictional criteria, in specific programs in this field, and in the daily actions of the State regarding human rights; they must, ultimately, be reflected in the national experience as a whole.[131]

44. The Court has applied the conventionality control in several cases, although its phraseology has not been always the same. In Almonacid, the Court addressed the judiciary. In the case of Alfaro Aguado *et al.* (Dismissed Congressional Employees), the Court again put the burden on the judges but added that the control should be done *ex officio*, which could have been read already in Almonacid.[132] In the Gelman case, the Court starts to address itself timidly to other State agents, in a manner uniting the conventionality control with the constant jurisprudence of the Court that all State agents must comply with the Convention and the Court is the only one with authority to interpret it. In this case, the usual formula is preceded by the sentence: "When a State has ratified an international treaty such as the American Convention, *all of its bodies*, including its judges, are also subject to such a treaty, and this obligates them to ensure that the effects of the provisions of the Convention are not diminished by the application of norms contrary to its object and purpose".[133] In Fernández

---

129 *Case of Almonacid v. Chile*, para. 124. See also *Case of Radilla Pacheco v. Mexico*, para. 114; *Case of Guerrilha de Araguai v. Brazil*, para. 176; *Case of the Dismissed Congressional Employees (Aguado-Alfaro et al.) v. Peru*, para. 128 and *Mendoza et al. v. Argentina*, para. 221.

130 For a thorough examination of conventionality, see the separate opinion of *ad hoc* Judge Ferrer MacGregor Poisot in the *case of Cabrera Montiel v. Mexico*.

131 *Case of Tibi v. Ecuador*, concurring vote of Judge García Ramirez, paras. 3 and 6.

132 *Case of the Dismissed Congressional Employees v. Peru*, para. 128.

133 *Case of Gelman v. Uruguay*, para. 193.

Ortega, the Court repeats this formulation.[134] In Ibsen Cárdenas and Ibsen Peña, the Court returns to its first formulation.[135] In Cabrera García and Montiel Flores, the Court repeats the formulation of the judgment in Gelman, adding at the end that the judiciary must take into account not only the provisions of the Convention but also the interpretation of the Court. In the Santo Domingo Massacre case, referring to the subsidiary role of the Court with respect to that of the States, the Court states: "These ideas have also been incorporated in recent case law based on the opinion that all the authorities and organs of a State Party to the Convention have the obligation to ensure 'control of conformity with the Convention'". In the case of Mendoza *et al.*, the Court clearly affirms that judges and any organ involved in the administration of justice, mentioning in particular the Office of the General Prosecutor, must exercise the conventionality control *ex officio*.[136]

In sum, all State agents must comply with their obligations under the Convention, because they are being interpreted by the Inter-American Court in strict conformity with international law and judges have the function of seeing to it that application of the law, if possible, does not infringe the Convention and the Court's case law. The development of the conventionality control enhances the idea that the interpretation of the Convention rights emanating from the Court's judgments is obligatory for States, even if they are not a party to the case.[137]

45. States have not contended the conventionality control. A court in Mexico asserted that the national courts must apply international treaties and *inter alia* the jurisprudence of the Inter-American Court of Human Rights and other organs. This obliges them to exercise conventionality control as the Mexico Supreme Court had decided.[138] The Mexican court reiterated this position, for example, in the case of Cabrera García and Montiel Flores v. Mexico.[139] Peru's Constitutional Court has also decided that the judgments of the Inter-American Court are legally binding for state organs, including not only the decisions but also the ratio decidendi (reasoning), even when Peru is not a party to the case.[140]

---

134 *Case of Fernández Ortega v. Mexico*, paras. 236–237.

135 *Case of Ibsen Cárdenas and Ibsen Peña v. Bolivia*, para. 202.

136 *Case of Mendoza et al. v. Argentina*, para. 221.

137 See in this regard, "Latinoamérica está avanzando en la democracia de ejercicio", interview in *El País* (Spanish newspaper) on December 15, 2013 with the then President of the Inter-American Court, available at: http://internacional.elpais.com/internacional/2013/12/15/actualidad/1387124578_658856.html.

138 Quoted by the Court in the *Case of Radilla Pacheco v. México*, para. 339.

139 *Case of Cabrera García and Montiel Flores. v. Mexico*, para. 21.

140 Tribunal Constitucional del Perú (00007-2007-PI/TC).

There have been some writings on this issue. Ariel Dulitzky labels this development by the Court's case law "an invention".[141] Perhaps the word exceeds what the Court has done, because what is behind this control is not much more than what the Court has said throughout its many years of work. With the decision that States must exercise conventionality control, the Court simply enhances the fact that States Parties to a treaty are obligated to ensure that the Convention's provisions are complied with by any and all State agents, and it is therefore necessary for them to take these obligations into consideration in all their performances. Of course, the Court will always have the final decision on whether the State before it has done this correctly or has committed a violation and the judgment will be binding for that State. Conventionality control is only a reminder and an explanation to States of how to fulfil their international duties.

4.8. RESTRICTIONS

46. Since human rights are, in general, not absolute, States have a non-discretionary power to regulate their exercise by all. These regulations are called restrictions. International law provides a frame within which States may impose them.

The first limit is that the general conditions and circumstances allowing a restriction of the exercise of a human right must be established by law, for reasons of general interest and in accordance with the purpose for which the restrictions are established.[142] The requirement that a law be put in place in order to regulate rights is a safeguard against potential governmental arbitrariness, as the expression "law" implies both formal[143] and material requirements.

---

141 See the interesting article by Ariel Dulitzky developing reasoned criticism of the conventionality control as it appears now to be. A.E. Dulitzky, "An Inter-American Constitutional Court? The Invention of the Conventionality Control by the Inter-American Court of Human Rights", *Texas International Law Journal*, Vol. 50, issue 1. See also K. Castilla: "El control de convencionalidad: Un nuevo debate en México a partir de la sentencia del caso Radilla Pacheco", Biblioteca Jurídica Virtual del Instituto de Investigaciones Jurídicas de UNAM.

142 For examples, see Articles 6, 9, 12, 19 and 22 of the ICCPR, and Articles 4, 7, 12, 13, 16 and 30 of the American Convention.

143 The word "law" has a clear meaning in the legal systems of the majority of the Latin American States that participated in the drafting of the Convention. In the majority of those States, the word is used to mean an instrument created by the legislature through the observance of specific procedural steps provided for in the Constitution (R. Medina and C. Medina Quiroga, *Nomenclature of Primary Legal Sources*, Library of Congress, Washington DC, 1979, pp. 2, 8, 16, 22, 38, 48, 65–66, 90, 95–96, 102, 112, 120–121). The majority of the other States define "law" as the content of the instrument created by the legislature in accordance with specific proceedings, while the instrument itself is called a "decree" (*ibidem*, pp. 54–55, 59–60, 72, 84–85 and 107–108). Mexico uses both words – "law" or "decree" – to indicate a decision of Congress (*ibidem*, p. 77). Therefore, they are all in agreement that "law" can only

Interpreting the word "law" as meaning a formal law is reasonable, as instruments coming from the legislature go through proceedings that are carefully designed to reflect the points of view of the majority and of minorities and represent, at least formally, the wishes of the majority. In light of the political reality of the American continent, it seems quite clear that the purpose of the safeguard is to prevent the imposition of restrictions by mere executive decrees. The word "law" incorporates as well the requirement of being enacted for "reasons of general interest", according to Article 30 of the Convention, which means "they must have been adopted for the 'general welfare' [...], a concept that must be interpreted as an integral element of public order (ordre public) in democratic states".[144] This would be called law in a material sense. Any other interpretation of the word would be contrary to Article 1(1) of the Convention, which establishes the general principle of non-discrimination.[145] The Court does not refer to the requirements that law must be foreseeable and accessible, as the European Court does. The foreseeability of a law, in Latin American terms, would equate to the principle of legality of Article 9 of the Convention regarding criminal offenses, and the accessibility would be provided by the fact that all laws are written. The requirements of an instrument to be qualified as law, suits only states with a civil law system. If there were a case affecting a common law States, the Court would have to revisit the issue, probably in similar terms as in Europe.[146]

The second limit on all restrictions is that the cause invoked to justify the restriction be one of those established in the Convention, whether through a general or a specific provision. The causes are the interest of national security, public order or security, or the protection of health and public morals and the freedoms of others.[147] One provision allows the restriction of the right to property for reasons of social interest.[148]

47. There is a third limitation in the inter-American system: restrictions must be "necessary in a democratic society". This requirement exists explicitly for the rights of peaceful assembly, freedom of association, and freedom of movement.[149]

be the result of the action of legislators (this being understood as one or two assemblies of representatives of the people plus, in general, the president of the Republic), carried out in accordance with a proceeding provided for at the highest level of law: the Constitution.

144 IACtHR, Advisory Opinion 6, *OC-6/86* of May 9, 1986. The word "laws" in Article 30 of the American Convention on Human Rights, para. 29.

145 The interpretation of the word "law" in the Convention was made by the Court in Advisory Opinion 6 (*OC-6/86*, paras. 27, 28, 29, 31 and conclusion).

146 Regarding foreseeability and accessibility, see P. van Dijk *et al.* (eds.), *Theory and Practice of the European Convention on Human Rights*, 4th edition, Intersentia, Antwerp/Oxford, 2006, pp. 652–657.

147 ACHR, Articles 15 and 16.

148 *Ibidem*, Article 21.

149 ACHR, Articles 15, 16 and 22.

However, its application as a limit to the restrictions of each of the rights of the Convention can be inferred from the context of the Convention itself, especially in light of its object and purpose[150] – both established in the preamble – and of Article 29(c) of the Convention. In the preamble, the American States reaffirmed their intention "to consolidate in this hemisphere, within the framework of democratic institutions, a system of personal liberty and social justice based on respect for the essential rights of man."

The European Court of Human Rights has interpreted the expression "necessary in a democratic society" at great length, and the Inter-American Court of Human Rights has offered a similar interpretation in its Advisory Opinion 5/85 that draws comparisons with European case law and incorporates it into the system. The Inter-American Court found that in the inter-American system, restrictions should comply with several conditions. First, the restriction must be in response to the "existence of an urgent social need" – that is, it must be oriented toward "satisfying an imperative public interest". Second, of the various options for achieving this objective, "the one must be chosen that restricts the protected right the least". Third, the restriction must be "proportional to the interest justifying it and closely aligned with the achievement of this legitimate objective".[151] In other words, the restriction must be intended to protect the value that can be protected through the restriction of this particular right and proportional, involve only the measures that are strictly necessary to achieve the intended purpose. In addition, there must be no other alternative to restricting this right for achieving the goal, meaning that if an alternative does exist, it must be used in place of the greater restriction.

4.9. TEMPORARY SUSPENSION OF OBLIGATIONS

48. In its Article 27, the Convention allows States Parties to temporarily suspend some of their human rights obligations in the event of war, public danger, or other emergency that threatens the independence or security of the State Party. In these cases, States generally turn to declaring the existence of a situation they often describe as "emergency" or "martial law" or other similar nomenclature. This provision has been key for many Latin American States to diminish or ignore the protection of the rights contained in the Convention. Effectively, according to a study prepared for the Commission, during the decade between 1950 and 1960 there were over a hundred occasions when Latin American States lived in a state of emergency.[152] In its 1981–1982 Annual Report,

150 In this sense, see Vienna Convention on the Law of Treaties (1969) (Vienna Convention), adopted in Vienna on May 23, 1969, entered into force on January 27, 1980, United Nations, *Treaty Series*, vol. 1155, p. 331. A/CONF.3 9/27, Article 31(1) and (2).

151 *OC-5/85*, para. 46.

152 IACHR, Doc. OEA/Ser.L/V/II.8, No. 6.

the Commission indicated "the declaration of states of emergencies was one of the most frequent human rights violations."[153] The situation is now different with States being in general under democratic rule.[154]

49. For this reason, and following the general trend, the Convention sets forth the guidelines according to which a State can declare a state of emergency. The guidelines establish: (i) the grounds on which certain treaty obligations can be suspended; (ii) the rights with respect to which the State cannot suspend any obligation; (iii) a requirement of proportionality as far as the duration and kind of suspensions ordered; (iv) a requirement that the measures cannot be discriminatory; and (v) the prohibition on suspending obligations when the suspension is not compatible with a State's other international obligations – this because the State, as noted previously, must apply the rule that most favors individuals. Finally, the Convention requires that the other States Parties be informed of the declaration of a situation of emergency.

4.9.1. Grounds for Authorizing Suspension

50. Article 27 of the Convention establishes that suspension is authorized in time of war, public danger, or other emergency that threatens the independence or security of a State Party. The drafting history of the provision does not clarify the specific meaning of the grounds that would allow suspension. This part of the provision originated in the European Convention, so the European precedents with regard to Article 15 of its Convention can be useful for its interpretation. However, the American Convention differs from Article 15 of the European Convention on replacing the European expression "the life of the nation" with "the independence or security of a State Party." This wording must be interpreted and developed in terms of the Inter-American system. We should take into consideration that these concepts are dangerously vague, particularly in view of the various interpretations – some rather extreme – of "national security" that have prevailed at certain times and in certain States on the American continent. This has made the supervision of regional organs crucial in every case in which the authority to suspend the observance of human rights is invoked.[155]

---

153 IACHR, *Annual Report of the Inter-American Commission on Human Rights*, 1981–1982, p. 133.

154 On emergency situations, see H. Faúndez, *El Sistema Interamericano de Proteccción de los Derechos Humanos. Aspectos institucionales y procesales*, 3rd edition, Instituto Interamericano de Derechos Humanos, 2004, pp. 95 ff.

155 See R.E. Norris and P.D. Reiton, "The suspension of guarantees: A comparative analysis of the American Convention on Human Rights and the Constitutions of the States Parties" (1980) 30 *American University Law Review* 189–223 (191–199).

The Court has been especially strict in limiting States' authority to take measures that can affect the rights of persons, and particularly those rights whose obligations, according to the Convention, are non-derogable.[156]

4.9.2. Obligations not Susceptible to Suspension

51. As far as obligations not susceptible to suspension are concerned, Article 27 itself prohibits suspending rights emerging from Articles 3, 4, 5, 6, 9, 12, 17, 18, 19, 20, and 23. In addition, nor are "the judicial guarantees essential for the protection of such rights" subject to suspension. It is not possible to deduce from the drafting history of the Convention the criteria used for selecting these rights. The list seems to include either rights that are in a way absolute, such as the right to life and the right not to be tortured, or rights whose suspension could not be relevant for dealing effectively with an emergency, such as for example the right to a name stipulated in Article 18 of the Convention.

52. The long history of threats to political participation on the American continent, in which the suspension of constitutional guarantees under emergencies has frequently resulted in the suspension of all political rights for long periods, is reflected in the rule that obligations regarding political rights are not susceptible to suspension in emergency situations.[157] It has been argued that the non-susceptibility of these rights to suspension can in practice be highly difficult to abide by, especially in times of war.[158] However, a reasonable interpretation where the provision's goal and purpose play a role leads to a different conclusion. Sections (a) and (c) of Article 27, which address the right to participate in the conduct of public affairs and equal access to public services respectively, present no problems. Both of them establish rights whose exercise should be possible under any circumstance. Furthermore, section (c) only addresses an aspect of the general principle of equal protection, which obviously is non-derogable. Only section (b), which sets forth the right to vote and to be elected, could present a problem, as it could be said that there are many circumstances in the life of the nation in which the organization of an election may be difficult or even impossible – for example, a natural disaster or a war. In order to analyze this point, one should consider that Article 27 refers to the

---

156 *Case of Loayza Tamayo v. Peru, para.* 57; *Case of Cantoral Benavides v. Peru*, para. 96; *Case of Bámaca Velásquez v. Guatemala*, para. 155.

157 Article 23 sets forth: "1. Every citizen shall enjoy the following rights and opportunities: a. to take part in the conduct of public affairs, directly or through freely chosen representatives; b. to vote and to be elected in genuine periodic elections, which shall be by universal and equal suffrage and by secret ballot that guarantees the free expression of the will of the voters; and c. to have access, under general conditions of equality, to the public service of his country."

158 T. Buergenthal, "The American Convention on Human Rights: Illusion and Hopes" (1971–72) 21 *Buffalo Law Review* 121–136.

willful temporary suspension of an obligation, meaning that the right could be materially exercised if it were not for the suspension. It could be argued that in the case of a natural disaster or a war, it would be impossible to exercise the right to vote due to events that are beyond the control of the authorities, not due to a suspension. The inclusion of Article 23 in Article 27(2) seems to have the clear goal of preventing measures such as the dissolution of the parliament or congress or the prohibition of political parties on the grounds of an emergency, or the suspension of the right to vote for reasons other than the material impossibility of holding an election.

53. Article 27 also prohibits the derogation (or suspension) of the judicial guarantees that are indispensable for the protection of rights whose obligations cannot be suspended. The Inter-American Court has elaborated upon this in two opinions. The first identifies Articles 7(6) and 25 of the Convention as guarantees that are non-derogable.[159] It considers that an emergency situation should not affect representative democracy, should not entail "the temporary suspension of the rule of law",[160] and should not authorize governments "to conduct themselves outside the legality to which they should adhere at all times", given that "the principle of legality, democratic institutions, and the rule of law are inseparable."[161] For this reason, independent and impartial judicial authorities suitable for determining the legality of actions taken during a state of emergency must be able to have oversight of the measures.[162]

In the second opinion, the Court reiterates its arguments and position with regard to Article 25. However, it pauses to examine Article 8 – which sets forth legal due process – noting, "it does not, strictly speaking, contain a judicial remedy, but rather a collection of requirements that must be met in the procedural instances in order to be called true and suitable judicial guarantees according to the Convention."[163] It concludes that the concept of legal due process "in its essence should be understood to be applicable to all judicial guarantees addressed in the American Convention, even under the suspension regime regulated by Article 27 of the Convention."[164]

In addition to the guarantees already mentioned, there are other guarantees that arise from Article 29(c)[165] of the Convention. These

159 *OC-8/87*, para. 20.
160 In this regard, see *infra* Chapters 4 and 7.
161 *OC-8/87*, para. 24.
162 *Ibidem*, para. 30.
163 *OC-9/87*, para. 27.
164 *Ibidem*, para. 29.
165 Article 29, titled "restrictions regarding interpretation", establishes: "No provision of this Convention shall be interpreted as: [...] precluding other rights or guarantees that are inherent in the human personality or derived from representative democracy as a form of government."

> "guarantees [...] derived from representative democracy as a form of government" referred to in Article 29(c) imply not only a particular political system against which it is unlawful to rebel, but the need that it be supported by the judicial guarantees essential to ensure the legality of the measures taken in a state of emergency, in order to preserve the rule of law.[166]

It reiterates once more that the rule of law, representative democracy, and the regime of personal freedom are innate characteristics of the Inter-American system and, in particular, of the system for the protection of the human rights set forth in the Convention.[167]

It concludes:

- The "essential" judicial guarantees which are not subject to derogation [...] include habeas corpus (Art. 7(6)), *amparo*, and any other remedy effective before judges or competent tribunals (Art. 25(1)) designed to guarantee the respect of the rights and freedoms whose suspension is not authorized by the Convention.
- The essential judicial guarantees which are non-derogable include those judicial procedures, inherent to representative democracy as a form of government (Art. 29(c)). These procedures must be provided for in the laws of the States Parties as suitable for guaranteeing the full exercise of the rights referred to in Article 27(2) of the Convention and whose suppression or restriction entails the lack of protection of such rights.
- The aforementioned judicial guarantees should be exercised within the framework and the principles of due process of law, expressed in Article 8 of the Convention.[168]

In sum, both the American Convention and the Court emphasize that the general rule is that rights should be respected and ensured; the suspension of States' international obligations to respect and ensure the exercise and enjoyment of rights when merited by very special circumstances is the exception. However, the guarantees of non-derogable rights cannot be suspended, nor can any suspension result in the invalidation of the principle of legality.

4.9.3. Proportionality of Measures of Suspension

54. Article 27 of the Convention sets forth the requirement of proportionality. This means that the Court allows suspensions "to the extent and for the period of time strictly required by the exigencies of the situation." If the exigency of the situation is what justifies the measures, international law requires that in addition to being proportional in length and form, the measures taken must be geared to the objective of overcoming the emergency that is taking place. This requirement is applicable both to the general measure of suspension of a right

166 *OC-9/87*, para. 37.

167 *Ibidem*, paras. 34 and 35. Here the Court repeats what it had expressed in Advisory Opinions 5, 6 and, naturally, 8.

168 *OC-9/87*, para. 41.

as well as to every specific measure taken by the authorities in the application of the general measure.[169] The principle of proportionality is thus linked with three ideas. The first is that the necessary measures taken must also be adequate; second, there must be a relationship between the danger facing the community and the measures for counteracting it.[170] Finally, actions taken by the authorities to limit fundamental rights and freedoms may never exceed the particular rational limit of any restrictive measure.[171]

For its part, the Inter-American Court has indicated that "the lawfulness of the measures taken to address each of the special situations referred to in Article 27(2) will thus depend on the character, intensity, depth, and particular context of the emergency, as well as the proportionality and reasonableness of the measures adopted."[172] The limits alluded to address the form in which the measures affect rights and individuals. Regarding the former, under no circumstance may the authorities overstep the severity of the measures, as they must constitute only those measures that are suitable for re-establishing normality. As regarding the persons affected, authorities must limit themselves to suspending the exercise of the rights of persons who are directly involved in the emergency, without affecting the rights of others.

55. The case of Zambrano Vélez seems to be the leading case on Article 27, although much of the interpretation is firmly based on the two Advisory Opinions examined above. Emergencies must be tailored to the exigencies of the situation. Therefore, "it is clear that what might be permissible in one type of emergency would not be lawful in another. The lawfulness of the measures [...] will depend, moreover, upon the character, intensity, pervasiveness, and particular context of the emergency and upon the corresponding proportionality and reasonableness of the measures".[173]

The reasons and motives for a declaration of a state of emergency must be determined in the declaration and the measures must be conducive to deal with them. Authorities must have effective control on the actions taken in an emergency considering the limitation that they will be carried out "to the extent and for the period of time strictly required by the exigencies of the

169 *OC-8/87*, para. 39.

170 *Ibidem*, pp. 95–97.

171 "This principle, like its justification – legitimate defence – presupposes the existence of an imminent threat and requires a proportional relationship between that threat and the measures used to avert it. These measures in turn, to be legitimate, must be proportional to the severity of the threat. Thus any excess in the use of the measures makes the 'defence' illegitimate and thus transforms it into aggression." Report of the Special Rapporteur of the Human Rights Subcommission on the *Question of Human Rights and States of Emergency*, E/CN.4/Sub.2/1997/19 of 23-VI-1997, para. 84.

172 *OC-8/87*, para. 22.

173 *Case of Zambrano Vélez v. Ecuador*, para. 45.

situation".[174] In the case of Zambrano Vélez, the domestic decree-law that declared the emergency, "neither fixed a time limit for the military intervention, which would allow knowing its duration; nor did it lay down the rights which would be suspended, that is, the material scope of the suspension".[175] This was incompatible with Article 27, and against the interpretation of a similar provision in the ICCPR.[176]

Given the history of the continent, the Court emphasized in Zambrano Vélez "the extreme care which States must observe when they decide to use their Armed Forces as a mean for controlling social protests, domestic disturbances, internal violence, public emergencies and common crime". It reminded Ecuador that the military "are trained to fight against enemies"; the police should carry out social control.[177] The Court found the scope of the military intervention in Ecuador, with purposes that were "broad and vague" and "exceeded the powers attributed to the States by the Convention", and so there had been a violation of Articles 25 and 27.[178]

4.9.4. Prohibition on Affecting Obligations not Subject to Suspension in Other International law Norms

56. Article 27 of the Convention sets forth the principle that the human rights enshrined therein and the State obligations regarding human rights are not exclusive of the content of other laws, ordering that measures suspending obligations during a state of emergency may not alter other obligations imposed by international law. This provision is repeated in both Article 4 of the ICCPR and Article 15 of the European Convention, both of which refer to the provisions of treaties – including humanitarian law treaties – and customary law.[179]

4.9.5. Prohibition of Discrimination

57. According to Article 27 of the Convention, the measures of suspension that the State can take during a state of emergency cannot entail any discrimination based on race, color, sex, language, religion, or social origin. This provision reproduces the grounds of discrimination enumerated in Article 4(1) of the ICCPR and it leaves out some of the grounds contained in Article 1 of the Convention. Political and other opinions, nationality, economic status, and

---

174 *Ibidem*, para. 47.
175 *Ibidem*, para. 48.
176 *Ibidem*, para. 48. See HRC, General Comment No. 29, adopted at the 1950th meeting, on July 24, 2001, CCPR/C/21/Rev.1/Add.11, August 31, 2001, para. 4.
177 *Ibidem*, para. 51.
178 *Ibidem*, para. 52.
179 See in this regard J. Fitzpatrick, *The International System for Protecting Rights During States of Emergency*, Procedural Aspects of International Law Series, Vol. 19, University of Pennsylvania Press, Philadelphia, 1994, pp. 59–60.

birth are not included in the wording of Article 27. The provision also does not mention the clause that allows for the incorporation of other not specified grounds of discrimination under the category of "any other social condition". There is nothing in the *travaux préparatoires* of the American Convention that would help explain the absence of these grounds. However, it should be taken into account that the application of the principles of necessity and proportionality, as well as the principle that all difference in treatment must be objective and reasonable, constitutes a powerful barrier to differences in treatment based on political opinions, absent in Article 27, or for that matter other possible reasons as well.[180]

58. Professor Fitzpatrick wondered in her excellent book on the topic of human rights during states of emergency if the inclusion of the prohibition on taking measures that affect other international obligations means that the oversight organs, in this case the Commission and the Court, have jurisdiction to hear the substance of these other obligations.[181] She argues, and I agree, that on supervising the application of Article 27, the Commission and the Court will be obligated to review whether the State has other obligations, the content and scope of those obligations, and whether the State is violating them on making use of Article 27. Finally, it could be concluded that should the State be found to be in breach of those obligations, it is also violating Article 27 of the Convention and that should be the finding of the Court.

4.9.6. Notification of Other States Parties and International Supervision

59. The Convention indicates that the State declaring a state of emergency "shall immediately inform the other States Parties, through the Secretary General of the Organization of American States" of the contents of the declaration, its motives and its duration. This is an evident reduction of the scope of domestic jurisdiction, as it means that a fact that has been imminently domestic and closely linked with the idea of statehood gives rise to an obligation to notify it to the international community. The notification requirement is a clear signal that the suspension of obligations is in the joint interest of States Parties to the Convention, and that they have the right to act upon the declaration of an emergency.

The Court considers that the notification is "a mechanism within the framework of the notion of collective guarantee underlying this treaty, which aim and purpose is the protection of human beings". This "allows

180 Paragraph 8 of General Comment No. 29 of the United Nations Human Rights Committee (CCPR/C/21/Rev.1/Add.11, August 31, 2001) is an interesting addition to the obligations that cannot be suspended pursuant to the ICCPR.

181 J. Fitzpatrick, *supra* n. 179, p. 60.

other State Parties to evaluate if the scope of this suspension is consistent with the provisions of the Convention" and the lack thereof is a violation of Article 27(3).[182]

60. International monitoring organs also have the authority to monitor whether the declaration of emergency and the specific measures taken based on that declaration violate the Convention, as part of their power to oversee and control the observance of Article 27.[183] A contrary interpretation would have the result of annulling the meaning of Article 27 and several other articles of the Convention, significantly diminishing the beneficial effect that the Convention can have on human rights in the Americas. It is likely that in the exercise of their jurisdiction, regional supervisory organs take into consideration the fact that governments could have more information available to them than oversight organs possess about the problems the States face and will take care to carry out their supervision in a reasonable manner. This also leads to the conclusion that – given that the decision on the justifiableness of the human rights suspensions imposed by the State is always in the end brought before the international organ supervising it[184] and that this international supervision is subsidiary – domestic courts must have control of the decision, both in its reasonableness and its legality.[185]

5. THE PRINCIPLE OF EQUALITY AND NON-DISCRIMINATION

61. Article 1 of the Convention sets forth that states must respect and ensure the full and free exercise of human rights without discrimination. The provision reflects an essential principle of human rights law: human rights are universal so all human beings are entitled to them; as a consequence, there can be no discrimination in respect of any human being on any grounds regarding these rights. The rights enshrined in the Convention are formulated in those terms, as they refer to "every person", "everyone", "no one" and "any one". The equality that we, human beings, are entitled to is in dignity and rights.[186] In

---

182 *Case of Zambrano Vélez v. Ecuador*, para. 70.

183 *Case of Neira Alegría et al. v. Peru*, para. 77.

184 The authorities of those organs are established in the corresponding treaties. Articles 44 and 45 of the American Convention give the Inter-American Commission the authority to hear petitions or complaints of any and all violations of the Convention; Article 62 gives the Inter-American Court authority to hear, under certain conditions, "all cases concerning the interpretation and application" of the Convention.

185 On suspension of obligations and international control, see *case of Espinoza Gonzales v. Peru*.

186 Universal Declaration of Human Rights, adopted and proclaimed by the UN General Assembly by Resolution 217 A (III) on December 10, 1948.

the inter-American system, dignity underlies all human rights. One could say that the human rights enumerated in the American Convention stand against different forms in which dignity may be transgressed. Those bound to respect and ensure human rights are the States and it is to them that the prohibition on discrimination is directed. The principle of non-discrimination has been found by the Court to be a *jus cogens* norm.[187]

62. Article 1(1) of the Convention directs States to respect and ensure the Convention rights "without discrimination". Article 24, in its turn, sets forth the right to "equality before the law" adding that "[c]onsequently, they are entitled, without discrimination, to equal protection of the law". Therefore, equality is not only ordered by the Convention with respect to human rights, but also regarding any matter regulated by the State. The Court has reiterated this in the Atala case, by affirming: "Article 24 of the American Convention prohibits discrimination, by law or *de facto,* not only with regard to the rights enshrined in said treaty, but also in regard to all laws approved by the State and their application".[188] Other words used in the Convention to express the same idea are: entitlement to minimum guarantees for the accused "with full equality" (Article 8), "equality of rights and the adequate balancing of responsibilities of the spouses as to marriage, during marriage, and in the event of its dissolution" (Article 17), and access "under general conditions of equality, to the public service of his country" (Article 23).

63. Sometimes the Court employs the two concepts, equality and non-discrimination, as apparent synonyms. However, in the Apitz case, the Court distinguishes between the two provisions – Articles 1(1) and 24 – affirming that Article 1(1) applies to the human rights set forth in the Convention, while Article 24 establishes "equal treatment before the law" with respect to all matters regulated by the State.[189] This means that the Court may decide to choose under which provision to examine a case.[190] This notwithstanding, the Court does not usually distinguish between equality and non-discrimination. This is the case, for example, of Advisory Opinion 4 of the Court, written at the request of Costa Rica. The Court had to give its opinion on the compatibility with the American Convention of amendments to the Costa Rican Constitution being discussed in Congress, which referred to certain requirements to grant naturalization. These requirements were different for different groups of people: men, women, persons from Central America, Spain and Ibero-America. One paragraph of the Opinion

---

187 Advisory Opinion *OC-18*, paras. 97–110.

188 *Case of Atala Riffo v. Chile*, para. 82. See also *Case of Apitz Barbera et al. v. Venezuela*, para. 209 and *Case Barbani Duarte et al. v. Uruguay*, para. 174.

189 *Case of Apitz et al. v. Venezuela*, para. 209.

190 See also *Case of Rosendo Cantú v. Mexico*, para. 183.

appears to make equality and non-discrimination equivalent concepts;[191] the equivalence is expressed unequivocally in the separate vote of Judge Piza Escalante. In it he affirms: "in the second place, it appears clear that the concepts of equality and non-discrimination are reciprocal, like the two faces of one same institution. Equality is the positive face of non-discrimination. Discrimination is the negative face of equality".[192] In Advisory Opinion 18, the Court observes that:

> Non-discrimination, together with equality before the law and equal protection of the law, are elements of a general basic principle related to the protection of human rights. The element of equality is difficult to separate from non-discrimination. Indeed, when referring to equality before the law, the instruments cited above[193] [...] indicate that this principle must be guaranteed with no discrimination.[194]

64. Much has been written on the principle of equality[195] and by now there is fairly widespread agreement that when one speaks of equality it is referring both to formal equality and material equality. This corresponds to the reality that society is not composed of homogenous persons but by people with a variety of particularities: some more talented than others; some have more education than others; some richer than others; we are all also of different sexes, different races, and different religions. The purpose of human rights is to respect and protect individuals in their own individualities. Luigi Ferrajoli sums this position up very eloquently: equality is "the equal right of everybody to the affirmation and protection of their own identity in virtue of the equal value associated to the differences that make of each person an individual different from all the others and of an individual a person as all the others".[196] A consequence of this is that, in order to respect individuality, distinctions

---

191 Advisory Opinion *OC-4*, para. 54.

192 *Ibidem*, para. 54. See also D. Shelton, "Prohibición de Discriminación en el Derecho Internacional de los Derechos Humanos", in *Anuario de Derechos Humanos*, Centro de Derechos Humanos, Facultad de Derecho, Universidad de Chile, available at: www.anuariocdh.uchile.cl.

193 Para. 71 of Advisory Opinion 18 refers to the OAS Charter, the American Declaration of the Rights of Man, the American Convention, the International Covenant on Civil and Political Rights and the Universal Declaration.

194 Advisory Opinion *OC-18*, para. 83.

195 See, for example, A. Sen, *Inequality re-examined*, Russell Sage Foundation, New York and Harvard University Press, Cambridge, Mass., 4th printing, 1997; S. Fredman, "Providing Equality: Substantive Equality and the Positive Duty to Provide" (2005) *South African Journal on Human Rights*; S. Fredman and S. Spencer, "Beyond discrimination: it's time for enforceable duties on public bodies to promote equality outcomes" (2006) *European Human Rights Law Review*; United Nations Development Programme, *Humanity Divided: Confronting Inequality in Developing Countries*, 2013.

196 L. Ferrajoli, "Igualdad y Diferencia" in L. Ferrajoli, *Derechos y garantías. La ley del más débil*, Editorial Trotta, pp. 73–96, available at: www.cubc.mx/biblioteca/libros/30 (author's own translation).

have to be made and some peoples may be catalogued in groups in order for the States to comply with their duties.

65. International law treaties have defined discrimination in similar terms in the International Convention on the Elimination of all forms of Racial Discrimination (CERD);[197] in the International Convention on the Elimination of All Forms of Discrimination against Women (CEDAW);[198] and in the Convention on the Rights of Persons with Disabilities (CRPD).[199] Because the definition of the treaties only dealt with discrimination on specific grounds, the Human Rights Committee, organ of the ICCPR, defined discrimination in its General Comment No. 18 in the following terms:

> "discrimination" as used in the Covenant should be understood to imply any distinction, exclusion, restriction or preference which is based on any ground such as race, colour, sex, language, religion, political or other opinion, national or social origin, property, birth or other status, and which has the purpose or effect of nullifying or impairing the recognition, enjoyment or exercise by all persons, on an equal footing, of all rights and freedoms.[200]

66. Jurisprudence of the Committee and of the European Court has provided criteria to decide when an action is discriminatory. The Committee observed in the same General Comment No. 18: "Not every differentiation of treatment will constitute discrimination, if the criteria for such differentiation are reasonable and objective and if the aim is to achieve a purpose which is legitimate under the Covenant".[201] In turn, the European Court has said that it:

> holds that the principle of equality of treatment is violated if the distinction has no objective and reasonable justification. The existence of such a justification must be assessed in relation to the aim and effects of the measure under consideration, regard being had to the principles which normally prevail in democratic societies. A difference of treatment in the exercise of a right laid down in the Convention must not only pursue a legitimate aim: Article 14 (art. 14) is likewise violated when it is clearly established that there is no reasonable relationship of proportionality between the means employed and the aim sought to be realised.[202]

---

197 International Convention on the Elimination of all forms of Racial Discrimination (CERD) adopted by the UN General Assembly on December 21, 1965, Article 1(1).

198 International Convention on the Elimination of All Forms of Discrimination against Women, adopted by the UN General Assembly on December 18, 1979, Article 1.

199 UN Convention on the Rights of Persons with Disabilities, adopted by the UN General Assembly on December 13, 2006, Article 2. This convention introduces a paradigm shift by adopting the "social model" of disability (instead of the medical model) and recognizing that the "denial of reasonable accommodation" constitutes discrimination on the basis of disability.

200 HRC, General Comment No. 18 on Discrimination, of 1989 (HRI/GEN/1/ Rev 7), para. 7.

201 *Ibidem*, para. 13.

202 European Court of Human Rights, *Case "Relating to certain aspects of the laws on the use of languages in education in Belgium" v. Belgium* (merits), judgment of July 23, 1968, para. 10.

Consequently, a difference will be discriminatory when the differentiation of a person or a group is not based on an objective criterion and is unreasonable and when it does not pursue a legitimate aim, compatible with the treaty.

67. The Court's Advisory Opinion 18 asserts that the State is bound to make distinctions and explains the criteria to be considered to decide whether an action is or is not discriminatory. It states that the differentiation must have "a legitimate purpose", "not lead to situations which are contrary to justice or the nature of things" – an extremely difficult criterion to identify – and that it is necessary that "there exists a reasonable relationship of proportionality between these differences and the aims of the legal rule under review. These aims may not be unjust or unreasonable, that is, they may not be arbitrary, capricious, despotic or in conflict with the essential oneness and dignity of humankind".[203] Some paragraphs later the Court writes that:

> there would be no discrimination in differences in treatment of individuals by a state when the classifications selected are based on substantial factual differences and there exists a reasonable relationship of proportionality between these differences and the aims of the legal rule under review. These aims may not be unjust or unreasonable, that is, they may not be arbitrary, capricious, despotic or in conflict with the essential oneness and dignity of humankind.[204]

Finally, in paragraph 119 the Court speaks of "differential treatment [that] is reasonable, objective and proportionate and does not harm human rights".

As can be observed, the Court abounds in adjectives and qualifications, which makes the establishment of a standard difficult.

68. Article 1(1) of the Convention has a non-exhaustive list of grounds based on which a State may not discriminate. The list contains race, color, sex, language, religion, political or other opinion, national or social origin, economic status, birth and ends with "any other social condition". The last mention opens up the possibilities of basing a claim of discrimination on grounds not provided for in Article 1(1). The Court had the opportunity of interpreting the expression "any other social condition" in the Atala case. The Court considered that when interpreting those words "it is always necessary to choose the alternative that is most favorable to the protection of the rights enshrined in said treaty".[205] The subject matter of the case was an alleged discrimination against Ms. Atala Riffo because she had lost custody of her children based on her sexual orientation. The Court resorted to the standards established by the European Court and

---

A similar ruling can be found in the *case of Burden v. United Kingdom*, judgment of April 29, 2008, para 60.

203 Advisory Opinion 18, *OC-18*, para. 91.

204 *Ibidem*, para. 91.

205 *Case of Atala v. Chile*, para. 84.

the mechanisms of the United Nations, and decided that sexual orientation is a category protected by the Convention. Consequently, it concluded that "any regulation, act, or practice considered discriminatory based on a person's sexual orientation is prohibited. Therefore, no regulation, decision, or practice of domestic legislation, whether by state authorities or individuals, may diminish or restrict, in any way whatsoever, the rights of a person based on their sexual orientation".[206] Although the Court quoted in its support the position of the Human Rights Committee in Toonen v. Australia, it did not follow it, as in those views the Committee places sexual orientation as being covered by the word "sex",[207] while the Court includes it under "any other social condition".

69. Since its first judgment the Court decided any violation of a substantive right would always be a violation of Article 1, as that article contains the obligations to respect and ensure the rights in the Convention *without discrimination*. Thus, any violation found by the Court may also be read as a violation of the prohibition to discriminate, without any specific analysis of its discriminatory part. However, I believe there is more to it than just the letter of the treaty. In my opinion, the Court correctly joins these two concepts (the obligations to respect and ensure on the one hand, and the prohibition on discrimination on the other) because one cannot be examined without the other.

In Advisory Opinion 18, the Court put it clearly: "There is an inseparable connection between the obligation to respect and guarantee human rights and discrimination". This can be read in the sense that all discrimination regarding a human right will bring about a violation of the right, but it could also be read in the sense that all violations of human rights are at the same time a violation of discrimination. Only the former interpretation seems to be the right one. This is clarified later when the Court adds: "Non-compliance by the State with the general obligation to respect and guarantee human rights, *owing to any discriminatory treatment,* gives rise to its international responsibility".[208] The examination of judgments shows, however, that the Court analyzes discrimination on the basis of the requirements for restrictions explained above.

The same Advisory Opinion mentions as one effect of the principle of equality and non-discrimination "the State's obligation to take affirmative action to reverse or change discriminatory situations that exist in their societies to the detriment of a specific group of persons".[209] In a relatively recent judgment, in the Furlán case, the Court considers that the right to equality and non-discrimination encompasses two concepts. A negative one relates to the prohibition of arbitrary differences of treatment. A positive one relates to the States' obligation to create

206 *Ibidem*, para. 91. See also paras. 82–90.

207 Human Rights Committee, *Toonen v. Australia*, Communication No. 488/199, Views adopted during the Fiftieth session of the Committee, 31 March 1994, para. 8.7.

208 Advisory Opinion 18, *OC-18/03*, para. 85.

209 *OC-18/03*, para 104.

conditions of real equality for groups that have historically been excluded or that find themselves at risk of being discriminated against,[210] and proceeds to examine the case in those terms. The Court's position places it in the vanguard of the protection of groups in a disadvantaged situation and has had a significant impact on the protection of the economic and social aspects of the civil and political rights as one can see in the reparations phase of each judgment.

70. An important facet of the Court's comprehension of discrimination is that it links the principle with what is now being called "structural discrimination" and thereby with the obligation to ensure rights. In effect, the Court has handled discrimination of individuals who are part of a group that is disadvantaged on the enjoyment of rights because of social prejudices based on sex or on the economic or social situation they suffer from.[211] This prejudice is embedded in the laws and policies of a State and in society itself and it cannot be solved without a clear effort by the State toward producing changes in all these areas. Roberto Saba speaks of a structural vision based on the idea that the law cannot be completely blind to the social, economic and political relations between different groups of people at a certain historical moment. There will always be situations of social exclusion or of subjection of some groups by other groups; women, persons with disabilities, indigenous people and others will be deprived of their human rights because of this.[212] The State has to take this into account in order to fulfil its obligations under Article 1 of the Convention.

Cases or opinions of the Court have dealt *inter alia* with discrimination against children, migrants, women, indigenous people and members of a group with a different sexual orientation than the majority. An example of structural discrimination is the case of Cotton Field. Mexico's authorities had not reacted to the disappearance of two young women and a child – all three poor – attributing the reason of their absence to the fact that they were "flighty" or had "run away with their boyfriends". The bodies of the victims appeared later tortured and dead. The Court found that:

> gender stereotyping refers to a preconception of personal attributes, characteristics or roles that correspond or should correspond to either men or women. Bearing in mind the statements made by the State [...], the subordination of women can be associated with practices based on persistent socially-dominant gender stereotypes, a situation that is exacerbated when the stereotypes are reflected, implicitly or explicitly, in policies and practices and, particularly, in the reasoning and language of the judicial

---

210 *Case of Furlán and family v. Argentina*, para. 267.

211 See, for example, *Case of the Yakye Axa Community v. Paraguay*, para. 51.

212 R. Saba, "(Des)igualdad estructural", in D. Caicedo Tapia and A. Porras Velasco (eds.), *Igualdad y no discriminación. El reto de la diversidad*, Serie Justicia y Derechos Humanos Neoconstitucionalismo y Sociedad, Ministerio de Justicia, Derechos Humanos y Cultos, Argentina, p. 57, available at: www.justicia.gob.ec/wp-content/uploads/2012/05/20-Igualdad-y-no-Discriminación.pdf.

police authorities, as in this case. The creation and use of stereotypes becomes one of the causes and consequences of gender-based violence against women.[213]

The stereotyping had lead Mexico to leave the victims without proper access to justice and this had, in turn, resulted in impunity, which "sends the message that violence against women is tolerated; this leads to their perpetuation, together with social acceptance of the phenomenon". In sum, the way Mexican institutions and society were organized constituted discrimination.[214]

71. In the case of Yatama, an indigenous organization, the Court found that, when regulating the political rights of these peoples, the State could not leave aside the special protection they were entitled to under the Constitution of Nicaragua and the Statute of Autonomy of the Atlantic Coast Region. The political rights of the members of Yatama had been seriously hindered when the new Electoral Law required the indigenous peoples – like of course the rest of the population – to create a political party in order to present candidates for local elections. This form of organization was alien to the customs, practices and traditions of the indigenous and ethnic communities involved, thus making it impossible for the Yatama members to participate because they could not fulfil all the requirements of the new law. The Court found that, although every State had the right to decide how to organize the country for carrying out elections, Nicaragua's law did not comply with the requirements of a democratic society. The State had imposed a disproportionate restriction that disregarded the particularities of indigenous communities for political participation and had thus violated Articles 23 and 24 of the Convention.[215]

In the case of the Saramaka people, the Court dismissed the argument put by the State reasoning that "it would be discriminatory to pass legislation [to indigenous peoples] that recognizes communal forms of land ownership". The Court said that persons in an unequal situation should be treated differently.[216] This agrees with the jurisprudence of the Court regarding the scope and content of the obligation to ensure.

In the case of Xákmok Kásek, the Court found discrimination against the Indigenous Community because of the "weak presence" of State institutions that failed to provide food, water, healthcare and education to the group. In addition, the State had given "pre-eminence of a view of property that grants greater protection to property owners over indigenous claims, thereby failing to recognize their cultural identity and threatening their physical subsistence".[217]

---

213 *Case of Cotton Field v. Mexico*, para. 401.
214 *Ibidem*, paras. 400–401.
215 *Case of Yatama v. Nicaragua*, paras. 205–206, 214, 220, 224–225.
216 *Case of the Saramaka People v. Suriname*, para. 103.
217 *Case of the Indigenous Community Xakmok Kásek v. Paraguay*, paras. 273–274.

In the case of Servellón García the Court dealt with the treatment of "*maras*" (young gangs) by State agents. There was evidence that within the framework of the state's response of preventive and armed repression of young gangs, a context of violence appeared at the beginning of the nineties. The *maras* are composed of children and youngsters in a situation of social risk and identified as causing an increase in public insecurity. 904 minors died as a result of State violence between 1995 and 2002.[218] The Court found several violations of the right to life and personal integrity of the victims, but invoked equality and non-discrimination to warn that a State "cannot allow that its agents, nor can it promote in the society practices that reproduce the stigma that poor children and youngsters are conditioned to delinquency, or necessarily related to the increase in public insecurity".[219]

Judgments that are more recent have dealt with discrimination in similar terms.[220]

72. Reviewing the Court's judgments, one comes to the conclusion that in dealing with, in particular, structural discrimination, the Court examines the situation placing the accent on the State's obligation to ensure. In my view, the Court starts from the following premises. The first premise is that society is by definition heterogeneous, comprising people with different characteristics. The second premise is that, given that society is heterogeneous, it is up to the States to see to it that discrimination does not occur: the prohibition of discrimination does not address the holders of rights but the duty-bearers, which are the States. It is up to States to take the necessary steps so that everyone can exercise their human rights without discrimination, and the manner of complying with this is by taking the measures that will be adequate and appropriate to making the enjoyment of rights equal. The measures themselves do not have to be equal; on the contrary, they must be different if we wish for equal enjoyment. Of course, States will have to ensure that this is also complied with by members of society, since they are responsible not only for their actions but also for their omission in protecting those under their jurisdiction from third parties.

73. Actually, in this matter of comparisons, it is hard for me to agree with the idea of dividing people between "equal" and "different". This distinction requires that we accept that equal is the general rule and those who are different are "deviant". This is a pejorative way of looking at the rich diversity of humanity. I am not even going to enter into the problem of how to decide, for example, whether we, women, are the equal and they, men, are the different or what to

---

218 *Case of Servellón García et al. v. Honduras*, paras. 79.1 and 79.2.

219 *Ibidem*, para. 112.

220 See, for example, *Case of Dominicans and Haitians expelled v. Dominican Republic* and *Case of Espinoza y Gonzáles v. Peru*.

consider we are equal on.[221] This position makes one wonder about what has been written regarding "affirmative actions", in the sense that they are supposed to be essentially temporal and, for some, voluntary. This is not necessarily so and more reflection on this subject would be welcome. Actions taken to allow people with disabilities to exercise their rights, for example, are neither temporal nor voluntary.

6. THE INTERPRETATION OF HUMAN RIGHTS TREATY PROVISIONS

74. The American Convention is a treaty and as such must be interpreted according to the rules for the interpretation of treaties of the Vienna Convention on Treaties of 1969.[222] The first subparagraph of Article 31 of the Vienna Convention establishes that "a treaty shall be interpreted in good faith in accordance with the ordinary meaning to be given to the terms of the treaty in their context and in the light of its object and purpose".

What constitutes the context of a treaty is set forth in Article 31(2)(a) and (b) of the Vienna Convention. The wording of the rules in Article 31 emphasizes the idea that those rules' various elements form an interpretative system without any hierarchy. This is different to the rules that are usually found to interpret legal norms in countries with a continental legal system. Here, all treaty provisions must be interpreted by simultaneously taking into account good faith, the common meanings of the terms, in the context of the treaty, and the treaty's objective and goal. Regarding the history of the adoption of the treaty (the *travaux préparatoires*), the Vienna Convention definitively gives it secondary interpretive status.[223]

75. In contrast to other international treaties, human rights treaties confer rights to individuals before the State, which in turn has obligations toward those individuals. The Inter-American Court had the opportunity to rule on this point in Advisory Opinion 2, where it expressed the following:

> The Court must emphasize, however, that modern human rights treaties in general, and the American Convention in particular, are not multilateral treaties of the traditional type concluded to accomplish the reciprocal exchange of rights for the mutual benefit of the contracting States [...]. In concluding these human rights

221 There has been much written on what would be the criteria to decide on equality and difference, but usually no agreement has been reached. See, for example, A. Sen, *supra* n. 195.

222 Vienna Convention, *supra* n. 150, p. 331.

223 Vienna Convention, Article 32. In this regard, the Inter-American Court has reached similar conclusions. See *OC-9/87*, paras. 49–50.

> treaties, States can be deemed to submit themselves to a legal order within which they, for the common good, assume various obligations, not in relation to other States, but towards all individuals within their jurisdiction.[224]

Thus, the establishment of rights and reciprocal obligations for States Parties is only a marginal purpose of human rights treaties.[225] The main purpose is the establishment of a system for the protection of human dignity. In the above-cited Advisory Opinion, the Court clearly expressed that clause 2 of Article 20 of the Vienna Convention is not applicable.[226] The main reason is that "the objective and goal of the [American] Convention is not the reciprocal exchange of rights among a limited number of States but rather the protection of the rights of all human beings residing in the Americas, independent of their nationality".[227]

76. If we take into account that one of the elements for the interpretation of international law is the consideration of the object and purpose of the treaty, and that object and purpose are the protection of human rights, it must be concluded that the interpretation must always be to the benefit of the individual (a *pro persona* interpretation). This being the case, it follows that the content and scope of rights must be interpreted broadly, while their restriction must itself require a restrained interpretation. This has been reiterated frequently by the Inter-American Court of Human Rights, which expressed in the first matter it heard that "balanced interpretation is achieved by orienting it as favorably as possible toward the beneficiary of international protection, as long as this does not imply altering the system".[228] *Pro persona* interpretation is thus an important characteristic of the interpretation of human rights law, constituting the guiding principle that must govern its interpretation at all times.

77. The mention of a treaty's object and purpose as an interpretive element also confers on it a dynamic character. A treaty must be read in such a way that the law is interpreted taking into account the situation at the moment at

---

224 *OC-2/82*, para. 29. For this same reason, Article 60(5) of the Vienna Convention establishes that the provisions of the article allowing a State to terminate or suspend a treaty by invoking a violation of the treaty by another State do not apply to treaties of a humanitarian nature.

225 However, there are rights and obligations between States. Article 27, for example, on emergency situations, orders that any declaration of an emergency must be notified through the OAS to all States parties, which will have the right to contest it because of an alleged incompatibility with the Convention. Also, it is possible, given certain circumstances, that a State complains before the inter-American organs against another State for the violation of the Convention.

226 Article 20 of the Vienna Convention, which regulates the acceptance of and objections to reservations, indicates the following in subparagraph 2: "When it appears from the limited number of the negotiating States and the object and purpose of a treaty that the application of the treaty in its entirety between all the parties is an essential condition of the consent of each one to be bound by the treaty, a reservation requires acceptance by all the parties."

227 *OC-2/82*, para. 27.

228 *Matter of Viviana Gallardo et al. v. Costa Rica*, para. 16.

which the interpretation occurs. The way to protect a person today may be, and frequently is, different from what was required in the past; the perception of what is impermissible for States to do and permissible in a person's conduct similarly varies with the passage of time. In the case of human rights, the object and purpose of treaties establishing or guaranteeing them is to protect human dignity, providing safeguards for individuals faced with the possibility of abuse from those governing them and granting those individuals the right to demand that the State organize society in such a way that the opportunity to enjoy and exercise those rights is guaranteed. The interpretation of each human right must allow for protection, even from possible violations not taken into consideration at the time the provision was established. The treaty provisions' freedom from those who drafted them is reflected in the fact that the *travaux préparatoires* are clearly only a supplementary means to determine the meaning of a norm.[229]

The International Court of Justice recognizes this dynamism on expressing in the Advisory Opinion entitled *Legal Consequences for States of the Continued Presence of South Africa in Namibia notwithstanding Security Council Resolution 276 (1970)* that "an international instrument must be interpreted and applied within the framework of the entire legal system prevailing at the time of the interpretation".[230] This dynamism, both in the interpretation of the content of human rights laws and in the context of treaties, also appears in the Inter-American Court's Advisory Opinion 10/89, whose text states as follows:

> the Court finds it necessary to point out that to determine the legal status of the American Declaration it is appropriate to look to the inter-American system of today in the light of the evolution it has undergone since the adoption of the Declaration, rather than to examine the normative value and significance which that instrument was believed to have had in 1948.[231]

Finally, this form of interpretation is firmly based on the European human rights system and can be found in innumerable rulings. These refer to both substantive and procedural law issued by the European Court of Human Rights, the international body with the fullest experience of ruling on cases of alleged human rights violations.[232]

---

229 Vienna Convention, Articles 31(1) and 32.

230 International Court of Justice, *Legal Consequences for States of the Continued Presence of South Africa in Namibia (South West Africa) notwithstanding Security Council Resolution 276 (1970)*, Advisory Opinion, ICJ Reports 1971, pp. 16–31, para. 53.

231 IACtHR, Advisory Opinion on "The interpretation of the American Declaration of the Rights and Duties of Man within the framework of article 64 of the American Convention on Human Rights", *OC-10/89* of July 14, 1989, para. 37. See also Advisory Opinion on "The right to information on consular assistance in the framework of the guarantees of the due process of law", *OC-16/99* of October 1, 1999, paras. 113–115.

232 For a general analysis on this point, see P. Van Dijk, "'Positive Obligations' Implied in the European Convention on Human Rights: Are the States Still the 'Masters' of the

Since the American Convention is mainly formulated in the form of principles and general norms, they require the interpreter to elaborate, detail and, in short, develop them to suit the circumstances of each case. This is also so because the *travaux préparatoires* of the Convention, as already explained, are only a supplementary means to determine the meaning of a norm.[233] In sum, dynamism and the *pro persona* rule provide judges with ample scope for a very creative interpretation.[234]

78. From a different point of view, the various sources of international law influence each other reciprocally. The general principles of law, customary law, the unilateral actions of States, and the resolutions of international organizations can pre- or post-date the provisions of treaties. Thus, it is impossible to attempt the application of a treaty without knowledge of the existing general principles of law or customary law, just as it is not possible when interpreting a treaty to ignore other sources of law that may have come afterward and that clarify or complement the treaty. This, which is specific to international law, is particularly important for international human rights law, which is always subject to a dynamic interpretation. In its Advisory Opinion 16/99, the Court supports this idea by indicating that "the *corpus juris* of international human rights law comprises a set of international instruments of varied content and juridical effects (treaties, conventions, resolutions and declarations)". It proceeds then to examine the subject of the opinion in "the context of the evolution of the fundamental rights of the human person in contemporary international law."[235]

Just as international sources of law influence each other, this kind of reciprocity also exists between those sources and domestic ones. From the point of view of international law, one should recall that general legal principles originate in the domestic law of States; this law, therefore, can be a source for international law, as well as guiding criteria for a broader interpretation of human rights contained in international provisions. Interpretation of international provisions can also benefit from the case law generated on this point in States Parties to the system, given that the application of domestic law in individual cases can also give a more precise scope and content to human rights provisions. Looking at this from another angle, on interpreting domestic human rights provisions, a domestic judge must also take international provisions and international case law into consideration.

Convention?", in M. Castermans, F. Van Hoof and J. Smith (eds.), *The Role of the Nation-State in the 21st. Century*, Kluwer Law International, 1998, pp. 17–33.

233 Vienna Convention, Articles 31(1) and 32.

234 On "creative interpretation", see C. Medina, "The Role of International Institutions: Law making or creative interpretation", in D. Shelton (editor and author), *The Oxford Handbook of International Human Rights Law*, Oxford Handbooks in Law, Oxford University Press, Oxford, 2013.

235 *OC-16/99*, para. 115.

Finally, knowledge of "judicial decisions and the teachings of the most highly qualified publicists of the various nations" is likewise relevant for interpretation. In fact, recognized doctrine and the rulings of international supervisory bodies represent auxiliary means for determining the rules of international law, pursuant to Article 38 of the Statute of the International Court of Justice.

79. In the inter-American framework, the idea of a system of interpretation is reflected and broadened in Article 29(c) and (d) of the Convention. The former prohibits the interpretation of any provision of the Convention in a way that precludes "other rights or guarantees that are inherent in the human personality or derived from representative democracy as a form of government." This rule clearly shows that the system is a single whole that goes beyond the mere letter of the specific treaty. This consideration of the human person is based on his or her dignity, an inherent quality of a human being that requires the respect of others in their relations with him or her. Dignity is a concept perhaps difficult to define but can be clearly identified in each case, in the light of an international human rights system that exists within a historical context.[236] Besides, Article 29(c) reflects the position of the inter-American system that treaties do not grant human rights but simply recognize them, and that human rights not formally recognized by a legal body can however exist.

Article 29(d) establishes that no provision of the Convention can be interpreted as "excluding or limiting the effect that the American Declaration of the Rights and Duties of Man and other international acts of the same nature may have." In addition to supporting the idea of the system as a whole, this provision furthers the position that the resolutions of international bodies can have legal value even when formally and in principle they do not appear to, indicating that the interpreter cannot ignore them.[237]

80. All of the above just serves to emphasize that the system for the promotion and protection of human rights is – as the word "system" would indicate – a collection of rules and principles connected rationally one to another that should be viewed as a whole when applying any of its parts. As an analogy for these ideas, we could say that national and international contributions to human rights flow into a crucible, resulting in a synergy from which human rights reappear broadened and perfected. It is to that crucible that the interpreters of human rights law must turn when performing their task.

---

236 On dignity, see D. Kretzmer and E. Klein (eds.), *The Concept of Human Dignity in Human Rights Discourse*, Kluwer Law International, The Hague/London/New York, 2002.

237 The Inter-American Court ruled on this point in Advisory Opinion No. 10, based in part on the arguments that an interpretation of the Declaration could be necessary when interpreting the American Convention due to the provisions of the Convention's Article 29. See *OC-10/89*, para. 36.

7. RESPONSIBILITY OF STATES

81. Responsibility is "the state of being answerable for an obligation".[238] The Draft Articles on Responsibility of States for Internationally Wrongful Acts (Draft Articles)[239] set forth the rules that are applied to find a State responsible, starting by providing: "Every internationally wrongful act of a State entails the international responsibility of that State". Article 2 of the Draft Articles defines when an international wrongful act exists, requiring two elements: it must be an action or omission attributable to the State under international law and it must constitute a breach of an international obligation. The characterization of such an act or omission will be carried out by international law.[240] The Draft Articles do not mention fault or malice as elements of responsibility.[241] In general, internationalists support this position: international responsibility is objective and determined by the causal relationship between the agent and the wrongful act.[242] Thus, the failure to comply with an international obligation through State action or omission results in State responsibility and this translates into the obligation to provide full reparations,[243] both pecuniary and non-pecuniary, for any damage the violation may have caused. In international human rights law, a wrongful act that results in responsibility consists in the violation of one of the obligations established in a human rights treaty to the detriment of an individual subject to the jurisdiction of the State responsible.

82. According to the Draft Articles, the conduct of any State organ makes the State responsible, "whether the organ exercises legislative, executive, judicial or any other functions, whatever position it holds in the organization of the State, and whatever its character as an organ of the central Government or of a territorial unit of the State".[244] The Inter-American Court has applied this rule in its judgments. In the case of the Ituango Massacres it affirmed: "This active protection of the right to life by the State involves not only its legislators, but also all State institutions and those who should protect security, whether they are its police or its armed forces".[245] Other conducts may make the State responsible and some of them have appeared in the Court's case law.[246] States have frequently

---

238 *Black's Law Dictionary*, 5th edition, 1979.

239 Draft Articles on Responsibility, *supra* n. 107.

240 *Ibidem*, Article 3.

241 On fault and malice, see I. Brownlie, *Principles of Public International Law*, 4th edition, Clarendon Press, Oxford, p. 440.

242 *Ibidem*, pp. 437–440.

243 International Court of Permanent Justice, *Usine de Chorzów*, judgment on merits, 1928, Series A No. 17, para. 13.

244 Draft Articles on Responsibility, *supra* n. 107, Article 4.

245 *Case of the Ituango Massacres v. Colombia*, para. 131.

246 Draft Articles on Responsibility, *supra* n. 107, Articles 5–11.

been found responsible for the actions of paramilitary organizations, as will be seen below.

83. In its judgments, the Inter-American Court follows the rules of the Draft Articles, including the theory of objective responsibility, in which it insists that it is not necessary to take into account "elements of a psychological nature intended to categorize the individual guilt of the perpetrators."[247] It has also established that State responsibility can exist for acts presumably committed by private individuals, concluding that the State can incur international responsibility directly, because of the actions of its agents, and indirectly, for failing to act in response to the actions of private individuals that infringe rights established in the Convention. Regarding direct responsibility, the Court has stated that "[a]ccording to Article 1(1) [of the Convention], any exercise of public power that violates the rights recognized by the Convention is unlawful. Whenever a State organ, official or public entity violates one of those rights, this constitutes a failure of the duty to respect the rights and freedoms set forth in the Convention".[248]

Regarding indirect responsibility, the Court has affirmed:

> A wrongful act which violates human rights and which is initially not directly imputable to a State (for example, because it is the act of a private person or because the person responsible has not been identified) can lead to international responsibility of the State, not because of the act itself, but because of the lack of due diligence to prevent the violation or to respond to it as required by the Convention.[249]

Applying this general provision to a specific case, the Court found that the disappearance of Velásquez Rodríguez was clearly attributable to State agents. However, even if that had not been the case, the attribution of responsibility could have been equally made. It was proven in the case that there was "a failure on the part of Honduras to fulfil the duties it assumed under Article 1(1) of the Convention, which obligated it to ensure Manfredo Velásquez the free and full exercise of his human rights".[250] The case of the 19 tradesmen referred to the fate of 19 people. They were abducted, made to disappear and subsequently killed and dismembered by paramilitary groups, which allegedly were part of the guerrilla. The Court found that Colombia had protected for many years the creation and activities of the paramilitary groups and the Armed Forces in the region had encouraged them to assume "an offensive attitude towards the guerrilla".[251] Once proven that public authorities had supported or tolerated a violation, nothing else was needed: neither the guilt nor the intentions of the perpetrators,

---

247 *Case of Velásquez Rodríguez v. Honduras*, para. 173.
248 *Ibidem*, para. 169.
249 *Ibidem*, para. 172.
250 *Ibidem*, para. 182.
251 *Case of the 19 tradesmen v. Colombia*, para. 124. See also paras. 134–135.

nor their identification.[252] In the case of the Mapiripán Massacre the Court notes that the acts in 1997 were committed by paramilitary groups, but they "could not have been prepared and carried out without the collaboration, acquiescence and tolerance" of the armed forces of the State.[253] The State was thus responsible for the violations.

84. When responsibility arises indirectly, so also arises the problem of determining which exact obligations the State must comply with to guarantee the exercise and enjoyment of the right in question – that is, what the content and scope of the obligation to guarantee each right is. It is impossible to give a general and abstract rule for this; the decision must be made case by case, establishing whether according to the circumstances, the State's conduct constitutes a violation of the Convention. Without prejudice to this, it is useful for the supervisory organs to be able to determine the standard of conduct required in order to guide interpretation and guide the State in complying with its obligations.

85. The Court has been consistent in finding States responsible where a situation of systematic violations and grave violations of the rights to life, personal integrity and disappearances exists. It stresses that the obligation to adopt positive measures of prevention and protection is increased in these circumstances.[254] The context in which a violation has been committed "permeates and conditions" the State's international responsibility.[255] This was clearly the case in Goiburú, a missing person in the context of a systematic practice of arbitrary detention, torture, executions and disappearance perpetrated by the intelligence and security forces of the dictatorship in Paraguay of Alfredo Stroessner under "Operation Cóndor". Operation Cóndor was carried out by "the intelligence services of several countries of the Southern Cone of the Americas [that] established a criminal inter-State organization with a complex assemblage, the scope of which is still being revealed today; in other words, there was a systematic practice of 'State terrorism' at an inter-State level".[256] The Court's judgment in Goiburú touched on interesting points regarding responsibility. The nature of the facts shows that Paraguay was but one of several States involved with the crime. The Court found that "the need to eliminate impunity establishes an obligation for the international community to ensure inter-State cooperation to this end". Consequently, the Court stated that the States Parties to the Convention "should collaborate with each other to eliminate the impunity of the violations committed in this case, by the

---

252 *Ibidem*, para. 141.

253 *Case of the Massacre of Mapiripán v. Colombia*, para. 120.

254 *Case of Ituango Massacres v. Colombia*, para. 137.

255 *Case of Goiburú v. Paraguay*, para. 94.

256 *Ibidem*, paras. 62 and 72. This judgment contains a thorough account of this criminal association.

prosecution and, if applicable, the punishment of those responsible". This was in tune with the collective guarantee ordered by the American Convention and other international instruments which bind "the States of the region to collaborate in good faith in this respect, either by conceding extradition or prosecuting those responsible for the facts of this case on their territory".[257]

86. Finding a State responsible for this type of violation has its limits. In Cotton Field the issue was the disappearance of two young women and an adolescent who were finally found tortured and dead. The authorities had not reacted with due diligence to investigate the events, which lead the Court to declare the State responsibility for its failure in ensuring the rights of the victims. However, the Court found no evidence that there had been participation of public officials in the disappearance or that public authorities had supported or tolerated private individuals when committing the illegal actions. As a result, it did not find a violation of the obligation to respect the substantive rights to life, personal integrity and personal liberty.[258]

87. International responsibility "arises immediately when the international illegal act attributed to it is committed, although it can be demanded once the State has had the opportunity to correct it by its own means".[259] If a case has begun before the inter-American system, a subsequent reparation by the State does not inhibit the regional organs from hearing the case.[260] This allows the Commission and Court to assess all the violations that have been perpetrated and their reparation.

In the case of Velásquez Rodríguez, the Court found categorically that "international protection of human rights must not be confused with criminal justice. States do not appear before the Court as criminal defendants." The purpose of the Court's examination is to protect the victims and provide reparations, which are due by the State responsible for the violation.[261] It can be deduced from this statement that international State responsibility is not criminal, and that as a consequence, the obligation to provide reparations is merely to compensate the damage caused by the failure to comply and should not be understood as a punishment inflicted on the State. This idea was reiterated in the judgment on reparations in the Velásquez case, in which the Court insisted that "under the current state of international law", indemnities could not be used to make an example or as a deterrent.[262]

---

257 *Ibidem*, paras. 131–132 and operative paragraph 5.

258 *Case of "Cotton Field" v. Mexico*, para. 242. See also *Case of Castillo González et al. v. Venezuela*, paras. 128 and 132.

259 *Case of Gómez Paquiyauri v. Peru*, para. 75.

260 *Ibidem*.

261 *Ibidem*, para. 134.

262 *Case of Velásquez Rodríguez v. Honduras*, judgment on reparations, para. 38.

In the case of Myrna Mack Chang, Judge Cançado Trindade challenged the Court's position. He argued that "a State's international responsibility includes elements of both civil and criminal nature in international law's current developmental stage",[263] a statement intended to advocate for the need for reparations established by the Court to eventually take on the status of penalties or deterrents.[264] Cançado Trindade argues that even when one acknowledges that State responsibility is objective, this does not dismiss the idea that responsibility based on the infraction or guilt be totally dismissed. In some cases, the intention of the State to cause damage or its negligence in avoiding it can be proven; fault or blame then becomes, here, the indispensable basis for responsibility of the State. The concurring opinion calls this aggravated responsibility a "State crime" that should result in obligations intended to "set an example or establish a deterrent".[265]

In that same case, the concurring opinion of Judge García Ramírez takes a different position. The judge admits that in the case of Myrna Mack Chang, there was "an objective aggravation of the facts" because it was not an isolated crime. Rather, it was the product of a plan prepared to deprive the victim of life, in which "both operatives and security officials presumably took part". Meanwhile, there were numerous obstacles in the investigation of those individuals and their criminal prosecution.[266] Despite this admission, he argues that the Court is not a criminal court.[267] Therefore, aggravation does not relate to changes in the nature of responsibility enforced by the Court. Without prejudice to this, the opinion finds that in the wording of the reproach it is necessary to take into account the greater gravity of the facts. This can be reflected in the reparations ordered by the Court, having an influence, for example, on acts of non-pecuniary compensation, circulation of the judgment, the expression of guilt or other similar actions.[268] What the opinion does not accept is an influence on monetary reparations through the establishment of "punitive damages". This was "a concept that has not been included in the case law of this Court, because it corresponds more to the idea of a fine than to that of the reparation of damage and, in any case, it would be payable by the Treasury, which implies an additional burden for the taxpayer and also a reduction in the resources that should go towards social programs."[269]

---

263 *Case Myrna Mack Chang*, concurring vote of Judge Cançado Trindade, para. 36.

264 *Ibidem*, concurring vote, para. 38. In para. 46, he argues that "reparations can perfectly function as both compensation and penalty, with the purpose of putting an end to impunity and ensuring that justice be carried out".

265 *Ibidem*, para. 40.

266 *Case of Myrna Mack Chang v. Guatemala*, concurring vote of Judge Sergio García Ramírez, paras. 44–45.

267 *Ibidem*, para. 44.

268 *Ibidem*, para. 47.

269 *Ibidem*, paras. 46–47.

The discrepancy between these two judges continued in the case of Goiburú. Judge García Ramírez gave powerful reasons that I find persuasive to substantiate his position. He argues against speaking of "aggravated responsibility", "State terrorism or crime or policy". In his opinion, that would imply in a literal examination, "attributing conducts to the State, concentrating responsibilities in the State, and categorizing criminal acts as policies". This attribution would exist as "a result of the conduct of those who occupied senior public posts and had or exercised excessive powers, and also the accumulation of responsibilities in the State itself."[270] Although he recognizes that this language is effective as it uncovers the characteristics of these criminal events and the potency for halting the arguments put forward by their authors, he prefers to speak of "crime originating in the State" or "terrorism originating in the State".[271] For him, this is a more precise way of distinguishing between those who commit the acts with the use of the State's power from the State as an entity. He argues, "[n]o official, however elevated his rank and determinant his authority, can concentrate in himself 'the whole State' – irrespective of the historical examples of absolutism – and register his crimes to the latter's account".[272] I agree with Judge García Ramírez and I find that it would be perhaps more precise still to speak of acts perpetrated by those illicitly holding power and employing for their actions the whole clout of the State.

In a later case, the Massacres of El Mozote and Nearby Places, concerning an incredibly violent situation with a significant quantity of victims during El Salvador's internal armed conflict, the Court found that El Salvador's international responsibility was aggravated because of this context. However, the Court did not elaborate on the issue.[273]

Whatever the ruling on the nature of responsibility and the effect of an "aggravated" violation, what seems to be clear is that proving intention on the part of the State agents who committed the violation facilitates the attribution of responsibility and can influence the determination of reparations. It seems that the Court must reflect on this point and discuss it further in order to reach a consensus on an issue that could be very important.

270 *Case of Goiburú v. Paraguay*, judgment of September 22, 2006, concurring vote of Judge García Ramírez, para. 17.

271 *Ibidem*, para. 23.

272 *Ibidem*, para. 28.

273 *Case of the Massacres of El Mozote and nearby places v. El Salvador*, paras. 156 and 208.

CHAPTER 2
DISAPPEARANCES*

1. INTRODUCTION

1. A few years ago I wrote: "[i]t is evident that although human rights are universal, every region finds modalities to adjust this universality, as far as protection systems are concerned, to the nuances necessary to deal with the people, the states and the culture in which they are immersed at a given time in order to fulfil their role as comptrollers of states' compliance with the obligations emerging from the respective treaties".[1] Implicit in this statement was the need to consider the political, social and economic situation in the States subject to supervision. A significant factor which influenced the nature of the nuances devised by the system was the phenomenon of disappearances in the region, a powerful weapon of the States to deal with political opposition and assert a grossly uncontrolled power over the people. The system had to address this problem, which required a new approach to what may have been envisaged when the Inter-American Commission on Human Rights (the Commission) and later the Inter-American Court of Human Rights (the Court) were created.

2. Disappearances are one of the worst atrocities that may afflict human beings. Their aim is to deprive a person of everything that makes life meaningful, short of killing them (although this usually happens too), and to spread terror in their direct environment, family and friends, and in society as a whole. Ultimately, it destroys the faith in institutions that constitute the essence of that which allows us to live in society. A person is deprived of his or her liberty; he or she is hidden, away from any contact with family or lawyers. Since frequently one of the aims of the exercise is to obtain information, the victim is ill-treated, usually tortured, and when this aim has been achieved or it is clear that it will not be achieved, the person is usually killed. In turn, the relatives experience, besides their loss, the desperation and impotence of not being heard by anyone, including executive

* For a comprehensive analysis of disappearances, see an interesting book by M. Lot Vermeulen, *Enforced Disappearance. Determining State Responsibility under the International Convention for the Protection of All Persons from Enforced Disappearance*, School of Human Rights Research Series, Intersentia, Antwerp, 2012.

1 C. Medina, "The Bumpy Road to Human Rights Enjoyment – the Americas", SIM lecture 2008, (2008) 26(4) *Netherlands Quarterly of Human Rights* 627–641.

authorities and the police. Moreover, they are ridiculed or even mistreated to discourage them from resorting to the legal channels that handle this type of complaint. Finally, there is no closure of the grief if the body of the disappeared person is not found and the truth is not known. The practice of this horror was frequent in the region. The idea behind it was to leave no trace, so it would be almost impossible to find out, even by private means, what had happened to the missing person. Those who made people disappear were State agents or civilians who worked under the control of the State or whose actions are acquiesced or tolerated by the State; in all cases, people who were in a position to engage the State's responsibility either by the State's action or omission.

3. In the case of Goiburú, among others, the Court affirmed that disappearance constitutes a crime against humanity involving a gross rejection of the essential principles on which the inter-American system is based.[2] It added that "[t]he State's international responsibility is increased when the disappearance forms part of a systematic pattern or practice applied or tolerated by the State". This may imply that there can be a disappearance outside a systematic pattern or practice.[3] In the sense I understand the phenomenon, which excludes missing persons in which the State is not involved through action or omission,[4] it is hard to imagine in real life a disappearance that is not part of a pattern. If a State tolerates or perpetrates a disappearance, it means that there must be a form of joint operation, through action or omission, between the executive, the legislature, and the judiciary. This may be voluntary cooperation or the result of the absolute submission of two of the organs to the third one, or of one organ to the other two. None of the cases before the Court indicates otherwise; all disappearances were committed in the framework of the absence of an effective rule of law. In this sense, they form part of what has been known for long as "a situation of gross, systematic violations".[5] Disappearances will be dealt with thus in this chapter.

4. The treatment of this phenomenon of disappearances has had a considerable impact on the development of the Court's interpretation of several rights of the

---

2 *Case of Guiburu v. Paraguay*, para. 82. See also *Case of Garcia and family v. Guatemala*, para. 92.

3 In the *Case of Osorio Rivera and family v. Peru*, the State objected to qualifying the situation of Mr. Osorio because there was no pattern of disappearances in Peru at the time. See paras. 106 and 127. The Court, in turn, examined and proved the systematic pattern, which was used for deciding on the case. See paras. 117–159.

4 I am aware that there are patterns of disappearance carried out by private individuals, such as drug dealers, of which one reads in Mexican papers. The only way that this situation could be covered by the Court would be if there was an omission of the State in their regard, in which case it would fall under the Court's jurisdiction.

5 For an old analysis of the expression, see C. Medina Quiroga, *The Battle of Human Rights. Gross Systematic Violations and the Inter-American System*, Martinus Nijhoff, Dordrecht/Boston/London, 1988, Chapter 2.

Convention and particularly on the rights to life, to personal integrity and to a fair trial. One important issue that will be treated in the chapter is the matter of the next of kin of a disappeared person. In doing this, I am aware that many questions belonging to these three rights will be examined here in advance, but I have preferred this organization in order to preserve the unity of the subject.

2. NORMATIVE FRAMEWORK

5. The graveness of the phenomenon and its frequent occurrence impelled the international community to react. In 1992, the UN Declaration on the Protection of all Persons from Forced Disappearance was adopted and in 2006 the International Convention for the Protection of all Persons from Forced Disappearance was signed, entering into force in 2010.[6] Article 1(2) of the Declaration establishes that:

> Any act of enforced disappearance places the person subjected thereto outside the protection of the law and inflicts severe suffering on them and their families. It constitutes a violation of the rules of international law guaranteeing, inter alia, the right to recognition as a person before the law, the right to liberty and security of the person and the right not to be subjected to torture and other cruel, inhuman or degrading treatment or punishment. It also violates or constitutes a grave threat to the right to life.

In Article 2 of the UN Convention,

> "forced disappearance" is considered to be the arrest, detention, abduction or any other form of deprivation of liberty by agents of the State or by persons or groups of persons acting with the authorization, support or acquiescence of the State, followed by a refusal to acknowledge the deprivation of liberty or by concealment of the fate or whereabouts of the disappeared person, which place such a person outside the protection of the law.

6. In 1994, the Inter-American Convention on Forced Disappearance of Persons (the Disappearance Convention) was adopted and gave the Court competence to supervise its compliance.[7] The gravity of the violation was the main consideration taken into account to qualify it as a "crime against humanity"[8] and to establish a series of provisions whose purpose was to prevent

---

6 UN Declaration on the Protection of All Persons from Enforced Disappearance, of December 18, 1992 and UN International Convention for the Protection of All Persons from Enforced Disappearance, entry into force on December 23, 2010.

7 Inter-American Convention on Forced Disappearance of Persons, adopted on June 9, 1994, in Belém do Pará. It entered into force on March 28, 1996. As of June of 2014, it had 14 States Parties.

8 Disappearance Convention, preamble.

forced disappearance by combating the impunity of those involved in it in a variety of ways. This Convention sets forth that:

> forced disappearance is considered to be the act of depriving a person or persons of his or their freedom, in whatever way, perpetrated by agents of the state or by persons or groups of persons acting with the authorization, support, or acquiescence of the state, followed by an absence of information or a refusal to acknowledge that deprivation of freedom or to give information on the whereabouts of that person, thereby impeding his or her recourse to the applicable legal remedies and procedural guarantees.[9]

7. The definitions of the Declaration, the UN Convention and the Inter-American Disappearance Convention do not contain exactly the same elements. The Declaration is wide in its conception of the legal effects of a disappearance; involved are the *right to recognition as a person* before the law, the right to liberty and security of the person and the right not to be subjected to torture and other cruel, inhuman or degrading treatment or punishment. As to the right to life, it considers that a disappearance can constitute a violation or a grave threat to life. The UN Convention, in its turn, refers mainly to the right of personal liberty and the refusal to acknowledge the deprivation of liberty or the concealment of the fate or whereabouts of the disappeared person, "which place such a person outside the protection of the law".

8. The Inter-American Disappearance Convention is nearer to the UN Convention's definition in that it places the accent on the deprivation of liberty followed by an absence of information or a refusal to acknowledge the action "or to give information on the whereabouts of that person, thereby impeding his or her recourse to the applicable legal remedies and procedural guarantees." The latter has a bearing on the right to due process and the right to personal liberty in its procedural aspect. The Inter-American Convention introduces a description of the actors who perpetrate a disappearance: they must be State agents or individuals acting on the authorization or with the support or acquiescence of the State. In its wording, the right to life is not an element of the disappearance. On the contrary, Article IV, paragraph 2 of the Convention refers to the possibility that a person might reappear,[10] a phenomenon that has actually occurred. In the case of Contreras *et al.*, there was a systematic pattern of forced disappearances of children and many of them went missing.[11] Members of the armed forces illegally abducted and retained these children, appropriating and

---

9 Disappearance Convention, Article II.

10 Article IV, paragraph 2 sets forth that: "The States Parties may establish mitigating circumstances for persons who have participated in acts constituting enforced disappearance when they help to cause the victim to reappear alive or provide information that sheds light on the forced disappearance of a person".

11 For a similar case, see *Rochac Hernández et al. v. El Salvador.*

registering some of them under their own names. At the time of the judgment, one of them had been found, and in 2013 the Court announced that two more were alive.[12]

9. Without prejudice to the Inter-American Disappearance Convention's definition, its preamble makes it clear that its drafters were aware that forced disappearance violates not only the right to personal liberty but also "multiple rights", without mentioning them. In addition, its preamble reaffirms "that the systematic practice of the forced disappearance of persons constitutes a crime against humanity".

The norms themselves contain a number of novel rules for the treatment of the phenomenon. In Article I, States undertake "[n]ot to practice, permit, or tolerate the forced disappearance of persons, even in states of emergency or suspension of individual guarantees" and "to cooperate with one another in helping to prevent, punish, and eliminate the forced disappearance of persons", the latter a clear reference to allow extradition. Article III sets forth that "[t]his offense shall be deemed continuous or permanent as long as the fate or whereabouts of the victim has not been determined." Articles IV–VI and VIII–X grant States universal jurisdiction to try a disappearance or to extradite a perpetrator. These provisions start by establishing an obligation for States Parties to pass a law that qualifies forced disappearance as a crime associated with an appropriate penalty[13] as a way of deterring individuals from participating in these types of actions. They set forth universal jurisdiction for the prosecution of this crime, ordering States Parties to adopt measures to establish jurisdiction – considering the definition found in Article II of the Convention on Disappearance – in order to be able to prosecute cases of disappearance.[14] To ensure that prosecutions are carried out, if the State does not try the accused it must extradite them.[15] Because the region's experience shows that impunity is often the result of the military jurisdiction handling these cases, Article IX of the Convention on Disappearance orders that cases of disappearance can only be brought to trial before the competent civilian jurisdiction and cannot be assigned to any special jurisdiction, particularly military. Neither can the facts leading to a disappearance be justified as having been perpetrated in the exercise of military duties, nor are privileges, immunities, or special exemptions allowed. Article VIII of the Convention on Disappearance prohibits due obedience from being ruled to provide exemption from criminal responsibility. As another way of preventing impunity, Article V of |the Convention on Disappearance establishes that forced disappearance will not be considered a political crime for the purposes of extradition and

---

12 See Resolution of the Inter-American Court of May 14, 2013 in the *case of Contreras et al. v. El Salvador.*

13 Disappearance Convention, Article III.

14 *Ibidem*, Article IV.

15 *Ibidem*, Article VI.

will always be included among crimes for which extradition is allowed, the Convention being sufficient legal basis therefor. The criminal action resulting from the disappearance – and the subsequent penalty – will not be subject to a statute of limitations unless it is established in a norm with the same hierarchy of the Constitution. In that case, the period of time in the statute of limitations shall be equal to that of the most serious crime in that State's legal system.[16] The Convention also contains some positive rules, such as the one on cooperation of States in combatting disappearances, as well as those relating to universal jurisdiction. Finally, the Convention establishes certain basic provisions for preventing forced disappearance. Persons deprived of liberty must be kept in places of detention that are officially recognized and brought without delay before the competent judicial authority. Updated official registries of detainees must be kept. Those registries must be made available to "any [...] person having a legitimate interest, as well as other authorities."[17] Judicial authorities must have free and immediate access to detention centers and any other place where they may have reason to believe that a disappeared person may be located, even those under military jurisdiction.[18] Finally, as another form of prevention, States must provide "the education necessary" on the crime of disappearance as part of the training of the personnel in charge of applying the law.[19]

10. The Disappearance Convention came into force in 1996. Most of what is in the Convention was already part of the development of the Court's case law. As of 2014, 15 States are parties to the former Convention so there are opportunities for the Court to apply that Convention instead of resorting to its own case law emerging from the American Convention. Even if the State is not a party to that Convention, the Court may resort to it, since the idea of a *corpus juris* is well settled in the Court's jurisprudence. This allows the Court to interpret the ACHR in the light of the Disappearance Convention to illuminate the obligations emerging from the former. The interplay between the norms of the Disappearance Convention and those developed by the case law of the Court has been very flexible. It could be fairly stated that the Court has not used the definition in the Disappearance Convention as a matter of course when dealing with a disappearance occurred in a State that is a party to the Convention.[20] On the contrary, it has frequently applied the obligations spelled out therein. The application of obligations reaffirms those that the Court had already imposed on the states when interpreting Article 1 jointly with that of the right violated, be it Article 4 on the right to life, Article 5 on the right to personal integrity or Article 8 on due process.

16 *Ibidem*, Article VII.
17 *Ibidem*, Article XI.
18 *Ibidem*, Article X.
19 *Ibidem*, Article VIII.
20 For example, it was used in the case of *Gómez Palominos v. Peru*, paras. 96–97.

3. THE PHENOMENON OF DISAPPEARANCES IN THE COURT

11. Disappearances, which proliferated in our region in the 1970s and 1980s, required of the Court its best ability to find a legal base compatible with the American Convention to address the phenomenon. It presented the complex problem of adjudicating over an alleged violation that did not exist as such in the Convention, nor in any another international instrument that the Court could use. The decisions taken by the Court on this regard have influenced, I would submit, the path of the Court's work thereafter.

12. The Court was called to deal with three cases of disappearances in 1986. Aside from the political challenges posed by a possible confrontation with reluctant States, the cases presented the Court with several legal challenges. A specific violation as complex as a disappearance did not exist in the Convention; it was necessary to decide whether a disappearance could be broken down into isolated specific human rights violations set forth in the Convention or if the violations might form part of a single phenomenon, which therefore had to be treated as a single violation. Evidence was necessary to prove something that the perpetrators were careful not to leave any traces of, which made it extremely difficult to ensure that the State where they occurred could be held responsible for them. There were complicated issues of jurisdiction depending on what would be considered the moment at which the phenomenon started and at which it concluded; and finally it seemed impossible to deal with a violation that had left some other people in a significantly distressing situation, usually not only emotionally but also financially, without taking them into consideration. The Court dealt with all this in an incredibly resourceful manner and, I believe, did a praiseworthy job.

3.1. ELEMENTS AND CHARACTERISTICS

13. When the Court received these cases, there was no international instrument containing any type of specific support on how to process the cases. In the cases of Velásquez Rodríguez and Godínez Cruz,[21] the phenomenon, a complex and explicitly non-existing violation, was decomposed and then composed by joining the violation of three rights: personal liberty, personal integrity and life. The Court reasoned that the violation of the right to personal liberty was clear: "The kidnapping of a person is an arbitrary deprivation of liberty, an infringement of a detainee's right to be taken without delay before a judge and to invoke the

21 I will refer only to *Velásquez Rodríguez*, because it was the first judgment and it was replicated in *Godínez Cruz v. Honduras*.

appropriate procedures to review the legality of the arrest, all in violation of Article 7 of the Convention".[22] The violation of the right to personal integrity was also clear: "prolonged isolation and deprivation of communication are in themselves cruel and inhuman treatment, harmful to the psychological and moral integrity of the person and a violation of the right of any detainee to respect for his inherent dignity as a human being", and is thus a violation of Article 5.[23] Besides, people who had been able to come back from similar experiences of torture and the like gave testimony of the ill-treatment that they themselves had undergone and of the ill-treatment of others who were with them but never returned.

14. The violation of the right to life was more difficult to ascertain, as usually the body of the disappeared person was missing. In its respect, the Court held that the "practice of disappearances often involves secret execution without trial, followed by concealment of the body to eliminate any material evidence of the crime and to ensure the impunity of those responsible. This is a flagrant violation of the right to life, recognized in Article 4 of the Convention". The Court gave several other reasons to find a violation of Article 4. First, it ruled that "the context in which the disappearance of Manfredo Velásquez occurred and the lack of knowledge seven years later about his fate create a reasonable presumption that he was killed.".[24] It explained that even if there was the slightest chance that Manfredo Velásquez was still alive, "his fate was decided by authorities who systematically executed detainees without trial and concealed their bodies in order to avoid punishment". This, in addition to the lack of investigation of the facts, constituted a violation of the duty to guarantee found in Article 1(1) of the Convention, with regard to Article 4(1) of the Convention.[25] Along with that, a violation of Article 4 could have taken place based on the sole fact that Manfredo Velásquez's life was put in danger when he was placed in the hands of authorities with a reputation for murdering those they detained – that is, the mere clear and imminent threat to life was enough to find a violation of that right. In sum, for the Court disappearance constituted a multiple and continuous violation of these rights under the Convention[26] and, regarding the right to life, a violation would exist in every instance of a disappearance, whether or not there was evidence of the death in the proceedings. A consequence of this finding is that a disappearance will continue to be such even if the person later reappears, thus bringing the concept closer to the definition in the Inter-American Disappearance Convention.

In terms of the elements of the disappearance, later on the Court added the right to recognition of the person before the law of Article 3 of the ACHR.

---

22 *Case of Velásquez Rodríguez v. Honduras*, para. 155.
23 *Ibidem*, para. 156.
24 *Ibidem*, para. 188.
25 *Case of Velásquez Rodríguez v. Honduras*, para. 157.
26 *Ibidem*, para. 155.

The Court did not explain the reason for including Article 3, except that the Commission had requested the violation of that right as an element of disappearances and responsibility for its violation was accepted by the State in question.[27]

15. The Court handled two more cases of disappearances after the adoption of the UN Declaration on Disappearances and before the Inter-American Disappearance Convention came into force. One was Caballero Delgado and Santana, where the Court did not follow its findings in Velásquez Rodríguez. The Court only found violations of Article 4 (right to life) and Article 7 (right to personal freedom), but not of Article 5 (right to personal integrity). Article 4 was violated on the basis that their death could be presumed.[28] In Garrido and Baigorria, the State had admitted all the facts, *inter alia* the violation of the three rights that composed a disappearance; by accepting this recognition, the Court accepted that those violations had been committed by Argentina.[29]

When the Court examined the case of Trujillo Oroza, the Disappearance Convention was already in force in Bolivia. However, the Court did not mention that Convention and addressed the disappearance of Mr. Trujillo Oroza as a single violation comprised of the rights to life, to personal integrity, to personal liberty and, for the first time, the right to juridical personality in Article 3 of the Convention.[30] This addition was not found consistently in some later cases. In Bámaca Velásquez, for example, the Court invoked the Inter-American Disappearance Convention to say that Article 3 is not included among the elements that typify a disappearance. It added "[t]he right to the recognition of juridical personality established in Article 3 of the American Convention has its own legal content, as do the other rights protected by the Convention". Therefore, it held that there had been no violation of Article 3 in the disappearance of Mr. Bámaca Velásquez.[31]

In Anzualdo Castro, the Court returned to its former interpretation, explaining that:

> given the multiple and complex nature of this serious human right violation, the Tribunal reconsiders its previous position and deems it is possible that, in this type of cases, the forced disappearance may entail a specific violation of said right: despite the fact that the disappeared person can no longer exercise and enjoy other rights, and eventually all the rights to which he or she is entitled, his or her disappearance is not only one of the most serious forms of placing the person outside the protection

---

27 *Case of Trujillo Oroza v. Bolivia*, paras. 1 and 41. See below for developments on Article 3.

28 *Case of Caballero Delgado and Santana v. Colombia*, paras. 53.b and 71.a.

29 *Case of Garrido and Baigorria v.* Argentina, paras. 10–19 and 24.

30 Article 3 sets forth the right to recognition as a person before the law.

31 *Case of Bámaca Velásquez v. Guatemala*, paras. 180–181. See also *Case of Benavides Cevallos v. Ecuador*, para. 43; *Case of La Cantuta v. Peru*, para. 121; and *Case of Ticona Estrada et al. v. Bolivia*, para. 71.

> of the law but it also entails to deny that person's existence and to place him or her in a kind of limbo or uncertain legal situation before the society, the State and even the international community.[32]

The Court found support for this assertion in several provisions and case law of other organs. One source used was Article 1 of the 1992 Declaration on the Protection of All Persons from Enforced Disappearance[33] where the right to recognition as a person before the law forms part of the rights violated in a disappearance. Another source was some decisions of the UN Human Rights Committee. Finally, several other international instruments used the phraseology of including as part of the definition of disappearance "impeding his or her recourse to the applicable legal remedies and procedural guarantees" or similar formulations. For the Court this meant precisely depriving the person of his right to legal recognition as a person.[34] Similar reasons were given in the cases of García and family[35] and Torres Millacura,[36] so this seems to have become a set precedent for the Court.[37] There have been a couple of attempts to include as an element of disappearances the violation of Articles 13 and 23 of the American Convention because the next of kin of a disappeared person had not been provided with information in the context of the criminal investigation at the domestic level. The Court has not accepted this petition, arguing that those facts were a violation of Article 8 on due process. It added that it had indeed found a violation of Article 13 but not on the basis of refusal to provide information on a trial.[38]

16. Strictly speaking, I would say that a disappearance occurs when a person is deprived of his/her liberty and the State refuses to give any information about it or does not even acknowledge it. Of course, to engage the responsibility of the State, this act must be perpetrated by agents of the State or by persons or groups of persons acting with the authorization, support, or acquiescence of the State.[39] As a consequence of the disappearance, other human rights of the victim are violated: life, personal integrity and the right to be recognized before the law. In addition, there may be other victims, in which case Articles 8 and 25 will probably come into play. This coincides with what the Court has said in the

---

32 *Case of Anzualdo Castro v. Peru*, para. 90. *See also Case of González Medina and family v. Dominican Republic*, para. 186, where the Court acknowledges that in the *case of Anzualdo Castro v. Peru*, it had returned to its position previous to the *case of Bámaca Velásquez v. Guatemala* and that this reasoning had been applied consistently since Anzualdo.

33 Adopted by the United Nations General Assembly in Resolution 47/133 of December 18, 1992.

34 *Case of Anzualdo Castro v. Peru*, paras. 88–101. See also *Case of the Massacres of Rio Negro v. Guatemala*, para. 118.

35 *Case of García and family v. Guatemala*, para. 12.

36 *Case of Torres Millacura v. Argentina*, para. 106.

37 See also *Case of Rodríguez Vera et al. v. Colombia*, para. 615.3.

38 *Case of "Diario Militar" v. Guatemala*, para. 268.

39 *Case of Osorio Rivera and family v. Peru*, para. 113.

case of Osorio Rivera and family: "acts that constitute enforced disappearance have a continuing or permanent character and [...] *their consequences* result in multiple violations of the human rights recognized in the American Convention while the whereabouts of the victim are unknown or his remains have not been found.[40] It is not clear that the violation of the right to life is an intrinsic element of the definition of a disappearance, unless "the mere clear and imminent threat to life" is enough to find a violation of that right. Otherwise, a disappearance exists even if the person remains alive and is released or is able to escape later on.

17. As to the characteristics of disappearances, a more recent judgment in the case of Gudiel Alvarez *et al.* reiterates the Court's original position that disappearances have a "permanent or continuing nature". The judgment indicated as concurrent and constituent elements of forced disappearance: (i) the deprivation of liberty, (ii) the direct intervention of State agents or their acquiescence, and (iii) the refusal to acknowledge the detention and to reveal the fate of the whereabouts of the person concerned. It emphasized that this characterization precedes the definition in the Inter-American Convention on Forced Disappearance, and is consistent with other definitions contained in different international instruments, mentioning the case law of the European human rights system, decisions of the UN Human Rights Committee, and decisions of domestic high courts.[41] It also stressed that:

> the individual's deprivation of liberty should be understood as merely the beginning of the constitution of a complex violation that is prolonged over time until the victim's fate and whereabouts are known. The analysis of a possible forced disappearance should not focus in an isolated, divided and fragmented manner only on the detention, or on the possible torture, or on the risk of loss of life, but rather the focus should be on all the facts that are present in the case being considered by the Court.[42]

Finally, the Court mentioned that, in cases of forced disappearance where there is evidence that the victim has died, the determination of whether this phenomenon existed and ceased, if applicable, necessarily entails finding the remains and establishing, as certainly as possible, the identity of the individual to whom the remains that have been found belong. In this regard, the corresponding authority must exhume them promptly, so that a competent professional can examine them. The forced disappearance continues to exist until the remains have been identified.[43]

---

40 *Ibidem*, para. 115 (emphasis added).

41 *Ibidem*, paras. 190–191. Some of this had already been said in *Heliodoro Portugal v. Panama*, para. 112 and in the *case of Contreras et al. v. El Salvador*, para. 84. It has also been repeated later in the *case of Gonzalez Medina and family v. Dominican Republic.*

42 *Ibidem*, para. 196. See also *case of Heliodoro Portugal v. Panama*, para. 112 and *case of Osorio Rivera and family v. Peru*, para. 165.

43 *Ibidem*, para. 207. See also *Case of Río Negro Massacres v. Guatemala*, para. 113.

18. Disappearances begin on the day the person is arrested or kidnapped and the State refuses to acknowledge the detention or simply does not give any information about it, and conclude when the person or their body is found and identified. The violation exists as long as the person or their body do not reappear, so the Court will have jurisdiction to deal with it because the disappearance is, in effect, happening every day, starting with the arrest or kidnapping. In such a situation, as the phenomenon of disappearance has not concluded, there is nothing to prevent the Court from ruling on the violation of the right to life, the right to personal freedom, and the right to humane treatment of the disappeared individual, handling the case as a single phenomenon.

The issue of the length of time after which a deprivation of liberty turns into a disappearance – for example, if the person reappears within a week – has not been an object of examination by the Court. In principle, one could say that a deprivation of liberty not acknowledged by the State, without there being any reason therefor, should technically be characterized as a disappearance. The consequences thereof in terms of reparations for the victim and for his or her next of kin would probably vary.

19. The way the Court proceeds to identify a disappearance is shown in a complicated case, Osorio Rivera, which required the need to prove a significant amount of facts. The case also shows how the Court handles the issue of weighing the evidence. The Court examined there whether the facts of the case constituted a disappearance. The State argued that military personnel had detained Osorio Rivera during a state of emergency, which was permitted by the Peruvian emergency law, and had released him later on. In addition, it denied a situation of gross, systematic violations in the area where the detention of the victim had been carried out.[44] After analyzing the evidence, the Court came to several conclusions. First, there was in Peru at the time a situation of gross systematic violations, and the case of Osorio was one case within this pattern.[45] Second, the release had not been proven. Further, an ostensible release order was an illegal device often used in situations of gross and systematic violations in order not to assume responsibility for a disappearance.[46] In addition, there was evidence that the soldiers at the Regiment, where the victim had been taken, had denied the detention of Osorio Rivera,[47] the family itself had seen when the victim had been taken handcuffed to a second destination, the Cajatambo Counter-subversive Base, and finally the State had admitted that it had released the victim. The Court found that the refusal to acknowledge the deprivation of liberty and to reveal the fate or whereabouts of the victim

[44] *Case of Osorio Rivera and family v. Peru*, paras. 108–109.
[45] *Ibidem*, paras. 145–154.
[46] *Ibidem*, para. 137.
[47] *Ibidem*, para. 69.

had been verified, which was an element to characterize a detention as the beginning of a disappearance. It further added that the way in which the deprivation of liberty is carried out is unimportant for the purposes of the characterization of an enforced disappearance.[48] Consequently, it considered that the deprivation of Osorio Rivera's liberty was just "a step prior to his disappearance". His transfer to a Counter-subversive Base without being placed before a court reflected that the "purpose was not to bring him before a judge or other competent authority and to make him available to them, but to execute him or make him disappear".[49] As a conclusion, the Court found that the facts of the case constituted a disappearance and that Peru was responsible for it, as State agents had carried out the actions.[50] Another interesting case also dealing with the identification of a disappearance is Rodríguez Vera *et al.*, decided at the end of 2014. The case of Rodríguez Vera *et al.* deals with the takeover of the Colombian Supreme Court of Justice by M19, a Colombian guerrilla movement, resulting in the taking of hundreds of hostages. The security forces of the State retook the Court, in an operation later qualified by Colombian courts and the Colombian Truth Commission as disproportionate. The State admitted responsibility for several forced disappearances but this recognition did not cover all the cases. According to the State, nine victims had not been subject to a forced disappearance. To start its examination, the Inter-American Court expressed that the fact that a person is missing, because his or her whereabouts are unknown, is not equivalent to them being the victim of a "forced disappearance". In order for the Court to accept this qualification, evidence was needed that the victims had left the Colombian Supreme Court alive under the custody of State agents who had subsequently refused to admit to the detention. In addition, their fate had to still be unknown.[51] By using all the requirements established in its previous case law, the Inter-American Court concluded these had indeed been forced disappearances and the State was responsible for them.

3.2. THE QUESTION OF JURISDICTION

20. What has been said so far appears to be a fairly coherent way to deal with disappearances. In the case before the Court, the victim is the disappeared person, the rights violated are those of the victim and some relatives may be beneficiaries. There is a clear legal beginning of the disappearance (when the person is detained and the State refuses to admit the detention and give information thereon), and a clear end (either when the disappeared reappears or his identified body is found).

48 *Ibidem*, paras. 124 and 158.
49 *Ibidem*, para. 167.
50 *Ibidem*, para. 159.
51 *Case of Rodríguez Vera et al. v. Colombia*, para. 226.

21. The handling of a case of disappearance that begun with the kidnaping of the victim before the Court acquired jurisdiction to receive individual cases[52] and the body had appeared after the recognition of the Court's jurisdiction blurred this apparently impeccable picture. Yet more confusion came with other cases related to the jurisdiction of the Court, which have not followed a clear and consistent route. The newness of the phenomenon in an international Court makes it understandable to find hesitations and contradictions in the process of arriving at the final goal. The confusion was apparently the consequence of two facts. One was the requirement of the Convention of an explicit State recognition of the jurisdiction of the Court to examine individual cases. The other was the decision of the Court, very early on in its work, that it could not have jurisdiction over a case that occurred after the entry into force of the Convention for the respective State but before the recognition of Article 62 granting the Court jurisdiction over these individual cases. This would constitute an obstacle to making the State responsible for all the violations of rights comprised in a disappearance and would interfere with the role the next of kin[53] were to have in the case.

22. I will examine here four cases of disappearances where the Court's competence *ratione temporis* complicates the development of a clear position on how a disappearance ought to be treated, who the victims in the case are and which the rights violated. In the case of Blake, the alleged victim disappeared on March 28, 1985, before Guatemala had recognized the Court's jurisdiction. Guatemala recognized this jurisdiction on March 9, 1987, "with the reservation that cases in which the competence of the Court is recognized are exclusively those that shall have taken place after the date that this declaration is presented to the Secretary General of the Organization of American States". The whereabouts of the victim were unknown until June 14, 1992, the date on which, thanks to the strenuous efforts of Blake's relatives, his body was found. The Court accepted as proven that the date of the abduction of Blake was also the date of his death, March 25, 1985.[54] Based on this background, Guatemala objected to the Court's jurisdiction to hear the case because the kidnapping, subsequent disappearance and taking of life of Mr. Blake predated recognition

52 See Article 62 of the American Convention.

53 For a wider examination of their treatment by the Court, see C. Medina, "'Family members' and the Inter-American Court", in G. Venturini and S. Bariatti (eds.), *Diritti Idividuali e Giustizia Internazionale, Individual Rights and International Justice, Droits Individuels et Justice Internationale, Liber Fausto Pocar*, Giuffré editore, 2009, pp. 557–572.

54 Judge Cançado Trindade objects to the supposed agreement between the State and the Commission with regard to the date of death, accepted by the Court as fact. He states in his separate opinion that there was no evidence on the acceptance by the Commission that the disappearance and death of Mr. Blake had taken place on the date indicated by the State. (*Case of Blake v. Guatemala*, judgment on preliminary objections, dissenting opinion of Judge Cançado Trindade, para. 7).

of that jurisdiction. This preliminary objection meant that Guatemala did not consider that an element of the violation amounting to a disappearance was the fact that it had refused to give any information to the next of kin and that the disappearance continued until the body had been found *after* Guatemala had recognized the jurisdiction of the Court. In turn, the Court accepted the objection presented by Guatemala and declared itself partially without jurisdiction over the violation of the victim's rights to life, to personal integrity and to personal liberty.[55] In arriving at this decision, it argued that the victim's deprivation of liberty and his death were completed in March 1985 and so could not be considered "*per se* to be continuous", meaning that the Court did not have jurisdiction with regard to these facts.[56] Without prejudice to this lack of jurisdiction, it ruled that principles of international law recognized by Guatemala establish that forced disappearance involves the violation of several rights and that the *effects* of the violations, even when they are committed previously, "may be prolonged continuously or permanently until such time as the victim's fate or whereabouts are established."[57] This is not exactly accurate, since the Court cites for support the United Nations Declaration on the Protection of All Persons from Enforced Disappearance of December 18, 1992, and the Inter-American Convention on Forced Disappearance of Persons of June 9, 1994 and neither of them refer to the "effects" of a disappearance but to the disappearance itself.[58]

The Court thus had partially accepted the preliminary objection of the State because the three violations involved in the disappearance were "not continuous". However, considering that the family of Blake did not know the victim's whereabouts until June 14, 1992, it denied the rest of the objection of lack of jurisdiction in two different paragraphs. In the first, it stated that "since the question is one of forced disappearance, the consequences of those acts extended to June 14, 1992",[59] the date the body appeared. Then it added:

> In the light of the above, as Mr Blake's fate or whereabouts were not known to his family until June 14, 1992, that is, after the date on which Guatemala accepted the contentious jurisdiction of this Court, the preliminary objection raised by the Government must be deemed to be without merit insofar as it relates to effects and actions subsequent to its acceptance. The Court is therefore competent to examine the possible violations which the Commission imputes to the Government in connection with those effects and actions.[60]

55 *Case of Blake v. Guatemala*, judgment on preliminary objections, para. 32.
56 *Ibidem*, para. 33.
57 *Ibidem*, para. 39.
58 *Ibidem*, paras. 36–37.
59 *Ibidem*, para. 34.
60 *Ibidem*, para. 40.

One has to notice here that the Court is ignoring the fact that a disappearance remains such until the person is freed or the body is found. For the Court, death appears as the main element to set the time of the disappearance and not the lack of knowledge of the whereabouts of the victim. The "effects and actions", as considered by the Court, consisted of complicity with and concealment of the detention and death of Mr. Blake, denial of the victim's death to his parents, and attempts to make the body disappear.[61] Reasoning along these lines, the Court decided it lacked jurisdiction to deal with the instant acts of the kidnapping of Blake and its assassination, but possessed jurisdiction to deal with the actions immediately following these two instants. This meant the Court could apply Articles 8 and 25 of the Convention to find whether the State had complied with the investigation of the case in a proper due process. Thus, in the Blake case the Court did not consider the phenomenon of disappearance as a multiple violation, because it left out the denial of the deprivation of liberty by the State, an essential characteristic of the phenomenon. In addition, it ruled that the date on which the kidnapping took place and on which, presumably, the death of the victim occurred, was the decisive date for establishing jurisdiction. Consequently, it failed to consider that the crime remained in progress and was therefore a "continuous violation" up until the moment the body was found, which happened after the State had recognized the jurisdiction of the Court.[62] I think it was a mistake of the Court's majority not to have rejected the first preliminary objection and consequently follow its concept of disappearance as construed in Velásquez. Two judges expressed the hope that this would be different in the future but did not dissent from the decision.[63] In addition, the Court found a violation of Article 5 on personal integrity of the next of kin,[64] "since the violation of those relatives' mental and moral integrity is a direct consequence of his forced disappearance. The circumstances of such disappearance generate suffering and anguish, in addition to a sense of insecurity, frustration and impotence in the face of the public authorities' failure to investigate."[65] With regard to the access to justice of the next of kin,[66] citing in support of its position the UN Declaration on the Forced Disappearance of Persons, the Court reached

61 *Ibidem*, para. 34.

62 But see in *ibidem* the separate – but not dissenting – opinion of Judge Cançado Trindade. There, he laments with resignation the Court's position of not treating the disappearance in an integral manner. He states this will have the effect of "renvoi or abandonment to the national jurisdiction of the issues of the investigation of the detention and death of a person, and the punishment of those responsible for them, after resorting to the international jurisdiction precisely in view of the shortcomings or insufficiencies of national jurisdiction to this effect".

63 *Case of Blake v. Guatemala*, judgment on preliminary objections, separate opinions of Judge Cançado Trindade and *ad hoc* Judge Alfonso Novales Aguirre.

64 For the next of kin, see below, section 4.

65 *Case of Blake v. Guatemala*, paras. 114–115.

66 For the right to personal integrity and access to justice of the next of kin, see below.

the conclusion that Article 8(1) of the American Convention includes the right of relatives of the victim to judicial guarantees. This meant investigating his disappearance, prosecuting those allegedly responsible, eventually punishing them and providing compensation for these violations.[67]

In conclusion, all these rights were derived from the right to due process and to judicial protection. The next of kin were also the holders of the right to have the violations of their right to personal integrity be examined by the courts. According to this, the disappeared person, Mr. Blake, was not a victim and the disappearance was not a multiple violation of rights that had to be considered as a whole.

The case of the Serrano Cruz sisters showed a more difficult situation in that El Salvador became a party to the Convention on June 20, 1978 and recognized the jurisdiction of the Court on June 6, 1995, with the caveat that it would not operate with respect to cases *begun* before the date of the deposit of the instrument of the recognition. This was meant obviously to prevent giving jurisdiction to the Court for disappearances that were still ongoing. The Court found that it should respect this recognition because it was clear that the disappearance had *begun* before that instrument existed.[68] Consequently, the Court would not examine the facts alleged by the Commission related to Articles 4, 5 and 7 of the Convention that had commenced in June 1982, that is, 13 years before El Salvador recognized the contentious jurisdiction of the Inter-American Court.[69] In addition, it eliminated from examination "those facts or acts that commenced prior to June 6, 1995, and that persist after that date when its jurisdiction was recognized". This meant that the Court "will not rule on the alleged forced disappearance of Ernestina and Erlinda Serrano Cruz and, thus, on any of the allegations concerning violations related to the disappearance".[70] However, it reasoned that all the subsequent facts were not excluded because "they refer to judicial proceedings that constitute independent facts". They could be "specific and autonomous violations concerning denial of justice occurring after the recognition of the Court's jurisdiction".[71] I concurred with my vote on that decision, but I think the Court, including myself, adhered to a wrong construction in that judgment. Article 62(2) of the Convention allows States to recognize the jurisdiction of the Court "unconditionally, on the condition of reciprocity, for a specified period, or for specific cases". It is doubtful that El Salvador's recognition is made for a specified period, or for specific cases; rather it purports to exclude certain individuals from the protection of the Court, so it could be categorized as discriminatory and therefore unacceptable under the

---

67 *Case of Blake v. Guatemala*, paras. 85–86 and 977.

68 *Case of Serrano Cruz sisters v. El Salvador*. But see the dissenting opinion of Judge Cançado Trindade.

69 *Ibidem*, para. 77.

70 *Ibidem*, para. 79.

71 *Ibidem*, para. 84.

Convention.[72] The inadmissibility was reiterated in the judgment on the merits, where the Court considered that:

> the substantial aspect of the dispute in this case before the Court is not whether the Serrano Cruz sisters were made disappear by the State, but whether the domestic proceedings from the moment of the State's recognition of jurisdiction on ensured access to justice according to the standards of the American Convention.[73]

The consequence of this is that the Court does not consider a trial as a whole; each part of the proceedings may be separated, which permits the Court to exercise jurisdiction at any stage thereof. In both these cases, then, the disappearance was actually not treated as such, but the proceedings turned on the lack of a proper criminal investigation that had been denied to the victims' families. Consequently, the Serrano sisters were not the victims in the case. In the judgment on merits, the Court found violations of Articles 5, 8 and 25 to the detriment of the Serrano sisters' next of kin. In the end, the Court did achieve the aim sought and found the State responsible for not having given justice in the case, but it did not find violations of the rights of the two sisters, which would have been a stronger response to such an abhorrent action against these children.

23. In the case of Heliodoro Portugal, also a disappearance, the detention occurred in 1970 and Panama recognized the Court's jurisdiction on May 9, 1990.[74] The Court considered that it could "exercise its competence *ratione temporis* to examine those facts that constitute violations of a continuing or permanent nature; in other words, those that occurred before the date on which the Court's competence was recognized, and that persist after that date".[75] In this case, there was no condition like the one of El Salvador in the acceptance of the jurisdiction of the Court. Accordingly, deprivation of liberty was considered as one of the facts under the Court's jurisdiction, "since this is related to his alleged forced disappearance, which continued after 1990, and until his remains were identified in 2000." The alleged failure to investigate the disappearance was also under the jurisdiction of the Court.[76] The right to life and the alleged violation of Mr. Portugal's personal integrity, however, were excluded from the competence. The Court had accepted the preliminary objection of Panama based on a *ratione temporis* ground and the Court decided that the death of the victim in 1970 was an extrajudicial execution and the possible ill-treatment must have occurred around that date.[77] Consequently, they did not share with detention

---

72 See in this regard the dissenting opinion of Judge Cançado Trindade in *case of Serrano Cruz sisters v. El Salvador*, judgment on preliminary objections.
73 *Case of Serrano Cruz sisters v. El Salvador*, judgment on merits, para. 55.
74 *Case of Heliodoro Portugal v. Panama*, para. 27.
75 *Ibidem*, para. 25.
76 *Ibidem*, paras. 37–38.
77 *Ibidem*, para. 36.

the quality of being continuous. The Court explicitly stated, "it finds that it is not empowered to rule on his alleged *extrajudicial execution*, as a violation that is independent of his right to life, particularly since this is a violation of an instantaneous nature."[78] It also rejected competence with regard to possible torture or other ill-treatment, because they were also instantaneous violations.[79]

As the Court handled the case on the basis that it was one of disappearance, it is difficult to understand why it was treated as if the right to life and the rights to personal integrity were not elements of such disappearance or were not caused by the disappearance. If Mr. Portugal's death and his ill-treatment were the result of an extrajudicial execution and actions taken at that time, this approach is adequate, but that was not what the Court said, as the case was handled as a disappearance. The Court states that the whereabouts and fate of Mr. Portugal became known when his remains were identified in August 2000 and Panama accepted the jurisdiction of the Court on May 9, 1990. It added, "[a]ccordingly, the Court has competence to rule on the alleged forced disappearance of Heliodoro Portugal, because it continued after May 9, 1990 and up until August 2000".[80] Later on, it insists that it is a "need to consider the offense of forced disappearance *in toto*, as an autonomous offense of a continuing or permanent nature with multiple intricately interrelated elements", quoting as its base Articles II and III of the Inter-American Convention on the Forced Disappearance of Persons.[81] Finally, it again reiterates that the examination of this violation "should not be approached in an isolated, divided and fragmented manner, considering merely the detention, or the possible torture, or the risk of loss of life, but rather the focus should be on all the facts presented in the case being considered by the Court".[82] Contrary to these considerations, the Court did not find violations of the rights to life and personal integrity of Heliodoro Portugal, excluding him as a victim of violations of Articles 4 and 5, both elements of a disappearance according to the Court's previous case law. Jurisdiction was assumed only with regard to Mr. Portugal's deprivation of liberty. The Court reasoned that it had jurisdiction to rule on the alleged violation of Article 7 of the Convention:

> inasmuch as it is alleged that this initiated the forced disappearance and continued until the alleged victim's fate and whereabouts became known in 2000, 10 years after Panama had accepted the competence of the Court to examine "all matters relating to the interpretation or application of the American Convention".[83]

---

78 *Ibidem*, para. 32 (emphasis added).

79 *Ibidem*, para. 36.

80 *Ibidem*, para. 35.

81 Inter-American Convention on Forced Disappearance of Persons. It entered into force on March 28, 1996.

82 *Case of Heliodoro Portugal v. Panama*, para. 112.

83 *Ibidem*, para. 104.

The application of the Inter-American Convention on Disappearance might have been used to explain a change in the jurisprudence, because it considers only deprivation of liberty surrounded by certain circumstances that constitute a disappearance, and not the possible violations of the rights to life and to personal integrity. However, the Court failed to explain the change of its position of using Article II of the Disappearance Convention instead of its consistent case law regarding the definition of a disappearance. In my view, this would not have been enough to base the decision in those terms. There was here an unexplained reversal of the Court's position. As to the rights violated, the Court found that Articles 5, 8 and 25 had been violated to the detriment of Heliodoro Portugal's next of kin.

There is still one case of a different order related to the jurisdictional problem, Gudiel Alvarez *et al.* (Diario Militar), which deserves examination. It appears that the Court took a different stand with regard to jurisdiction when the deprivation of liberty is prior to the recognition of the Court's competence to deal with the substantive violation of the rights to personal freedom, personal integrity and life of the disappeared person. I use the verb "appear" here because the submission of the case by the Commission, the partial recognition of the State and some of the considerations of the Court are somewhat confusing.

The Commission presented the case to the Court on the disappearance of 26 persons in Guatemala plus "the [alleged] forced disappearance and *extrajudicial execution* of Rudy Gustavo Figueroa Muñoz, and the [alleged] detention and *torture* of the child, Wendy Santizo Méndez."[84] The submission stated that this was a case of "multiple and continuing offenses, *with the exception* of the *forced disappearance* and subsequent extrajudicial execution of Rudy Gustavo Figueroa Muñoz, as well as the detention and torture of Wendy Santizo Méndez." It

> clarified that the facts on which those [two latter] violations are based, relating to the effects on the respective family units, the lack of access to information, the denial of justice, the absence of an effective investigation and the consequent impunity of both *the forced disappearance followed by the extrajudicial execution of Rudy Gustavo* Figueroa Muñoz, as well as the detention and torture of Wendy Santizo Méndez, fall within the temporal jurisdiction of the Court.[85]

However, the request to the Court included the violations of, among others, Articles 3, 4, 5 and 7 not only to the detriment of the 26 victims but also of Rudy Gustavo Figueroa Muñoz. The Court qualified the action as a disappearance followed by an execution. Here one finds the first contradiction: the case can be either one of disappearance or one of extrajudicial execution but not both. Extrajudicial execution has the primary aim of the killing of a person; death, as an element of a disappearance, is not the primary aim of the action; taking an

---

84 *Case of "Diario Militar" v. Guatemala*, para. 3 (emphasis added).
85 *Ibidem*, para. 4 (emphasis added).

individual from circulation so that the State can terrorize through it or obtain information is. Consequences of a death as an element of a disappearance will be treated legally in a different way. Death may follow a disappearance but not an extrajudicial execution. The formulation of the judgment seems to be inclined toward an extrajudicial execution since it refers to the impact of the actions perpetrated against Rudy Figueroa on his next of kin, not qualifying the facts of his case as multiple and continuing offenses.

In its turn, Guatemala acknowledged its responsibility. In reference to the Court's competence to examine the case, it indicated that it was for the Court to determine if it had competence to examine the facts on which the violations of the Convention alleged in the case were founded. It mentioned as facts to be determined "the arbitrary detention and subsequent extrajudicial execution of Rudy Gustavo Figueroa Muñoz and the illegal detention, torture and rape of the minor, Wendy Santizo Méndez". Following this statement, it partially acknowledged the alleged violations of Articles 3, 4, 5 and 7 of the American Convention, in relation to Article 1(1) of this instrument, to the detriment of Rudy Gustavo Figueroa Muñoz. It gave as a reason that the facts of the case "may be examined by the Court as of the date on which the State recognized its competence". The Court's examination of these facts should be "based on the Court's temporal competence".[86] The novelty in this regard is that the State admitted the possibility of finding a violation of substantive rights (personal freedom, personal integrity and life) based on a violation of a procedural nature. In paragraph 25, the Court added that Guatemala's recognition was "solely to determine the State's responsibility for the presumed omissions arising from the lack of an investigation", a reading that one does not find *prima facie* in the paragraph mentioned above. The Court accepted this position[87] with its own reading of the State's submission, and stated that it "only has competence to assess the consequence that the failure to investigate the facts that occurred to the said victims had for their next of kin".[88] Consequently, in the operative paragraphs of the judgment it declared the responsibility of the State in the violation of Articles 7, 5(1), 5(2), 4(1) and 3 of the Convention, plus Articles 1, 6 and 8 of the Torture Convention to the detriment of Rudy Figueroa for not effectively investigating his death.[89] In accordance with this declaration, it did not grant compensation for the loss of earnings of Rudy Figueroa but, strangely enough, it did grant compensation for non-pecuniary damages in his favor.[90] This means that the Court recognized Rudy Figueroa as a holder of the rights to life, personal integrity, personal liberty and the right to recognition as a person before the law. This is also a departure from the way the Court handled the three

86 *Ibidem*, para. 17.
87 *Ibidem*, para. 26.
88 *Ibidem*, para. 290.
89 *Ibidem*, para. 391.3.
90 *Ibidem*, paras. 363 and 374.

cases examined above, where it was only the next of kin who were found to be victims in the case. In this judgment, then, the Court accepted the positions held for long by the European Court of Human Rights in the sense that certain rights, such as life, have two types of obligations for the States: one substantive and another procedural.

In short, the Court has not yet given an appropriate response to deal with disappearances when the jurisdiction *ratione temporis* interferes. Perhaps new cases will be necessary for the Court to find the right way to deal with them in a manner that does justice to the definition of this phenomenon that the Court itself has produced.

3.3. EVIDENCE AND STATE RESPONSIBILITY

24. Disappearances are committed with the perpetrators being careful not to leave traces; this inevitably causes difficulties in the matter of evidence, both to prove the existence of a disappearance and to ascribe responsibility to a State. In Velásquez, the Court admitted evidence of the practice of disappearances as a general phenomenon in the country at the time of Velásquez's abduction. Evidence took the form of testimony of "members of the Legislative Assembly of Honduras, Honduran lawyers, persons who were at one time disappeared, and relatives of disappeared persons". These testimonies purported to show that "in the period in which the events took place, the legal remedies in Honduras were ineffective in obtaining the liberty of victims of a practice of enforced or involuntary disappearances [...] ordered or tolerated by the Government. In addition, the record also contains dozens of newspaper clippings which allude to the same practice".[91] The evidence showed that, from 1981 to 1984, more than one hundred persons were illegally detained, and their whereabouts were unknown. Of those, many of them never reappeared, and, in general, the legal remedies that the government claimed were available to the victims were ineffective. The Court admitted that many of the press clippings offered by the Commission could not be considered documentary evidence as such. However, many contained events that were public knowledge, others reproduced statements given by various state agents and yet others corroborated evidence given by witnesses.[92] It was also shown that of those abducted, some of them reappeared not as "the result of any of the legal remedies which, according to the Government, would have been effective, but rather the result of other circumstances, such as the intervention of diplomatic missions or actions of human rights organizations".[93] Subsequently, the Court received evidence showing that Mr. Velásquez's disappearance

91 *Case of Velásquez Rodríguez v. Honduras*, para. 76.

92 *Ibidem*, para. 146.

93 *Ibidem*, para. 77.

matched the elements of the other disappearances, therefore being just one instance of a pattern of disappearances that had afflicted Honduras at the time. The pattern showed similar features of the *modus operandi* of the detention (weapons and vehicles), of the way detention had taken place, of the type of victim that were affected by the pattern (usually social leaders or students), of the ineffectiveness of complaints to any judicial organ. The silence of the State did not play in its favor; on the contrary, the Court decided that it would interpret it as an acceptance of the facts, because the defense of the State could not rest on the impossibility of the complainant to present evidence that often is only in its hands.[94] This way to ascertain the evidence has been constantly used by the Court.[95] Such approach to the case allowed the Court to attribute responsibility for the disappearance of Velásquez to Honduras. The Court relied on Article 1 of the Convention that sets forth the obligations of States and particularly on the obligation to ensure. The Court used the first part of this judgment to develop the State's responsibility by saying:

> An illegal act which violates human rights and which is initially not directly imputable to a State (for example, because it is the act of a private person or because the person responsible has not been identified) can lead to international responsibility of the State, not because of the act itself, but because of the lack of due diligence to prevent the violation or to respond to it as required by the Convention.[96]

The Court added that the intent or motivation of the agent violating the right is irrelevant and a violation could be found "even if the identity of the individual perpetrator is unknown". The violation will exist when there is support or acquiescence of the State or when "the State has allowed the act to take place without taking measures to prevent it or to punish those responsible".[97] The State has an obligation to investigate the event in order to identify those responsible, impose the appropriate punishment and ensure the victim adequate compensation.[98] An indissoluble link between disappearances and the struggle against impunity was born.

25. In Velásquez Rodríguez, the Court set other legal standards to treat a disappearance. In the judgment on reparations, the relatives were found to be beneficiaries because of the psychological impact they suffered for the dramatic characteristics of the involuntary disappearance of Manfredo Velásquez, who

94 *Ibidem*, paras. 135–136 and 138.

95 One has to keep in mind that the Court is not a criminal court but an organ that decides whether a State has complied with its obligations under the Convention, compliance that sometimes require an action and sometimes an omission. The evaluation, consequently, cannot follow the strict lines required in a criminal trial.

96 *Ibidem*, para. 172.

97 *Ibidem*, para. 173.

98 *Ibidem*, para. 174.

was never found.[99] The only victim recognized by the Court was Manfredo Velasquez, for the violations of his rights to life, personal integrity and personal liberty. In this case, the disappearance was treated as a multiple violation where all the elements referred before were taken into account. In addition, the Court did consider "the failure of the judicial system to act upon the writs brought before various tribunals in the instant case" and the "complete inability of the procedures of the State of Honduras, which were theoretically adequate, to carry out an investigation into the disappearance of Manfredo Velásquez". It also ordered "the fulfillment of its duties to pay compensation and punish those responsible, as set out in Article 1(1) of the Convention". It did not find a violation of Article 8 on due process, leaving aside, apparently, the obligation to investigate further.[100]

This notwithstanding, in the judgment on reparations, the Court recalled that "in its judgment on the merits [...] the Court has already pointed out the Government's continuing duty to investigate so long as the fate of a disappeared person is unknown [...]. The duty to investigate is in addition to the duties to prevent involuntary disappearances and to punish those directly responsible". It also clarified that "[a]lthough these obligations were not expressly incorporated into the resolutory [sic] part of the judgment on the merits, it is a principle of procedural law that the bases of a judicial decision are a part of the same. Consequently, the Court declares that those obligations on the part of Honduras continue until they are fully carried out."[101] With this, the Court made it clear that there was an obligation on the part of the State to investigate the disappearance "so long as the fate of a disappeared person is unknown", although its resolution on the merits did not mention any right of the next of kin of Velázquez to demand this.

3.4. PREVENTION AND INVESTIGATION

26. Disappearances experienced in Latin America occur in a situation of absence of the rule of law. Therefore, preventing them means a major change in the arrangement of power, something that exceeds the mere changing of laws. The global political situation has to change and usually the social and economic situation has to be transformed drastically. Nevertheless, law can help. The international law on disappearances incorporated in the various conventions described above has come to life after the repetition of instances of the phenomenon. As has been seen above, under the Inter-American Disappearance Convention States must establish disappearances as a crime. The Court has

99 *Case of Velásquez Rodríguez v. Honduras*, judgment on reparations, para. 50.
100 *Case of Velásquez Rodríguez v. Honduras*, judgment on merits, para. 179.
101 *Case of Velásquez Rodríguez v. Honduras*, judgment on reparations, paras. 34–35.

ordered compliance with this obligation in the case of Trujillo Oroza.[102] The same was ordered by the Court in the case of Osorio.[103]

Disappearances violate all the basic principles of international human rights law; for them to occur, the rule of law must be nonexistent at least for a certain group of people; a true conspiracy, willingly or unwillingly, of all the main organs of the States (executive, legislative and judicial) has to be present. Hence, international courts and laws have categorized disappearances as *jus cogens* and as a crime against humanity, forbidding any statute of limitations to be applied in relation to them. In the face of these characteristics, it seems imperative that disappearances be investigated in a due process of law. A State where disappearances have occurred must *ex officio* start a judicial process to investigate, prosecute the persons involved in the crime and eventually punish them. In this process, the victims surviving these violations or their relatives must have ample opportunity to participate in the judicial procedures and be heard, although of course responsibility for the investigation will never depend on the procedural initiative of the individuals but on the State and its judicial apparatus.[104] The Court has decided that the next of kin are the holders of the right to access to justice in these events.

27. The Court states the obligation to investigate disappearances with extreme precision. First, it characterizes the obligation as "an inherent juridical obligation" that must be carried out independently of the activities of the interested parties. Second, the investigation "must endeavor to ensure the pursuit, capture, prosecution and eventual punishment of all the authors of the facts, especially when State agents are or may be involved".[105]

The case law also incorporates in the investigation what is considered essential for these situations of massive and systematic human rights violations. The Court has held that:

> It is not sufficient to be aware of the scene and material circumstances of the crime; rather it is essential to analyze the awareness of the power structures that allowed, designed and executed it, both intellectually and directly, as well as the interested persons or groups and those who benefited from the crime (beneficiaries) [...] [I]t is not a question of examining the crime in isolation, but rather of inserting it in a context that will provide the necessary elements to understand its operational structure.[106]

---

102 *Case of Trujillo Oroza v. Bolivia*, para. 98.

103 *Case of Osorio Tivera and family v. Peru.*

104 *Case of the "Mapiripán Massacre" v. Colombia*, para. 219.

105 *Ibidem*. See also *Case of the Pueblo Bello Massacre v. Colombia*, para. 143 and 145; *Case of Radilla Pacheco v. Mexico*, para. 143; *Case of Anzualdo Castro v. Peru*, para. 65; *Case of the Pueblo Bello Massacre v. Colombia*, para. 143; *Case of González et al. ("Cotton Fields") v. Mexico*, para. 290; and *Case of Valle Jaramillo et al. v. Colombia*, para. 101.

106 *Case of Manuel Cepeda v. Colombia*, para. 118; *Case of González et al. ("Cotton Fields") v. Mexico*, para. 454; and *Case of Valle Jaramillo et al. v. Colombia*, para. 101.

In the case of González Medina and family, the Court found the Dominican Republic in violation of the obligation to investigate a disappearance because the investigating judge decided that in order to investigate a disappearance it was necessary first to file a civil action to declare Mr. González a "disappeared person". The Court found that subordinating the attribution of criminal responsibilities to a civil procedure showed the judge had no understanding of what a disappearance is.[107]

3.5. IMPUNITY

28. From all that has been said about the obligation to investigate, try and punish those responsible for disappearances, it transpires that impunity in these cases is not compatible with the Convention. The Court has defined impunity in a case on disappearance as the "total lack of investigation, prosecution, capture, trial and conviction of those responsible for violations of the rights protected by the American Convention".[108] It has firmly repeated that "if a violation goes unpunished in a State, in such a way that the victim's full enjoyment of such rights is not restored as soon as possible, the State has failed to comply with its obligation to ensure the free and full exercise of those rights to the persons within its jurisdiction."[109] In general, one determining factor for impunity is the non-responsive attitude of the domestic court responsible for hearing a case of an alleged violation by means of a disappearance. It is unlikely that a situation of impunity can happen without the cooperation of the judiciary, stemming either from fear or from acquiescence with those exercising political power in the country. A lack of democratic rule of law, at least regarding certain sectors or certain individuals, is needed for impunity to prosper.

Jurisprudence on impunity has been constant "in cases of extrajudicial executions, enforced disappearances, torture and other serious human rights violations".[110] This formulation of the Court leaves open the possibility of applying the jurisprudence to instances other than those referred above and this will require extreme care. In some cases, it is doubtful that the rules given for massacres, disappearances and such should have been applied as they were, for example in the case of Bulacio, a minor in Argentina who was detained in a razzia on a discotheque, taken to jail and beaten, as a consequence of which he died. There the Court held that "no domestic legal provision or institution, including [the statute of limitations], can oppose compliance with the judgments of the Court regarding investigation and punishment of those responsible for

107 *Case of González Medina and family v. Dominican Republic*, para. 228.
108 *Case of Paniagua Morales et al. v. Guatemala*, para. 173.
109 *Case of Garrido and Baigorría v. Argentina*, judgment on reparations, para. 73.
110 *Case of Manuel Cepeda v. Colombia*, para. 117.

human rights violations".[111] The wording seems to suggest that all human rights violations should be treated equally, although I would venture to say that this is not what the Court wishes to imply. In fact, my general impression is that the situations in which the notion of impunity has been applied so far deserved to be so treated.[112] A couple of examples follow.

29. The long period of nondemocratic rule of law in Central America and in the Southern Cone caused an immense number of victims – most dead, disappeared or tortured – and atrocities beyond description. As just one example from Central America, one could refer to the Massacres of El Mozote and nearby villages, which occurred in the context of an internal armed conflict in El Salvador between 1980 and 1991 in which an estimated 75,000 individuals died.[113] According to national organs, the counterinsurgency followed a strategy of "*tierra arrasada*".[114] This consisted "in the indiscriminate annihilation of one or more villages followed by the destruction of crops, dwellings and other property of the victims which had been previously executed or who had fled, in order to destroy essential social relations in communities that might give logistical support to the guerrilla".[115] Accepting responsibility, the Government of El Salvador, appearing before the Court in 2012, said: "In three days and three nights the greatest massacre against a civilian population of contemporary Latin American history was perpetrated; there were almost a thousand victims half of them less than 18-years-old; among other atrocities, people were tortured, executed and raped or disappeared".[116]

30. In the Southern Cone, a notable example is that of Operation Cóndor, "a code name given to the alliance of the security forces and intelligence services of the Southern Cone dictatorships in their repression of and fight against individuals designated 'subversive elements'". In the beginning, Argentina, Bolivia, Chile, Paraguay and Uruguay were the members of the alliance. Brazil provided at least intelligence input. This was an operation that "systematized and improved clandestine coordination between the 'security forces and military personnel and intelligence services' of the region". The Court studied Operation Cóndor in depth in the case of Goiburú *et al.* v. Paraguay.[117] Goiburú was a Paraguayan kidnapped by Paraguayan agents in Argentina and taken back to Paraguay, where he disappeared. In another case, Gelman v. Uruguay, the victim was a young pregnant Argentinian woman, kidnapped in Argentina

---

111 *Case of Bulacio v. Argentina*, para. 117.
112 I would take exception with its application in the *Case of Bulacio v. Argentina*.
113 *Case of the Massacres of El Mozote and nearby villages v. El Salvador*, para. 63.
114 The equivalent in English is "scorched earth policy."
115 *Case of the Massacres of El Mozote v. El Salvador*, para. 70.
116 *Ibidem*, para. 77.
117 *Case of Goiburú et al. v. Paraguay*, paras. 61(1) to (14).

and taken to Uruguay where she disappeared. The collaboration between the military and non-military security organs was proven beyond doubt with a series of documents revealed in Paraguay, better known as the "Terror Files", an important and irrefutable source of evidence of the grave abuses committed during the dictatorship of General Stroessner in collusion with other dictators. Uruguay admitted its responsibility in the Gelman case.

31. The most obvious impunity is the consequence of the passage of amnesty laws. As a conclusion to a long debate on the subject, there is a widely shared agreement that these laws, when referring to certain classes of violations, are not compatible with a human rights treaty such as the Convention. In the inter-American system, the Commission was the first to address this subject. It raised the alarm in 1985 about an amnesty decree in Guatemala, arguing that it could hinder and make courts ineffective in their work of investigating the crimes and punishing the guilty parties.[118] However, it was in response to amnesties in Uruguay and Argentina that the Commission developed a detailed basis for concluding that these laws were in violation of Article XVIII (right to justice) of the American Declaration and of Articles 1, 8, and 25 of the American Convention.[119]

The judgment handed down in the case of Barrios Altos v. Peru, a leading case on disappearances, is categorical in holding that all provisions on amnesty, application of a statute of limitations and any other measure designed to eliminate responsibility are inadmissible, because they violate non-derogable rights recognized by international human rights law.[120] Subsequently, the Inter-American Court has ruled all amnesties incompatible with the Convention, whether they are self-amnesties, such as the one in Peru[121] or amnesties approved by a majority of the population of a State, such as the amnesty in Uruguay. In the case of Gelman v. Uruguay, the Court gave a long account of the pronouncements of international bodies and supreme courts of the region on the matter of amnesties. It stated that the *ratio legis* of amnesties, whichever way they are passed, is "to leave unpunished serious violations of international law", so their incompatibility "does not stem from a formal question [...] but rather from the material aspect in what regards the rights enshrined in Articles 8 and 25, in relation to Articles 1(1) and 2 of the Convention."[122] This marks a difference with

118 IACHR, Annual Report 1985–1986.

119 Case on the expiry of the State's punitive intention (Uruguay), Nos. 10029, 10036, 10145, 10305, 10372, 10373, 10374,10375, Resolution 29/92, October 2, 1992 (IACHR, Annual Report 1992–93) and Cases No. 10147, 10181, 10240, 10262, 10309 and 10311 (Argentina) Resolution 28/92, October 2, 1992 (IACHR, Annual Report 1992–93).

120 *Case of Barrios Altos v. Peru*, paras. 41–43.

121 *Ibidem*, paras. 41–43.

122 *Case of Gelman v. Uruguay*, para. 229. This case referred to the disappearance of Juan Gelman's daughter occurred within Operation Condor. An account of the various pronouncements on this issue can be also found in *Case of the Guerrilha of Araguaia v. Brazil*, paras. 149–164.

the Inter-American Disappearance Convention, which falls short of the Court's case law. Article VII of the Convention states that in disappearances, criminal prosecution and the penalty judicially imposed shall not be subject to statutes of limitations, unless "the statute is set forth in a norm of a fundamental character". If that is the case, the period of limitation shall be equal to that which applies to the gravest crime in the domestic laws of the corresponding State Party. The Court's case law plainly rejects any application of a statute of limitations to deal with this crime.

The Court faced in the case of the Massacres of El Mozote and nearby places a different type of amnesty law, one passed at the end of an internal armed conflict. The decision involved consideration of Additional Protocol II to the 1949 Geneva Conventions, "as well as of the specific terms in which it was agreed to end hostilities, which put an end to the conflict in El Salvador and, in particular, of Chapter I ('Armed Forces'), section 5 ('End to impunity'), of the Peace Accord of January 16, 1992".[123] In such a situation, the Protocol directs the authorities to grant "the broadest possible amnesty". The Court interpreted the provision as referring to amnesties "in relation to those who have taken part in the non-international armed conflict or who are deprived of liberty for reasons related to the armed conflict". However, this could not include facts that can be categorized as war crimes or crimes against humanity.[124] The National Reconciliation Law passed subsequently applied that interpretation, but a following Law of General Amnesty for the Consolidation of Peace granted an extensive amnesty precisely to those that the National Reconciliation Law has exempted from the benefit of an amnesty.[125] The Court found a violation of the obligation to investigate.[126]

32. The Court's rulings have been issued in addressing situations of political violence carried out by the State or at least tolerated by it; these are the types of cases that have been brought before the Court to date. Nevertheless, the principles developed in its case law can be applied to other situations. Other phenomena such as, for example, lynching,[127] "social cleansing",[128] so-called "honor crimes",[129] domestic violence against women resulting in the death of

---

123 *Case of the Massacres of El Mozote and nearby places v. El Salvador*, para. 284.
124 *Ibidem*, para. 287.
125 *Ibidem*, paras. 289 and 291.
126 *Ibidem*, para. 295.
127 IACHR, Report on the human rights situation in Guatemala (OEA/Ser.L/V/II.111, Doc. 21 rev., April 6, 2001), pp. 89–95.
128 *Ibidem*, pp. 95–98.
129 The uxoricides committed by men against their partners in response to alleged infidelity are known as "honor crimes". There are countries in which these crimes are not punished because courts have found that the motive exempts perpetrators from criminal responsibility. See IACHR, Report on the human rights situation in Brazil (OEA/Ser.L/V/II.97, Doc. 29 rev. 1, September 29, 1997), p. 140.

the victim or a serious threat to her life[130] and so on also require the State to comply with its obligation to investigate, try and punish the guilty parties. In those cases, it is also necessary to take into account the whole situation within which these violations occur.

33. It is not far-fetched to think that in the future a new type of situations be admitted as constituting a similar phenomenon as that of disappearances. This has been insinuated in the case of massacres. The Court has for the first time characterized massacres as entailing "a complex violation of rights recognized in the American Convention". In the case of El Mozote and nearby places it included as having been violated not only the rights to life and personal integrity and liberty but also Articles 19 and 21(1) and 21(2) of the American Convention.[131] I do not know if this idea is sensible or if it can have a useful purpose. We will have to wait and see whether this will become a trend.

4. THE NEXT OF KIN AS VICTIMS OF A DISAPPEARANCE

34. The concept of the "next of kin" is a development from the Court's interpretation of the Convention to address the phenomenon of disappearance, reflecting the concern of the Court in the personal integrity of people who appear not to have been necessarily the prime desired targets of a State action or omission. Given the devastating effects that a disappearance has on those with a close link to the disappeared persons – grief, uncertainty, impotence at the contempt with which the authorities reacted to their plight – it was unthinkable the Court would stay unmoved by their situation and interpret the Convention in a way that would have left their human rights unsheltered. I believe the violation of the personal integrity of certain relatives (now called the next of kin) is the main violation of their rights. First, it is nearly impossible to fathom the suffering the next of kin endure trying to imagine the horror their relatives may be undergoing. Second, the refusal of the authorities to investigate what has happened to their relatives amounts to a humiliation of their basic dignity. In order to find and then repair this violation, it seems necessary to give the next of kin access to the Court. The only way to diminish their suffering is for the courts to find out what has happened to the disappeared person and consequently order the prosecution of those responsible and a punishment once they are identified, also punishing those responsible for their failure in imparting justice. Actually,

130 For a pioneering case on domestic violence, see *Case 12.051, Maria da Penha Maia Fernández v. Brazil*, Report 54/01, Resolution of April 16, 2001, published in the IACHR 2000 Annual Report.

131 *Massacre of El Mozote and nearby places v. El Salvador*, para. 203.

for the next of kin the reparation begins when they can have their day in court and this is clearly perceived when they appear before the Court and tell their stories. I would say that this is in essence the way the Court has addressed the situation.

4.1. THE NEXT OF KIN AND ARTICLE 5

35. The next of kin are certain family members of persons who have suffered particularly serious violations and who have been found by the Court to be themselves victims of a violation of Article 5 as a consequence of a main violation having been committed against a third person related to them. It is necessary to examine several issues in this regard. One is the type of violation that can produce a new violation against other persons. Another is the determination of who can be considered "next of kin" for this effect. A third is to determine what sort of attack on their personal integrity they must bear to be considered victims of the violation of this right.

36. The first judgment recognizing the violation of Article 5 of certain relatives of victims of particular human rights violations was in the case of Blake, where the Court found that Guatemala had violated Article 5 of the Convention with regard to the relatives of Mr. Blake, whose lives had been seriously altered by the disappearance of their relative. This fact had caused them "suffering and anguish, in addition to a sense of insecurity, frustration and impotence in the face of the public authorities' failure to investigate."[132] The Court also found that incineration of Mr. Blake's mortal remains, done in order to destroy any trace of them, was an attack on Guatemalan society's prevailing cultural values and had likewise contributed to an intensification of the family's suffering.[133] According to the Court there had been a violation of Article 5 of the relatives of Mr. Nicholas Blake, the disappeared person.

Several cases have followed. An analysis of the judgments of the Court up to now shows that the Court has consistently recognized the violation of Article 5 with respect to certain next of kin. This is always the case when the primary violation is one of disappearance,[134] extrajudicial execution,[135] torture[136] and prolonged arbitrary detention.[137] There are, however, instances of a different kind. For example, in the case of Yean and Bosico, the main violation – that

---

132 *Case of Blake v. Guatemala*, paras. 113–114.

133 *Ibidem*, para. 115.

134 *Case of 19 Merchants v. Colombia*; *Case of Anzualdo Castro v. Peru*; and *Case of Gómez Palomino v. Peru.*

135 *Case of Gómez Paquiyauri v. Peru* and *Case of Uzcátegui v. Venezuela.*

136 *Case of Baldeón García v Peru* and *Case of Bueno Alves v. Argentina.*

137 *Case of De la Cruz Flores v. Peru.*

against two girls born to Haitian parents – was the State not providing them with a birth certificate and consequently making it extremely difficult for them to remain in that State, of which the mothers and a sister were nationals. This had caused the latter uncertainty and insecurity with regard to the permanence of the family as a union; the Court found that the three of them were victims of a violation of Article 5.[138] In another instance, the rape of a young indigenous woman brought about the violation of the right of personal integrity of the husband, the children and other family members.[139] In the case of Albán Cornejo the main victim was a woman who died as a consequence of medical negligence. The Court found a violation of Article 5 because "the lack of a judicial answer to clear up the death of Laura Albán impaired the right to humane treatment of her parents, Carmen Cornejo de Albán and Bismarck Albán-Sánchez".[140]

37. The determination of who can be called "next of kin" has evolved. At the beginning, it was difficult to see a clear position on the type of relationship that must exist between the primary victim and their next of kin to allow the latter to become victims of a violation of Article 5. However, in the case of Bámaca Velásquez, and in the context of a forced disappearance, the Court delved more deeply into the circumstances in which the relatives of a person whose human rights had been violated could be considered for their own part as victims of a violation of Article 5 of the Convention. Using the case law of the European Court, it found that when a person's fundamental rights are violated, including the right to life or the right to physical integrity, those closest to that person also become victims. It added that in order to decide who should be considered as belonging to that category, it was necessary to examine

> the closeness of the family relationship, the particular circumstances of the relationship with the victim, the degree to which the family member was a witness of the events related to the disappearance, the way in which the family member was involved in attempts to obtain information about the disappearance of the victim and the State's response to the steps undertaken.[141]

The development of the jurisprudence brought with it a precedent clarifying the Court's position.

38. The position of the Court is as follows: mothers and fathers, daughters and sons, husbands and wives and permanent companions are the "direct next of kin". In their regard, the Court may apply a rebuttable presumption, "provided

---

138 *Case of Yean and Bosico v. Dominican Republic*, paras. 205 and 206.

139 *Case of Fernández v. Mexico*, para. 149.

140 *Case of Albán Cornejo v. Ecuador*, para. 50.

141 *Case of Bámaca Velásquez v. Guatemala*, paras. 162–163. The European case law cited by the Court is: European Court, *Case of Kurt v. Turkey*, judgment of May 25, 1998, Reports of Judgments and Decisions 1998-III, paras. 130–134; *Case of Timurtas v. Turkey*, judgment of June 13, 2000, para. 95; and *Case of Cakici v. Turkey*, Judgment of July 8, 1999, para. 98.

this responds to the specific circumstances of a case, as has happened, for example, in the cases of various massacres, forced disappearance of persons and extrajudicial executions".[142] In relation to those who are not direct next of kin, the Court must assess, for example, whether there is a particularly close tie between them and the victims in the case that would allow the Court to declare a violation of their right to personal integrity. The Court can also assess whether the alleged victims have been involved in seeking justice in the specific case, or whether they have endured special suffering because of the facts of the case or of subsequent acts or omissions of the State authorities in relation to the facts.

The case of the Guerrilha do Araguaia is a good example of the way in which the Court applies these rules. The case deals with the "arbitrary detention, torture, and enforced disappearance of 70 persons, members of the Communist Party of Brazil [...] and peasants of the region". The events were the result of the operations of the Brazilian Army between 1972 and 1975, which attempted to eradicate the Guerrilha do Araguaia in the time of the military dictatorship in Brazil (1964–1985).[143] The Court found a violation to the right to personal integrity of the direct family members of the disappeared persons, regarding whom the State had not rebutted the presumptions of closeness with the main victims.[144] With regard to the siblings, not considered direct family members, the Court found that one or several circumstances obtained; either they had a close connection with the disappeared, constituting a single nuclear family or were involved in actions seeking truth and justice for the victim.[145] Consequently, their right to personal integrity had also been violated.

In the case of Tarazona Arrieta *et al.*, the Court established that the presumption *iuris tantum* concerning the "direct next of kin" could be applied only if this responds to the particular circumstances of the case, such as in massacres, disappearances or extrajudicial executions. The presumption that there is a violation of the personal integrity of the next of kin does not apply in all types of cases nor with respect to every member of the family. In cases other than those concerning a serious violation of human rights, the pain and suffering must be proven.[146]

39. As to the sort of actions that would amount to a violation of Article 5 for the next of kin, they are of a various nature. The first is the suffering that the next of kin endure for the anguish and uncertainty about the situation of the person who has, for example, disappeared or been submitted to torture. A variety of formulations are found throughout the judgments. The second is the impotence they feel and the suffering to which they are submitted by a State

---

142 *Case of Valle Jaramillo v. Colombia*, para. 119.
143 *Case of Guerrilha de Araguaia v. Brazil*, para. 2.
144 *Ibidem*, para. 236 They amounted to over forty individuals.
145 *Ibidem*, paras. 237–238.
146 *Case of Tarazona Arrieta et al. v. Peru*, paras. 145 and 146.

which ignores or directly impedes the actions of the next of kin to obtain justice and information leading thus to impunity. Almost invariably, these two causes of suffering are present.

In general, in cases of disappearance, massacres, torture and extrajudicial executions just the facts of the main violations are enough to ascertain the anguish and suffering of the next of kin that will make them victims of a violation of Article 5. In some, the anguish involves the lack of knowledge of the situation the main victims are in; the impotence vis-à-vis the authorities which either ignore the pleas for investigation and justice or, at its worst, place obstacles of every kind, not excluding threats to the next of kin or physical and mental violence. In disappearances and massacres, the complexity of the situation makes it impossible not to have permanent sequels for the next of kin and while impunity remains, the suffering remains as well.[147] In another case, the Court has found that the deprivation of access to the truth about the location of a disappeared person constitutes a form of cruel and inhumane treatment.[148] In torture cases, the suffering may come from the next of kin having been a witness to torture, as in Fleury.[149] In execution, it may come from the threats or criminal actions to which the next of kin were submitted when they tried to find out what had happened.

40. In cases other than disappearances, massacres, executions and torture the origin of the suffering varies. For example, in Rosendo Cantú, an indigenous woman raped by military men, the victim had to move to another village as her husband and the community rejected her. As a result, her next of kin (her daughter) had to leave with her and live in various villages and in the city, which meant the loss of her culture and of her family.[150] There was then a violation of the right to personal integrity of the child. In a case of prolonged arbitrary imprisonment, the Tibi case, Mr. Tibi was detained more than six hundred miles from his family's residence. The mother of the children, his partner, could not earn enough to keep the family together and had to send one of her children to her family in France. In sum, as the Court said, the detention contributed to breaking up the family nucleus and to frustrating their personal and collective plans.[151]

In a case of the death by fire of 107 inmates,[152] there were two considerations to find that the next of kin were victims of a violation of Article 5: first, the

---

147 See for example, *Case of the 19 Trademen v. Colombia*, paras. 210–216; *Contreras et al. v. El Salvador*, paras. 122–123; *Goiburú v. Paraguay*, para. 103; *Guerrilla de Aruguaia v. Brazil*, paras. 240–243; *Mapiripán Massacre v. Colombia*, para. 144.

148 *Case of Guerrilha de Araguaia v. Brazil*, para. 243.

149 *Case of Fleury v. Haiti*, para. 88.

150 *Case of Rosendo Cantú et al. v. Mexico*, paras. 133 and 138.

151 *Case of Tibi v. Ecuador*, paras. 160–161.

152 In the case, the State had accepted responsibility for the 107 deaths due to a lack of appropriate prevention. *Case of Pacheco Teruel v. Honduras*.

suffering they experienced due to the atrocious death of their relatives, and second, the negligence of the authorities in identifying the bodies and allowing the next of kin a proper burial and closure.[153]

41. In the Court's case law, then, the next of kin are victims in a direct sense; the Court deems them victims of a violation of Article 5. This jurisprudence is wide, containing degrees both of the type of violation that will cause the next of kin to be a victim and the type of relationship of the person with the main victim. The mere suffering of what has happened to the main victim may be enough, but frequently the next of kin are also directly subjected to actions or omissions of the State regarding the main victim that would amount to a violation of Article 5. The level of suffering required, as has been shown, is very flexible. The Court does not bind itself with a set criterion, being guided only by what Article 5(1) sets forth, that is, to examine if in their opinion the right to personal integrity of a person, be it physical, mental or moral, has been affected and there are no reasons for the State to justify its action or omission.

4.2. THE NEXT OF KIN AND ACCESS TO JUSTICE

42. The notion of the next of kin developed with disappearances and was later extended to other serious violations of human rights. The next of kin started to be considered as victims in their own right of a violation of their right to personal integrity. The violation consisted, in what is relevant for this section, in the failure of the State organs to do their duty in the prosecution of these serious violations that affected one of their relatives. In the case of Blake, the Court stated that Article 8(1) on due process should be interpreted broadly, basing its argument – in addition to the letter and spirit of the provision – on Article 29(c) of the Convention, "whereby none of its provisions shall be interpreted as precluding other rights or guarantees that are inherent in the human personality or derived from representative, democratic form of government".[154] It continued indicating that, at least in the case of disappearances, Article 8(1) of the Convention grants certain victims' relatives judicial guarantees, since a disappearance causes grave suffering "to him and to his family".[155] Therefore, Mr. Nicholas Blake's relatives had the right to have his disappearance and death effectively investigated by the Guatemalan authorities, those found responsible should be properly prosecuted and punished and the relatives should be

153 *Ibidem*, paras. 73–75.

154 *Case of Blake v. Guatemala*, para. 96.

155 The Court quotes Article 1(2) of the United Nations Declaration on the Protection of All Persons Against Enforced Disappearance. Adopted by General Assembly Resolution 47/133 of December 18, 1992. See in this same sense, the *Case of the 19 Merchants v. Colombia*, para. 186.

compensated.[156] With this interpretation, the Court establishes that the victim or the victim's relatives have the right to a hearing in a criminal trial, along with the right to demand that a criminal proceeding be pursued. This includes actors in the criminal proceeding that would not seem *prima facie* to have been included in the provision, which appears to be based on the adversarial system. In the case of Villagrán Morales, the Court reiterated this position, indicating that "it is evident from Article 8 of the Convention that the victims of human rights violations or their next of kin should have substantial possibilities of being heard and acting in the respective proceedings, both in order to clarify the facts and punish those responsible, and to seek due reparation."[157] In the case of Las Palmeras, the Court concluded that "the use of the military courts in this case did not guarantee due process in the meaning of Article 8(1) of the American Convention, which recognizes the right of the victims' next of kin to a hearing by a competent, impartial and independent court".[158] In the case of Juan Humberto Sánchez, the Court established in its judgment that "[t]he next of kin of the victim must have full access and the capacity to act, at all stages and levels of said investigations [referring to investigations into the extrajudicial execution of the victim], in accordance with domestic laws and the provisions of the American Convention."[159] In the case of Bulacio, in considering forms of reparation for the violations for which Argentina was responsible, the Court found that the situation was one of grave impunity. Thus, the State must pursue and conclude the investigation into the facts and punish those responsible, specifying that the relatives of the victim must have full access and capacity to take action at all stages of the investigation and trial.[160]

43. The Court has always invoked Articles 8 and 25 of the Convention as the legal basis for the next of kin's access to justice. Article 8 is the basis for the right of access to justice, granting this right to those who seek a determination of a right or an obligation of any nature, or to those who are subject to a criminal trial in which their innocence or guilt is decided. In order to invoke it, one must first either have "a right or an obligation that needs to be determined" or be subject to an accusation. I do not share the interpretation of the Court that Article 8 by itself grants "the right that must be determined". In my opinion, the right of the next of kin in these cases arises from the State's obligation to ensure substantive human rights. In principle, these rights are of two different natures. The first is the right of everyone to an effective recourse "for protection against acts that violate his fundamental rights recognized by the constitution or laws of

156 *Case of Blake v. Guatemala*, para. 97.

157 *Case of Villagrán Morales et al. v. Guatemala*, para. 227. It ruled likewise in the *Case of Durand and Ugarte v. Peru*, paras. 128–130.

158 *Case of Las Palmeras v. Colombia*, para. 54.

159 *Case of Juan Humberto Sánchez v. Honduras*, para. 186.

160 *Case of Bulacio v. Argentina*, paras. 121 and 137, No. 5.

the state", set forth in Article 25. The Court has asserted this in some cases. In García Prieto, the Court affirms that "[i]t is important to note that the obligation to investigate does not derive solely from the Treaty norms of International Law binding upon the States Parties, but also from the domestic legislation that makes reference to the duty to investigate certain unlawful conducts, and from the norms that allow the victims or their family members to present a complaint such that they may participate in the criminal proceedings in order to establish the truth of the events".[161] In a more recent case, Vélez Franco *et al.* v. Guatemala,[162] the Court states that the obligation to investigate *ex officio* certain illicit conducts and the right of the next of kin to present "*querellas*" and participate in the trials derive from domestic legislation. The second rights are those affecting the next of kin in their personal integrity, that is Article 5 of the Convention, violated by the suffering that the violation of the rights of their disappeared or executed family member causes them and the frustration and impotence to which the State subjects them when they try to find justice for the disappearance, execution or other serious violations of the human rights of that relative. Although the Court does not make the connection explicit, all its judgments follow that pattern.

44. As can be observed, the phenomenon of disappearances has had an enormous impact on the evolution of the obligations of States with regard to Articles 4, 5 and 8. Part of this evolution has also permeated the treatment of other serious violations, even when they are of a lesser scale.

161 *Case of García Prieto v. El Salvador*, para. 104, See also, for example, *Vera Vera v. Ecuador*, para. 86.

162 *Case of Véliz Franco et al. v. Guatemala*, para. 184.

CHAPTER 3
RIGHT TO LIFE

Article 4. Right to Life

1. *Every person has the right to have his life respected. This right shall be protected by law and, in general, from the moment of conception. No one shall be arbitrarily deprived of his life.*
2. *In countries that have not abolished the death penalty, it may be imposed only for the most serious crimes and pursuant to a final judgment rendered by a competent court and in accordance with a law establishing such punishment, enacted prior to the commission of the crime. The application of such punishment shall not be extended to crimes to which it does not presently apply.*
3. *The death penalty shall not be reestablished in states that have abolished it.*
4. *In no case shall capital punishment be inflicted for political offenses or related common crimes.*
5. *Capital punishment shall not be imposed upon persons who, at the time the crime was committed, were under 18 years of age or over 70 years of age; nor shall it be applied to pregnant women.*
6. *Every person condemned to death shall have the right to apply for amnesty, pardon, or commutation of sentence, which may be granted in all cases. Capital punishment shall not be imposed while such a petition is pending decision by the competent authority*

1. INTRODUCTION

1. Paragraph 1 of Article 4 of the Convention sets forth the right of all persons to have their lives respected. After this extensive assertion, the Convention limits it by stating that "no one shall be arbitrarily deprived of his life". "Arbitrarily" qualifies the deprivation of life; the right is not absolute, as situations exist in which it is permissible to take the life of a person without violating Article 4(1) of the Convention. A possible way to do so is through the imposition of the death penalty by a court. Another possibility would include a private individual taking a life in legitimate self-defense or in legitimate defense of a third party. A third possibility would be the undesired taking of a life by law enforcement personnel as the result of licit use of force in pursuit of a legitimate aim. There is the question of whether the right to life exclusively covers the protection from arbitrary deprivation of life through the imposition of the death penalty by the State or through the abuse of force by a State agent, as the reading of the five subsequent clauses might insinuate; or if it protects from the arbitrary deprivation of life whatever the manner in which it is carried out. If the latter, does the right to life allows a person to demand a certain minimum quality of life from the State or does the Convention's protection stop short of this idea? Put in different words, do social, economic or cultural rights play a role in the interpretation of the right to life? This and other queries will be addressed in this chapter. According to Article 1, States must also ensure life and the scope of this obligation has to be determined. Like every other right, Article 4 generates for the State negative and positive obligations. It must prevent its violations, investigate them, repair the victims, and guarantee their non-repetition. The measures the State takes will vary according to the situation. They will be different for an isolated killing from those needed in case of a massacre, or a disappearance. Consequently, Article 4(1) states that the right to life "shall be protected by law", thus establishing a positive obligation for the State to broaden its area of concern, insofar as this protection extends to actions that can affect the conduct of both State agents and private individuals.

By virtue of its positive obligations, the State must take the necessary measures – legislative or other – to prevent violations of the right to life and when violations do take place, to examine their cause, to remedy them and – when necessary – to mete out punishment. The American Convention and the development of its provisions through case law must guide all these steps.

The Court constantly mentions these positive obligations of the State. It usually holds that they involve all State institutions, including police and armed forces. States must adopt the necessary legislative, administrative and judicial measures, for example establishing criminal norms and a justice system that will punish deprivation of life, both by State agents and by private individuals.[1]

2. This chapter will examine these various obligations. It will start with the death penalty, and continue with the protection of the right to life in general and the use of force by State agents acting in functions proper to their position and deprivation of life by non-State agents, that is to say, private individuals. After this, it will examine the jurisprudence on the protection of life of persons that find themselves in a disadvantaged social or economic condition, which will bring the reader to the subject of indigenous peoples and children, two groups that require particular measures of prevention by the State. The Court is

1 *Case of the Ituango Massacre v. Colombia*, para. 131, quoting *Case of Baldeón García v. Peru*, para. 85; *Case of the Sawhoyamaxa Indigenous Community v. Paraguay*, para. 153; and *Case of the Pueblo Bello Massacre v. Colombia*, para. 120.

bound by the Convention to develop international standards that transcend the domestic legal orders to achieve the aim of a common standard for all of those under their jurisdiction. The Court has dealt already with several of these issues and they will be the main subject of the study of Article 4 in this chapter.

3. Finally, the chapter will deal with the difficult issue of the fetus vis-á-vis human rights. Examining this matter is a complex task in the American Convention, as Article 4(1) states: "[t]his right shall be protected by law and, in general, from the moment of conception". This idea brings up the question of its meaning: is the unborn child a holder of the right or should the protection mentioned be given on a different basis? This chapter will not address the question in depth, since that would likely require a long monograph. The accent will be mainly on a legal interpretation and the so far scarce case law of the Court on this point.

2. THE DEATH PENALTY

4. Even though the imposition of the death penalty clearly constitutes, in my view, cruel and inhuman treatment of a human being and conflicts directly as well with the provisions of Article 5(6) of the American Convention,[2] Article 4 of the Convention allows it, due to the lack of consensus among the States that drafted the treaty to abolish it.[3] However, its acceptance has a clear abolitionist slant: paragraph 3 of Article 4 establishes that "the death penalty shall not be re-established in states that have abolished it" and paragraph 4 says that nor "shall capital punishment be inflicted for political offenses or related common crimes." The protection of the right to life, in this case, consists in the many requirements with which the State must comply in order to be able to sentence a person with the death penalty.

As the Inter-American Court ruled in its Advisory Opinion 3/83, the last part of the second paragraph of Article 4[4] establishes a true freeze on the death penalty as of the moment the Convention enters into force for a particular State. The Inter-American Commission requested an Opinion concerning a reservation made by Guatemala on ratifying the Convention, which excluded from the prohibition in Article 4(4) the "related common crimes" established

2 This provision establishes that "punishments consisting of deprivation of liberty shall have as an essential aim the reform and social readaptation of the prisoners".

3 There are many reasons invoked to abolish the death penalty. I will not deal with these here, aside from the fact that in my opinion one obvious, legal reason is that it is not conducive to any improvement in the conduct of people who seriously break the law, and thus cannot be justified as a compatible restriction to the right to life.

4 The paragraph provides that "the application of such punishment shall not be extended to crimes to which it does not presently apply."

therein. According to Guatemala, this reservation allowed it to impose the death penalty for new common crimes related to a political crime. However, the Court clarified that such an interpretation of the reservation was in contradiction to Article 4(2). The Court expressed that the latter "imposes a definite prohibition on the death penalty for all categories of offenses as far as the future is concerned".[5] The *travaux préparatoires* only confirm this abolitionist slant, which furthermore is part of a global trend.[6] In the same Advisory Opinion, the Court references the drafting history of the Convention to argue its stand. It says that although the proposal to abolish the death penalty did not achieve majority support as required under the rules of procedure, there was on the other hand no vote against it. Fourteen of the 19 delegations participating in the Plenary Closure Session of the Specialized Conference where the Convention was drafted made a solemn declaration of their "firm hope of seeing the application of the death penalty eradicated from the American environment" and their intention to sign an additional protocol enshrining that abolition.[7] In compliance with this aspiration, in 1990 the Protocol to Abolish the Death Penalty was approved.[8]

In the case of Raxcacó Reyes, the Court dealt with an amendment of the application of the death penalty in the case of kidnapping. At the time of ratification of the Convention, the Criminal Code of Guatemala punished kidnapping with deprivation of liberty and with death if the kidnapped person had died because of the kidnapping or while being held. The law applied to Raxcacó Reyes, however, allowed the extension of the death penalty to abductions that did not result in the death of the victim. The Court found that this amendment constituted a violation of Article 4.[9]

5. Article 4 of the Convention establishes strict conditions for States to be able to impose the death penalty, meaning that not all crimes punishable by the death penalty when the Convention entered into force for a State are compatible with it. If the rules regulating its application do not meet all the conditions, there will be a violation, unless a State makes a reservation to Article 4(2).[10]

---

5 *OC-3/83*, paras. 56 and 68. Also see *Case of Hilaire, Benjamin, Constantine et al. v. Trinidad and Tobago*, para. 99.

6 The European Convention on Human Rights, which was drafted in 1950 and also allows the death penalty, was amended with a Protocol – No. 6 – on the abolition of the death penalty, adopted on April 28, 1983. As of June 2014, 46 States have accessed to or ratified it. The International Covenant on Civil and Political Rights also has a Protocol – No. 2 – for the abolition of the death penalty, adopted on December 15, 1989, and as of June 2014, it has 81 States Parties.

7 *OC-3/83*, paras. 58.

8 Protocol to the American Convention on Human Rights to Abolish the Death Penalty, approved on June 8, 1990, entered into force on August 28, 1991. As of June 2014, 13 States have ratified or adhered to the Protocol.

9 *Case of Raxcacó Reyes v. Guatemala*, para. 66.

10 *OC-3/83*, paras. 70 and 71.

Based on the text of Article 4 of the Convention, the Inter-American Commission has grouped the limitations on the death penalty in countries that have not abolished it. The first is substantive, as "its scope of application must be reduced to the most serious of crimes", understanding that political crimes and common crimes connected with political crimes cannot be included in that category. The second refers to certain conditions of persons, as death sentences cannot be applied to minors under the age of 18, those over the age of 70, or pregnant women. The third constitutes a procedural limitation: the State must comply with certain procedural rules, "respect for which must be strictly guarded and required."[11]

6. The determination of what are considered "the most serious crimes" is made according to the fact that the death penalty is only acceptable "under truly exceptional conditions";[12] it is not enough for a crime to be serious for the death penalty to be applied: the crime must be "among the most serious". The United Nations Human Rights Committee has addressed the subject both in its views on individual cases and in its examination of the reports that States submit pursuant to Article 40 of the International Covenant on Civil and Political Rights (ICCPR).[13] Its members have stated that crimes against property,[14] economic crimes,[15] political crimes, and in general, crimes in which there has been no force against persons[16] cannot be punished by the death penalty. More recently, the Committee has not only urged States to restrict the application of the death penalty to the "most serious crimes", but has also invited States to take measures to abolish it completely.[17]

The case law of the inter-American system has not addressed the point of which crimes are considered "one of the most serious crimes". The Inter-American Commission has found that rulings issuing the death penalty, among other requirements, must be "individualized".[18] This means that they

11 IACHR, Case 9647, Report 3/87, Resolution of March 27, 1987, published in 1986–1987 Annual Report, para. 55.

12 *Ibidem*, para. 54. In the same sense see HRC, General Recommendation 6 (on Article 6 of the ICCPR), of July 12, 1996, para. 7.

13 The ICCPR was adopted on December 16, 1966 and entered into force on March 23, 1976. As of June 2014 it has 168 State Parties.

14 HRC, *Concluding Observations: Republic of Korea*, A/47/40 (1992) 113, para. 517.

15 HRC, *Concluding Observations: Algeria*, A/47/40 (1992) 61, para. 297.

16 HRC, *Concluding Observations: Iran*, A/48/40 Vol. I (1993) 44, para. 255; HRC, *Concluding Observations: Iraq*, A/53/40 Vol. I (1998) 18, para. 99.49. See also M. Nowak, *UN Covenant on Civil and Political Rights. CCPR Commentary*, N.P. Engel Publisher, Kehl/Strasbourg/Arlington, 1993, p. 118.

17 HRC, *Concluding Observations: Republic of Korea*, A/47/40 Vol. I (2001) 98, para. 86.13; HRC, *Concluding Observations: Guatemala*, A/47/40 Vol. I (2001) 93, para. 85.17.

18 The problem is addressed in IACHR, *Case of McKenzie et al. v. Jamaica*, Nos. 12023, 12044, 12107, 12126, 12146, Report No. 41/00 of April 13, 2000, published in the 1999 Annual Report; and IACHR, *Case of Joseph Thomas v. Jamaica*, No. 12183, Report No. 127/01 of December 3, 2001, published in the 2001 Annual Report.

"may include some factors as the offender's character and record, subjective factors that might have motivated his or her conduct, the designed and manner of execution of the particular offense, and the possibility of reform and social readaptation of the offender".[19] In the case of rulings where a death sentence is the only punishment allowed, the judge cannot consider this factor, lest the ruling becomes an arbitrary one and thus is in violation of Article 4(1) of the Convention.[20] In its turn, the Court has indicated that to decide whether a crime is in that category, it is not enough to consider the type of crime: possible attenuating circumstances, the degree of participation of the alleged perpetrator, and the motive, circumstances and methods used must be examined. This approach allows for a graduated assessment of the seriousness of the offense, so that it will bear an appropriate relation to the graduated levels of gravity of the applicable punishment. As a consequence legislation cannot order that the death penalty be applied automatically.[21] Stated thusly, the limitation on the State applies not only to legislators, requiring that they establish the death penalty only with regard to certain crimes. It also applies to judges intending to issue the death penalty in a particular case, requiring them to weigh the results of the unlawful action, the odiousness of the crime, and its perversity, among other circumstances of any specific case. Consequently, any provision making the death penalty mandatory without allowing any alternative sentence is not compatible with the Convention.[22] Mandatory application of the death penalty in these cases therefore would violate Article 4(2) of the Convention.[23] Finally, a mandatory death penalty also deprives the accused of the possibility of having a judicial review, as it is a punishment fixed by the law.[24] It also implies treating the accused "not as individual, unique human beings, but as undifferentiated and faceless member of a mass who will be subjected to the blind application of the death penalty."[25]

---

19 *Case of McKenzie et al. v. Jamaica*, paras. 208–212 and *Case of Joseph Thomas v. Jamaica*, para. 104.

20 *Ibidem*, para. 234 and para. 109, respectively.

21 *Case of Boyce et al. v. Barbados*, para. 61; *Case of Hilaire, Benjamin, Constantine et al. v. Barbados*, paras. 102–103, 106 and 108; *Case of Raxcacó Reyes v. Guatemala*, paras. 81 and 82; and *Case of Dacosta Cadogan v. Barbados*, para. 46.

22 *Case of Hilaire, Benjamin, Constantine et al. v. Trinidad and Tobago*, paras. 103 and 104.

23 Similarly, the Human Rights Committee has highlighted in its concluding observations on Barbados that "it remains concerned that the State party's laws make the imposition of the death penalty mandatory in respect of certain crimes, thus depriving the sentencing court of any discretion in imposing the penalty in the light of all the circumstances of the case." UNHRC, *Consideration of Reports submitted by States Parties under Article 40 of the Covenant, Concluding Observations on Barbados* (Eighty-ninth session, 2007), CCPR/C/BRB/CO/3, May 11, 2007, para. 9.

24 *Case of Boyce et al. v. Barbados*, para. 60.

25 *Case of Raxcacó Reyes v. Guatemala*, para. 80, quoting from the *case of Hilaire, Constantine and Benjamin et al. v. Trinidad and Tobago*, para. 105.

7. Neither is there any case law defining political crimes, nor criteria for establishing when a common crime is linked to a political one. In fact, there was intense debate over this provision during the discussion of the text. The Dominican Republic indicated that in order to keep this provision, a definition of "political crimes" was indispensable.[26] Brazil suggested the provision be eliminated, arguing that it could not be separated from a definition of the concept of political crime, "regarding which no positive international law text or jurist of the inter-American system has been able to reach a consensus".[27] The United States agreed with Brazil, adding that if the provision were not removed, an effort would have to be made to define the term.[28] Unsuccessfully, El Salvador attempted a definition,[29] while Uruguay stated that political crimes are defined and codified in domestic legislation and that "everyone knows what a political crime is".[30] In the end, the paragraph in question was approved and the concept of political crimes remained undefined. To this day, there is still debate over what criteria should serve as a basis for deciding whether a crime is political, as well as which crimes can be classified as "related" to political crimes. The Inter-American Court will have eventually to rule on the concept of political crime or other crimes connected therewith on a case-by-case basis.

8. Certain personal circumstances can exempt particular individuals from being subjected to the death penalty. In keeping with Article 4(5) of the American Convention, those over 70 years old and pregnant women cannot be sentenced to the death penalty, nor can those younger than 18 years old. This provision, like others in the Convention, allow for reservations. However, a *jus cogens* provision of international law prohibits the execution of minors. This prohibition appears in the Convention on the Rights of the Child (CRC)[31] and in the ICCPR.[32] Additionally, a significant number of domestic legal systems establish the elimination of the death penalty for minors. All this prevents States from making reservations with regard to Article 4(5) in order to subject minors to the death penalty.

In a 1986 case against the United States, the Inter-American Commission accepted the United States' argument that as of that date, there was no customary international law norm establishing the age of 18 as the minimum age for the imposition of the death sentence. However, it noted that the norm

26 Inter-American Specialized Conference on Human Rights, San José, Costa Rica, November 7–22, 1969, Minutes and Documents, General Secretariat, OAS, Washington DC, 1979, p. 57.

27 *Ibidem*, p. 121. Translation by the author.

28 *Ibidem*, p. 164.

29 *Ibidem*, p. 165.

30 *Ibidem*, p. 166.

31 Convention on the Rights of the Child, by General Assembly Resolution 44/25 of November 20, 1989, entry into force September 2, 1990, Article 37(a). Only Somalia and the United States have not ratified this Convention.

32 ICCPR, Article 6(5).

was emerging in light of the growing number of countries that have ratified the American Convention and the ICCPR.[33] Because of ratification, those countries had modified their domestic legislation in order for it to conform to those instruments.[34] During a Human Rights Committee hearing in 1995, the US delegation agreed that "[i]t was generally accepted that children below a certain age should not suffer the death penalty no matter how terrible the crime". However, this age varied and in the US, it had been set at 16.[35] The Committee itself expressed its concern over the application of the death penalty to those under the age of 18 and urged the United States to take all necessary measures to address the situation.[36] In its turn, based on various treaties and domestic practice of several States, including the United States, the Inter-American Commission concluded that by 2002, a clear international definition existed establishing the age of an adult for the purposes of the death penalty at 18.[37]

9. The third condition that the State must meet in order to avoid violating the Convention in its application of the death penalty refers to the trial itself. A competent court must carry out the trial in accordance with a law establishing such punishment enacted prior to the commission of the crime. The wording of this requirement is somewhat unfortunate. The provision does not make the need for the trial to be carried out with strict respect for due process explicit; rather, it simply accentuates certain elements of due process, failing even to mention that the principles of non-retroactivity of criminal law and interpretation of the law in a way most favorable to the accused cannot be violated.[38] The fact that Article 4(2) of the Convention accentuates only certain aspects of these guarantees, and not all of them, does not help to convey the idea of the strictness with which procedural requirements must be met in order to apply the death penalty in a manner that is compatible with the Convention. The inescapable need to rigorously comply with all procedural requirements has led the Human Rights Committee to find that if certain requirements are not met, not only has the due process provision – Article 14 of the ICCPR – been violated, but so has the provision on the right to life, Article 6 of the ICCPR.[39]

---

33 The Children's Convention also determines the age of children at 18 years.

34 IACHR, *Case of Roach and Pinkerton v. United States*, No. 9647, Resolution No. 3/87, September 22, 1987, para. 60.

35 HRC, *Summary record of the 1405th meeting* (CCPR/C/SR.O405, April 24, 1995), paras. 13 and 14.

36 See HRC, *Concluding Observations: United States*, A/50/40 Vol. I (1995) 52, paras. 281 and 296.

37 IACHR, *Case of Michael Domínguez v. United States*, No. 12285, Report No. 62/02, October 22, 2002, published in *2002 Annual Report*.

38 Regarding Article 9, see Chapter 7 of this book.

39 From a legal point of view, it is not necessary to specify some elements explicitly since Article 8 of the American Convention clearly states that no punishment can be applied absent all the requirements established therein. For a full list of the elements of due process, see Chapter 6.

The Inter-American Court took the same position in its Advisory Opinion No. 16/99 requested by Mexico. Mexico wished the Court to opine whether failing to inform a foreign accused person of his or her right to have contact with legal counsel in his or her country in a proceeding in the host country that could – and in fact did – lead to a death sentence constituted both a violation of due process and of life.[40] The Court ruled that, given the irreversibility of the penalty, "the strictest and most rigorous enforcement of judicial guarantees is required" for its application; a sentence of death ordered without this information amounted to an arbitrary deprivation of life.[41] In the case of DaCosta Cadogan, the Court found a violation of Articles 8 and 4 arising from the national courts' lack of diligence in assessing and presenting to the jury the mental condition of the accused. This was a consequence of the fact that since "Mr. DaCosta Cadogan [had been] afforded state-appointed legal counsel, the presiding judge had the duty to adopt a more active role in ensuring that all necessary measures were carried out in order to guarantee a fair trial".[42] The Convention's abolitionist leaning and the care it takes in regulating the imposition of the death penalty extend even beyond conviction and sentencing.

Article 4(6) of the Convention provides that every person condemned to death shall have the right to apply for amnesty, pardon, or commutation of sentence, noting that any of these may be granted in all cases. In the case of Fermín Ramírez v. Mexico, the Court found that if no State body has the power to know of and decide upon the measure of grace, there is a violation of the right to life.[43]

3. PROTECTION OF THE RIGHT TO LIFE IN GENERAL

3.1. THE DUTY TO PREVENT

10. The first level of protection of the right to life is the duty to prevent. It includes all those means of a legal, political, administrative and cultural nature that promote the protection of life and ensure that any violations are considered and treated as illegal acts. Once a death has occurred, it is necessary for the State to investigate the matter, eventually punish and give reparation.[44] Finally, guarantees of non-repetition will be in order, so as to prevent future actions of that nature. The State is required to prevent possible violations of the right to

40 HRC, *Mbenge v. Zaire*, Communication 016/1977, report dated March 25, 1983, para. 17; also see *Case of Wright v. Jamaica*, Communication 349/1989, report dated August 18, 1992, para. 8.7.

41 *OC-16/99*, paras. 136 and 137.

42 *Case DaCosta Cadogan v. Barbados*, para. 84.

43 *Case of Fermín Ramírez v. México*, paras. 107, 109 and 110.

44 *Case of Velásquez Rodríguez v. Honduras*, para. 175.

life by its own agents or by private individuals. Its obligations in this regard are varied. One is the establishment of deterrents for private individuals with respect to threats to life. These generally will consist in establishing as a crime a variety of forms of homicide,[45] as well as the strict statutory regulation of legitimate self-defense and the establishment of pertinent procedural provisions in order for courts of law to be able to hear cases of deprivation of life at the hands of private individuals. In principle, one could argue that when the State prevents the commission of acts that violate Article 4, it does so not to the benefit of one particular subject but of the population in general. The deterrence is meant for the whole of society.[46]

In several cases, the Court has traced the line separating the State's responsibility with respect to prevention from lack thereof. In Velásquez it said:

> The Court is convinced, and has so found, that the disappearance of Manfredo Velásquez was carried out by agents who acted under cover of public authority. However, even had that fact not been proven, the failure of the State apparatus to act, which is clearly proven, is a failure on the part of Honduras to fulfill the duties it assumed under Article 1 (1) of the Convention, which obligated it to ensure Manfredo Velásquez the free and full exercise of his human rights.[47]

According to the Court, the responsibility of the State to prevent all deprivation of life perpetrated by private individuals is not unlimited. The obligation is "conditional on its awareness of a situation of real and imminent danger for a specific individual or group of individuals and the reasonable possibility of preventing or avoiding that danger."[48] In other words, even though the legal consequence of an act or omission of a private individual is the violation of certain human rights of another private individual, responsibility cannot be attributed automatically to the State, because the specific circumstances of the case and the discharge of such obligation to prevent must be taken into account. In the case of the Kichwa people, an oil company, "with the State's acquiescence and protection, cleared trails and planted nearly 1400 kilograms of pentolite explosives in Block 23, which includes the Sarayaku territory". This action was taken notwithstanding a provisional measure ordered by the Court previously to clear up the territory, thus creating "a permanent situation of risk and threat

45 *Case of Caballero Delgado and Santana v. Colombia*, judgment on reparations, para. 56.

46 The European system faced this problem more than once. See Communication 9348/81, *W. v. United Kingdom*, D&R 32 (1983) and Communication 9829/82, *X. v. United Kingdom and Ireland* (not published) on the general situation of security in Northern Ireland (cited by P. van Dijk and G.J.H. van Hoof, in collaboration with A.W. Heringa, J.G.C. Schokkenbroek, B.P. Vermeulen, M.L.W.M. Viering and L.F. Zwaak, *Theory and Practice of the European Convention on Human Rights*, 3rd edition, Kluwer Law International, The Hague/London/Boston, 1998, p. 298, footnote 23).

47 *Case of Velásquez Rodríguez v. Honduras*, para. 182.

48 *Case of González et al. (Cotton Field) v. Mexico*, para. 280. See also *Case of the Kichwa Indigenous People of Sarayaku v. Ecuador* and *Case of Hermanos Landaeta v. Venezuela*, para. 184.

to the life and physical integrity of its members".[49] Although the Court reasoned that "the State's positive obligations must be interpreted in such a manner that an impossible or disproportionate burden is not imposed upon the authorities", it found a violation here. The State was responsible for a violation of Articles 4 and 5 because of the risks to life and physical integrity it had placed on the Sarayaku people.[50]

On the contrary, in the case of González *et al.* (Cotton Field) v. Mexico, the Court did not go so far as to find a violation of Article 4, or eventually of Article 5 on personal integrity, when dealing with the lack of preventive general policies in Ciudad Juárez to curtail the situation of violence surrounding young, poor women. The difference of circumstances accounts for this: in the case of Cotton Field, the issue was the absence of general policies. This notwithstanding, it affirmed that the lack of these policies was "a failure of the State to comply in general with its obligation of prevention".[51] This would suggest that there is some form of responsibility, but the Court would have no jurisdiction to pass judgment on it because it would be an abstract issue. The Court did not feel it could go further, but still decided that it was allowed to call the State's attention to this, since it is the State's duty to comply with prevention.

Aside from women, children and indigenous peoples,[52] the Court assigns a special need of protection to human rights defenders or advocates. There have been several cases where the Court has dealt with violations of the rights to life and personal integrity of these defenders, stating generally that the type of activities they carry out puts them in a situation of risk that should be considered by the State when complying with its obligations to guarantee these rights.[53] In the case of Human Rights Defenders v. Guatemala, the Court recalled its case law alluding to the special State duties determined by the functions the defenders exercised, but only when the State is aware of a real and immediate risk to them and there are reasonable possibilities to prevent or avoid the risk.[54] This is a "reinforced obligation" toward this category of individuals.[55] The Court emphasizes in this judgment and others the important role human rights defenders have in strengthening democracy and the rule of law.[56] Other

---

49 *Case of the Kichwa Indigenous People of Sarayaku v. Ecuador*, para. 246.

50 *Ibidem*, paras. 248–249.

51 *Case of González et al. v. Mexico*, para. 282. *Massacre of Pueblo Bello v. Colombia*, para. 123. See also ECHR, *Kiliç v. Turkey*, judgment of March 28, 2000, Application No. 22492/93, paras. 62 and 63; *Osman v. United Kingdom*, judgment of October 28, 1998, Reports of Judgments and Decisions 1998-VIII, paras. 115 and 116, all quoted by the Court.

52 Women, children and indigenous peoples will be treated separately.

53 See, *inter alia*, cases of *Valle Jaramillo v. Colombia*, *Nogueira de Carvahlo v. Brazil* and *Luna López v. Honduras*.

54 *Case of the Human Rights Defenders v. Guatemala*, para. 141.

55 *Ibidem*, para 142.

56 *Ibidem*, para. 128. See IACHR, Report on the Situation of Human Rights Defenders in the Americas (OEA/Ser.L/V/II.124 Doc. 5 rev.1, 7 March 2006) and Second Report on the Situation of Human rights Defenders in the Americas (OEA/Ser.L/V/II. Doc.66,

groups of people may find themselves in the same predicament and require more personalized protection of the right to life in order to prevent potential violations thereof aimed at specific individuals whose lives are apparently being threatened, so long as the danger of death is clear and individualized. This is not a hypothetical problem in Latin America. There have been situations in many countries in which people who are part of a group have seen their lives threatened simply because they belonged to that group. This was the case, for example, of political and union leaders during the time of dictatorships, or with human rights defenders in situations of massive violations. It is also possible for a specific person to face a threat to his or her life in connection with some specific event, such as being, for example, a witness of a massacre or other grave human rights violation. The risk, of course, must be clear and imminent. In a similar sense, the Court has referred to the fourth of the Principles on the Effective Prevention and Investigation of Extra-legal, Arbitrary and Summary Executions,[57] which "provides that effective protection must be ensured, by means of judicial or other remedies, to persons who are in danger of being executed in an extra-legal, arbitrary, or summary manner."[58] Again, in González *et al.* (Cotton Field) v. Mexico, the Court made it clear that Mexico should have taken measures to prevent the sexual abuse, ill-treatment and killing of three victims who had been kidnapped, given that the prevalence of violence existing in the region at the time where kidnappings in the area occurred usually resulted in torture and death. It was the State's duty to presume the kidnapped person to be alive "until there is no longer any uncertainty" about their fate.[59]

3.2. THE DUTY TO PREVENT THE MISUSE OF FORCE

11. The loss of life due to the frequent abuse of force has plagued Latin American States. Of course, the misuse of force was rampant during dictatorships; it was the easiest, most effective way of exercising political power. It not only did away with political opponents through killing them; through fear, it also prevented others from even attempting opposition. There was also misuse of force in otherwise democratic States, or perhaps in non-dictatorship situations. Force has been, and I think still is, a political instrument in some Latin American countries. Given that the State has a monopoly on the legitimate use of force, the provisions regulating its use must be drafted carefully in

December 31, 2011. This importance and the special concern the States should have with regard to these activities has made the Inter-American Commission of Human Rights issue two reports dealing with this matter.

57 UN, ECOSOC, Principles on the Effective Prevention and Investigation of Extra-legal, Arbitrary and Summary Executions, Resolution 1989/65 of May 24, 1989.

58 *Case of Juan Humberto Sánchez v. Honduras*, para. 133.

59 *Case of González et al. (Cotton Field) v. Mexico*, para. 283.

order to prevent any abuse that could lead to the death of a person, whether intentionally or because of negligence. Of course, not all deaths resulting from the use of force by State agents constitute a violation of the Convention; it is possible for State agents with authority to use force to take a human being's life through actions outside the imposition of the death penalty without generating international responsibility because there has been no violation of the American Convention. Even though it can result in the taking of a life, the Inter-American Court acknowledged the legitimacy of the State's right to use force. States have the important tasks of establishing rules regulating the conduct of their agents in the use of force and of informing both those agents and the rest of society of those rules. The Inter-American system has no provision indicating generally or specifically what the content of these rules should be, but certainly the Court has developed a framework within which States may operate. A significant contribution has been made to this task by the universal system created under the umbrella of the United Nations. A series of instruments have been created specifying State obligations in this area, addressing both the use of firearms and the treatment of persons subjected to detention or prison, rules that protect the individual's right to life and the right to humane treatment.[60]

12. The rules must be established according to the standards of absolute necessity and proportionality that every interference with a human right requires in order not to become a violation. Furthermore, it is the State's obligation to demonstrate that it has complied with these principles. As it found in Cabrera García and Montiel Flores, the Court specified that any use of force that is not strictly necessary to ensure proper behavior on the part of the detainee constitutes an assault on the dignity of the person in violation of Article 5 of the American Convention.[61] In Uzcátegui the Court found a violation of Article 4 because the State had failed to present consistent, coherent, varied, reliable and sufficient evidence to prove that the use of lethal force against Mr. Uzcátegui was legitimate. In addition, it had not proved that the force used was not "absolutely necessary and proportional", or that the police officers who participated in this operation attempted to use other less lethal means.[62]

13. The authorities must order the use of force by law enforcement officials – including the military – only in exceptional circumstances, must plan it carefully and limit it proportionally. As such, the Tribunal has considered that force or coercive means can only be used once all other methods of control have

60 See, for example, Basic Principles on the Use of Force and Firearms by Law Enforcement Officials, adopted by the Eighth Congress of the United Nations Congress on the Prevention of Crime and the Treatment of Offenders, held in Havana (Cuba) on August 27–September 7, 1990.

61 *Case of Cabrera García and Montiel Flores v. Mexico*, para. 133.

62 *Case of Uzcátegui et al. v. Mexico*, para. 141.

been exhausted and have failed.[63] The use of lethal force and firearms against individuals by law enforcement officials or military – which is forbidden as a rule – is only justified in extraordinary cases. The exceptional circumstances shall be determined by law and restrictively construed, so that they are used to the minimum extent possible in all circumstances and never exceed the use which is "absolutely necessary" in relation to the force or threat to be repelled.[64] When excessive force is used, any resulting deprivation of life is arbitrary.[65] Excessive or disproportionate use of force by law enforcement officials and military that result in the loss of life therefore amounts to an arbitrary deprivation of life. The principle of necessity justifies only those measures of violence permitted by international law and that are relevant and proportionate to ensure the prompt subjugation of the enemy with the least possible cost of human and economic resources. The principle of humanity complements and inherently limits the principle of necessity by forbidding those measures of violence which are not necessary (i.e. relevant and proportionate) to the achievement of a definitive advantage. In peacetime situations, State agents must distinguish between persons who, by their actions, constitute an imminent threat of death or serious injury and persons who do not present this threat.[66] The Court has applied these principles in the investigation of every case where the force has been excessive.

14. The existence of rules on the use of force requires that States train its agents on the content of the rules governing the use of force and the obligations imposed on security forces by the right to life. Psychological training to prevent agents from responding emotionally in a way that exceeds the limits established by the rules also seems indispensable. Article VIII of the Inter-American Convention on Forced Disappearance of Persons makes explicit the obligation to train personnel. It holds that "[t]he States Parties shall ensure that the training of public law-enforcement personnel or officials includes the necessary education on the offense of forced disappearance of persons".

In the case of Bámaca Velasquez, the Inter-American Court ordered Guatemala to comply with the obligation to train State agents.[67] In the case of Suárez Rosero, the petitionary asked the Court to order the State to "adopt measures to avoid a repetition of the violations in the future, including provision of human rights training to the officials in charge of applying the law."[68] In

---

63 *Case of Montero Aranguren et al. (Detention center of Catia) v. Venezuela*, para. 67.

64 *Ibidem*, para. 68.

65 *Ibidem*, para. 68. See also the Basic Principles on the Use of Force and Firearms by Law Enforcement Officials, adopted by the Eighth Congress of the United Nations for the Prevention of Crime and the Treatment of Criminals, Havana, Cuba, August 27–September 7, 1990, Principle 9.

66 *Case of Zambrano Vélez v. Ecuador*, paras. 83–88. See also *Case of Nadege Dorzema v. Dominican Republic*, paras. 81–85.

67 *Case of the Bámaca Velásquez v. Guatemala*, judgment on reparations, para. 86.

68 *Case of the Suárez Rosero v. Ecuador*, judgment on reparations, para. 84.

response to the petition, the Court reiterated its judgment on the merits handed down in the same case. It told Ecuador that it should "adopt such measures as may be necessary to ensure that violations such as those established in the instant case never again occur in its jurisdiction",[69] from which one can conclude that the Court found training of law enforcement personnel to be necessary and obligatory.[70] The Court reiterated and detailed this obligation in a judgment handed down in the case of the Caracazo. There it ordered the State to prevent a repetition of this situation by making provisions for the education and training of all members of its armed forces and its security agencies on principles and provisions of human rights protection and regarding the limits to which the use of weapons by law enforcement officials is subject, even in a state of emergency.[71] Additionally it stated that "[t]he State must, also, adjust operational plans regarding public disturbances to the requirements of respect and protection of those rights, adopting to this end, among other measures, those geared toward control of actions by all members of the security forces in the very field of action to avoid excess."[72] This has become a standard order of the Court in similar cases.

15. The use of force has been the subject of the Court's decisions in other type of situations. A mentally ill person, Ximenes Lopes, died while interned in an institution due to mistreatment inflicted by employees of the institution. Another factor impinging on the situation was the lack of medical care in general. When addressing the abuses committed within the institution, the Court approached the subject of restraint of patients, stating, "the use of restraint poses a high risk of doing harm to the patient or causing his or her death [...] falls and lesions during such procedure are quite common".[73] Considering restraint as an "aggressive measure", it stated that "it should be used as a last resort and with the only purpose of protecting the patient, or else the medical staff or third persons, when the behavior of the patient involved is such as to pose a threat to their safety".[74] The Court proceeded in this case to specify the duties of a State with regard to protecting the life and the personal integrity of mental patients as the duties to take care, to regulate and supervise and to investigate.[75] With this

69 *Ibidem*, para. 87.

70 Also noteworthy is that the Human Rights Committee reminds all States almost uniformly of their obligation to train law enforcement personnel on their obligations regarding human rights in general. See, for example, *Concluding Observations: Bolivia* (CCPR/C/79/Add.74, May 5, 1997, para. 33); *Concluding Observations: Brazil* (CCPR/C/79/Add.66, July 24, 2007, para. 19), *Concluding Observations: Cyprus* (CCPR/C/79/Add.39, August 3, 1994, para. 22), *Concluding Observations: Kyrgyz Republic* (CCPR/CO/69/KGZ, July 24, 2000, para. 6).

71 *Case of the Caracazo v. Venezuela*, judgment on reparations, para. 127.

72 *Ibidem*.

73 *Case of Ximenes Lopes v. Brazil*, para. 133.

74 *Ibidem*, para. 134.

75 *Ibidem*, paras. 138–149.

judgment, the Court started to tread the path toward considering the economic, social and cultural aspects of civil and political rights. Additionally, it began to examine the behavior of individuals, not directly a part of the State,[76] and apply the regulations on the use of force to them.

3.3. PREVENTION AT THE INTER-AMERICAN LEVEL

16. Another means of prevention involves the international level. In Article 63(2) of the American Convention sets forth that, "[i]n cases of extreme gravity and urgency, and when necessary to avoid irreparable damage to persons, the Court shall adopt such provisional measures as it deems pertinent in matters it has under consideration." The Court may grant provisional measures in any matter that it is hearing, or in matters that have not been yet submitted before the Court if the Inter-American Commission requests them.[77] The central purpose of this provision is probably not to require the State to protect specific lives, without denying the importance of this, but rather to prevent international justice from being frustrated. The Court, however, has extended provisional measures to include as beneficiaries, for example, not only individuals singled out by name but also groups of people that are potentially identifiable, even when the purpose is not to ensure that the objective sought in a case before the system is not frustrated. In this respect, one case to cite is the request for and granting of provisional measures in the case of the Miguel Agustín Pro Juárez Human Rights Center *et al.*, before the Inter-American Commission. The Commission cited the murder of a human rights lawyer as background in its petition and asked the Court to order provisional measures for all members of the aforementioned Human Rights Centre without naming them individually. One of the arguments used to request the measure was that "the State is responsible for taking all necessary measures to guarantee the safety of all citizens, in particular the safety of those who dedicate themselves to defending and promoting human rights." In addressing these issues, the Court raised two important considerations. In the first, it held that the purpose of provisional measures in international human rights law is to protect effectively fundamental rights, insofar as they seek to prevent irreparable damages to persons.[78] In the second, it expressed that Article 1(1) of the American Convention sets forth the general obligations of States Parties to respect the rights and liberties enshrined in the Convention and to guarantee the free and full exercise of these rights for

---

[76] In order to understand the relationship between the health institution and the State, it is unavoidable to read the whole case. This is not the purpose of this book.

[77] ACHR, Article 63(2).

[78] *Matter of Miguel Agustín Pro Juárez Human Rights Center et al.*, Provisional Measures requested by the Inter-American Commission on Human Rights with regard to the United Mexican States, decision of the IACtHR of November 30, 2001, para. 8 (emphasis added).

all individuals subject to their jurisdiction. This would imply a duty to take the security measures necessary for their protection. These obligations become even more evident but not exclusive with respect to individuals linked to proceedings before the supervisory organs of the American Convention.[79]

Furthermore, there have been also provisional measures to protect rights that go beyond life and personal integrity, such as the right to freedom of expression.[80] With this case law, provisional measures are very near to *amparo*, a Latin American remedy set forth in Article 25 of the Convention.[81]

3.4. THE DUTY TO INVESTIGATE THE MISUSE OF FORCE

17. When a death is apparently the unintentional result of the use of force, it is the responsibility of the supervisory agency to examine the facts in light of the framework established in the Convention for deciding whether affecting a human right is compatible with the obligations of the Convention. All the rules explained above must be followed in the investigation of the events. The examination must include whether there is an authorizing legal norm; whether there was a clear aim permitted by the law; whether there is a plan for the specific use of the force; and finally, whether the measure itself that resulted in the taking of a life is "necessary in a democratic society". For this, it is indispensable to examine whether the measure is appropriate and proportional and whether there was any other alternative to achieve the objective.[82] The Court has applied this standard on more than one occasion.

The judgment in Neira Alegría weighed the legitimacy of the death of 118 prisoners in a cellblock of the San Juan Bautista Prison because of an order given by the Peruvian Navy to demolish the cellblock after the prisoners, who had been rioting, had surrendered. The Court found that Peru had the right and the duty to put down the riot. The riot had apparently been planned beforehand and had already resulted in the capture of three security guards as hostages, injuries to another four security guards, and a shootout where several members of the security forces attempting to end the uprising had died. The Court found that the aim for which force had been used was compatible with the American Convention, but applying the standard of "necessity in a democratic society", it added that Peru's right did not allow for the exercise of unlimited power.[83]

79 *Matter of the Urso Branco Prison*, Provisional Measures requested by the Inter-American Commission on Human Rights regarding the Federal Republic of Brazil, decision of the IACtHR of June 18, 2002, para. 5 (emphasis added).

80 See, for example, provisional measures in the *case of Ríos et al. v. Venezuela*, para. 29.

81 On provisional measures, see, for example, H. Faúndez Ledesma, *The Inter-American System for the Protection of Human Rights. Institutional and procedural aspects*, 3rd edition, San José, Costa Rica, Inter-American Institute of Human Rights, pp. 484–556.

82 *Case of Neira Alegría et al. v. Peru*, para. 74.

83 *Ibidem*, paras. 61 and 75.

Based on abundant evidence, including reports from the Peruvian Congress, the Court concluded that the elements of the case did not justify the degree of force that Peru used.[84] The case of Durand and Ugarte referred to a similar situation. Therein, the Court ruled that it had been proven "that Cell Block Blue had been demolished by forces of the Peruvian Navy, who used force disproportionate to the danger presented by the uprising [...] This resulted in many of the inmates being crushed to death". The Court also found that the authorities had had no interest in rescuing those that remained alive and there had been no diligence in the identification of the bodies. Furthermore, the process of recovering the bodies took approximately nine months.[85] In the case of Castro Castro, a prison in Peru raided by the military, the Court decided that it had not been proven that there was any cause that called for the legitimate use of force by State agents in the attack carried out by the military on the women's cellblock. The Court acknowledged the State had the power and even the obligation to guarantee security and maintain public order even by the use of force, but this power was limited by the need to respect human rights. In this case, there had been no mutiny and no "cause that called from [sic] the legitimate use or force by the state agents in that first act of the attack".[86]

18. A case in which the Court put together and explained these requirements is that of Nadege Dorzema. There the Court considers that, "when analyzing the use of force by State agents, three fundamental moments must be considered: (a) preventive actions, (b) actions accompanying the events, and (c) actions subsequent to the events".[87] It explained that appropriate measures compatible with the Convention, required the application of "the principles of legality, absolute necessity, and proportionality". Legality meant that the force must have a legitimate goal, which was absent in the case, as weapons were used to stop a vehicle that failed to stop at a checkpoint. Absolute necessity was also absent here; quoting the European Court, the judgment states that "even when the lack of the use of force would result in the loss of the opportunity to capture them", that was not enough to legitimize the killing of seven people. These people did not pose a direct threat.[88] Proportionality means that the "level of force must be in keeping with the level of resistance." It also means that the operation to use force must be planned according to the circumstances.[89] The Court establishes that agents must apply the criteria of differentiated and progressive use of force, determining the degree of cooperation, resistance or violence of the subject against whom the intervention is intended and, on this basis, employ negotiating

84 *Ibidem*, para. 74. Unofficial English version.
85 *Case of Durand and Ugarte v. Peru*, para. 68.
86 *Case of Castro Castro v. Peru*, paras. 240–241.
87 *Case of Nadege Dorzema v. Dominican Republic*, para. 78.
88 *Ibidem*, para. 80.
89 *Ibidem*, para. 88.

tactics, control or use of force, as required.[90] Similar considerations were made in the case of Montero Aranguren.[91]

19. The Court decided on the use of force from a different angle in the case of the Landaeta brothers.[92] Eduardo Landaeta was under the age of 18, was taken prisoner by the police and died while he was being transferred for a second time to another place of detention. The State argued that the vehicle in which the police was transporting Eduardo had been ambushed by masked individuals who shot and killed him. The first issue the Court examined was the State's obligation to protect the detainee, especially because he was underage and clearly was in a situation of real and imminent risk. From the record, it appears that this was the case since the same police that had detained Eduardo had threatened him more than once.[93] Furthermore, the Court considered, *inter alia*, that there was at the time a situation of police abuse, that the same police corps that held Eduardo had killed his brother, that Eduardo's detention had been illegal, and that the evidence showed that his killers were the same police that were transferring him.[94] The Court, deciding that this death was a result of the misuse of force, dealt in depth with the requirements to make death resulting therefrom compatible with the Convention. For this, it relied on the judgment in the Dorzema case.[95] I find the Landaeta brothers case to be more one of an extrajudicial execution than of an excess of force, but that is not the Court's position.

It is possible that State agents might use force when not carrying out their functions or that other individuals might be the ones exercising the force. The obligation to investigate is important in this case, since it has been a constant in the region, particularly in the cases of disappearances or massacres.[96] As has been noted, the Court's case law in this field is abundant, and fortunately its rulings have been able to define this aspect of the obligation to ensure in detail.

20. The obligation to protect is not fulfilled when the existing provisions are not applied consistently and without discrimination. Therefore, a new area for State action opens, related to the establishment of adequate procedural regulation for overseeing its agents, the establishment of an independent and impartial organ to carry out that oversight, and the consistent application of that oversight, without discrimination, in order to deter potential offenders. It is crucial that all taking of life due to the actions of third parties that is not

90 *Ibidem*, para. 85.
91 *Case of Montero Aranguren v. Venezuela*, para. 67.
92 *Case of the Landaeta brothers v. Venezuela.*
93 *Ibidem*, paras. 185–190. See also *case of the Landaeta brothers v. Venezuela*, para. 130.
94 *Ibidem*, para. 196.
95 *Ibidem*, paras. 125–136.
96 *Case of Myrna Mack v. Guatemala*, para. 156.

the result of a death sentence be treated with absolute respect for the guidelines indicated in the Convention for carrying out the investigation, that the accused be brought to trial, and that those found guilty be punished.[97] The European Court of Human Rights has considered that in cases of violations to the right to life or to personal integrity:

> the idea of an "effective remedy" implies, in addition to the payment in compensation, where applicable, and without detriment to any other available remedy in the national system, the obligation of the respondent State to carry out an exhaustive and effective investigation, which allows for the identification and punishment of those responsible, as well as the effective access for the petitioner in the investigation procedures.[98]

In its turn, the former United Nations Commission on Human Rights recognized that demanding the responsibility of the perpetrators of serious violations of human rights is a key factor for a fair and equitable justice system. It also helps reconciliation and stability of society, particularly of societies in a situation of conflict or post-conflict.[99]

21. In the consideration of the obligation to investigate, one cannot forget that the Court has been handling cases of which many directly involved complicity of State organs. Even today, investigations are hindered due to the weakness found in so many Latin American courts and police, with a past mixed with prejudices and discrimination, which has been difficult to eradicate.[100] In cases where grave violations form a systematic pattern, the Court is extremely rigorous when it is proven that there has been no investigation at all or an ineffective remedy that results in impunity. This has led the Court to highlight the importance of compliance with the obligation to investigate in several rulings.

The Court has often explained what exactly and how facts should be investigated when there has been a violation of the right to life in a context of gross, systematic violations. A thorough view was given in the Cotton Field case. It started by examining the creation of the report on the discovery of the bodies, preservation of the crime scene, and collection and handling of evidence.[101] Then it continued with the performance of autopsies and the identification and

---

97 See, *inter alia*, *Case of Velásquez Rodríguez v. Honduras*, para. 174; *Case of Godínez Cruz v. Honduras*, para. 184; *Case of the El Amparo v. Venezuela*, judgment on reparations, para. 61 and operative paragraph 4; *Case of Castillo Páez v. Peru*, para. 90; *Case of Suárez Rosero v. Ecuador*, para. 107 and operative paragraph; *Case of Blake v. Guatemala*, para. 121 and operative paragraph 3; *Case of Paniagua Morales et al. v. Guatemala*, para. 178 and operative paragraph 6.

98 *Case of Guerrilla de Araguarai v. Brazil*, para. 192.

99 *Ibidem*, quoting Commission on Human Rights. Impunity. Order 2005/81, 61st Period of Sessions, UN Doc. E/CN.4/RES/2005/81, April 21, 2005.

100 See, for example, HRC, *Concluding Observations: Chile* (CCPR/C/CHL/CO/5, May 18, 2007 or *Concluding Observations: Honduras* (CCPR/C/HND/CO/1, December 13, 2006).

101 *Case of Cotton Field v. Mexico*, paras. 298–306.

return of the bodies.[102] Attention was also paid to the fragmentation of the investigations and its alleged impact on creating impunity,[103] with particular reference to the fact of having investigated each case of the three victims separately.[104] This prevented the courts from considering carefully the context within which these events had taken place. The case law of the Inter-American Court "indicated that certain lines of inquiry, which fail to analyze the systematic patterns surrounding a specific type of violations of human rights, can render the investigations ineffective".[105] A review of all these observations by the Court showed the lamentable state of domestic courts in this respect. In the Uzcátegui case, the situation is *mutatis mutandis* similar. The Court again refers to the relevance of taking into account the context in which the particular case took place. The death of Mr. Uzcátegui occurred in the context of extrajudicial executions carried out by police squads or units, a situation of which the State organs were aware.[106] The Court emphasized that in this type of cases

> it is essential to analyze the information concerning the power structures that permitted, planned and executed it, both intellectually and directly, and concerning the individuals or groups that were interested in or would benefit from the crime (beneficiaries). This, in turn, would lead to theories and lines of inquiry and to an examination of the crime scene, witnesses and other probative elements. Hence, in cases such as this, it is not a question of examining the crime in isolation, but rather of inserting it in a context that will provide the necessary elements to understand its operational structure.[107]

22. When speaking of the obligation to investigate cases of serious human rights violations, the Court enters into the issue of impunity.[108] It holds that the application of the statute of limitations (leading to the extinction of punitive possibilities owing to the passage of time) "or any other domestic legal obstacle that attempts to impede the investigation and punishment of those responsible for human rights violations are inadmissible".[109] The statement is somewhat overreaching, as it does not make any distinction between the different kinds of violations. However, a thorough examination of the case law on the rights to life, to personal integrity and others points to cases of grave human rights violations.[110] Later judgments have nuanced this assertion. In Vélez Restrepo,

---

102 *Ibidem*, paras. 310 and 313–333.

103 *Ibidem*, paras. 354–363.

104 *Ibidem*, paras. 364–370.

105 *Ibidem*, para. 366.

106 *Case of Uzcátegui v. Venezuela*, para. 139.

107 *Ibidem*, para. 222.

108 On impunity, see also Chapter 2.

109 *Case of Bulacio v. Argentina*, para. 116. In the same sense, *Case of Trujillo Oroza v. Bolivia*, judgment on reparations, para. 106; *Case of Barrios Altos v. Peru*, para. 41.

110 The Guidelines of the Committee of Ministers of the Council of Europe on eradicating impunity for serious human rights violations, defines serious human rights violation as those

the Court stated that "in certain circumstances international law considers that application of the statute of limitations is inadmissible and inappropriate".[111] It mentions as examples the forced disappearance of persons, extrajudicial execution, and torture. The Court considered that in this case the appropriate circumstances did not concur and the necessary presumptions did not exist to apply any of the exceptions and therefore the statute of limitations should have been applied and no violation of Article 4 existed. However, being aware of the existing impunity in Vélez Restrepo's killing, the Court "finds it necessary to order the State to advise whether, under Colombian law, it is possible to adopt other measures or actions that allow the responsibilities in this case for the said acts to be determined and, if so, to take these measures or actions".[112] The Court is here conducting a function more extensive than just solving a case. It is attempting to make justice prevail, although it has no power to order appropriate reparations.

23. There has been a trend in the region and in other parts of the world to establish truth commissions,[113] bodies officially empowered by the State to investigate patterns of systematic and gross violations in a particular State, both to learn the truth and to help bring about reconciliation between victims and perpetrators. Among the States party to the American Convention several States have set up these Commissions. The Court has pronounced on them, stating that if they are correctly organized they "can contribute to build and safeguard historical memory, to clarify the events and to determine institutional, social and political responsibilities in certain periods of time of a society."[114] However, the Court finds that "this mechanism should not be understood as a substitute to the obligation of the State to ensure the judicial determination of individual and state responsibilities through the corresponding jurisdictional means, or as a substitute to the determination, by this Court, of any international responsibility".[115]

3.5. THE DUTY TO PUNISH AND MAKE REPARATION

24. Investigation can lead to punishment of the author of an illegal deprivation of life. The subject has been examined in Chapter 1. The obligation to punish is

that "concern those acts in respect of which states have an obligation under the Convention, and in the light of the Court's case law, to enact criminal law provision". See Article II.3. Also relevant is Article V.

111 *Case of Vélez Restrepo v. Colombia*, para. 283.

112 *Ibidem*, para. 284.

113 An interesting source on Truth Commissions is found in Beyond Intractability, a Collaborative Learning Community. See www.beyondintractability.org/.

114 *Case of Zambrano Vélez v. Ecuador*, para. 128.

115 *Ibidem*.

dependent on the type and circumstances of the violation occurred. Violations of the right to life will likely generally carry the State's obligation to punish, but of course only if there is somebody found guilty in a court of law. I will deal with this further in the chapter on due process.

25. Finally, if a violation has taken place, has been investigated, and the conclusion is that it is attributable to the State, it seems indispensable that any guarantee of the right include reparations. The right to life thus requires the State to have mechanisms and measures of reparation available should that right be violated. In the case of Bámaca Velásquez, the Court set forth the reparations without distinguishing the different violations, and in setting its amount took into consideration the need to ensure that the violations that took place do not happen again. The Court ruled that if *restitutio in integrum* is not possible, reparation is made by ordering "indemnification or monetary compensation, to which positive measures on the part of the State must be added to ensure that damaging acts such as the ones in this instant case do not take place again".[116]

The Court has always ordered monetary reparations for the relatives of the deceased victim. Before, the amount was normally set in a procedural stage subsequent to, and separate from, the judgment on the merits. Now, the Court usually fixes reparations together with the preliminary objections and the merits. In addition, in the beginning, the procedure was carried out between the State and the Commission, without including the victim. This led to a dissenting opinion from Judge Piza in Velásquez Rodríguez.[117] A change to the Rules of Procedure, which entered into force on January 1, 1997, allowed for the autonomous participation of the victim, his or her relatives, or his or her representatives in the stage establishing the amount of reparations.[118] Should the parties not be able to reach an agreement, it is for the Court to set the amount,[119] decide who the beneficiaries are, and establish how the compensation is distributed.

Aside from compensation, the Court can establish other possible reparations.[120] In the case of Bámaca Velásquez, it found that the State had the duty to locate the remains of Efraín Bámaca Velásquez and turn them over

116 *Case of Bámaca Velásquez v Guatemala*, judgment on reparations, para. 40.

117 *Case of Velásquez Rodríguez v. Honduras*, dissenting opinion of Judge Piza Escalante.

118 IACtHR, Rules of Procedure, Article 23, approved in its 34th Regular Period of Sessions, held on September 9–20, 1996. The Rules of Procedure of the Court have been amended so that they currently allow the victim and his or her relatives to act autonomously in the process (see Rules of Procedure of the Court, approved during its 85th Regular Period of Sessions held on November 16–28, 2009, Articles 25 and 40(d)).

119 *Case of Velásquez Rodríguez v. Honduras*, para. 191. With the exception of the *case of Neira Alegría*, where the Court ruled that the Commission and the State (operative paragraph 4) must set the indemnity, the trend subsequent to the *case of Caballero Delgado* has been to set it directly.

120 *Case of Trujillo Oroza v. Bolivia*, judgment on reparations, paras. 94–97.

to his relatives "to be buried in accordance with their customs and religious beliefs". The Court also "considers that the State must implement [...] a national exhumations program, as the State itself mentioned in its brief with observations on the reparations", something that the State itself had offered in its response regarding reparations.[121] This latter measure clearly shows an attempt to resolve by means of reparations an aspect of the problems arising from situations of massive and systematic violations.[122] In the case of Juan Humberto Sánchez, the judgment orders the State to carry out "a public act of acknowledgment of its responsibility in connection with the facts in this case and of amends to the victims". Additionally, it must "publish in the official gazette Diario Oficial and in another national-circulation daily, once only, the operative part of this Judgment and the chapter on proven facts in this same Judgment".[123] As mentioned above, the Court also includes the State obligation to carry out a serious investigation into the facts, bring those allegedly responsible to trial and punish those it finds guilty to be a form of reparation.

26. The Court usually orders guarantees of non-repetition, particularly with regard to deprivations of life resulting from the illegal use of force. In a 2013 case, the Court directed the State to adapt its domestic law to the American Convention, incorporating therein the international standards on the use of force by law enforcement agents.[124] The adaptation had to follow "the principles of legality, proportionality, necessity and exceptionality, as well as the criteria for the progressive and differentiated use of force. This legislation must include the specifications indicated in Chapter VII-1 of this Judgment."[125]

27. In sum, we can say that the obligation to ensure the right to life requires the State to carry out a collection of dissuasive actions, preventative actions, oversight of the taking of lives by third parties, and finally, reparation of violations of the right. These actions cannot be described in detail for each case, but they must respond to the central purpose of the obligation to guarantee. First, they should attempt in the best way possible to diminish the possibility of violations of the right to life. When one occurs, States must take the necessary measures to ensure that the infraction does not remain in impunity, and to redress the moral and material damages suffered by the victims.

---

121 *Case of Bámaca Velásquez v. Guatemala*, judgment on reparations, paras. 79–83.

122 I refer here to the enormous injustice that only one case out of many come to the Court and persons suffering from the consequences of similar acts do not receive the justice they deserve.

123 *Case of Juan Humberto Sánchez v. Honduras*, para. 188.

124 *Case of Montero Aranguren et al. (Retén de Catia) v. Venezuela*, para. 144.

125 *Case of Nagdege Dorzema v. Dominican Republic*, para. 275.

4. LIFE, PERSONAL INTEGRITY AND ECONOMIC, SOCIAL AND CULTURAL RIGHTS

28. The extent of the right to life is not exhausted with what we have examined thus far. Like other rights, the right to life has economic, social and cultural aspects that the bodies applying it in specific cases have no reason not to consider. Thus, a measure of prevention that is completely different from the ones examined thus far involves keeping people alive by providing an economic and social situation or special care that enables persons to prevent death by starvation or lack of medical care. It also means being respectful to and caring for cultures existing within the State, which is, according to the Court, intrinsically associated with the right to life. The economic, social and cultural aspects also belong to the right to personal integrity. The Court has developed its case law mainly on the basis of the human rights of children and of indigenous peoples.

4.1. CHILDREN

29. The socio-economic aspect of the rights to life and personal integrity evolved in international organs in the area of children. The Human Rights Committee considered the State obligation in this area in its General Comment No. 6. There it expressed that the right to life cannot be understood in a restrictive manner and that "the protection of this right requires that States adopt positive measures", recommending them to take "all possible measures to reduce infant mortality and to increase life expectancy, especially in adopting measures to eliminate malnutrition and epidemics".[126] This initial approach was reaffirmed and refined over time as the Committee and States gained experience regarding compliance with the obligations under the ICCPR. The Committee uses the right to life together with the prohibition of discrimination to give this right the social and economic content it should always have had.[127]

30. In the Inter-American Court's case law, perhaps the most significant judgment on this point is that of the case of Villagrán Morales *et al.* (the Street Children), in which the Court found that it is inadmissible to have a restrictive approach to the interpretation of the right to life. It considered that it "includes not only the right of every human being not to be deprived of his life arbitrarily,

---

126 HRC, General Comment No. 6, A/37/40 (1982) Annex V (pp. 93–94), para. 5.

127 HRC, *Concluding Observations: United States* (A/50/40 Vol. I (1995) 52, paras. 291 and 302); *Concluding Observations: Guatemala* (A/51/40 Vol. I (1996) 33, paras. 221); *Concluding Observations: Israel* (A/53/40 Vol. I (1998) 45, paras. 308 and 310); *Concluding Observations: Canada* (A/54/40 Vol. I (1999) 48, para. 242).

but also the right that he will not be prevented from having access to the conditions that guarantee a dignified existence".[128]

The concurring opinion of Judges Cançado Trindade and Abreu Burelli in the same ruling goes even further. These judges affirm: "[t]his perspective conceptualizes the right to life as belonging to the domain of civil and political rights while at the same time it belongs to the domain of economic, social and cultural rights, thus illustrating the interrelation and indivisibility of all human rights".[129] On this unprecedented basis, the jurisprudence of the Inter-American Court evolved. Some relevant milestones in this development relate to the interpretation of the rights in the Convention.

31. The right to life in Article 4 and the right to personal integrity in Article 5 have been interpreted widely because of their joint reading with Article 19 of the Convention. The Convention sets forth the right of every minor child to "the measures of protection required by his condition as a minor on the part of his family, society and the state". The American Convention and the Convention on the Rights of the Child form part of a very comprehensive international *corpus juris* for the protection of the child. Therefore, the latter helps the Court "establish the content and scope of the general provision established in Article 19 of the American Convention".[130] The Court addressed the issue of State obligations toward children and children's rights in more depth in an Advisory Opinion where it laid down the foundation for future contentious cases. The Court opined: "children's rights require that the State not only abstain from unduly interfering in the child's private or family relations, but also that, according to the circumstances, it take positive steps to ensure exercise and full enjoyment of those rights. This requires, among others, economic, social and cultural measures."[131]

32. In the case of the Juvenile Re-education Institute (Panchito López),[132] the Court, quoting from this Advisory Opinion, said that Article 19 had to be construed as an additional right for those who, because of their physical and emotional development, require special protection.[133] Consequently, it proceeded to interpret Articles 4 (right to life) and 5 (right to personal integrity) in the light not only of the Convention on the Rights of the Child but also of the International Covenant on Economic, Social and Cultural Rights.[134] The Court

---

[128] *Case of Villagrán Morales (the Street Children) v. Guatemala*, para. 144.

[129] *Ibidem*, paras. 3–6 of the concurring opinion (emphasis added).

[130] *Case of the "Street Children" v. Guatemala*, paras. 191–194.

[131] Advisory Opinion *OC-17/02*, Juridical Condition and Human Rights of the Child, para. 88.

[132] *Case of the "Juvenile Re-education Institute" (Panchito López) v. Paraguay*, paras. 149, 160–162, 172–176, 209–213.

[133] *Ibidem*, para. 147.

[134] International Covenant on Economic, Social and Cultural Rights (1966), 993 UNTS 3.

said that the measures in Article 19 went "well beyond the sphere of strictly civil and political rights" and "encompass economic, social and cultural aspects that pertain first and foremost, to the children's right to life and right to humane treatment".[135] The Court stated, for example, that in interpreting Article 4 in conjunction with these other treaties, it could be concluded that it was a State obligation to provide children deprived of their freedom with special periodic health care and education programs.[136]

The Court joined the protection of children under Article 19 with the rights to life and personal integrity in the Santo Domingo Massacre case, finding that the State had not provided the necessary special protection in a context of a non-international armed conflict.[137]

33. The importance the Court assigns to the protection of children is noticeable in the case of Véliz Franco, a 15-year-old girl whose disappearance had been reported by her mother on the same day that she went missing. It also addresses the situation of violence still existing in several countries of the region. The case was similar to the Cotton Field case:[138] it took place in a context of violence against women and girls. The Court had affirmed that a disappearance of a girl, in a context of widespread violence against women and girls, required immediate action to prevent a violation of the rights to personal integrity and life. This case also reaffirms the importance of the context in which a case occurs. The Court here acknowledges that it is not within its powers to assess the way a State gathers and systematizes information on the situation of girls in the country. However, the State has the duty to have the necessary information to comply with its international obligations in respect of situations such as the one in the case. There were clear indications of the context of violence against women prevailing in the country, of which the State must have been aware, and yet the State had not taken immediate action to look for the victim.[139] Consequently, there was a violation of Articles 4 and 5.[140]

34. The Court issued a new Advisory Opinion on children and immigration, answering the request of several States. They wished the Court to "determine the precise obligations of the States in relation to the possible measures to be adopted regarding children, their immigration status or the status of their parents in light of the interpretation of Articles 1(1), 2, 4(1), 5, 7, 8, 11, 17, 19, 22(7), 22(8), 25 and 29 of the American Convention on Human Rights; Articles 1, 6, 8, 25 and 27 of the American Declaration of the Rights and Duties

135 *Case of Panchito López v. Paraguay*, para. 149.
136 *Ibidem*, para. 172.
137 *Case of the Massacre of Santo Domingo v. Colombia*, para. 241.
138 See Chapter 1, para. 40.
139 *Case of Véliz Franco v. Guatemala*, para. 152.
140 *Ibidem*, paras. 134, 147 and 158.

of Man; and Article 13 of the Inter-American Convention to Prevent and Punish Torture".[141] The Opinion is long and detailed and will be touched upon in other chapters. It links the situation of migrant children to many human rights in the Convention, where the right to life is of course paramount. It repeats and develops the standards set forth in previous jurisprudence but adapts them to the problems of migration.

4.2. INDIGENOUS PEOPLES

35. Latin America has an indigenous population that fluctuates among the countries between a little over 50% of the population (in Bolivia) to a little over 1% (in Argentina). The economic and social situation of these peoples has always been highly problematic. There is frequent discrimination against them; they are mostly poor and their level of health is low; their culture has at best been ignored.[142] Consequently, if one wishes human rights to reach every person without discrimination, the interpretation of the Convention needs to take heed of the diversity of these peoples and the disadvantaged position in which they find themselves. Because of this, the rights of indigenous peoples have also been part of the wide interpretation of Articles 4 and 5. Not only have economic and social conditions been taken into consideration; an important point of the right to life is the culture of these peoples.

36. The case of Yakye Axa was a significant milestone for the importance of the economic, social and cultural rights of indigenous peoples. First, the Court reasserted that the State, as a guarantor of life, must generate "minimum living conditions that are compatible with the dignity of the human person" and not create conditions to hinder or impede the right to life. The measures must be "geared toward fulfilment of the right to a decent life, especially in the case of persons who are vulnerable and at risk, whose care becomes a high priority".[143] Second, the Court linked the rights to life and to personal integrity with the right to health and both with the right to food and access to clean water. Subsequently, the rights were connected with the right to education and culture.[144] Finally, it found that not guaranteeing the right of the members of the community to communal property had a negative effect. It deprived them "of the possibility of access to their traditional means of subsistence, as well as to use and enjoyment

---

141 Advisory Opinion *OC-21/14* of August 19, 2014.

142 See, for example, Centro Latinoamericano y Caribeño de Demografía (CELADE) – División de Población de la Comisión Económica para América Latina y el Caribe (CEPAL). Pobreza infantil en pueblos indígenas y afrodescendientes de América Latina. Available at: www.cepal.cl/cgi-bin/getProd.asp%3Fxml%3D/publicaciones/xml/9/47289/P47289.xml%26xsl%3D/p.

143 *Case of Yakye Axa v. Paraguay*, para. 164.

144 *Ibidem*, para. 167.

of the natural resources necessary to obtain clean water and to practice traditional medicine to prevent and cure illnesses".[145] Consequently, the Court found that Paraguay had violated Article 4 "to the detriment of the members of the Yakye Axa Community, for not taking measures regarding the conditions that affected their possibility of having a decent life".[146]

In the Sawhoyamaxa case, also regarding indigenous peoples, the Court recalled that, "in the light of its obligation to secure the full and free enjoyment of human rights, the States shall adopt all appropriate measures to protect and preserve the right to life (positive obligation)."[147] Therefore, the Court found a violation of Article 4 because the State had failed to carry out the measures "which could reasonably be expected to prevent or avoid risking the right to life of the members of the Sawhoyamaxa Community".[148]

37. Among indigenous peoples, the right to personal integrity of children should in particular be safeguarded, as they are extremely vulnerable. In the case of the Massacres of Rio Negro, the Court held that Article 19 "must be understood as an additional, complementary right that the treaty establishes for individuals who, based on their physical and emotional development, require special protection." The State "must take special measures based on the principle of the best interest of the child",[149] taking into consideration Article 30 of the Convention on the Rights of the Child. The Court also invoked General Comment No. 11 of the Committee on the Rights of the Child which states that "empowerment of indigenous children and the effective exercise of their rights to culture, religion and language provide an essential foundation of a culturally diverse State."[150]

38. The Court's decisions on the right to life of indigenous communities are intrinsically linked with the right to communal property of their land. The first case on an indigenous people handled by the Court was that of Mayagna (Sumo) Awas Tingni Community (Mayagna). The Community complained that in spite of Nicaraguan law granting the property on ancestral land,[151] the national courts had been ineffective in procuring for them the use and enjoyment of their

---

145 *Ibidem*, para. 168.

146 *Ibidem*, para. 176.

147 *Case of the Sawhoyamaxa Indigenous Community v. Paraguay*, para. 152.

148 *Ibidem*, para. 178.

149 *Case of the Rio Negro Massacre v. Guatemala*, para. 143. See also case of the *Santo Domingo Massacre v. Colombia*, para. 241.

150 *Ibidem*, para. 143.

151 The Constitution of Nicaragua "recognizes communal property of indigenous peoples, but has not regulated the specific procedure to materialize that recognition, and therefore no such title deeds have been granted since 1990". See *Case of Mayagna (Sumo) Awas Tingni Community (Mayagna) v. Nicaragua*, para. 152.

property. The main issue for the Court was the interpretation of the right in Article 21. It concluded that:

> Through an evolutionary interpretation of international instruments for the protection of human rights, taking into account applicable norms of interpretation and pursuant to article 29(b) of the Convention – which precludes a restrictive interpretation of rights – it is the opinion of this Court that article 21 of the Convention protects the right to property in a sense which includes, among others, the rights of members of the indigenous communities within the framework of communal property, which is also recognized by the Constitution of Nicaragua.[152]

One reason for the interpretation was the fact that the provision recognizes the right to use and enjoyment of property and not of "private" property. Furthermore, the Court was aware of the meaning of land for indigenous peoples. The Court evoked this in the subsequent paragraph, referring to the indigenous communitarian tradition regarding a communal form of collective property. It stated that ownership of the land is centered on the group and its community and not on an individual. Land was the fundamental basis of their cultures, their spiritual life, their integrity, and their economic survival.[153]

39. In subsequent cases, the Court continued to link the right to property with the right to life of the indigenous communities. The Court always states that "the way of life" of these communities must be respected. In this regard, the Court said in the case of Xákmok:

> Indigenous peoples, as a matter of survival, have the right to live freely on their own territory; the close ties of indigenous people with the land must be recognized and understood as the fundamental basis of their cultures, their spiritual life, their integrity, and their economic survival. For indigenous communities, [their relationship with] the land is not merely a matter of possession and production but a material and spiritual element, which they must fully enjoy to preserve their cultural legacy and transmit it to future generations.[154]

In a 2012 judgment in the case of the Kichwa Indigenous People, the Court examined the right to property of this people. The Court affirmed that lack of access to the territories and their natural resources and to other traditional activities expose them "to poor or inhumane living conditions, to increased vulnerability to diseases and epidemics". All these things harm the preservation of their way of life, customs and language.[155]

---

152 *Case of Mayagna v. Nicaragua*, para. 148.

153 *Ibidem*, para. 149.

154 *Case of Xákmok Kásek Indigenous Community v. Paraguay*, para. 86. See also *Case of Yakye Axa v. Paraguay*, para. 135.

155 *Case of the Kichwa Indigenous People v. Ecuador*, para. 147.

40. No State has rejected the Court's interpretation of Article 21. What has been contended is the categorization of certain people as indigenous. Suriname argued that the voluntary inclusion of some of the members of the Saramaka people in "modern society" had affected their cultural distinctiveness, such that it would be difficult to define them as having a distinct legal personality. That is, the State did not think the Saramaka could be legally defined in a way that takes into account the different degrees to which various self-identified members of the Saramaka people adhere to their tradition, particularly those living in Paramaribo or outside the territory claimed by the Saramaka.[156] In response, the Court found that the Saramaka people "can be defined as a distinct tribal group, whose members enjoy and exercise certain rights, such as the right to property, in a distinctly collective manner." The way they live "does not affect the distinctiveness of this tribal group nor its communal use and enjoyment of their property"; it is for the Saramaka people themselves to decide whether an individual forms part of their people. Furthermore, it referred to a second problem that the Saramaka people had: the lack of recognition of their legal personality, which would allow them to exercise their rights collectively. The Court stressed that "a violation of the right to juridical personality entails an absolute failure to recognize or acknowledge the capability of a person to exercise and enjoy said rights and obligations, which in turn places the person in a vulnerable position in relation to the State or third parties."[157] It added that "the State is bound to guarantee to those persons in situations of vulnerability, exclusion and discrimination, the legal and administrative conditions that may secure for them the exercise of such right, pursuant to the principle of equality under the law".[158]

This would allow them to exercise the attributes of their collective property safeguarded by national law.[159] One can conclude that, concerning indigenous peoples, the Court has read the right to life and the right to personal integrity as containing a right to enjoy their culture. Since land is intrinsically linked to their culture, the lack of enjoyment of their collective land will profoundly affect both the lives and personal integrity of the members of the community. The suffering and the deterioration of their capacity to feed the community, provide assistance to health, and live according to their ancient culture will amount to a violation of the rights to life and to personal integrity.

---

156 *Case of the People of Saramaka v. Suriname*, para. 164.

157 *Ibidem*, para. 166.

158 *Ibidem*, paras. 166–167.

159 This is just a brief glimpse of a difficult subject. For a wider treatment of the Court's jurisprudence with regard to indigenous peoples see T.M. Antkoviak, "Rights, Resources, and Rhetoric: Indigenous peoples and the Inter-American Court" (2014) 35 *U. Pa. J. Int'l L.* 113–87, Seattle University School of Law Legal Paper Series, available at: http://ssrn.com/abstract=2390405; O. Ruiz Chiriboga, "The right to cultural identity of indigenous peoples and national minorities: a look from the inter-American system" (2006) *Sur: International Journal on Human Rights*, issue 5, 2006, available at: www.surjournal.org.

4.3. HEALTH, LIFE AND PERSONAL INTEGRITY

41. The Court under the provisions of Articles 4 and 5 has also addressed the right to health of persons other than those who are members of an indigenous community. As stated in this book[160] the States have a duty to care for the life and personal integrity of inmates; this is a consistent position of the Court. In the case of Vera Vera, for example, the Court stated: "the rights to life and personal integrity are directly and closely linked with human health care".[161] In the case of Ximenes Lopes, an individual who died while interned in a medical center for a mental illness, the Court set forth that since health is a matter of public interest, States must regulate and supervise all activities related to health care "regardless of the public or private nature of the entity giving such health care".[162] States may delegate the rendering of health assistance but the State will "continue being responsible for providing such public services and for protecting the public interest concerned."[163] Additionally States must "guarantee the provision of effective health care services to all persons with mental illness".[164] In the case of Laura Albán, a young woman who died in a private hospital due to medical negligence, the Court establishes explicitly that "the rights to life and humane treatment are directly and immediately linked to human health care". The Court recalls its former case law on the State's responsibility for its failure to take measures to prevent conduct of third parties from impairing human rights.[165] This leads the Court to decide that the State incurs international responsibility when it does not supervise the rendering of health services.[166]

The case of Suárez Peralta is similar to that of Ximenes Lopes as it finds a violation of Articles 4 and 5 by the State due to lack of control over health care establishments. The Court sets out some indications as to how to create this control by pointing out "that the State's supervision and inspection should be designed to ensure the principles of availability, accessibility, acceptability, and quality of the medical services."[167] Ecuador, however, did have regulations in this regard and the problem here was the lack of implementation of these rules.[168] The Court does not refer to Article 26 in this judgment, but "recalls the interdependence and indivisibility of civil and political rights, and economic, social and cultural rights, because they must be understood integrally as human rights without any specific ranking between them, and as rights that can be

---

160 See Chapter 5.

161 *Case of Vera Vera v. Ecuador*, para. 43.

162 *Case of Ximenes Lopes v. Brazil*, para. 89.

163 *Ibidem*, para. 96.

164 *Ibidem*, para. 128.

165 *Case of Albán Cornejo v. Ecuador*, para. 117.

166 *Ibidem*, para. 119.

167 The directives are taken from United Nations, Economic and Social Council, Committee on Economic, Social and Cultural Rights, General Comment No. 14, para. 12.

168 *Case of Suárez Peralta v. Ecuador*, paras. 138, 141, 144 and 154.

required in all cases before those authorities with the relevant competence".[169] In addition, it recalls that using international instruments and sources other than the American Convention is common practice in the Court, and thus it is possible to use the Protocol of San Salvador "to give content and scope to the [...] rights derived from Article 26."[170]

Judge Ferrer MacGregor expressed a different opinion in a 37-page concurring vote suggesting that "the implications in the case for the right to health could have been examined autonomously".[171] He states that the intention of this separate opinion is to encourage further thought on the necessary development that should take place in inter-American case law toward the full normative effectiveness of Article 26 of the Pact of San José.[172] He bases his position mainly on the former judgments of the Court examined above,[173] stating that the reading of Article 26 as providing the basis for the justiciability of the right to health and other social rights requires, on the one hand, further scrutiny of the interpretation of this provision and the inter-American normative system in general,[174] and on the other hand, "a progressive vision and interpretation, in keeping with the times, which requires considering the progress made in comparative law".[175] He also advocates the use of the Protocol of San Salvador as well as other sources to expand the scope of the rights of individuals and the State obligations in the Convention.[176] In his vote, Judge Ferrer MacGregor examines the justiciability of economic, social and cultural rights, including the right to health; the way to interpret Article 26 of the American Convention for the direct justiciability of economic, social and cultural rights; and the *iura novit curia* principle in relation to the direct justiciability of the right to health in this case. Many of his arguments come from the Court's jurisprudence, *inter alia* the idea of using a *corpus juris* approach to interpret Article 26. I find this vote in a way similar to the one of former Judge Macaulay in the case of Furlán, but with more detailed reasons.[177]

The vote of Judge Pérez Pérez in the same case of Suárez Peralta argues in the opposite direction. He agrees with the Court's decision, but wishes to make clear "that the references to the right to health contained in the judgment do not mean that the Court is assuming competence with regard to this right

169 *Ibidem*, para. 131.

170 *Ibidem*, para. 56.

171 For a different view, see O. Ruiz Chiriboga, "The American Convention and the Protocol of San Salvador: Two intertwined treaties. Non-enforceability of Economic, Social and Cultural Rights in the Inter-American System" (2013) 31(2) *Netherlands Quarterly of Human Rights* 156–183.

172 *Case of Suárez Peralta v. Ecuador*, concurring vote of Judge Ferrer MacGregor, para. 10.

173 *Ibidem*, concurring vote, para. 6.

174 *Ibidem*, concurring vote, para. 7.

175 *Ibidem*, concurring vote, para. 8.

176 *Ibidem*, concurring vote, para. 10.

177 See Chapter 1.

in particular, or to the economic, social and cultural rights in general. The contentious competence of the Court is established in Article 62 of the American Convention, and in paragraph 6 of Article 19 of the Protocol of San Salvador, without prejudice to the pertinent provisions in other inter-American human rights conventions."[178] I believe that the Court has advanced more than what Judge Pérez Pérez maintains in his vote.

By now, the introduction of the economic, social and cultural aspects of the rights to life and to personal integrity is well established in the Court's jurisprudence in issues on health. This may allow other rights, be they civil and political or economic, social and cultural, to slowly come together as they were in the fundamental instrument of human rights, the Universal Declaration of Human Rights of 1948. One could hardly disagree with this union.

5. PROTECTION OF LIFE FROM THE MOMENT OF CONCEPTION

42. In contrast to the ICCPR[179] and the European Convention on Human Rights,[180] the American Convention introduces in Article 4(1) the obligation to protect the right to life, in general, as of the moment of conception. This seems to have been an unsuccessful attempt by the drafters to introduce what can be described as a religious stand[181] in a Convention that was destined to operate for many States which had long since separated themselves from the Catholic Church. In this matter, the drafters abandoned the neutral position they held regarding all other guaranteed rights. However, the text is here and it requires interpretation, as it is necessary to establish, on the one hand, the contents of the obligation arising from Article 4(1), and on the other, who is entitled to demand its application from the State. The effects of this interpretation are not trivial, as this article has an inextricable link with the issue of the criminalization of abortion.[182] The high rate of maternal mortality resulting from back-alley

---

178 *Ibidem*, concurring opinion of Judge Pérez Pérez, para. 1.

179 ICCPR Article 6.

180 ECHR Article 2. The ECHR was adopted on November 4, 1950 and entered into force internationally on September 3, 1953.

181 I say "religious" because the Catholic faith permeates the legal systems of all our countries. A small evidence of this are the speeches given by the President of Costa Rica and the Minister of Foreign Affairs of that country during the Inaugural Session of the Specialized Conference of San José. See Inter-American Specialized Conference on Human Rights, *supra* n. 26, pp. 407–417, and the very explicit dissenting opinion of one Commissioner in the IACHR's views in the Baby Boy case.

182 On the mistake of recurring to a religious faith as a base for the prohibition of abortion, see David Boonin, *A Defense of Abortion*, Cambridge University Press, Cambridge, 2003, pp. 27 and following.

abortions in Latin America and throughout the world[183] is a cause for great concern, as are the varied and difficult consequences a woman faces for various reasons when carrying an unwanted pregnancy to term – leaving aside for the moment the often brutal consequences for children brought into life in these circumstances.[184] Because of this, international supervisory bodies whose area of supervision includes the rights of women have advocated at least for the elimination of the total criminalization of abortion.[185] The Human Rights Committee has repeatedly indicated that both when a pregnancy puts the life of the mother in danger and when pregnancy is the result of rape, total criminalization of abortion is a violation of Articles 6 and 7 of the ICCPR. The Human Rights Committee states that this would be a failure to protect the mother's life or to abide by the absolute ban on torture and cruel, inhuman or degrading treatment.[186]

43. The reality on the American continent has not prevented Spanish- and Portuguese-speaking States Parties to the Convention from deciding to criminalize abortion altogether[187] or to decriminalize only certain types. Normally these States accept only those abortions performed to protect the life of the mother or to end a pregnancy resulting from rape, leaving aside other causes or considerations which might be similar in relation to the burden on the mother, such as being very young or living in poor economic conditions. Where abortions under certain conditions are allowed, they are in practice very difficult to obtain: States often permit hospitals, for example, including public ones, to create innumerable obstacles that women have to deal with and that are sometimes unsurmountable, thus generally creating a clear risk to the life

---

183 See R. Cook, "Human Rights Dynamic of Abortion Law Reform" (2003) 25(1) *Human Rights Quarterly* 1–59, with abundant information based principally on the research of the World Health Organization.

184 It seems that children have rights before they are born but not after: the fate of the sixth child to a poor woman whose partner is a drunkard and violent is a terrible fate. This example is certainly not far-fetched on the American continent. On this, see for example a 2011 study of the Economic Commission for Latin America and the Caribbean (ECLAC) and the United Nations Children's Fund (UNICEF) titled *Child Poverty in Latin America and the Caribbean.*

185 Committee on the Elimination of Discrimination against Women (CEDAW), General Recommendation No. 24: Woman and Health (1999), para. 31(c), and HRC, General Comment No. 28, Article 3: The equality of rights between men and women (2000), paras. 10 and 11. Also see *Bringing Rights to Bear: An analysis of the Work of UN Treaty Monitoring Bodies on Reproductive and Sexual Rights,* Center for Reproductive Law and Policy and University of Toronto International Programme on Reproductive and Sexual Health Law, 2002, Chapter III E.

186 HRC, *Concluding Observations: Ecuador,* August 18, 1998, para. 11; *Concluding Observations: Chile,* March 30, 1999. *Llantoy v. Peru,* Communication No. 1153/2003 (2005), paras. 6.3 and 6.6; *Concluding Observations: Peru,* November 15, 2000, para. 20.

187 Chile, El Salvador and Honduras are in this situation.

and personal integrity of women.[188] An important factor in the imposition of these rules and practices is the fact that the Convention covers a continent where the Catholic Church holds great power, power which it has used to advance the struggle against abortion and, often, against all forms of family planning – a subject that is a priority in its activities domestically and internationally. This notwithstanding, what is important to remember is that the Convention rules over a population with differing views and so the Convention has to transcend these views to achieve a result that is faithful to the object and purpose of the treaty and does not destroy the rights of some in order to follow a certain ideology or religious creed.

44. These circumstances make the issue of abortion a particularly difficult one; for some, it is not simply a problem of law and human rights. Rather, what is at issue is a subject in which the position taken on it represents religious ideas that some groups attempt to impose as legal rules. These ideas go to extremes, for example, preventing a 9-year-old girl who was raped from obtaining an abortion or girls with a disease requiring treatment that might result in the interruption of a pregnancy.[189] At the end of 2012, legislation was passed in Uruguay to legalize abortion in the first trimester of pregnancy. Even though steps have been taken in that direction, as shown by the judgments of the Supreme Courts of Mexico,[190] Colombia,[191] Brazil[192] and Argentina,[193] judges continue to operate as usual, considering every form of abortion a crime. A judge in Chubut, for example, in Argentine Patagonia, refused to accept the termination

---

188 For more information, see Center of Reproductive Rights, www.reproductiverights.org.

189 A 16-year-old girl died in August 2012 in the Dominican Republic due to the unjustified delay to treat her acute leukemia diagnosed when she was seven months pregnant. She died in agony because the hospital refused to give her treatment arguing any treatment would affect the embryo's development (www.womenslinkworldwide.org/wlw/new.php). In El Salvador a young woman could not obtain an interruption of her pregnancy of an anencephalic fetus, although she had a severe case of lupus and a lupus derived nephritis, due to the opposition of part of the country's population and of the Catholic Church.

190 In April 2007, Mexico City's Congress amended the Criminal Code to legalize abortion on the first trimester on a pregnancy. In August 2008, Mexico's Supreme Court upheld Mexico City's law legalizing abortion in the first trimester, striking down a challenge that the abortion law violated constitutional and international principles on the right to life.

191 Colombia, Constitutional Tribunal, Decision C-355/06. The Constitutional Court of Colombia struck down the State's total abortion ban as "a blatantly disproportionate measure" that not only violates international human rights treaties, but also the State's Constitution.

192 In 2012 the Federal Supreme Tribunal of Brazil issued a judgment in which the majority of its members declared the unconstitutionality of a legal interpretation of some Penal Code provisions that would criminalize abortions in cases of fetal anencephaly. Federal Supreme Tribunal of Brazil, Arguição de Descumprimento de Preceito Fundamental (ADPF 54), April 12, 2012.

193 Argentina, Judgment of the Supreme Court, CSJA-ANP-13 March 2012.

of the pregnancy of a 12-year-old girl who had been raped in the mountains.[194] Other States have become still stricter with women: El Salvador's Constitution was amended to prevent any possibility of abortion by recognizing human beings as legal persons from the moment of conception, thus as human beings bearing all human rights.[195] In 2006, Nicaragua's Congress passed a complete ban on abortion. The ban offers no exceptions for women's health, for victims of rape or incest – or even for women whose lives are at risk. Later on, in July 2008, it incorporated the law into the Penal Code itself.[196] In 2012, Honduras criminalized the use of the morning-after pill.[197] Whether or not to criminalize abortion is currently a burning issue. What is surprising is that a majority of the people do not share the position that abortion should be criminalized, even many who are Catholics.[198] The position is that of the rulers in Latin America who have a conservative perspective on women's place in society and their role in the family, firmly supported and perhaps instigated by the Catholic Church.[199]

45. In 2012, the Inter-American Court passed its first judgment on Article 4 in the case of Artavia *et al.* v. Costa Rica. This was not a case on the problem of abortion, but on the prohibition in Costa Rica on performing in vitro fertilization. Ms. Artavia and others complained before the Court against this prohibition.[200] The Supreme Court of Costa Rica had argued that in this fertilization procedure embryos are discarded and this, according to the State, would be a violation of the obligation of the State to protect life, in general from the moment of conception. The Inter-American Court found in favor of the complainant in an extensive judgment where it explored and used all the elements of interpretation.

---

194 Diario La Jornada, September 10, 2012, reporting the news about a procedure to which the judge was being submitted before the Council of the Judiciary.

195 Constitution of El Salvador, Decree 38, Article 1. This article was expressly amended in 1999 to avoid the possibility of abortion.

196 See Law 603 of October 2006. The law repealed a provision in the then in force Criminal Code on therapeutic abortion. In 2007, the same provision was eliminated in the new Criminal Code.

197 See Center for Reproductive Rights in www.reproductiverights.org for this and other information. For a journalist's view see Tim Padget, "Uruguay Diverges from a Continent Where Abortion Is Worse than Rape", October 19, 2012, available at: http://world.time.com/2012/10/19/uruguay-diverges-from-a-continent-where-abortion-is-a-crime-worse-than-rape/#ixzz2IGRdJ0wJ.

198 See http://catolicasporelderechoadecidir.net/cdd_derecho.php; a non-governmental organization with members of most Latin American States plus Spain. The last editorial of the Latin American net, in 2013, contains a letter to Pope Francisco requesting him to defend the primacy of conscience and to acknowledge women's capacity and autonomy to take moral decisions over their bodies, sexuality and reproduction.

199 See Encyclical Letter Evangelium Vitae, John Paul II, March 25, 1995; Encyclical Letter Redemptoris Mater, John Paul II, March 25, 1987; Apostolic Letter Mulieris Dignitatem, John Paul II, August 15, 1988.

200 *Case of Artavia Murillo et al. v. Costa Rica.*

The first step was to interpret the terms "conception" and "human being" according to the ordinary meaning of the words. For this, the Court heard several experts, based on which it took two decisions. One was that it concurred with domestic and international courts that there is no one agreed definition of the beginning of life. Nevertheless, it was "clear to the Court that some opinions view a fertilized egg as a complete human life". The second is that the Court considered that the term "conception" cannot be understood as a moment or process that excludes the woman's body,[201] given that an embryo has no chance of survival if implantation does not occur. Proof of this is that it is only possible to establish whether pregnancy has occurred once the fertilized egg has been implanted in the uterus. In addition, when Article 4 of the American Convention was drafted, the dictionary of the *Real Academia Española* differentiated between the moment of fertilization and the moment of conception, understanding conception as implantation.[202] The American Convention does not mention fertilization as equal to conception. Many embryos are spontaneously lost between fertilization and implantation and it is only at the latter moment that a pregnancy can be detected, so the Court understands the term "conception" as the moment at which the egg is implanted in the woman's womb.[203] Secondly, the words "in general" allow deviation from the rule, but do not give guidance on specifying which deviations are acceptable.[204] As a result, it concludes that Article 4 cannot be applied before implantation happens, thus it is inapplicable to the instant case, which deals with a stage prior to conception.

46. This notwithstanding, since Article 4 was invoked by the State, which held the Convention to contain an obligation to States to ensure an absolute protection of the "right to life of the embryo", the Court thought it pertinent to interpret the idea *in toto*. Next, the Court proceeded to a literal interpretation on the expression "in general", stating that "[t]he literal interpretation indicates that the expression relates to anticipating possible exceptions to a particular rule. The other methods of interpretation would suggest the meaning of a provision that contemplates exceptions".[205] Subsequently it applied a systematic and historical interpretation, explaining that norms should be interpreted as part of a whole, the meaning and scope of which must be defined based on the legal system to which they belong. Thus, the Court considered that "the interpretation of a treaty should take into account not only the agreements and instruments formally related to it (Article 31(2) of the Vienna Convention), but also the system of

201 *Ibidem*, para. 187. I have not used the English translation here. The Spanish text speaks of "exclusion" and not "exclusive".

202 *Ibidem*, para. 181.

203 *Ibidem*, paras. 186–187.

204 *Ibidem*, para. 189.

205 *Ibidem*, para. 188.

which it is part",[206] in other words, international human rights law. Most of the analysis, however, is historical.

The Court found that an interpretation of the *travaux préparatoires* in the inter-American system cast no useful light for interpretation. This was in contrast to what the Inter-American Commission said in the case of Baby Boy where it attached much importance to the *travaux préparatoires*.[207] In the case of Artavia *et al.*, the Court found that the embryo could not be considered "a person"[208] in the Convention, so protection to it should be given through the mother.[209] A similar method of interpretation was applied to the various treaties and international supervisory organs within the United Nations and Europe including the views and decisions of those organs, and the same conclusion was reached.[210] Among others, the Court quoted a judgment of the European Court of Human Rights, which held that "[a] prohibition of abortion to protect unborn life is not therefore automatically justified under the Convention on the basis of unqualified deference to the protection of pre-natal life or on the basis that the expectant mother's right to respect for her private life is of a lesser stature".[211]

47. Since in vitro fertilization was a procedure unknown when the Convention was drafted, the Court considered that it was indispensable to have recourse to a progressive interpretation and to comparative law.[212] In doing so, the Court started from the premise that the Convention is a live instrument, as had been held in many of its judgments and in decisions of other international organs. First, the Court examined the legal status of the embryo. Mainly based on European case law, the Court observed that the regulatory trends in international law do not lead to the conclusion that the embryo should be treated in the same way as a person, or that it has a right to life.[213]

The Court also examined the practice of States with regard to in vitro fertilization, finding that nowhere had it been considered that Article 4 could be understood to prohibit any technique of assisted reproduction. Additionally, it

---

206 The Right to Information on Consular Assistance in the Framework of the Guarantees of the Due Process of Law, Advisory Opinion *OC-16/99* of October 1, 1999, Series A No. 16, para. 113; and *Case of the "Street Children" (Villagrán Morales et al.) v. Guatemala*, reparations and costs.

207 See IACHR, *Case of Baby Boy v. the United States*, IACHR Annual Report 1980–1981, Resolution 23/81, Case 2142 of March 6, 1981. Of course, there were other reasons in the case to find against the complainant, as the United States was not a party to the Convention.

208 *Case of Artavia Murillo et al. v. Costa Rica*, para. 223.

209 *Ibidem*, paras. 223–224.

210 *Ibidem*, para. 244.

211 *Ibidem*, para. 239, quoting from ECtHR, *Case A, B, and C v. Ireland*, Application No. 25579/05, judgment of December 16, 2010, para. 238.

212 *Ibidem*, para. 246.

213 *Ibidem*, para. 253.

found that this generalized practice[214] is associated with the principle of gradual and incremental – rather than absolute – protection of prenatal life and with the conclusion that the embryo cannot be understood as a person.[215]

The mention of the existence of a "principle of gradual and incremental – rather than absolute – protection of prenatal life" allows the reader to understand that the interpretation does not recognize the fetus to have a "right to life". The final reflections on the principle of the most favorable interpretation, and the object and purpose of the treaty, reinforce this interpretation. The Court first categorically found that the right to life is not an absolute right "the alleged protection of which can justify the total negation of other rights."[216] Then it referred to some examples from Europe and the United States where "a legitimate interest in protecting prenatal life is recognized, but where this interest is differentiated from entitlement of the right to life".[217] The Court concluded that "the object and purpose of the expression 'in general' in Article 4(1) of the Convention is to allow, as appropriate, an adequate balance between competing rights and interests".[218] The rights will be those of the mother and the eventual interests those of the State, as set forth in Article 4(1). As a final example of this, I recall that in 2013 the Court was asked for a provisional measure to protect the life and integrity of a 22-year-old Salvadorian woman who was pregnant with an anencephalic fetus. She had been unable to terminate her pregnancy, even though she had a severe case of lupus and lupus-derived nephritis, due to the opposition of part of the country's population and of the Catholic Church. In El Salvador, abortion is forbidden. Finally a provisional measure ordered by the Inter-American Court of Human Rights on May 29, 2013, supporting the Salvadorian doctors' decision to intervene, resulted in an operation on a fetus who died after five hours because of its condition.[219]

48. It is well known that an intense debate is ongoing on the meaning of the phrase "in general from the moment of conception". Academics and activists have discussed what the drafters of the Convention intended to express by adding the phrase that is – as said above – not found in any other human rights treaty. It was clear that the reason behind adding "from the moment of conception" was to prohibit all types of abortion, as it is clear that the reason to add the words "in general" was to allow legalization of abortion as the Inter-

214 Article 31(3)(b) of the Vienna Convention establishes that: "[t]here shall be taken into account, together with the context: any subsequent practice in the application of the treaty which establishes the agreement of the parties regarding its interpretation."

215 *Case of Artavia Murillo et al. v. Costa Rica*, para. 256.

216 *Ibidem*, para. 258.

217 *Ibidem*, para. 260.

218 *Ibidem*, para. 263.

219 *Matter of B. regarding El Salvador*, Order of the Inter-American Court of Human Rights of May 29, 2013.

American Commission held in the case of Baby Boy v. the United States.[220] The end of the debate leaves, as the Court says, vagueness, not unusual in the way treaties are written, expecting and hoping that the interpreters will unveil the real meaning taking into account the moment at which they are doing the interpretation.

It is clear that, as the Court says, the interpretation of Article 4 may not exclude women's rights. No interpretation could imply a complete distortion of the system and the negation of the rights of women, as the task of the interpreter is to harmonize the different human rights set forth in the treaty together with the eventual interests that the State must protect. In examining this provision, I will start with two basic ideas. The first is that the mother is a person, a human being, both in the legal systems of States Parties to the Convention and under the Convention itself. She is therefore the holder of all the human rights set forth in the Convention. The second is that a fetus is dependent on the mother while it is in the womb; it is not a person or a human being in the sense of the Convention and therefore cannot have rights. The fact that the mother is a person in both the legal systems of States Parties to the Convention and under the Convention itself, and that she is therefore the holder of all the human rights in the Convention, need be neither demonstrated nor reasoned out. In addition, it is clear that human rights constitute a limit on State action, meaning that any State action taken with regard to a woman's body has necessarily to consider her rights. The fact that a fetus is not entitled to any right under the Convention, even the right to life, would need some reasoning.

49. If one looks at the formulation of all the human rights in the Convention one observes that none, except the right in Article 4(1), incorporate in their formulation the need to respect and protect the right; this is not necessary since all the rights of the Convention must be respected and ensured according to Article 1. On the contrary, Article 4(1) sets forth that "[e]very person has the right to have his life respected. This right shall be protected by law and, in general, from the moment of conception". There may be several reasons that might explain this accent on the protection of law, which is prescribed only for this right. One could be that the Convention saw the right to life as the basic one and the one with most value and therefore did not wish to leave its protection to the general formulation of Article 1, in the sense that all rights had to be respected

220 See the *travaux préparatoires* of the Specialized Conference of San José, *supra* n. 26. See the thorough analysis made by the Inter-American Commission in the *Case of Baby Boy*, IACHR Annual Report 1980–1981, Resolution 23/81, case 2142 of March 6, 1981 (OEA/Ser.L/V/II.54, Doc. 9 rev. 1, October 16, 1981, pp. 187–209). On the religious grounds of one of the two dissenters in *Baby Boy*, see Monroy Cabras's dissenting vote: "The maternal womb in which the flame of life is lighted is sacred and may not be profaned to extinguish what God has created in his image and in his likeness".

and ensured. Since the right was so geared toward regulating the death penalty, it was obvious that laws must be passed to regulate its protection. Another reason, linked to this and for me a very important one, is that in the time of the adoption of human rights treaties, there was almost a dogma that civil and political rights only created passive obligations for the State, contrary to economic, social and cultural rights, which required State actions. From another angle, it is agreed that the right to life's obligation to protect addresses only the legislative power and so the discussion should be centered on the question of how the legislature must comply with this duty to protect. Based on this formulation, the Human Rights Committee for example "has extended the scope of protection to include other threats to human life" and states that "the protection of this right requires that States adopt positive measures".[221] Looked at in this way, the mention of Article 4 of the obligation to the legislature to protect the right seems adequate. There could perhaps be other reasons.

What is not acceptable is the notion that the words under consideration add the fetus as a holder of a human right in a part where the Convention is in fact regulating what the domestic law must do to protect the right to life by law. I think it is clear that if the Convention had truly wished to give the fetus the status of a human being, being a holder of the right to life, it would have written this idea at the beginning of the article, immediately after the words "every human being", because this is where the entitlement to the right is given. Because it did not consider the fetus a human being, and wished to protect it, the Convention added the sentence "in general, from the moment of conception" in its current place.

In short, the American Convention sets forth a different rule for the fetus: it is not a bearer of the right but must be protected by law.[222] The reason for this protection has to do, *inter alia*, with the respect that a legal system owes to a woman embarking on the important task – both for her and for society – of bringing a child into the world. Therefore, the direct subject of the protection is the pregnant mother. The protection of the fetus is carried out indirectly through her, as established in the provisions of Article 15(3)(a) of the Protocol of San Salvador. That provision requires States Parties to "provide special care and assistance to mothers during a reasonable period before and after childbirth". The same sense can be found in Article VII of the American Declaration, which establishes the right of a pregnant woman to protection, care, and special aid. The Convention imposes on the State not only an obligation to allow the woman to carry out unhindered the task of procreating; it must also help the pregnancy to reach full term in different ways. The protection might consist of any measure

---

221 M. Nowak, *U.N. Covenant on Civil and Political Rights, CCPR Commentary*, N.P. Engel Publisher, Kehl/Strasbourg/Arlington, 1993, pp. 105–107.

222 On this issue, read V. Undurraga, *Aborto y protección del que está por nacer en la Constitución Chilena*, Legal Publishing, Thomson Reuters, Santiago, Chile, 2013.

required by the mother to reach this objective: medical assistance, the provision of basic foodstuffs necessary during the pregnancy, or other measures of this nature.[223] These measures give content to the obligation found in Article 4(1) of the American Convention. When the Convention in Article 4(5) prohibits the application of the death penalty to pregnant women, it is not protecting the fetus (this can be a consequential protection) but the mother's endeavor to have a child, a task that, as noted above, is important not only to her but to society.

Only the mother may demand the obligation to protect. Third parties cannot invoke it should the mother wish to terminate her pregnancy. This is because State action in these cases affects the rights of the woman.[224] The failure to protect women's human rights in this regard brings about, aside from the probable violation of rights, particularly serious consequences for the future. Bringing a child into the world constitutes a commitment that includes obligations the woman can never excuse herself from, except were she to renounce her motherhood completely. The State cannot impose this obligation on any human being and, certainly, it is not the Convention that imposes it; the Convention only imposes the obligation to protect on the law of the State. Also with the purpose of protecting the mother, and taking into consideration the fact that the circumstances in which a pregnancy is terminated can present a high degree of risk to the life of the mother, the State must regulate those circumstances in order to protect her health.

50. The situation is different when the fetus ceases to be completely dependent on the pregnant woman and one could assume with a degree of certainty that it would survive upon removal from her womb. Given that when separated from the woman the fetus legally becomes a human being to whom the right to life established in Article 4(1) of the Convention applies, the State has an interest and a reason to intervene. Here it seems appropriate to refer to the solution provided by the Supreme Court of the United States. Should a pregnancy be terminated at a stage at which the fetus has no chance of surviving outside the mother's body (theory of viability), the act of abortion wished for by the mother would be permissible, as the mother would have freedom to decide what happens to

---

223 This is the sense in which Article 15(3)(a) of the Protocol of San Salvador, among others, should be interpreted.

224 The rights that can be affected by decisions made by the State regarding a woman's pregnancy come from various sources. The rights to a woman's life and personal integrity come from the Convention itself and from Articles 6 and 7 of the ICCPR. Subsumed within them is the right to health, which is also set forth in Article 10 of the Protocol of San Salvador and Article 12 of the International Covenant on Economic, Social and Cultural Rights. The right of a woman to decide the number of children she wants, on the basis of equality with the man, is derived from Article 10(h) and Article 12(1) of the Convention on the Elimination of All Forms of Discrimination Against Women. The right to privacy, which allows for decisions to be made freely as regarding one's own person, is established in Article 11(2) of the American Convention and Article 17 of the ICCPR.

her body.[225] Any other action would be arbitrary and thus incompatible with Article 4(1).

Without prejudice to this, there are circumstances that make it necessary to allow the termination of a pregnancy of a viable fetus if it will injure the pregnant woman by remaining in her womb. This case presents a situation in which the goal is to protect the life or health of the woman, not necessarily to eliminate the fetus. Cases like this can result in a conflict between the woman's rights and the public interest, a conflict that must be resolved through the application of the general rules of international human rights law. The conflict normally arises from the risk to the life or health of the woman by the permanence of a potentially viable fetus in her uterus. I have no doubt that given a choice between the right to life or health of the mother and the potential risk to the continuity of the pregnancy, the decision should be to terminate the pregnancy. The State cannot cease to protect the right to life of someone who is at the time of the conflict a person in order to diminish the risk to a fetus, which is not a person, and therefore a human being, in the legal sense. Of course, this formulation requires the woman to have had unrestrained access in all senses to plan her future family, including legal and safe abortion within the time allowed in order to bring about a timely resolution to a risky or unwanted pregnancy. If this is the case, it is reasonable to limit the legality of late-term abortion to this case, which is justified on the grounds of their supervening nature.

51. In sum, arguing that the American Convention requires the State to criminalize abortion altogether is erroneous. In my opinion, supported by arguments based on the interpretation of both its text and drafting history, the Convention does not establish this obligation. There is no basis to argue that a prohibition on abortion must be applied in all cases. On the contrary, in certain cases – such as a pregnancy that puts the life or health of the mother in danger or that was the result of rape, for example – the criminalization of abortion constitutes a gross violation of the State's obligation to protect the life of the mother and her physical, mental and moral integrity. In all other cases, the criminalization of abortion would be a violation of the rights referred to above[226] – unless, of course, the fetus is viable, as in that situation the State has an interest to intervene. In addition, as the State must protect the life of the mother to the same extent as it protects the lives of others – without discrimination – it must provide her with access to health services such that any termination of a pregnancy that falls within the guidelines that have been set forth can be performed without putting her life in danger.

225 Supreme Court of the United States, *Case of Roe v. Wade*, 410 U.S. 113 (1973). See, with regard to the position of the European system, European Commission of Human Rights, *Bruggemann and Scheuten v. Federal Republic of Germany*, No. 6959/75.

226 See *supra* n. 224.

52. This section has taken up the controversial issue of abortion and the – until now – less controversial issue of in vitro fertilization,[227] according to the present state of the knowledge on this matter. It will fall to others subsequently to move forward in the interpretation of the provision or to modify it properly in order to adjust it to the changes that have already begun to take place in the field of human reproduction. I have no doubt that very soon scientific and technological progress will present new challenges for how human life can come to be or to end, and the law, as often happens, will fall behind.

227 From the "expert" testimonies in the case, it transpires that Costa Rica is the only country in the world that prohibits this form of assisted reproduction.

CHAPTER 4
RIGHT TO HUMANE TREATMENT

Article 5. Right to Humane Treatment

1. *Every person has the right to have his physical, mental, and moral integrity respected.*
2. *No one shall be subjected to torture or to cruel, inhuman, or degrading punishment or treatment. All persons deprived of their liberty shall be treated with respect for the inherent dignity of the human person.*
3. *Punishment shall not be extended to any person other than the criminal.*
4. *Accused persons shall, save in exceptional circumstances, be segregated from convicted persons, and shall be subject to separate treatment appropriate to their status as unconvicted persons.*
5. *Minors while subject to criminal proceedings shall be separated from adults and brought before specialized tribunals, as speedily as possible, so that they may be treated in accordance with their status as minors.*
6. *Punishments consisting of deprivation of liberty shall have as an essential aim the reform and social readaptation of the prisoners.*

1. INTRODUCTION

1. One important reason for the consecration of the right to personal integrity at an international level is the reaction of the international community to the existence of torture, the atrocious treatment to which individuals have been subjected to confess their alleged crimes, part of the history of the world for centuries. The legal international reaction to torture in the last century started with the Universal Declaration of Human Rights and continued with numerous instruments intended specifically to prohibit it. These instruments regulated not only torture but also cruel, inhuman or degrading treatment. In 1975, the Declaration on the Protection of All Persons from Being Subjected to Torture and Other Cruel, Inhuman or Degrading Treatment or Punishment was adopted in the United Nations.[1] The

---

1 Declaration on the Protection of All Persons from Being Subjected to Torture and Other Cruel, Inhuman or Degrading Treatment or Punishment, approved by the General Assembly of the United Nations on December 9, 1975 (Resolution 3452 (XXX)).

United Nations also subsequently adopted the Convention against Torture and Other Cruel, Inhuman, or Degrading Punishment.[2] Inhuman treatment is one of the acts that constitute the crime of apartheid.[3] In the framework of the OAS, the Inter-American Convention to Prevent and Punish Torture (the Inter-American Torture Convention) was adopted.[4] In 1987, Europe approved a European Convention for the Prevention of Torture and Inhuman or Degrading Treatment or Punishment.[5] Torture constitutes a severe violation of the Geneva Conventions of 1949, which establish the requirement of humane treatment of all along with the prohibition of torture and similar acts.[6] Other international instruments regulate different aspects of this phenomenon.[7] Although the instruments speak of torture as a different phenomenon from other ill-treatment, most of its rules also apply to cruel, inhuman and degrading treatment or punishment.

It is not only the number of international instruments specifically regulating this phenomenon that illustrates its gravity.[8] The gravity of the situation is also reflected by the fact that, first, perpetrators will incur criminal responsibility

---

2 Convention against Torture and Other Cruel, Inhuman, or Degrading Punishment (CAT), approved on December 10, 1994 (Resolution 39/46) UN Doc. A/39/51 (1984). The Convention entered into force on June 26, 1987.

3 Convention on the Suppression and Punishment of the Crime of Apartheid, approved on November 30, 1973, Article 2; entered into force on July 18, 1970.

4 Inter-American Convention to prevent and Punish Torture, approved on December 9, 1985. The Convention entered into force on February 28, 1987.

5 European Convention for the Prevention of Torture and Inhuman or Degrading Treatment or Punishment, approved in the framework of the Council of Europe on November 26, 1987. The Convention entered into force on February 1, 1989.

6 Also see Additional Protocol to the Geneva Conventions dated August 12, 1949, relating to the Protection of Victims of Non-International Armed Conflicts, approved on June 8, 1977. The Protocol entered into force on December 7, 1978.

7 Other instruments referencing torture include: Standard Minimum Rules for the Treatment of Prisoners, adopted by the First United Nations Congress on the Prevention of Crime and the Treatment of Offenders, held at Geneva in 1955, and approved by the Economic and Social Council by its Resolutions 663 C (XXIV) of July 31, 1957 and 2076 (LXII) of May 13, 1977; Body of Principles for the Protection of All Persons under Any Form of Detention or Imprisonment, adopted by the General Assembly in its Resolution 43/173, of December 9, 1988; Principles of Medical Ethics relevant to the Role of Health Personnel, particularly Physicians, in the Protection of Prisoners and Detainees against Torture and Other Cruel, Inhuman or Degrading Treatment or Punishment, adopted by the General Assembly in its Resolution 37/194 of December 18, 1982; Declaration on the Protection of All Persons from Being Subjected to Torture and Other Cruel, Inhuman or Degrading Treatment or Punishment, adopted by the General Assembly in its Resolution 3452 (XXX), of December 9, 1975; Basic Principles on the Use of Force and Firearms by Law Enforcement Officials, adopted by the Eighth United Nations Congress on the Prevention of Crime and the Treatment of Offenders, held in Havana (Cuba) from August 27–September 7, 1990.

8 The word "conduct" denotes an action or omission attributable to an individual. In this regard, see M. Novak, *U.N. Covenant on Civil and Political Rights. CCPR Commentary*, N.P. Engel Publisher, Kehl/Śtrasbourg/Arlington, 1993, p. 128.

for the conduct.[9] Furthermore, there is universal jurisdiction to judge it.[10] In principle, it is not subject to the application of a statute of limitations.[11] Finally, the prohibition of torture constitutes a *jus cogens* norm[12] – that is, a peremptory norm of international law from which a State cannot exempt itself by, for example, making a reservation upon committing itself to a human rights treaty.[13] In addition, in contrast to other rights, this right not to be tortured is absolute – that is, it cannot be restricted or suspended under any circumstances.[14] Unlike with other rights, there are no grounds that would allow a State to restrict this right.[15] Finally, the Convention does not allow this prohibition to be suspended during emergency situations. The Inter-American Court has reiterated, for example, that circumstances in which a State is faced with terrorism must not lead to restrictions on the protection of the physical integrity of persons.[16]

2. Article 5 of the American Convention deviates from the rule that the right to personal integrity amounts only to the prohibition on certain specific conducts, as is the case in Article 7 of the International Covenant on Civil and Political Rights (ICCPR)[17] and Article 3 of the European Convention.[18]

---

9 See, among others, Article 6 of the Charter of the Nuremberg Tribunal; Article 50 of Convention I; Article 51 of Convention II; Article 13 of Convention III; Article 147 of Convention IV; Article 75 of Protocol I; Article 4 of Protocol II; Article 3 part 1(a) of the four Geneva Conventions and Article 7(1)(f) of the Statute of the International Criminal Court.

10 Article 5.1 CAT; Principles of international co-operation in the detection, arrest, extradition and punishment of persons guilty of war crimes and crimes against humanity (Resolution 3074 (XXVIII) of the General Assembly, dated December 3, 1973); United States Court of Appeal for the Second Circuit: *Case of Filartiga v. Peña-Irala*, 630 F 2d 876 (2nd Cir. 1980).

11 Convention on the Non-Applicability of Statutory Limitations to War Crimes and Crimes Against Humanity. Adopted and opened for signing, ratification and adherence by the General Assembly in its Resolution 2391 (XXIII); entered into force on November 11, 1970.

12 ICJ, *Case of East Timor (Portugal v. Australia)*, Reports 1995, p. 90, at p. 102, para. 29; ILC, Report of the International Law Commission on the work of its fifty-third session, United Nations, Geneva, 2001, pp. 208 and 284 (commentaries on Articles 26 and 40); C. Villán Durán, "La Convención contra la Tortura y su contribución a la definición del derecho a la integridad física y moral en el derecho internacional" (1985) 37(2) *Revista Española de Derecho Internacional* 381–384. Also see *Case of Maritza Urrutia v. Guatemala*, para. 92.

13 E. Schwelb, "Some aspects of international jus cogens as formulated by the International Law Commission" (1967) 61 *American Journal of International Law* 946–975; A. Cebada Romero, "Los conceptos de obligaciones *erga omnes, ius cogens* y violación grave, a la luz del nuevo proyecto de la CDI sobre responsabilidad de los Estados por hechos ilícitos" (2002) *Revista Electrónica de Estudios Internacionales* 2–10, available at: www.reei.org/reei4/reei.4.htm.

14 Regarding torture, see *Case of Maritza Urrutia v. Guatemala*, para. 89.

15 I refer to grounds such as public order, public health or other similar ones.

16 *Case of Cantoral Benavides v. Peru*, para. 96, reiterating what had already been found in the *case of Castillo Petruzzi et al. v. Peru*, para. 197 and *case of Loayza Tamayo v. Peru*, para. 57.

17 International Covenant on Civil and Political Rights, Article 7 states: "No one shall be subjected to torture or to cruel, inhuman or degrading treatment or punishment. In particular, no one shall be subjected without his free consent to medical or scientific experimentation."

18 Convention for the Protection of Human Rights and Fundamental Freedoms, Article 3: Prohibition of torture: "No one shall be subjected to torture or to inhuman or degrading treatment or punishment".

Article 5 of the Convention establishes in its first clause the right of all people to have their physical, mental and moral integrity respected, while its second clause establishes a prohibition on the specific conduct mentioned. Article 5 also includes several provisions on conditions that persons deprived of liberty must enjoy and sets forth the purposes that sentences of deprivation of liberty must serve. All this shall be examined in this chapter.

The enshrining of a *right* to personal integrity (or humane treatment as labelled in the Convention) reveals two aspects of this provision. The first alludes to the status of every individual as a being who deserves respect, with no one allowed in principle to interfere with that individual or that individual's personal decisions. This suggests that the individual is personally autonomous and therefore has the authority to make decisions in that regard. Approaching the right in this way, Article 5 is closely related to the right to private life in Article 11, which is no surprise given that the rights established in the Convention seek jointly to protect the dignity of persons from many different angles.[19] The second generates an obligation for the State to respect and ensure the right to personal integrity of each person as it has to do with regard to any other right. It is not necessary for the Court to assess the seriousness of an action against personal integrity; it is enough that personal integrity has been affected and the State cannot provide a reasonable explanation for its conduct. This being so, analysis of the right should deviate from the usual approach in two ways. One is the connection between Article 5 and Article 11, with which I will deal later. The other is the consequence of Article 5 in the way the State treats individuals or protects them from the treatment of third parties, in compliance with its obligation to ensure.

3. The existence of the Inter-American Torture Convention[20] and the Inter-American Convention on the Prevention, Punishment and Eradication of Violence against Women (the Belém do Pará Convention),[21] and the fact that Article 5 of the Convention contains such broad provisions, complicate the approach to the article. From a variety of different options, I have selected the following structure for this chapter. First, I will examine the contents of the right in Article 5(1) of the Convention. The second issue to be handled will be the prohibited conduct in Article 5(2), which will first be analyzed in general and then in particular in the Court's case law. Subsequently, I will deal with how

19 For a similar position, see *Case of Martín de Mejía v. Peru*, No. 10.970, Report 5/96, of March 1, 1996, published in Annual Report of the Inter-American Commission on Human Rights 1995, pp. 168–214 (200–201).

20 Inter-American Convention to Prevent and Punish Torture, adopted on December 9, 1985 and in force since February 28, 1987.

21 Inter-American Convention on the Prevention, Punishment and Eradication of Violence against Women "Convention of Belém do Pará", adopted in Belém do Pará, Brazil, on June 9, 1994, at the twenty-fourth Regular Session of the General Assembly); entered into force on March 5, 1995.

States must treat people deprived of liberty. Although the required State conduct is set forth in Article 5(2), this section does not deal precisely with the prohibited conduct found in paragraph 2. The conduct of States regarding women deserves a separated examination in the light of both the American Convention and the Belém do Pará Convention. Briefly, since much on this matter has already been said in Chapter 3, the obligations to investigate, prosecute, punish and to make reparations once a violation has occurred will be examined here. Paragraphs 4, 5 and 6 of Article 5 of the Convention will be examined finally and separately, as they are in some ways outside the core of the article in question.

2. ARTICLE 5(1) OF THE AMERICAN CONVENTION

4. Article 5(1) of the American Convention establishes a *right* to personal integrity, so far unknown in universal and European human rights treaties,[22] a right of each person to have its physical, mental and moral integrity respected. This right is not absolute and allows for restrictions by the State. At the beginning of this chapter I stated that Article 5(1) has a facet, closely related to the personal autonomy that every individual possesses. The Court has used Article 5(1) in that sense relating it closely with Article 11 on privacy. In Artavia Murillo, a case dealing with Costa Rica's prohibition to allow in vitro fertilization in the country, the Court considered that the case was a particular combination of various aspects of private life. It related to the right to form a family, the right to physical and mental integrity, that is, Article 5, and specifically with an individual's reproductive rights.[23] Although the Court did not find a violation of Article 5, it held that "there is a connection between personal autonomy, reproductive freedom and personal and psychological integrity".[24] In the case of Manuel Cepeda, the Constitutional Court of Colombia declared that "accusing an individual or a group of individuals of killing and injuring civilians, without providing evidence to justify such serious statements, goes beyond the limits of freedom of expression".[25] On this basis, the Inter-American Court found that Manuel Cepeda's next of kin had been exposed to a situation of stigmatization for a long period. This had led to the State incurring international responsibility for the violation of Articles 5(1) and 11.[26] In the case of the Massacres of Río

22 The African Charter on Human and Peoples' Rights has an Article 4 that sets forth: "Human beings are inviolable. Every human being shall be entitled to respect for his life and the integrity of his person…"

23 *Artavia Murillo et al. v. Costa Rica*, para. 144. The section under which this was expressed intended to analyze the right to private and family life with the right to personal integrity in relation to personal autonomy, sexual and reproductive health and others.

24 *Ibidem*, para. 147.

25 *Case of Manuel Cepeda v. Colombia*, para. 209.

26 *Ibidem*, para. 210.

Negro, the Court linked personal integrity and the right to privacy of Article 11 stating that, because of the consequences of the rape suffered by one of the victims, the State had violated the rights of Articles 5(1), 11(1) and 11(2) of the American Convention.[27] One may expect that perhaps new cases will reach the Court that will permit it to elaborate on this further.

5. In its other facet, Article 5(1) is an improvement on the protection of human beings. If all individuals have the right for the State or private parties not to interfere with them or their decisions that affect only themselves, any interference that is not reasonably justified[28] would constitute a violation of that provision. There would be no need to examine whether or not the State's conduct falls under the classification of prohibited conduct of Article 5(2). It would only be necessary to examine the State's conduct in regard to its suitability and proportionality and confirm the absence of an alternative for achieving its aim deciding if the conduct of the State is or is not *necessary in a democratic society*. As noted, this is the test which all interferences on human rights have to go through to determine whether they are justified or constitute a violation, a test to which prohibited conduct, as set forth in the European Convention, the International Covenant on Civil and Political Rights and Article 5(2) of the American Convention, may not be subjected. The Inter-American Court interprets Article 5 in this manner when it finds that "any use of force that is not strictly necessary to ensure proper behavior on the part of the detainee constitutes an assault on the dignity of the person [...] in violation of Article 5 of the American Convention."[29] As can be noted, the Court does not indicate here any requirement for a purpose or a specific level of severity. Thus, it belies the idea that if the conduct of a State or private parties enjoying the State's acquiescence or tolerance does not include the elements of purpose, severity or others required to categorize a conduct as prohibited, the conduct will be legitimate. One could only conclude that while the conduct is not prohibited under Article 5(2) of the Convention absent these requirements, it may constitute still a violation of Article 5(1) of the Convention.

In the case of the Pacheco Tineo family, detained and transported to the border between Bolivia and Peru, the Court did not find that they had suffered cruel, inhuman or degrading treatment. This notwithstanding, their documents had been retained and Ms. Tineo had been illegally detained, causing "anxiety, frustration and anguish" to the family. Furthermore, they had suffered a proceeding for expulsion without any respect for due process, when it was known to the Bolivian authorities that Chile had given them refuge and had provided them assistance to come back to Chile. All this constituted a violation

27 *Case of the Massacres of Rio Negro v. Guatemala*, paras. 132–135.
28 See Chapter 1 on restrictions.
29 *Case of Loayza Tamayo v. Peru*, para. 57.

of the mental and moral integrity of the victims.[30] On the contrary, in the case of Norín *et al.*, the Court found that, although hunger strikes provoke serious emotional and physical consequences and affect personal integrity, these facts cannot be imputed to the State and thus there was no violation of Article 5(1).[31]

3. DIFFERENT KINDS OF PROHIBITED CONDUCT IN HUMAN RIGHTS TREATIES

6. The American Convention does not define the different types of conduct prohibited by its Article 5(2), nor are these terms defined in Article 7 of the ICCPR or in Article 3 of the European Convention. The treaties do not give any elements for guiding an interpreter toward determining when we are in the presence of such conduct, except for the obvious fact that conduct constituting a violation is that which endangers the physical, mental or moral integrity of a person. Rather, it leaves it up to the interpreter to determine whether the specific facts in a complaint amount to a violation of this provision. The supervisory body applying the treaty must decide which elements in a case allow it to determine whether a particular instance of conduct is among those expressly prohibited by the three provisions just mentioned. Since the supervisory bodies do not judge individual conducts, there is, in principle, no need to distinguish if the conduct that violates the prohibition is labelled torture, cruel, inhuman or degrading treatment. Whatever the prohibited conduct committed, there is a State violation of the corresponding provision and there is no need to make a distinction. The distinction will have to be made when the supervisory body is applying a treaty in which the prohibited conduct is already defined – as with torture – and where there are provisions making reference solely to that conduct.

7. It is often said that a distinction between different types of conduct must be made in order particularly to highlight torture, as the term torture has a greater stigma associated with it that must be expressed. This probably has to do with the fact that the history of the prohibition of torture is related to its use by State agents as a means of obtaining information.[32] It was, as a consequence, a response to the intentional actions of State agents toward a subject who is necessarily under their power and who is made to suffer severely. Torture viewed in this way becomes more serious because the State uses its power against a defenseless subject, and naturally the approach that it deserves should be in accordance with these circumstances. Aside from the stigma of being considered

30 *Case of Pacheco Tineo family v. the Plurinational State of Bolivia*, paras. 206–208.

31 *Case of Norín et al. v. Chile*, paras. 393–394.

32 N. Rodley, *The treatment of prisoners under international law*, 2nd edition, Oxford University Press, Oxford, 2002, pp. 7–11.

a torturer, the distinction can serve for the purposes of determining reparations for the victim, although it is possible to make this determination according to the specific circumstances of each case without need for giving a specific name to the conduct.

It is no wonder then that of all the conduct prohibited by international law, torture is the one that has been defined by international instruments. Universally, this is done by both the Declaration on the Protection of All Persons from Being Subjected to Torture and Other Cruel, Inhuman or Degrading Treatment or Punishment and the Convention against Torture and Other Cruel, Inhuman, or Degrading Punishment. Both definitions, which are relatively similar, take into consideration the following: (i) the agent, a public official, who causes or instigates it (according to the Declaration), or a public official or other person in the exercise of public authority who, in addition to causing it or instigating it, tolerates it or is aware of it (in the Convention); (ii) intent; (iii) the conduct's effects on the victim: severe pain or suffering, physical or mental (in the Declaration), or serious pain or suffering, physical or mental (in the Convention); and (iv) the purpose of the conduct: obtaining information or a confession from the victim or a third party, punishment or intimidation (in the Declaration) or, in addition to these purposes, coercion or discrimination (in the Convention).[33]

The Committee against Torture (CAT), a body established by the United Nations Convention, has not particularly analyzed the elements of torture in applying the Convention to a specific case. However, it has stated that "the definitional threshold between ill-treatment [an expression that encompasses cruel, inhuman or degrading treatment] and torture is often not clear" which leads it to consider that prohibition of ill-treatment is, like torture, non-derogable.[34] This shows that torture has a highly symbolic significance but it does not have much importance in legal terms.

8. The ICCPR does not define torture or other prohibited conduct. The Human Rights Committee of the United Nations, which supervises the application of this international instrument, has generally tried not to distinguish among the conduct prohibited by its Article 7, perhaps to emphasize that all such conduct is prohibited. In its General Comment No. 20, which replaces General Comment No. 7, it indicates that:

> The Covenant does not contain any definition of the concepts covered by article 7, nor does the Committee consider it necessary to draw up a list of prohibited acts or to establish sharp distinctions between the different kinds of punishment or treatment; the distinctions depend on the nature, purpose and severity of the treatment applied.[35]

---

33 For detailed analysis of these elements, see N. Rodley, *supra* n. 32, pp. 75–106.

34 CAT, General Comment No. 2: Implementation of Article 2 by States Parties, thirty-ninth session (2007).

35 HRC, General Comment No. 20, Article 7 (A/47/40 (1992), Annex VI (pp. 193–195), para. 4).

Accordingly, when the Committee finds that there has been a violation of Article 7 of the ICCPR, it rules as much, without specifying whether the facts constitute torture or another form of prohibited conduct.[36]

9. In contrast, in the European system, which also does not provide normative definitions, the distinction has generally been made in order to develop the concept of torture as an aggravated form of inhuman treatment, with this latter expression often appearing as a generic concept. The defunct European Commission of Human Rights conceptualized each conduct, finding that:

> The notion of inhuman treatment covers at least such treatment as deliberately causes severe suffering, mental or physical, which, in the particular situation, is unjustifiable. The word "torture" is often used to describe inhuman treatment, which has a purpose, such as the obtaining of information or confessions, or the infliction of punishment, and it is generally an aggravated form of inhuman treatment. Treatment or punishment of an individual may be said to be degrading if it grossly humiliates him before others or drives him to act against his will or conscience.[37]

Thus, the Commission addresses the severity of the treatment and the purpose it pursues to distinguish between torture and inhuman treatment.[38] As far as degrading treatment, it is defined by the humiliation it causes to the one receiving it.[39] Nothing in the European Commission's opinion indicates the parameters to be used for measuring when suffering is severe or humiliation is serious.

The European Court found in the judgment handed down in the case of Ireland v. United Kingdom that degrading treatment is treatment capable of "arous[ing] in [the] victims feelings of fear, anguish and inferiority capable of humiliating and debasing them and possibly breaking their physical or moral resistance."[40] This opinion has been confirmed in recent rulings.[41] The explanation seems to place emphasis on the victim's reaction to the treatment

---

36 HRC, *Boodlal Sooklal v. Trinidad and Tobago*, Communication 928/2000, ruling of October 25, 2001, A/57/40, Vol. II (2002), Annex IX, sect. EE (pp. 264–269), para. 4.6; *Michael Freemantle v. Jamaica*, Communication 625/1995, ruling of March 24, 2000, A/55/40, Vol. II (2000), Annex IX, sec. A., (p. 11–21), para. 7.2.

37 European Commission of Human Rights, *Greek Case*, Yearbook XII (1969), p. 186.

38 The European Convention does not make any mention of cruel treatment, but its case law is considered to include it under the term inhuman (D.J. Harris, M. O'Boyle and C. Warbrick, *Law of the European Convention on Human Rights*, Butterworths, London/Dublin/Edinburgh, 1995, p. 58).

39 This concept of degrading treatment was also used by the European Court in the case of *Tyrer v. UK*, Application No. 5856/72, judgment of April 25, 1978, para. 30.

40 European Court of Human Rights, *Ireland v. United Kingdom*, judgment of January 18, 1978, A 25, pp. 167, cited by J. Barquin Sanz, *Los delitos de tortura y tratos inhumanos o degradantes*, EDERSA, Madrid, 1992, p. 89.

41 See, for example, European Court of Human Rights, *Jalloh v. Germany*, Application No. 54810/00, judgment of July 11, 2006 and European Court of Human Rights, *Stanev v. Bulgaria*, Application No. 36760/06, judgment of January 17, 2012, para. 203.

in question, but does not make any reference to the fact that a prevailing social standard in the international community might be taken into consideration when determining whether conduct is prohibited and which could be used as a threshold not to be crossed. If these two elements are to be used, both the reaction of the victim and the social standard must be considered with extreme caution. If not, it could lead to reasoning – in my opinion unacceptable – like that of the European Commission in the Greek Case, where it found that:

> A certain roughness of treatment by both the police and military authorities is tolerated by most detainees and can even be taken for granted. Such roughness may take the form of slaps or blows of the hand on head or face. This underlines the fact that the point up to which prisoners and the public may accept physical violence as being neither cruel nor excessive, varies between different societies and even between different sections of them.[42]

A look at the case law of the European Court shows that it is difficult to find the criteria taken into consideration in deciding whether a conduct is sufficiently severe and cruel to constitute torture. Nor is it simple to differentiate by examining the purpose sought by the act, as according to the ruling of the European Court in the case of Ireland v. United Kingdom, inhuman or degrading treatment can have the same intent as torture. In this case, for example, the European Court found that the five techniques used in Northern Ireland – consisting of keeping individuals on tiptoe for long hours, covering heads with hoods, subjecting detainees to intense and constant noise, and depriving them of sufficient sleep, food and drink – "do not reach the level of torture but rather inhuman treatment, as the term torture attach a special stigma denoting "deliberate inhuman treatment causing very serious and cruel suffering".[43] In the case of Aksoy v. Turkey, the European Court ruled that conduct consisting of undressing an individual and hanging him by the arms, which were tied behind his body, constituted torture. The reason was that it had to have been inflicted deliberately and apparently with the purpose of getting the subject to admit a fact or give information and had caused temporary paralysis in both arms. The cruel and severe nature of the action could only be classified as torture.[44]

10. Up to this point, we have looked only at *treatment* that can be considered torture or cruel, inhuman or degrading. However, *punishments* with these characteristics are prohibited as well. Normally, the punishments most apt

42 *Greek Case*, ruling of November 5, 1969, Yearbook XII, 1969.

43 The fact that the European Commission of Human Rights, in the proceeding prior to the Court's hearing of the case, had classified these techniques as "torture" reflects the difficulty and subjectivity of the distinction (report of January 25, 1976, B.23-I, 1980), p. 411, cited in P. van Dijk *et al.* (eds.), *Theory and Practice of the European Convention on Human Rights*, 4th edition, Intersentia, Antwerp/Oxford, 2006, pp. 406.

44 European Court of Human Rights, *Ireland v. United Kingdom*, judgment of January 18, 1978, A 25, pp. 66–67, and *Akzoy v. Turkey*, judgment of December 18, 1996, Reports 1996-VI, Vol. 26, para. 64, both cited in *ibidem*, pp. 406–407.

to being considered as belonging to one of these categories are corporal in nature. In contrast to treatment, punishments are institutionalized, accepted by legislation, ordered by a court and applied by an agent of the State. The European Court indicated as much in the case of Tyrer in ruling that:

> The very nature of judicial corporal punishment is that it involves one human being inflicting physical violence on another human being. Furthermore, it is institutionalised violence that is in the present case violence permitted by the law, ordered by the judicial authorities of the State and carried out by the police authorities of the State. Thus, although the applicant did not suffer any severe or long-lasting physical effects, his punishment – whereby he was treated as an object in the power of the authorities – constituted an assault on precisely that which it is one of the main purposes of Article 3 (art. 3) to protect, namely a person's dignity and physical integrity.[45]

This leads Barquin to deduce from the judgment of the European Court that all institutionalized violence is by nature intrinsically degrading.[46] However, the European Court has not gone so far as to find that all corporal punishment is *per se* degrading. Rather, it indicates that it depends on the degree of humiliation or debasement caused, given that all punishments can have this effect. The European Court finds that this interpretation is, "in the nature of things, relative: it depends on all the circumstances of the case and, in particular, on the nature and context of the punishment itself and the manner and method of its execution." An attack on decency or shame can be a factor that aggravates the punishment and makes it degrading.[47] Without ruling on what kind of conduct is prohibited, the Human Rights Committee has taken the same position, finding that whippings violate Article 7 of the ICCPR.[48] The Inter-American Court, based on all these precedents, decided in the case of Caesar that the very nature of corporal punishment "reflects an institutionalization of violence" and makes it a punishment incompatible with the Convention.[49]

11. From this, it could be concluded that, while there have been attempts to distinguish between the different prohibited conduct, the distinctions have not been consistent. In addition, it should be recalled that with regard to personal integrity, as well as with regard to other rights, what is monitored internationally is State compliance with all obligations found in the respective provision of

---

45 European Court of Human Rights, *Tyrer v. United Kingdom*, *supra* n. 39, para. 33.

46 Cited in J. Barquin Sanz, *supra* n. 40, p. 92.

47 *Tyrer v. United Kingdom*, *supra* n. 39, para. 30. It should be noted that the punishment in the Tyrer case, consisted of being struck on the naked buttocks with a rod.

48 HRC, *Boodlal v. Trinidad and Tobago*, Communication 928/2000, ruling of November 8, 2000, A/57/40, Vol. II (2002), Annex IX, sec. EE (pp. 264–269), para. 4.6; *Osbourne v. Jamaica*, Communication 759/1997, ruling of March 13, 1999, A/55/40, Vol. II (2000), Annex IX, sec. L (pp. 133–139), para. 9.1.

49 *Case of Caesar v. Trinidad and Tobago*, para. 73.

the various conventions. Since the responsibility is the State's, as a logical consequence and as has already been stated, the distinction between one conduct and another is not, in principle, relevant for establishing a violation and can only be significant in weighing reparations or for the reputation of the State against which the supervisory body is ruling.

The attempts to differentiate between types of prohibited conduct have failed not only to do so, but also to assist efficiently in deciding when conduct meets the minimum standards for inclusion in the expression "torture or other cruel, inhuman or degrading treatment or punishment", which is what will make the conduct become a violation. Nevertheless, if only certain conduct is prohibited, this determination is crucial, as it is possible to conceive of treatments that affect personal integrity without violating the prohibition. To start with, we can admit that if legitimate self-defense is allowed as a justification for the taking of a life, a similar approach could be used to justify acts affecting personal integrity.[50] If punishments that include deprivation of liberty are allowed – which can very likely cause mental and moral suffering, as well as physical suffering at times – the circumstances that transform a deprivation of liberty into a violation of personal integrity must be defined.

12. If we allow ourselves to be guided by the aforementioned definitions and by case law, we note that torture and inhuman treatment require willful action that results in a degree of suffering that must be very severe for the former and severe for the latter. In the case of degrading treatment, the action must result in severe humiliation or must lead the victim to act against his or her will or conscience, in the opinion of the European Commission. Although the European Commission does not mention intent, it must be concluded that degrading treatment also requires intent to cause that particular effect.

Drawing the dividing line based on the harmlessness or severity of the conduct is not easy. The European Court in the case of Ireland v. the United Kingdom found that the treatment of a person must reach a minimum level of severity in order to be classified as prohibited conduct.[51] In one case, the European Court issued more explicit criteria on this point. It found that Article 3 required for "ill-treatment" a minimum level of severity and actual bodily injury or intense physical or mental suffering. In addition, degrading treatment shows a lack of respect for, or a diminishing of, his or her human dignity, "or arouses feelings of fear, anguish or inferiority capable of breaking an individual's moral and physical resistance".[52] The European Court established in the case

---

50 In this sense, see the separate opinion of Judge Fawcett in *Ireland v. United Kingdom*, B 23-I, p. 502, Com. Rep. (1976), cited by D.J. Harris *et al.*, *supra* n. 38, p. 56.

51 European Court of Human Rights, *Ireland v. United Kingdom*, A 25 (1978), cited in D.J. Harris *et al.*, *supra* n. 38, p. 61.

52 See European Court of Human Rights, *Pretty v. United Kingdom*, Application No. 2346/02, judgment of April 29, 2002, para. 52.

of Stanev v. Bulgaria that the assessment of the minimum is relative. It will depend "on all the circumstances of the case, such as the nature and context of the treatment, the manner and method of its execution, its duration, its physical or mental effects and, in some instances, the sex, age and state of health of the victim". It gives some examples of inhuman treatment, such as treatment that was premeditated and applied "for hours at a stretch and caused either actual bodily injury or intense physical or mental suffering".[53]

I believe that the various examples are very dissimilar in nature and do not differentiate torture from degrading treatment. I wonder how treatment that arouses feelings of fear, anguish or inferiority capable of breaking an individual's moral and physical resistance could be just "degrading treatment".

This element of the severity or intensity of suffering must be weighed with particular care, and it is possible this will continue to be done on a case-by-case basis, making it impossible to draw from it standards that can be transformed into an abstract norm; in any case, this point will surely continue to evolve over the coming years. This may be what the European Court is referring to when it admits a gradation in severity between torture and other kinds of treatment in ruling

> that certain acts which were classified in the past as "inhuman and degrading treatment" as opposed to "torture" could be classified differently in the future. It takes the view that the increasingly high standard being required in the area of the protection of human rights and fundamental liberties correspondingly and inevitably requires greater firmness in assessing breaches of the fundamental values of democratic societies.[54]

While these two criteria might help, robust case law is needed to be able to draw elements from it and establish the dividing line more precisely.

4. PROHIBITED CONDUCTS IN THE AMERICAN CONVENTION (ARTICLE 5(2))

4.1. LEGAL FRAMEWORK

13. The main task of the Inter-American Court is the application of the American Convention on Human Rights. Article 5(2) thereof sets forth that "[n]o one shall be subjected to torture or to cruel, inhuman, or degrading punishment or treatment". Like other Conventions, it does not give definitions of this prohibited conduct nor does it establish any specific obligations, so leaving the States with the general obligations of Article 1 which directs them to respect

53 European Court of Human Rights, *Stanev v. Bulgaria*, Application No. 36760/06, judgment of January 17, 2012, paras. 202–203.

54 European Court of Human Rights, *Selmouni v. France*, judgment of July 28, 1999, para. 95, cited in the *case of Cantoral Benavides v. Peru*, para. 99.

and ensure the right of individuals not to be subjected to any of these prohibited acts. The American Convention, however, is not the only inter-American treaty establishing a prohibition on torture and cruel, inhuman or degrading treatment or punishment. As mentioned previously, subsequent to the American Convention on Human Rights, in 1985 the Inter-American Convention to Prevent and Punish Torture was adopted. As there are two treaties addressing the same subject and it is difficult to imagine that they are not related to each other and cannot reciprocally influence each other, I will examine first the Inter-American Torture Convention itself and the relationship that could exist between this treaty and the American Convention. An important reason for this examination is that, despite the fact that the Torture Convention does not contain a clear and explicit provision granting jurisdiction to the Inter-American Court to hear cases in which a violation has been alleged, the Court has asserted jurisdiction and applied this treaty in some of the cases brought before it. An analysis of this application can help the reader answer a number of questions that arise regarding the relationship between the Inter-American Torture Convention and the American Convention: (i) Does the Court have jurisdiction to apply the Torture Convention in the cases before it? (ii) Does the application of this treaty depend on whether the State being accused is also a party to this treaty? (iii) May the Court use the Torture Convention as an element for interpreting State obligations under Article 5(2) of the American Convention even when the State against which the case has been brought is not part of that Convention? The questions refer both to the definition and the obligations contained therein.

14. To start with, it should be noted that the Torture Convention does not replace Article 5 of the American Convention but rather complements it. Article 16 of the Torture Convention establishes that "[t]his Convention shall not limit the provisions of the American Convention on Human Rights, other conventions on the subject, or the Statutes of the Inter-American Commission on Human Rights, with respect to the crime of torture." In addition, its Preamble establishes a link with the American Convention by indicating that States that adopt the Convention are "[a]ware of the provision of the American Convention on Human Rights that no one shall be subjected to torture or to cruel, inhuman, or degrading punishment or treatment." This link also extends to the OAS Charter, the United Nations Charter, the American Declaration of the Rights and Duties of Man and the Universal Declaration of Human Rights. The States also indicate that "in order for the pertinent rules contained in the aforementioned global and regional instruments to take effect, it is necessary to draft an Inter-American Convention that prevents and punishes torture." It thus appears evident that the intent of the States that approved the Torture Convention was to use this new treaty to make the provisions on torture established in the American Convention – among other instruments – more effective.

15. Article 2 of the Torture Convention offers the following definition:

> For the purposes of this Convention, torture shall be understood to be any act intentionally performed whereby physical or mental pain or suffering is inflicted on a person for purposes of criminal investigation, as a means of intimidation, as personal punishment, as a preventive measure, as a penalty, or for any other purpose. Torture shall also be understood to be the use of methods upon a person intended to obliterate the personality of the victim or to diminish his physical or mental capacities, even if they do not cause physical pain or mental anguish.

The definition's failure to identify the perpetrator of the conduct is remedied in Article 3 of the Convention, which states:

> The following shall be held guilty of the crime of torture:
> 1. A public servant or employee who acting in that capacity orders, instigates or induces the use of torture, or who directly commits it or who, being able to prevent it, fails to do so.
> 2. A person who at the instigation of a public servant or employee mentioned in subparagraph (a) orders, instigates or induces the use of torture, directly commits it or is an accomplice thereto.

The definition differs somewhat from the universal system definitions already mentioned. One difference is that it identifies as perpetrators both public officials and private parties who commit, instigate or induce torture, but requires the necessity of a link, a tenuous one, between the private party and the public official. In addition, this Convention qualifies certain acts as torture without requiring as an essential element that they have a specific purpose, given that its Article 2 uses the all-inclusive wording "any other purpose". This seems sensible as, in the end, the purpose of torture is to subject a person to the will of the torturer. What the torturer might do with that person once the person's will is broken can be more varied than one might think and is surely irrelevant for deciding whether the conduct is reproachable and should be prohibited by international law. Finally, it establishes that the act must cause physical or mental suffering to the victim, but does not specify any degree of severity. In addition, it states the possibility that if the purpose of the torture is to "obliterate the personality of the victim or to diminish his physical or mental capacities", the suffering of physical pain or mental anguish is not required as part of the definition. This gives the definition of torture considerable breadth that frees it from the restrictions imposed by the classic concept of torture,[55] but makes it

[55] This idea coincides with the concerns expressed by a judge of the European Court in the case of *Ireland v. United Kingdom* in the sense that on requiring the existence of suffering in the victim, and a significant level of suffering, the European Court could be excluding new forms of suffering from the definition of torture that have little to do with the physical suffering of

useless as a tool to distinguish torture from other ill-treatment that can be cruel or inhuman, since the degree of severity and the precise purpose are lacking.

16. The State obligations to prevent and punish torture are set forth in Article 1 of the Torture Convention and developed in several provisions.[56] Torture must become a criminal offense in the national legal order and States must take other measures with regard to other prohibited conduct (Article 6). Police officers and others responsible for the custody of persons deprived of liberty must receive training in order to ensure proper treatment (Article 7). State authorities must, either at the petition of a party or *ex officio*, carry out an investigation and launch the corresponding criminal proceeding where appropriate (Article 8) and domestic regulations on reparations must be in place (Article 9). Extradition of an alleged or demonstrated torturer must be granted (Article 11), or, failing that, the State must investigate the conduct of the alleged torturer and, where appropriate, launch the corresponding criminal proceeding (Article 14). Finally, States must establish their jurisdiction over the crime in accordance with specific rules (Article 12).

Once domestic remedies have been exhausted, the Torture Convention also authorizes a case of torture to be brought before "the international fora whose competence has been recognized by that State" (Article 8(3)). In addition, it establishes explicitly that nothing in the Convention[57] can be interpreted in a way that limits the right to asylum or modifies the obligations of States parties with regard to extradition (Article 15). Furthermore, the Inter-American Commission on Human Rights is empowered to monitor compliance with the Convention. The mechanism consists in studying the reports that States must send on the legislative, judicial, administrative and other measures they have adopted in applying the provisions of the Convention. The Commission is empowered to examine the situation of torture not only in States parties to the Convention but also in all OAS Member States (Article 17).

4.2. THE COURT'S CASE LAW

17. Since the American Convention does not give a definition of the various prohibited acts, it has been the Court's task to interpret them throughout its jurisprudence and the Court does not seem to have felt compelled to develop and have its own consistent concept of one or more types of prohibited conduct. Nor has the Court used to the letter the definition provided in the Inter-American

traditional torments but aim "at inducing even temporarily the disintegration of the human personality, the destruction of man's mental and psychological balance and the annihilation of his will" (cited in D.J. Harris *et al.*, *supra* n. 38, p. 61).

56 The provisions of the Inter-American Convention on Torture that regulate aspects of cruel, inhuman or degrading treatment or punishment are contained in Articles 6, 7, 13, 14, 15 and 17.

57 Regarding extradition, see also the provisions of Article 13 of the Convention.

Torture Convention in most cases.[58] It is not surprising that differentiating between one type of prohibited conduct and another is not an exercise that the Inter-American Court engages in frequently. The existence of Article 5(1) actually supersedes the necessity of having prohibited conduct. The flexibility with which the Court applies Article 5 shows that often the Court does not only leave aside a differentiation of the type itself – torture or cruel, inhuman or degrading treatment. It also disregards paragraphs 1 and 2 of Article 5, concluding at the end of a case that both paragraphs or simply Article 5 have been violated, quite independently of the circumstances of the case. Nevertheless, sometimes the Court attempts to classify the conduct into one of the types, so differentiation should be examined. When the Court makes a distinction, often with regard to torture, it is not easy to figure out which elements it considers for this task. Frequently, on classifying an action or omission as torture, the Court does so based on the elements of all the previously examined definitions. However, the variety of cases that the Court has heard on violations of that provision allow us to take note of different kinds of facts that, in the Court's opinion, violate Article 5(2) of the Convention, and thus we can identify some elements of these types of conduct.

There is one case – that of the forced disappearance of Mr. Bámaca Velásquez – in which the Inter-American Court takes a clear path toward defining the conduct as torture. In examining a possible violation of Article 5 of the Convention, it uses Article 1 of the United Nations Convention against Torture and Other Cruel, Inhuman or Degrading Punishment and Article 2 of the Inter-American Torture Convention. In this case, the Court found that the acts alleged – serious acts of physical and psychological violence – caused severe anguish and intense suffering for the victim and were perpetrated over a long period, deliberately, with the purpose of obtaining information that was relevant for the army. This constituted physical and psychological torture and the violation of Article 5 of the American Convention.[59] Here one can note the presence of the elements of severity of the actions, degree of suffering of the victim, deliberateness and purpose of the act, and the perpetration of the acts over a long period. The latter may be an addition that is not an element of the definition of torture but just a circumstance of the case itself. In the case of Loayza Tamayo, the Inter-American Court follows the position of the European Court that uses the severity of the conduct as an element of differentiation. It begins by drawing distinctions between different levels of severity on finding that:

> The violation of the right to physical and psychological integrity of persons is a category of violation that has several gradations and embraces treatment ranging from torture to other types of humiliation or cruel, inhuman or degrading treatment

58 I will deal with this Convention in the following section.

59 *Case of Bámaca Velásquez v. Peru*, paras. 156–158.

> with varying degrees of physical and psychological effects caused by endogenous and exogenous factors which must be proven in each specific situation.[60]

It also puts forward the concept of degrading treatment on finding that "the degrading character [of other types of conduct] is expressed through feelings of fear, anxiety and inferiority in order to humiliate, degrade and breakdown the physical and moral resistance of the victim."[61]

Latin America has provided more than enough examples of egregious, severe conduct that fits one of these types. For example, long incommunicado detention, being exhibited through the media wearing a degrading garment, solitary confinement in a tiny cell with no natural light, blows and ill-treatment, including total immersion in water, intimidation with threats of further violence, and a restrictive visiting schedule were all, according to the Court, "forms of cruel, inhuman or degrading treatment in the terms of Article 5(2) of the American Convention".[62] In the case of the Gómez Paquiyauri brothers, the Court held they had received physical and psychological maltreatment that consisted of being thrown on the ground, kicked, beaten with shotgun butts and subsequently murdered by gunshots to the head, thorax and other parts of the body, "with evidence of more injuries and bullet wounds than would have sufficed to cause their death, if that had been the only intention of the agents of the Peruvian National Police".[63] Therefore, the degree of violence varies and it is not possible to determine clearly the threshold of severity that the conduct must have to qualify as conduct prohibited by Article 5(2). As said above, this is not particularly relevant, as the first paragraph of Article 5 contains a general right to personal integrity. In a different approach, in the case of Mendoza *et al.*, where several children were sentenced to life imprisonment, the Court found that "punishments considered radically disproportionate, such as those that can be described as atrocious fall within the sphere of application of the articles that contain the prohibition of torture and cruel, inhuman and degrading treatment."[64]

18. The Court has applied the Torture Convention in many cases. The first time it did so was in the case of Paniagua Morales *et al.*, where it did not state the legal basis for asserting its jurisdiction. The Commission asked the Court to find that Guatemala had violated Article 5 of the American Convention as well as the obligations established in Articles 1, 6 and 8 of the Inter-American Convention on Torture. It argued on the one hand that Guatemala had not investigated the torture inflicted on the victims as required by Article 8 of that

---

60 *Case of Loayza Tamayo v. Peru*, para. 57.

61 *Ibidem*, citing the judgment of the European Court in the case of *Ireland v. United Kingdom*, Series A No. 25, para. 167.

62 *Case of Loayza Tamayo v. Peru*, para. 58.

63 *Case of Gómez Paquiyauri v. Peru*, para. 110.

64 *Case of Mendoza et al. v. Argentina*, para. 174.

Convention.[65] On the other hand, it indicated that almost all the victims have been subjected to "intentional acts that produced pain and physical and mental suffering in order to intimidate and punish them",[66] fitting the definition of torture found in Article 2 of that Convention. It also examined possible violations of Articles 1, 6, and 8, as raised by the Commission, in the section on the violation of Article 5 of the American Convention. However, it did not use the definition of torture found in Article 2 of the Torture Convention, nor did it invoke that article in ruling that the torture of the victims – who later had their lives taken – had been proven irrefutably.[67] The Court concluded that Guatemala had violated Article 5(1) and (2) of the American Convention and the obligations found in Articles 1, 6 and 8 of the Torture Convention;[68] that is the judgment directly applied the obligations derived from the Torture Convention, but not its definition of torture. Curiously, it also applied Article 8 of the Torture Convention – a provision that refers only to torture – to both victims of the conduct classified by the Court as torture and to two of the victims of violations classified in the judgment as cruel, inhuman or degrading treatment.[69]

In the case of Villagrán Morales *et al.*, the Court decided to go one step further. Along with explicitly affirming its jurisdiction to apply the Torture Convention, it dedicated a section exclusively to examining possible violations of Articles 1, 6, and 8 of that Convention and concluded that the State in question (Guatemala) had violated these provisions with actions that were being subject to international adjudication.[70] With regard to its jurisdiction, based on the Report of the Committee on Political and Juridical Affairs on the draft Convention, it held that:

> As some member countries of the Organization of American States were still not parties to the American Convention and had not accepted the jurisdiction of the Court, the drafters of the Convention against Torture decided not to include in it an article that made express and exclusive reference to the Inter-American Court in order not to indirectly bind them to the former Convention and the aforementioned jurisdictional organ.[71]

The Court added that what was important was to attribute jurisdiction of the Torture Convention to an international body, present or future, and that as this case was before the Inter-American Court, it was the Court's responsibility to exercise jurisdiction. This was the Court's interpretation of Article 8.

---

65 *Case of Paniagua Morales et al. v. Guatemala*, paras. 126 and 130.
66 *Ibidem*, para. 129.
67 *Ibidem*, para. 134.
68 *Ibidem*, para. 136.
69 From a substantive point of view, the Court could also have turned to its general case law on the obligation to ensure to reach the conclusion that the State must investigate, try and punish.
70 *Case of Villagrán Morales et al. v. Guatemala*, paras. 239–252.
71 *Ibidem*, paras. 247–248.

In the case of Cantoral Benavides, the Court again dedicated a special section to examining compliance with the Torture Convention, concluding that Peru had violated Articles 2, 6 and 8 of that Convention by having failed to carry out an investigation into the acts of torture proven during the trial.[72] In that judgment, the Court directly established a violation of Article 2, which defines torture, despite the fact that, when the Court examined the State's conduct according to Article 5(2) of the American Convention, it was not guided exclusively by that definition.[73] This meant that the Court analyzed the facts under Article 5(2) of the American Convention, where the definition of Article 2 of the Torture Convention was but one of several that it used to conclude that torture was committed. The Court limited itself in section XVI to finding a violation of only the Torture Convention. In the judgment handed down in the case of Bámaca Velásquez, the Court once more examined the existence of torture, turning to the two conventions that are in force on the subject – the United Nations Convention on Torture and the Inter-American Torture Convention. Subsequently it dedicated another section, section XVIII, to examining possible violations of Articles 1, 2, 6 and 8 of the latter. The section reproduces the Inter-American Commission's argument that the Inter-American Torture Convention "develops the principles contained in Article 5 of the American Convention in greater detail and, therefore, constitutes an auxiliary instrument to the Convention". The Commission notes that Guatemala had ratified that Convention in 1989 – that is, on a date prior to the date on which the facts of the case took place.[74] The Inter-American Court did not rule on this argument. Yet it concluded that as torture had been proven and Guatemala had not immediately moved *ex officio* to carry out an investigation and punish those guilty, the State had failed to comply with its obligation to prevent and punish torture, in the terms of Articles 1, 2, 6 and 8 of the American Convention.[75] In the case of Maritza Urrutia, the Inter-American Court found a violation of Article 5 (in general) of the Convention for a variety of types of conduct by State agents. They included "hooding" of the victim, the use of noise to prevent the victim from sleeping, and the threatening of the victim with physical torture and with death for her and members of her family.[76] However, later on in the judgment the Court used the same facts to weigh whether there was a violation of Article 2 of Inter-American Convention on Torture – which defines torture. It concluded that "the acts alleged in this case were prepared and inflicted deliberately to obliterate the victim's personality and demoralize her, which constitutes a form of mental torture", in violation of Article 5(1) and (2) of the American Convention and Articles 1 and 6 of the Inter-American Convention

72 *Case of Cantoral Benavides v. Peru*, paras. 180–191.
73 *Ibidem*, paras. 95–106.
74 *Case of Bámaca Velásquez v. Peru*, para. 215(a).
75 *Ibidem*, paras. 220–223.
76 *Case of Maritza Urrutia v. Guatemala*, paras. 85–88.

on Torture.[77] In the case of the Gómez Paquiyauri brothers, the Court appeared to follow the UN Torture Convention definition with regard to the severity of the treatment. These facts "intentionally carried out" were the cause of "grave physical and mental suffering on the alleged victims". As to the purpose, the Court stated that "[i]n general, in situations of massive human rights violations, [the case at the time in Peru] the systematic use of torture has the aim of intimidating the population".[78] In Bueno Alves, the Court examined the case in the light of its intentionality and the purpose and suffering caused. Additionally, it gave some guidelines to assert the degree of suffering. The determination of the suffering requires examination of the objective and subjective factors in the case. As objective factors, it mentions the "duration, method and manners used to inflict harm and the physical and psychological effects such harm may cause".[79] Subjective factors refer to the characteristics of the ill-treated person: age, gender, health condition and so on. Additionally, it marks a clearer understanding of the Court's position regarding torture and its independence with respect to the definition of the Torture Convention. The Court makes explicit in the judgment that it will consider not only the definition of the Inter-American Torture Convention but several other international instruments, citing as a basis Article 31(2) of the Vienna Convention. It then decides that the elements of torture are the following: "a) an intentional act; b) which causes severe physical or mental suffering; c) committed with a given purpose and aim".[80] The evidence in the case plus the acceptance of the facts by the government sufficed for the Court to find that torture had been perpetrated. In the case of Fleury, the Court reiterated these same elements.[81]

19. An analysis of this case law leads to several conclusions. First, the Court has found that it has jurisdiction to examine and apply in its judgments the Torture Convention. Even so, the role that Convention plays in its judgments is not clear. It is perfectly possible that the Court uses it as an auxiliary means of interpreting Article 5 of the American Convention, but in that case the wording of its considering paragraphs and conclusions should be different.[82] Second, the Court applies this Convention directly to those States Parties to it.

77 *Ibidem*, paras. 89–98.

78 *Case of Gómez Päquiyauri*, para. 115.

79 *Case of Bueno Alves v. Argentina*, para. 86.

80 *Ibidem*, para. 79.

81 *Case of Fleury v. Haiti*, para. 72.

82 The Court makes these criteria explicit in another judgment where it expresses that: "Although the Court has broad authority to hear human rights violations, they must address the rights protected by the Convention, except for cases in which an international instrument ratified by the State grants jurisdiction to weigh violations of rights protected by that same instrument", mentioning that it has acted thusly in the *cases of Bámaca Velásquez v. Peru, Cantoral Benavides v. Peru, Villagrán Morales et al. v. Guatemala*, and *Paniagua Morales et al. v. Guatemala* (all cited in the case of *Baena Ricardo et al. v. Panama*, para. 97).

Although there is no indication that this is because the States in question are parties to that Convention, it is clear that there is no other reason that would allow the Court to rule that a State has violated the obligations of a treaty than the fact that the State is a party thereto. It is also possible that even when that Convention is not invoked in a case, whether by the victim or during the proceedings before the Commission, the Court can invoke it by applying the principle of *iura novit curiæ*.[83] Third, with regard to the States that are not party to the Inter-American Torture Convention, the Court nevertheless seems to use the Torture Convention, insofar as its provisions align with the provisions of the American Convention or make explicit lines of interpretation that have begun to be developed through case law, as an auxiliary means of interpretation.[84] This action is based on the fact that the system for the protection of human rights is an integrated whole that allows the development of the corresponding human rights in any other international treaty or any other case law, whether domestic or international, to be used for the interpretation of any of its rules. Fourth, the Court applies the obligations of the Torture Convention in earnest, but is reticent to apply the definition of torture in Article 2 of that Convention.

20. I do not advocate here for the Court to differentiate between torture and other forms of ill-treatment. However, if the Court wishes to place the stigma of torture on certain actions of States – taking into consideration that it is not obliged to apply the various existing definitions and that there is no *jus cogens* definition of it[85] – the Court should not use the definition of Article 2 of the Inter-American Torture Convention. This definition is inefficient. The Court should have a definition of torture of its own and be consistent in requiring the same theoretical elements for all cases. Taking into account the long jurisprudence of the Court on this subject, I would maintain my position in the sense that the Court does indeed have independence to define torture and that this position is the one that has prevailed in the Court's jurisprudence.

5. TREATMENT OF PEOPLE DEPRIVED OF LIBERTY (ARTICLE 5(2))

21. The Inter-American Convention connects humane treatment with the right to personal liberty of Article 7. Article 5 and its paragraphs 2 and 4 include the effects of deprivation of liberty as possible infractions to the detriment of

---

83 *Case of Five Pensioners v. Peru*, paras. 153–155; *Case of Myrna Mack Chang v. Guatemala*, para. 224.

84 For example, see the considering paragraphs in the judgment handed down in the *case of Villagrán Morales* in relation to the Convention on the Rights of the Child. See *case of Villagrán Morales et al. v. Guatemala*, paras. 192–196.

85 For a detailed reasoning on the matter, see my vote in the *case of "Cotton Field" v. Mexico*.

personal integrity, introducing the right of all persons deprived of liberty to be treated "with respect for the inherent dignity of the human person". The Convention uses on this paragraph the expression "deprived of liberty" and not the word "detention". This implies that whatever form deprivation of liberty takes, whether detention (according to the meaning given to the word in the criminal procedural law of many Latin American countries), internment in a psychiatric hospital or deprivation of liberty of any other kind, the rule found in Article 5(2) of the Convention is always applicable.

22. In a number of judgments, the Inter-American Court has found that the State has a responsibility and duty to guarantee the personal integrity of the individual while that individual is being held in custody.[86] Personal integrity, or humane treatment, protects the physical, mental and moral integrity of the person and therefore conditions of detention must comply with several requirements. Not only must there be no form of ill-treatment, but the State has an obligation to keep prisoners within a certain level of infrastructural conditions, such as space, water, food, lighting, open air activities and others of that kind. In addition, medical care must be provided and security of the person must be ensured: the prisoner must be protected from attacks by State agents, inmates or even from him or herself.

23. The situation of jails in the region is deplorable, so the Court has had to handle this type of violation of Article 5 quite often. One of the conditions of deprivation of freedom the Court has stressed in terms of humane treatment is the problem of infrastructure and overcrowding. An instructive example is the case of Montero Aranguren (Retén de Catia in Venezuela). In its judgment, the Court details the horrible conditions in which prisoners live: 30 square centimeters per inmate were available in the cells;[87] the solitary confinement cells where some inmates were sent were deplorable and extremely small.[88] The sanitary conditions were appalling, I would say beyond endurance.[89] The State itself admitted that medical assistance did not meet the minimum requirements.[90] Overturning an old case where the Court did not find a violation when the State prevented a prisoner from being assisted by a doctor of his choice,[91] the judgment emphasizes that "[a]ssistance by a physician not related to

86 *Case of Neira Alegría et al. v. Peru*, para. 60; *Case of Cantoral Benavides v. Peru*, judgment on merits, para. 87; *Case of Hilaire, Benjamin, Constantine et al. v. Trinidad and Tobago*, para. 165.
87 *Montero Aranguren v. Venezuela*, para. 91.
88 *Ibidem*, para. 93.
89 *Ibidem*, paras. 95–100.
90 *Ibidem*, para. 101.
91 *Case of Cesti Hurtado v. Peru*, paras. 153–160.

prison or detention center authorities is an important safeguard against torture and physical or mental ill-treatment of inmates".[92]

In a case of migrants in Panama, the Court found that the State has a duty to guarantee the health and welfare of the inmates, seeing to it that their deprivation of liberty does "not exceed the unavoidable level of suffering inherent to the detention".[93]

24. The Court has dealt with some frequency with the issue of solitary confinement, also used with some regularity in the States in the region. The Inter-American Court ruled in its first judgment on the merits – the case of Velásquez Rodríguez – that "the mere subjection of an individual to prolonged isolation and deprivation of communication is in itself cruel and inhuman treatment which harms the psychological and moral integrity of the person, and violates the right of every detainee [...] to treatment respectful of his dignity."[94] In Suárez Rosero, another form of suffering emerges provoked by this kind of solitary confinement: that of being prevented from seeking a lawyer or communicating with family.[95] In Bámaca Velásquez, the Court linked this confinement with the particularly vulnerable position in which the prisoner is left, and the increased risk of aggression and arbitrary acts the prisoner can be subjected to.[96] Solitary confinement – also known as "incommunicado" detention – has apparently not been banned by the Court, but its findings are in sometimes confusing language. In the case of Suárez Rosero, it finds that solitary confinement is an exceptional measure.[97] The same is said in the cases of the Street Children,[98] De la Cruz Flores,[99] Bulacio[100] and others,[101] which

---

92 *Montero Aranguren v. Venezuela*, para. 102. See also *Case of Vélez Loor v. Panama*, paras. 67–69.

93 *Case of Vélez Loor v. Panama*, para. 198.

94 *Case of Velásquez Rodríguez v. Honduras*, para. 187. Other rulings of the Court in which it finds likewise include: *Case of Suárez Rosero v. Ecuador*, para. 91; *Case of Loayza Tamayo v. Peru*, para. 57; *Case of Castillo Petruzzi et al. v. Peru*, paras. 192–194; *Case of Villagrán Morales et al. v. Guatemala*, paras. 163–164; and *Case of Cantoral Benavides v. Peru*, paras. 180–191. The Court departed from this ruling only in the *case of Caballero Delgado and Santana* – also on a disappearance – in which it found that Article 5 had not been violated "as in its judgment there is not sufficient evidence that the detainees were tortured or subjected to mistreatment" (*Case of Caballero Delgado and Santana v. Colombia*, para. 65). For other cases in which forms of solitary confinement in inhuman conditions and/or for prolonged periods are found to constitute a violation, see *Case of Castillo Petruzzi et al. v. Peru*, paras. 192–194; *Case of Hilaire, Benjamin, Constantine et al. v. Trinidad and Tobago*, para. 164; and *Case of Lori Berenson v. Peru*, para. 103.

95 *Case of Suárez Rosero v. Ecuador*, paras. 90–91.

96 *Case of Bámaca Velasquez v. Guatemala*, para. 150.

97 *Ibidem*, para. 51.

98 *Case of Villagrán Morales et al. (the Street Children) v. Guatemala*, para. 164.

99 *Case of De la Cruz Flores v. Peru*, para. 129.

100 *Case of Bulacio v. Argentina*, para. 87.

101 *Case of De la Cruz Flores v. Peru*, paras. 127–128.

means that in certain conditions it could be allowed. However, in Castro Castro and in Montero Aranguren (Retén de Catia) the language is different. In Castro Castro, the Court states that "prolonged isolation and coercive solitary confinement are, *in themselves*, cruel and inhuman treatments, damaging to the person's psychic and moral integrity and the right to respect of the dignity inherent to the human person." Immediately thereafter it finds that "solitary confinement is allowed exceptionally "taking into account the gross effects it generates".[102] In Montero Aranguren, first the Court deems that solitary confinement must be used only as a disciplinary measure or for the protection of persons "only during the time necessary and in strict compliance with the criteria of reasonability, necessity and legality". They should have minimum standards of comfort "and they can only be used if a physician certifies that the prisoner is fit to sustain it". This notwithstanding, in the same paragraph it emphatically points out that "confinement in a dark cell and incommunication are *forbidden*".[103] It is not clear whether the two circumstances – prolonged isolation and coercive solitary confinement in Castro Castro and darkness and solitary confinement in Montero Aranguren – must coincide in order to be forbidden.[104] The same happens in Fermín Ramírez: the Court joins imprisonment in isolation with lack of communication or with unjustified restrictions on the regime of visits, to conclude that this constitutes a violation of Article 5.[105]

Perhaps an illustrative example of the type of regimes that make solitary confinement a clear violation of Article 5(2) is the case of De la Cruz Flores. Dr. De la Cruz Flores spent a whole month in incommunicado detention, which meant that she could not see or talk even with her family and lawyers. Later, her conditions were "improved" and she was in solitary confinement: she could be visited once every three months by her children (which they did not do to prevent the psychological consequences of them seeing their mother in the condition she was); once a month, she had thirty minutes to write to her family. She had no face-to-face visits where she could enter into physical contact with her visitors. During the first year of imprisonment, she was allowed once a day to go to the

102 *Case of Castro Castro v. Peru*, para. 323.

103 *Case of Montero Aranguren v. Venezuela*, para. 94. The Court resorts here to the Standard Minimum Rules for the Treatment of Prisoners. Adopted by the First United Nations Congress on Prevention of Crime and Treatment of Offenders, held at Geneva in 1955, and approved by the Economic and Social Council through its Resolutions 663C (XXIV) of July 31, 1957 and 2076 (LXII) of May 13, 1977.

104 *Case of Castro Castro v. Peru*, para. 323. In the same sense see *Case of García Asto and Urcesino Ramírez v. Peru*, paras. 229 and 235; *Case of De la Cruz Flores v. Peru*, para. 128; *Case of Maritza Urrutia v. Guatemala*, para. 87; and *Case of Bámaca Velásquez v. Peru*, para. 150.

105 *Case of Fermín Ramírez v. Guatemala*, para. 118. See also *Case of Cantoral Benavides v. Peru*, para. 84; *Case of Bámaca Velásquez v. Peru*, para. 155; and *Case of Maritza Urrutia v. Guatemala*, para. 87.

exercise yard.[106] The Court found a violation of Article 5 of the Convention. In the case of Montero Aranguren, quoting the United Nations Committee against Torture, the Court found that "confinement cells measuring 60 x 80 centimeters, where no light or ventilation exists, and where the prisoner can only be standing or crouched down, 'are torture instruments'".[107]

25. Part of the obligations of the State is providing a prisoner with adequate medical assistance. The necessity of proper medical care is a constant in the jurisprudence of the Court. In a number of judgments, the Inter-American Court has found that the State has a responsibility and duty to guarantee the personal integrity of the individual while that individual is in custody.[108] In the case of Juan Humberto Sánchez, the victim was detained, and his body appeared later bearing clear indications of torture. In the judgment handed down in that case, the Inter-American Court established that if a person is in normal physical condition when detained, it is up to the State to provide a reasonable explanation for why there were marks of torture on the person's body following the detention.[109] Prisoners must have regular medical check-ups and attention and adequate treatment when this is required. The Court cites as a source Principle 24 of the Body of Principles for the Protection of All Persons under Any Form of Detention or Prison. The provision stipulates: "[a] proper medical examination shall be offered to a detained or imprisoned person as promptly as possible after his admission to the place of detention or imprisonment, and thereafter medical care and treatment shall be provided whenever necessary. This care and treatment shall be provided free of charge."[110] In Díaz Peña, the Court gives a more precise account of what is to be expected from the States. It found that, according to Article 1, obligations must be determined "on the basis of the particular needs for protection of the subject of law, owing either to his personal situation or to the specific situation in which he finds himself".[111] It reiterated this by saying in the case of Vera Vera that the lack of appropriate medical care could be a violation of Article 5, depending

---

106 *Case of De la Cruz Flores v. Peru*, paras. 73.55, 125–127.

107 Committee against Torture's Report on Turkey, United Nations, 48th Session Term (A/48/44/Add.1), 1994, para. 52, quoted in *Case of Montero Aranguren v. Venezuela*, para. 94.

108 *Case of Neira Alegría et al. v. Peru*, para. 60; *Case of Cantoral Benavides v. Peru*, para. 87; and *Case of Hilaire, Benjamin, Constantine et al. v. Trinidad and Tobago*, para. 165.

109 *Case of Juan Humberto Sánchez v. Honduras*, para. 100. A similar position is taken in the *case of Bulacio v. Argentina*, both in the judgment, para. 138, and in paragraphs 22 through 25 of the separate concurring opinion of Judge Sergio García Ramírez.

110 United Nations, Body of Principles for the Protection of All Persons under Any Form of Detention or Imprisonment, adopted by the General Assembly in Resolution 43/173, December 9, 1988, Principle 24. See also, Rule 24 of the United Nations Standard Minimum Rules for the Treatment of Prisoners.

111 *Case of Diaz Peña v. Venezuela*, para. 137.

on the circumstances.[112] The Court reasserts that "[c]are by a doctor who does not have links to the prison or detention authorities is an important safeguard against the torture or physical or mental ill-treatment of the persons deprived of liberty".[113]

26. As was said above, prisoners are not to be subject to any ill-treatment that is not justified as a legitimate restriction of the right to personal integrity. In several cases the Court just mentions various things that would constitute a violation of Article 5(2) (second part). In the case of Loayza Tamayo, for example, the Court lists treatment that should be prohibited, including public display in humiliating clothing via the media, restrictions on visitation, and isolation in a small cell without ventilation or natural light.[114] Such a violation would be also committed by the sole threat of being hung at any moment because of a death penalty sentence.[115] In the case of Castro Castro, the Court qualified as sexual violence the fact that the victims were naked, covered only by a sheet and had to use toilet facilities with the door opened, all this while being watched by male guards.[116] This amounted to a violation of Article 5.

Closely related to personal integrity is the issue of security. In the case of Bulacio, the State itself recognized its responsibility for having failed to "appropriately exercise the duty of custody".[117]

With regard to the organization within prisons, the case of Castro Castro shows an example related to the need to have different regulations for different situations. It stated that the rules to decide when to distribute personal care facilities among prisoners should be adapted for "female detainees with their period, pregnant, or accompanied by their children", instead of having the same rule for all inmates.[118] Thus, one understands that otherwise there would be a violation of Article 5.

27. In addition to treatment related to detention conditions, the Court has put forward the idea that subjecting a person to an illegal detention places that person in an "exacerbated situation of vulnerability creating a real risk that his other rights, such as the right to humane treatment and to be treated with dignity, will be violated."[119] This constitutes a violation of Article 5 of the Convention. It could thus be understood from this that if a detention is carried

---

112 *Case of Vera Vera v. Ecuador*, para. 44.

113 *Case of Díaz Peña v. Venezuela*, para. 137. Other cases in this sense are the *Case of Tibi v. Ecuador*, judgment of September 7, 2004, Series C No. 114, para. 156; and *Case of Vélez Loor v. Panama*, para. 220.

114 *Case of Loayza Tamayo v. Peru*, para. 58.

115 *Case of Hilaire, Benjamin, Constantine et al. v. Trinidad and Tobago*, paras. 167–169.

116 *Case of Castro Castro v. Peru*, paras. 303, 306 and 308.

117 *Case of Bulacio v. Argentina*, paras. 32–33 and 38(c).

118 *Case of Castro Castro v. Peru*, para. 331.

119 *Case of Villagrán Morales et al. v. Peru*, para. 166; *Case of Bulacio v. Argentina*, para. 127.

out in an illegal place, other cruel or inhuman treatment is not necessary for the Court to conclude that this article has been violated. This interpretation is honed with the Court's position in the case of Juan Humberto Sánchez. That judgment establishes that a short time period in illegal detention is enough for a violation of the mental and moral integrity of the victim to have taken place.[120] The judgment in this case modifies the ruling handed down in the case of Gangaram Panday, in which the Inter-American Court did not assign responsibility to the State for the violation of his personal integrity despite having established a violation of Article 7 of the Convention on the illegality of Gangaram Panday's detention.[121]

6. THE BELÉM DO PARÁ CONVENTION AND ITS INTERACTION WITH ARTICLE 5 OF THE AMERICAN CONVENTION

28. As can be noted, the violations of personal integrity examined by the Court have so far and often been the result of political violence and been executed with the clear direct or indirect participation of State agents. However, this does not mean that what was said in the above sections is valid only for those types of cases. According to the case law on the obligation to ensure, ever since Velásquez Rodríguez it can be argued that the way the obligation has been developed also makes it applicable when the violence is perpetrated by private actors. This was discussed previously,[122] where it was noted that in general, it is the responsibility of the State to prohibit illicit conduct that can be committed by private parties and to regulate compliance with that prohibition, incurring international responsibility should it not carry out these actions. The State is responsible for its omissions. It should be recalled that the Inter-American Court established in the judgment handed down in the case of Velásquez Rodríguez that:

> An illegal act which violates human rights and which is initially not directly imputable to a State (for example, because it is the act of a private person or because the person responsible has not been identified) can lead to international responsibility of the State, not because of the act itself, but because of the lack of due diligence to prevent the violation or to respond to it as required by the Convention.[123]

29. These words are pertinent for the introduction of the subject of unpunished violence against women, which undoubtedly affects (apart from other rights) their right to humane treatment. In principle, it would not be necessary to

---

120 *Case of Juan Humberto Sánchez v. Honduras*, para. 98.

121 *Case of Gangaram Panday v. Suriname*, paras. 51 and 57–62.

122 On restrictions, see *infra* Chapter 1.

123 *Case of Velásquez Rodríguez v. Honduras*, para. 172.

examine this problem separately, as the provisions of the American Convention cover the protection of these rights. However, because of State negligence (fortunately in decline) in ensuring women's human rights, for many years women have not enjoyed protection of the rights granted to them.[124] One need not delve too deeply into the past to find evidence of this negligence. Domestically, in Latin America's traditional legal codes, provisions against rape – which is normally considered a criminal infraction – did not have the protection of the woman's physical integrity or her personal freedom as their principal purpose, but rather generally protected the honor of the woman's husband or family.[125] In addition, the punishment of these crimes in some countries increased along with the "honesty" or "chastity" of the woman, with punishments also increasing if the woman was married. Rape within a marriage, another type of conduct that violates personal integrity, is in many countries only just now considered as such. Until very recently, mistreatment of women by their husbands or parents and brothers was also not a subject of State concern, nor was the harassment that many women suffer from their superiors or co-workers in their workplaces. All these different expressions of violence are understood to fall within the realm of the private, and the distinction between public and private – the latter being the area in which the State must refrain from acting – was applied rigorously.[126]

30. The causes behind the phenomenon of violence against women are complex, as they are intimately linked to the subordination of women to men and women's position in society, these being the manifestations of a culture whose change will necessarily be slow. A clear sign of the difficulty in changing attitudes is found in what happened and may be still happening in murders of women by their husbands in Brazil, where the "husband's honor" defense still works to excuse the perpetrators of responsibility despite repeated judgments from the Supreme Court finding that this defense lacks

---

124 Paragraph 5 of the preamble of the Declaration on the Elimination of Violence against Women of the United Nations expresses that the General Assembly is "concerned about the long-standing failure to protect and promote those rights and freedoms in the case of violence against women." Text of the Declaration in document A/RES/48/104 dated February 23, 1994.

125 In the Chilean Criminal Code, in force as of July 2013, abortion, rape, rape of a minor, and incest, among other things, are crimes "against family order and public morality".

126 See C. Medina, "Women's Rights as Human Rights: Latin American Countries and the Organization of American States," in M. Díaz-Diocaretz and I. Zavala (eds.), *Women, Feminist Identity and Society in the 1980's*, John Benjamins Publishing Company, Amsterdam, 1985; C. Medina, "Toward a More Effective Guarantee of the Enjoyment of Human Rights by Women in the Inter-American Systems", in R.J. Cook (ed.), *Human Rights of Women*, University of Pennsylvania Press, Philadelphia, 1994, Chapter 10, pp. 257–284. Also C. Medina, "The Inter-American Commission on Human Rights and Women, with Particular Reference to Violence," in M. Castermans, F. Van Hoof and J. Smith, *The Role of the Nation-State in the 21st Century*, Kluwer Law International, the Netherlands, 1998, pp. 117–134.

all legal value.[127] Another sign is the judgment in 1998 of the Supreme Court of the Netherlands, a progressive country in many respects. In addressing a criminal complaint of rape from a woman against her ex-lover, there was no inquiry into whether there had been violence in carrying out the sexual acts. Rather, the Court examined whether the accused "was aware" that the stable relationship he had had with the victim had concluded,[128] as the crime of rape can only be committed when the victim and offender are not married or in a comparable stable relationship. As that Court found that this point was not clearly proven, it acquitted the accused.[129] I have no doubt this position has by now been overturned. This happened not only in Brazil and the Netherlands; it also took place in Maryland – in the United States – as recently as the 1990s. In October 1994, in a Baltimore county court, a judge ruled to convict a husband who had murdered his wife several hours after finding her apparently lying with another man, sentencing him to the minimum punishment established by law: three years in prison. The judge also suspended half of the sentence. On handing down his ruling, the judge stated: "I seriously wonder how many married men would have the strength to walk away [...] without inflicting some corporal punishment, whatever that punishment might be. I shudder to think what I would do".[130]

Violence against women forms definitely part of the international agenda and has found its way in the national legal order. Many instruments have been adopted to eradicate this plague from the world. The UN, *inter alia*, has a Declaration on the Elimination of Violence against Women,[131] a Convention on the Elimination of All Forms of Discrimination against Women with a Supervisory Committee,[132] and a Special Rapporteur on violence against women, its causes and consequences.[133] In 2008, a campaign was launched by the UN Secretary-General to raise public awareness to prevent and end all forms of violence against women. In addition, there is now a Special Rapporteur on Sexual Violence in Conflict. Until recently, general international supervisory bodies had kept their distance from the problem. The curious thing about

127 A documentary report on this can be found in Americas Watch, Criminal Injustice, Human Rights Watch, New York, 1991. Also see IACHR, Report on the human rights situation in Brazil (OEA/Ser.L/V/II.97, Doc. 29 rev. 1, September 29, 1997), Chapter VIII, para. 27.

128 It was proven during the trial that the woman had told the accused that the relationship had ended, but the Court had doubts as to whether he understood her clearly.

129 Judgment of June 16, 1987, handed down in a cassation proceeding against the judgment of the Court of Amsterdam dated February 11, 1986, in the criminal trial of Leslie Luciano A., reproduced in *Nederlandse Jurisprudentie*, 1988, No. 156, pp. 667–673. The judgment caused a stir in the Netherlands legal community, which reacted strongly against the Court (NJD, June 1, 1988, afl. 23, pp. 819–820).

130 The information was provided by Igualdad Ya, Acción Mujeres 7.1, December 1994.

131 UN Resolution 48/104/ of December 20, 1993.

132 UN Convention on the Elimination of All Forms of Discrimination against Women, adopted in New York on December 18, 1979.

133 UN Resolution 1994/45, adopted on March 4, 1994.

this is that from its beginning, international human rights law has offered a legal instrument appropriate for addressing the subject of violence against women.[134] From the perspective of rights affected, it is clear that violence against women violates, at the least, their right to physical and mental integrity, their personal security, and at times their right to life, all of which are ensured in all international human rights treaties.[135] This means that violence against women can and should be a subject of international concern, given that it can affect and violate three rights found in catalogues of international rights that are obligatory for very many States. This reticence has obviously delayed the treatment of a situation that still is a main concern in the world.

31. All this background was the driving force in the region behind the drafting of a special treaty on violence against women, the Inter-American Convention on the Prevention, Punishment and Eradication of Violence against Women (Belém do Pará), which constitutes, according to those who drafted it, "a positive contribution to protecting the rights of women and eliminating violence against them."[136]

Although this Convention refers to all the human rights found in the American Convention, it is clear that the main purpose of its adoption is to prevent attacks on the physical, psychological, and mental integrity of women. The extension of the Convention's content to other rights is a result of the fact that violence against women is nothing but a culmination, the most serious manifestation of the situation of subordination faced by women. In order to diminish it in a meaningful way, women's position in society must be improved, requiring action to be taken in order for them to be able to exercise all their human rights in full freedom. Because of this, the Convention of Belém do Pará does not replace general treaties but rather complements them, playing the role of specifying the State obligations derived from Article 5 of the American Convention with the purpose of protecting the personal integrity of women. From this point of view, it plays a role similar to that of the Inter-American Convention to Prevent and Punish Torture.

32. The definition of violence given by the Convention of Belém do Pará places us directly in the field of Articles 4 and 5 of the American Convention. Article 1 establishes that violence against women is understood to be "any act or conduct,

---

134 See in this sense, J. Fitzpatrick, "Utilización de las normas internacionales sobre derechos humanos para combatir la violencia contra la mujer", in R.J. Cook (ed.), *supra* n. 126, pp. 530–567.

135 ICCPR, Articles 6, 7 and 9; ACHR, Articles 4, 5 and 7.

136 The Inter-American Convention on the Prevention, Punishment and Eradication of Violence against Women, the "Convention of Belém do Pará", was adopted by the General Assembly of the OAS in a resolution dated June 9, 1994. Text at OAS/Ser. P, AG/Doc. 3115/94 rev. 2, June 9, 1994.

based on gender, which causes death or physical, sexual or psychological harm or suffering to women, whether in the public or the private sphere".[137] Article 2 of this Convention complements the definition by clarifying that for the purposes of the international instruments application, violence against women covered by the Convention is violence:

1. that occurs within the family or domestic unit or within any other interpersonal relationship, whether or not the perpetrator shares or has shared the same residence with the woman, including, among others, rape, battery and sexual abuse;
2. that occurs in the community and is perpetrated by any person, including, among others, rape, sexual abuse, torture, trafficking in persons, forced prostitution, kidnapping and sexual harassment in the workplace, as well as in educational institutions, health facilities or any other place; and
3. that is perpetrated or condoned by the state or its agents regardless of where it occurs.

The definition is not ideal from a legal point of view because it inadequately mixes the elements of place with the elements of the type of personal relationship and the specific form the violence can take. Despite these problems, it constitutes a valuable contribution to the determination of these State obligations on giving clear indications with regard to what they must "prevent," "punish" and "eradicate" in order to protect the personal integrity of women.

33. From the definition, it can be deduced that it is not enough to be a woman who suffers violence to fall under the protection of Belém do Pará. The Court affirmed in the case of Ríos *et al.* that it was necessary to clarify that:

> not all violations of human rights committed in detriment of a woman necessarily implies a violation of the stipulations of the Convention of Belém do Pará. Even though female journalists were attacked in the facts of this case, in all of the cases they were attacked along with their male colleagues. The representatives did not prove how the attacks were "especially direct[ed] against women," nor did they explain the reasons why women became a greater target of attack "based on their condition [of being women]." Therefore, it has not been proven that the facts were based on the gender or sex of the alleged victims.[138]

It stressed this position by stating that there was no evidence that "the proven facts "were aggravated by their female condition."[139]

From the point of view of the protected rights at issue for the examination of Article 5 of the American Convention, the Convention of Belém do Pará sets forth in its Article 3 a woman's right to live a life free of violence, both in her public and private life. Article 6 of this instrument precisely specifies the content

---

137 *Ibidem*, Preamble.
138 *Case of Ríos et al. v. Venezuela*, para. 279.
139 *Ibidem*, para. 280.

of this right, establishing that it includes the right to not be discriminated against and to be assessed and educated free from stereotypical patterns of social and cultural behavior and practices that are based on concepts of inferiority or subordination.[140]

34. The Convention of Belém do Pará establishes two types of obligations for States. One kind, indicated in Article 7, is to be complied with immediately and complaints must be allowed to be made regarding this kind before the Inter-American Commission on Human Rights. The other, found in Article 8, describes obligations whose content is progressive, and complaints cannot be made over failures to comply with this provision, although the Inter-American Commission of Women through the examination of the reports that States submit to it will at least supervise the obligations.[141]

Article 7 of the Convention of Belém do Pará reiterates the obligation to respect the physical integrity of women and expands on the obligation to guarantee personal integrity. Letters (a), (b) and (c) of the article repeat obligations that have already been indicated previously: prohibition on violating rights contained in the Convention (letter (a)), and obligation to act with due diligence to prevent, investigate and punish violence against women (letter (b)), through both legislative and administrative actions (letter (c)). The following specify other measures: preventative measures to warn aggressors to refrain from harassing, intimidating, threatening, damaging or putting in danger the life of a woman (letter (d)); and the establishment of just and effective procedures so that women can have effective access to protective measures and a fair trial (letter (f)) and to reparations (letter (g)). Finally, letter (h) contains the all-encompassing obligation to "adopt such legislative or other measures as may be necessary to give effect to this Convention".

The obligations of Article 8 of the Convention of Belém do Pará, on the contrary, are a step backwards with regard to the protection derived from Article 5 of the American Convention, such as it has been developed by the case law of the Inter-American Court. Among the obligations that States must comply with progressively are some that should be complied with immediately.

140 See HRC, General Comment No. 28 (Article 3 equality of rights between men and women) 29/03/2000, CCPR/C/21/Rev.1/Add.10, para. 5. In the same sense see: *Concluding Observations: Chile*, CCPR/C/79/Add.104, of March 30, 1999, para. 3.

141 The Inter-American Commission of Women is a specialized body of the OAS made up of 34 Permanent Delegates, one for each Member State, designated by their respective governments. Its mission is to promote and protect the rights of women and support member States in their efforts to ensure full access to civil, political, economic, social and cultural rights, allowing women and men to participate under equal conditions in all areas of social life. There is now a Follow-up Mechanism to the Belém do Pará Convention (MESECVI). MESECVI is a systematic and permanent multilateral evaluation methodology based on exchange and technical cooperation between the States Party to the Convention and a Committee of Experts.

They include education of justices, police and other law enforcement officials, as well as the personnel in charge of policy in this area (letter (c)); the establishment of services for attending to women subjected to violence (letter (d)) and for their rehabilitation (letter (f)); and the means of informing the public about the violence, the legal remedies available for filing complaints against it and the methods for obtaining reparations (letter (e)). This notwithstanding, the Court still has competence to deal with these issues when supervising compliance with the American Convention's obligation to ensure all rights without discrimination, resorting directly to its own jurisprudence on Articles 4 and 5 of the American Convention. Additionally, the Court may have recourse to letter (h) of Article 7 of the Convention of Belém do Pará which, in reality, allows for the inclusion of all the measures found in Article 8 should it be necessary and compatible with the Inter-American Court's development of Article 5 thus far.

35. The Court did not apply the Belém do Pará Convention directly until 2006. Similar to the Inter-American Torture Convention, the Convention of Belém do Pará can be used by the Court as part of the *corpus juris* in the matter of the personal integrity of women. From that point of view, there seems to be no need for the Court to assert jurisdiction over it. Belém do Pará details the obligations of the States emerging from Article 5 with regard to violence against women. It is a direct message to the States that women are as much human beings as the rest of the population, an obvious assertion but one States do not understand so easily. However, in 2006, the Court established its jurisdiction to apply that Convention after hearing some cases of violence against women. The first case was that of Castro Castro, dealing with a massacre in a women's section of a jail of Lima, Peru, where women were ill-treated to such an extent that Court found crimes against humanity had been perpetrated.[142] The events leading to the case had occurred before the Convention of Belém do Pará had entered into force for Peru, but the Court, applying its jurisprudence with regard to the obligation to investigate *ex officio* acts of this nature, found Peru had violated, among other provisions in the American Convention, Article 7(b) of the Convention of Belém do Pará, that is, the lack of access to justice to protect human rights.[143]

After Castro Castro, in several other cases the Court has followed this path. In the case of González *et al.* (Cotton Field) v. México – a party to the Convention of Belém do Para – answering a preliminary objection by Mexico arguing the Court had no competence to deal with violations of that Convention, a thorough reasoning was given to assert that jurisdiction. The first argument to sustain this position was the text of the Convention itself. Article 12 allows the Commission to consider petitions under Article 7, "in accordance with the norms and procedures established by the American Convention [...] and the Statute and

142 *Case of Castro Castro v. Peru*, para. 404.
143 *Ibidem*, paras. 378 and 470.6.

Regulations of the Inter-American Commission [...] for lodging and considering petitions". The norms for considering petitions in the American Convention give the Commission the power to send the cases to the Court. A systematic perusal does not show the existence of any provision either in the American Convention nor in the Convention of Belém do Pará that prohibits the Commission to do so.[144] The preparatory works of Belém do Pará are, according to the Court, "completely insufficient to provide solid grounds to reject the interpretation made of Article 12 of the Convention of Belém do Pará".[145] After examining a systematic and teleological interpretation and the principle of effectiveness, the Court came to the conclusion that it had jurisdiction to apply the Convention.[146]

Other cases of violence against women have followed suit and the Court has often considered the Belém do Pará Convention.[147] In the case of Juan Gelman, the issue was the disappearance of his pregnant daughter-in-law; the baby born to her was given to a Uruguayan family, all this in the context of Operación Cóndor.[148] The Convention of Belém do Pará was invoked in the case, but although the Court strongly affirmed that the acts perpetrated then "can be classified as one of the most serious and reprehensible forms of violence against women", it decided not to find a violation thereof.[149] Almost every other case, as it is shown below, has directly applied this Convention.

36. Apparently, the issue of rape or sexual violence has received a stricter interpretation, I believe, with the application of the Torture Convention definition, something that, as examined above, the Court does not often do.[150] The subject of rape as a violation that deserved to be investigated was referred for the first time in the case of the Massacre of Plan de Sánchez.[151] When examining torture, I pointed out that Bueno Alves was the case where the Court clearly stated that it would not exclusively use the Torture Convention definition of torture. The Court indicated, moreover, that the elements to decide if torture had occurred were intentionality, purpose and suffering caused. In the case of "Cotton Field", dealing with the disappearance, ill-treatment and finally death of two young women and an adolescent, the Court did not find it appropriate to consider that the victims had been subjected to torture. This decision was taken in spite of the fact that, with regard to one victim,

---

144 *Case of Cotton Field v. Mexico*, paras. 40–41, 54–56.
145 *Ibidem*, para. 73.
146 *Ibidem*, para. 77.
147 See *Case of Fernández Ortega* and *Case of Rosendo Cantú et al.* both v. Mexico.
148 See Chapter 2 of this book, paragraph 76.
149 *Case of Juan Gelman v. Uruguay*, para. 312.7.
150 See in *ibidem*, my concurring opinion where I argue that the Court has not followed consistently the definition in the Torture Convention which includes as an element the participation or inducement of State agents.
151 *Case of the Plan de Sánchez Massacre v. Guatemala*, judgment on reparations and costs, para. 49.19.

Esmeralda, the judgment states that "she must have endured such cruelty that it had to have caused her severe physical and mental suffering before she died",[152] and with respect to the other two victims it said that "the women showed signs of sexual violence". The reasons given by the Court were that the lack of evidence of "whether the perpetrators were public officials, or private individuals acting with their support and tolerance, cannot lead this Tribunal to presume that there were in fact public officials involved".[153] This judgment leaves aside the way the Court and international law assign responsibility to the State: responsibility may arise from an action or an omission, as, for example, the failure to ensure that there has been due diligence and promptness in the investigation of this type of violation, which was proven in the case. This, of course, is a deviation from the Court's position regarding the elements of torture, which do not contemplate requirements for the perpetrators like those mentioned in this judgment.

Later on, the Court has found torture or other ill-treatment in instances of rape, but there has been a lack of consistency in the judgments. In the case of Miguel Castro-Castro Prison (Castro Castro), a woman was submitted to "a finger vaginal inspection" at the Police Sanity Hospital, by several hooded people.[154] Using case law from other bodies,[155] the Court considered that this was sexual rape. The Court affirmed: "[t]he sexual rape of a detainee by a State agent is an especially gross and reprehensible act, taking into account the victim's vulnerability and the abuse of power displayed by the agent". It asserted that, in addition, "it causes great physical and psychological damage that leaves the victim 'physically and emotionally humiliated'".[156] Peru was found responsible for the torture of the victim in violation of Article 5(2) of the American Convention[157] and Article 7 of the Belém do Pará Convention was mentioned, without declaring a violation of that treaty.[158]

In the cases of Rosendo Cantú and Fernández Ortega, both against Mexico, the victims were indigenous women – one of them underage – who were assaulted by soldiers. The Court applied the method used in Bueno Alves – intentionality, severe physical or mental suffering and purpose – and found that rape may constitute torture even if it is just one act that took place outside State facilities. Although it was proven that the authors were soldiers, it did not mention this as a necessary element of torture and declared that Mexico was responsible for the

---

152 *Case of Cotton Field v. Mexico*, para. 219.

153 *Ibidem*, para. 242 dealing with the obligation to respect personal integrity and not with that of ensuring the right.

154 *Case of Castro Castro v. Peru*, para. 309.

155 Among others, ICTR, *Case of Prosecutor v. Jean-Paul Akayes*, judgment of September 2, 1998, Case No. ICTR-96-4-T.

156 *Ibidem*, para. 311.

157 *Ibidem*, para. 312.

158 *Ibidem*, para. 292.

torture of the victim having violated Article 5(2) of the American Convention and Article 2 of the Torture Convention.[159] In the case of the Massacre of the Dos Erres, the Court found "that the lack of investigation of grave facts against humane treatment such as torture and sexual violence in armed conflicts and/or systematic patterns, constitutes a breach of the State's obligations in relation to grave human rights violations, which infringe non-revocable laws (*jus cogens*)". However, the Court did not find a violation of Article 5, but of Articles 8 and 25 of the American Convention, Articles 1, 6, and 8 of the Torture Convention and Article 7(b) of the Convention of Belém do Pará.[160] In the case of the Río Negro Massacres, the Court considered that "rape is an extremely traumatic experience that has severe consequences and causes great physical and mental harm that leaves the victim 'physically and emotionally humiliated'". Therefore, it can be understood that the severe suffering of the victim is inherent in rape, even when there is no evidence of physical injury or disease. Women who are victims of rape also experience severe psychological and even social harm and after-effects. In addition, the Court established that, in certain circumstances, rape could also constitute a form of torture of the victim.[161] This notwithstanding, the Court only found a violation of Articles 5(1) and of 11 of the American Convention[162] and of Article 7 of the Convention of Belém do Pará.[163] The violation of Article 11 was explained in terms of the concept of privacy that comprises, according to the Court, sexual life.[164] In the case of the Massacres of El Mozote and other nearby places, the Court declared that "[i]n order to characterize a rape as torture, it is necessary to analyze the intent, the severity of the suffering and the purpose of the act, taking into consideration the specific circumstances of each case". As can be seen, for the Court not all rapes amount to torture; other elements are needed to deserve that qualification. Here it stated that several international bodies recognized as a specific circumstance the existence of an armed internal conflict. The Court added that the purpose might be varied, from a symbolic means of humiliating the enemy or to punish and repress; it may, for example, be "intended to produce an effect on society".[165] Contrary to the judgment in Río Negro, the Court found that the rape suffered by women in El Mozote amounted to a violation of Articles 5(2) and 11. On that occasion, it did not mention a violation of Article 7 of the Convention of Belém do Para for the rape of the women, but it found a violation of Article 7 with respect to those who had been

159 *Case of Fernández Ortega v. Mexico*, paras. 117–128; and *Case of Rosendo Cantú v. Mexico*, paras. 107–121. Both cases examine with detail the issue of rape.

160 *Case of the Massacre of the Two Erres v. Guatemala*, paras. 152–153.

161 *Case of the Rio Negro Massacre v. Guatemala*, para. 132.

162 *Ibidem*, para. 135.

163 *Ibidem*, para. 324, para. 6.

164 *Ibidem*, para. 133.

165 *Case of the Massacres of El Mozote and nearby places v. El Salvador*, para. 164.

executed.[166] In the case of J. v. Peru, J. being one of the detainees in the case of the Castro Castro Prison handled by the Court previously, it was accepted that "the sexual abuse was a generalized practice that was surreptitiously tolerated, but in some cases openly permitted by the immediate superiors".[167] The Court found that the various ill-treatments to which Ms. J. was subjected violated Article 5(1) and (2) of the Convention. In the case of Espinoza Gonzáles, the Court found that State agents had used sexual violence as a strategy to combat a subversive group called MRTA (*Movimiento Revolucionario Tupac Amaru*). This amounted to sexual discrimination regarding her rights under Articles (5)(1) and (2) and 11 of the Convention.[168]

It is clear the Court has not been consistent in the qualification of rape. Sometimes it refers to it as torture; other times as degrading treatment. Yet, in other cases, it only finds rape as a violation of Article 5(1), not as a type of violation that falls under any of the prohibited conduct Article 5(2).

7. THE OBLIGATION TO INVESTIGATE, PROSECUTE, MAKE REPARATIONS AND PUNISH

37. The obligation to investigate, prosecute and punish those involved in actions prohibited under Article 5(2) of the American Convention has been developed by the Inter-American Court jointly with the obligations to guarantee the right to life. The obligation to investigate, prosecute and punish violations of Article 5 is similar to the obligation analyzed in Chapter 3 of this book on the right to life. As noted therein, the obligation to investigate, prosecute and punish the guilty parties should be exercised, according to the Court, *ex officio*; it constitutes a legal duty of the State, derived from the obligation to ensure, and does not depend on the activity of the victim or the victim's relatives for its compliance.[169] The Court reiterated this in the case of J., where it considered that the fact that the offense of rape was subject to a private right of action was no impediment to starting an *ex officio* investigation immediately.[170] In addition, it rejected the State's arguments as to not to investigate, because usually sexual violence complaints were false, there was no sexual violence context at the time and not all rapes or sexual violence caused verifiable physical lesions.[171] In the case of García Lucero, the State closed the criminal procedure investigating the

166 *Ibidem*, para. 400.3.
167 *Case of J. v. Peru*, para. 316.
168 *Case of Espinoza Gonzáles v. Peru*, para. 229.
169 See Chapter 2.
170 *Case of J. v. Peru*, para. 350.
171 *Ibidem*, para 352.

allegation of torture, because Mr. García had not appeared before the domestic court "by means of a complaint or any other action". The Court deemed this action as running counter to the State's obligation to investigate the events *ex officio*.[172] Furthermore, it stressed that to investigate torture it was essential to obtain information from the victim itself and also from "the physical and psychological forensic examinations performed on him or her".[173]

38. In the cases in which the Court has used the Inter-American Convention on Torture, it has applied Article 8 of that Convention to develop the obligation to investigate, prosecute and punish. In its pertinent part, Article 8 establishes the obligation for the State to ensure the right of alleged victims to have their case heard impartially; and the obligation to ensure that the State authorities proceed *ex officio* to carry out an investigation and launch, where pertinent, the corresponding criminal proceeding.

In the case of Villagrán Morales *et al.*, for example, the Court found Guatemala had violated the aforementioned Article 8. It stated that Guatemala had not taken "any formal decision to initiate a criminal investigation into the alleged perpetration of the crime of torture, neither did they investigate it in the practice", although there was "a great deal of concurring evidence on it".[174] The case of Cantoral Benavides included similar reasoning.[175] In the case of Bámaca Velásquez, the Court employed the same reasoning, but it added an obligation for the State to disclose the investigation publicly.[176]

In the systematic rape of women in the case of Dos Erres against Guatemala, the Court applied the same rationale as in cases of systematic violation of the rights to life. It held that:

> the lack of investigation of grave facts against humane treatment such as torture and sexual violence in armed conflicts and/or systematic patterns [...] constitutes a breach of the State's obligations in relation to grave human rights violations, which infringe non-revocable laws [...] (*jus cogens*) and generate obligations for the States [...] such as investigating and punishing those practices, in conformity with the American Convention and in this case in light of the CIPST and the Convention of Belém do Pará.[177]

In the case of Espinoza Gonzáles, the Court found fault in the way Ms. Espinoza had been interrogated, because there had been no consideration for her.[178] It also observed that the medical exam practiced on the victim took place three

172 *Case of García Lucero v. Chile*, para. 137.
173 *Ibidem*.
174 *Case of Villagrán Morales et al. v. Guatemala*, paras. 250–252.
175 *Case of Cantoral Benavides v. Peru*, paras. 188–190.
176 *Case of Bámaca Velásquez v. Peru*, judgment on reparations, paras. 77 and 87.
177 *Case of Two Erres v. Guatemala*, para. 140.
178 *Case of Espinoza Gonzáles v. Peru*, paras. 249 and 250.

weeks from the time the State knew of the sexual violence suffered by her.[179] The conduct of the State doctors was also incompatible with their obligations; in spite of the progressive deterioration of the physical conditions of Ms. Espinoza, shown by four physical exams, doctors did not make the condition known to the authorities and simply made the victim return to the same agents of DINCOTE who had perpetrated the torture and other ill-treatment.[180] Thus, the physicians had not been independent, which should have been ensured by the State and it was for the State to prove otherwise.[181] All this amounted to a violation of Articles 5 and 11, as well as a violation of Article 8.[182]

8. SEPARATION OF CONVICTED PERSONS FROM ACCUSED PERSONS (ARTICLE 5(4))

39. Paragraphs 4 and 5 of Article 5 of the American Convention establish certain requirements for detention: accused persons must be separated from convicted persons, and minors must be separated from adults; in addition, accused persons must be treated in a way that is appropriate to their status as individuals who have not been convicted. During discussion of the American Convention, the Government of Chile made an observation to the effect that this article is intended "to regulate a subject that seems more appropriate to entrust exclusively to the corresponding domestic criminal legal systems than to an International Convention on Human Rights", and suggested it be deleted.[183] It shared this position with the Dominican Republic, the United States and Mexico,[184] but the proposal was struck down. Reasons can be given for these paragraphs: mixing the accused with the convicted is unfair and detrimental to the dignity and integrity of the former; in the case of children and adolescents, their separation from the adults is designed to avoid placing them at risk of violations of their personal integrity.[185] Actually, national rules sometimes segregate not only convicts from accused persons, but separate the prisoners into categories according to the degree of violence they might have perpetrated. All this is in agreement with the obligation of States to ensure all human rights.

40. In order to be able to decide on whether the rules have been complied with properly in a particular case, the specific circumstances of the separation must

---

179 *Ibidem*, para. 257.
180 *Ibidem*, para. 259.
181 *Ibidem*, paras. 260 and 261.
182 *Ibidem*, para. 348 in its paragraphs 4, 5 and 6.
183 Inter-American Specialized Conference on Human Rights, San Jose, Costa Rica, November 7–22, 1969, *Minutes and Documents* (OEA/Ser.K/XVI/1.2), p. 39.
184 *Ibidem*, pp. 59, 94 and 175, respectively.
185 The Court in the Bulacio case made this latter point. *Case of Bulacio v. Argentina*, para. 136.

be examined. The Human Rights Committee, for example, opined in one case that the fact that accused and convicted persons were in the same building, but in separate sections, with the accused having contact with the convicted because some of the convicted served the food or cleaned the sections where the accused were being held, did not constitute a violation of Article 10(2)(a) of the ICCPR (similar to Article 5(4) of the American Convention).[186]

The Inter-American Commission has expressed particular concern over the requirements necessary to consider whether there is separation of accused from convicted persons.[187] Its interest is also reflected in the establishment of a Work Group on Detention Conditions in the Americas,[188] assigned the task of monitoring States' compliance with their international obligations in this area. The Court has dealt with the issue of separation, but has no case law to elucidate when a situation could be called one of proper separation.[189]

41. The American Convention also requires that accused persons be given separate treatment appropriate to their "status as unconvicted [sic] persons". It seems evident that an individual who is only accused enjoys the presumption of innocence established in Article 8(2) of the American Convention, and that this should have consequences for that person's treatment. Other consequences were mentioned by the Court in the case of Panchito López where accused and convicted persons were not separated and both received the same treatment. The Court held that "[t]his created a climate of insecurity, tension and violence in the Center".[190]

The American Convention says nothing on the separation of men from women, but it seems obvious that in order to protect the personal integrity of women, they should be separated from the men and guarded by personnel of their own sex. In this sense, in its report on the human rights situation in Mexico, published in 1998, the Inter-American Commission indicated:

---

186 HRC, *Larry James Pinkney v. Canada*, Communication 27/1978, report of November 25, 1977 (UN Doc. Supp. N°, 40 (A/37/40) (1982), p. 101).

187 See, for example, IACHR, Fifth Report on the human rights situation in Guatemala (OEA/Ser.L/V/II.111Doc.21 rev., April 6, 2001), Chapter VIII, paras. 34–45. This report details detention conditions with special reference to separation of the prison population, establishing criteria for separating the condemned from the accused and minors from adults, as well as for separating prisoners according to the seriousness of the crime. It also examines requirements regarding the physical and mental health of the prisoners and their sexual orientation. In addition, it highlights the lack of oversight of the physical condition of the individuals entering the penitentiary system and the lack of registry of inmates to allow for them to be properly separated. A second Report of the IACHR was published in 2011: Informe sobre los derechos humanos de las personas privadas de libertad (OEA/Ser.L/V/II.Doc. 64, December 1, 2011).

188 The Work Group was established during the 85th and 86th Periods of Sessions of the IACHR (see IACHR, 1996 Annual Report (OEA/Ser.L/V/II. 95 doc. 7 rev., March 14, 1997), p. 785).

189 See, for example, *Case of Tibi v. Ecuador.*

190 *Case of Panchito López v. Paraguay*, para. 169.

> Likewise, Article 18 of the Constitution [of Mexico] indicates that the women's prison must be separated from that of the men. However, this has not been effectively put into practice, with the presence of women in several male facilities having been confirmed. As alleged, this is a source of abuse and undesirable consequences.[191]

Regarding women, the Court made an extensive analysis of their treatment while in detention at a police hospital in the case of Castro Castro.

9. SPECIAL PROVISIONS FOR CHILDREN AND ADOLESCENTS (ARTICLE 5(5))

42. Article 5(5) of the American Convention regulates not only the separation of children and adolescents from adults, but also delves into their rights during legal proceedings, establishing that special juvenile courts are required before which the minors must be brought "as speedily as possible, so that they may be treated in accordance with their status as minors." The wording must be understood as requiring that the time period for ruling on the situation of children be less than the reasonable period of time mentioned in Article 8(1) of the American Convention for adults. This paragraph is obscure and may induce the reader to error. What does "treated" mean? A Uruguayan proposal during the Specialized Conference wished to change the word into "tried", which gave a more clear idea in the sense that speediness would refer to the definitive conclusion of a trial. However, this amendment was rejected and it is impossible to know the reasons why, if there are any, because they are not found in the text of the *travaux préparatoires*.[192] The term treatment is suggestive of the way in which children and adolescents were, or in some cases still are, handled when under control of a State facility even though they had not infringed any law. In that situation, there could be *treatment* without judicial processing or judgment, which means, among other things, deprivation of liberty. One cannot but conclude that this provision is understandable and right only if intended for those children and adolescents who must be submitted to a criminal trial. Today, the provisions of the American Convention and the provisions of the Convention on the Rights of the Child constitute a minimum to which States are bound, and therefore neither regulations nor proceedings can be applied that do not at least guarantee the basic institutions of due process established in those instruments. In that sense, the American Convention should be read as requiring the establishment of special courts for processing children and adolescents, application of the principle of legality, the presumption of innocence, the right to legal counsel, and the right to appeal a conviction, if the proceeding and

---

191 IACHR, Report on the human rights situation in Mexico (OEA/Ser.L/V/II.100 Doc. 7 rev. 1, September 24, 1998), para. 259.

192 Specialized Conference, *supra* n. 183, p. 176.

conviction are allowed according to the age of the accused.[193] With the entry into force of the Convention on the Rights of the Child and scientific progress in the field of psychology, it is possible to argue that children and adolescents need more than special courts. They also require specialized laws and, to apply them, specialized personnel who have been trained to communicate with children and adolescents, as proceedings for a criminal infraction must conclude with punishments and/or measures that promote the reintegration of the child and allow the child to "assum[e] [...] a constructive role in society."[194] The American Convention does not contain any provisions on these points, possibly because it was drafted near the end of the 1960s, when the legal status of members of this age group as rights holders had yet to be explicitly recognized, or even discussed.

43. The Inter-American Court plays an important role in integrating the provisions of the Convention on the Rights of the Child with the provisions of Article 5(5) of the American Convention and the interpretation of Article 19 of the same American Convention.[195] In the case of indigenous children, it used the Convention on the Rights of the Child to reiterate that the American Convention and the Convention on the Rights of the Child "are part of a very comprehensive international *corpus juris* for the protection of children that must be used [...] to establish the content and scope of the general provision defined in Article 19 of the American Convention".[196]

In the case of Mendoza *et al.*, César Alberto Mendoza, Lucas Matías Mendoza, Ricardo David Videla Fernández and Saúl Cristian Roldán Cajal, all of them children, were sentenced to life imprisonment and Claudio David Núñez, also a child, to reclusion for life.[197] The Court found violations of Article 5(2), (5) and (6) of the Convention. It admitted that the Convention does not include a list of punitive measures for children, but it thought it pertinent to apply the principle of proportionality, that is to say, to find a balance between the premises of the criminal reaction and the punishment itself, both as regards the individualization of the punishment and its judicial application. This means that the penalty must be adjusted to their status as minors and to the offense, and priority must be given "to reintegration with the family and/or society".[198] Imprisonment for life and perpetual reclusion are "radically disproportionate

193 *Case of Mendoza et al. v. Argentina*, para. 146. See also Article 40 of the Convention on the Rights of the Child, United Nations, adopted on November 20, 1989. The Convention entered into force on December 2, 1990, and only two States in the world are not parties to it: the United States and Somalia. See as well the United Nations Standard Minimum Rules for the Administration of Juvenile Justice ("the Beijing Rules"), adopted by Resolution 40/33 of the General Assembly of the United Nations on November 28, 1985, Article 7.

194 Convention on the Rights of the Child, Article 40.

195 *Case of Villagrán Morales et al. v. Guatemala*. paras. 192–196.

196 *Case of the Rio Negro Massacre v. Guatemala*, para. 142.

197 *Case of Mendoza et al. v. Argentina*, para. 1.

198 *Ibidem*, para. 151. Beware that the English formulation in this paragraph is wrong.

[and] fall within the sphere of torture and cruel, inhuman or degrading treatment."[199] The Court repeated here most of its findings in the case of the Río Negro Massacres, and pointed out that the children taken from that community during the Pacoxom massacre were forced to work in the homes of members of the Civil Self-defense Patrols. They had thus "suffered an increased impact on their mental integrity, the consequences of which remain until today".[200]

The separation of children from their families that occurred in the case of Contreras *et al.*, at a time when there was a systematic pattern of forced disappearances of children during the armed conflict in El Salvador, provoked serious effects on the personal integrity of the children. The separation was carried out by formal (a majority when abroad) or *de facto* adoptions; appropriations by soldiers, usually for domestic or agricultural tasks; sending them to orphanages; or the children remaining and growing up on military bases. In almost all these cases, the separation itself was aggravated by the treatment these children received from the adults who took them. This was a violation of Article 5.[201]

10. INDIVIDUALIZATION AND PURPOSE OF A SENTENCE (ARTICLE 5(3) AND (6))

44. Given that no one can be convicted and sentenced without due process that has led to a ruling issued based on unequivocal evidence that a person is guilty of a specific crime, it is clear that the sentence cannot transcend the criminal him or herself, as set forth in Article 5(3) of the American Convention. The Inter-American Court has not yet had an opportunity to examine cases in which a failure to comply with this provision has been alleged. The Commission ruled very tangentially on this in the case of Alan García v. Peru. Alan García's house was searched by the Peruvian military and the former Peruvian president's wife and young children were subjected to house arrest by the military. This was not a punishment, but only a human rights violation on the part of State agents. However, the Commission expressed that it wished to recall that "there is a special prohibition in the Convention that proscribes extending punishment to the family of the person alleged to be guilty of a crime." Without prejudice to this, the Commission did not find that Article 5(3) of the American Convention had been violated.[202]

199 *Ibidem*, para. 175.
200 *Case of the Río Negro Massacres v. Guatemala*, paras. 142–150.
201 *Case of Contreras et al. v. Guatemala*, paras. 54 and 100.
202 IACHR, *Case of Alan García v. Peru*, No. 11.006, Report 1/95, published in the 1994 Annual Report.

45. Article 5(6) of the American Convention establishes peremptorily that punishments consisting of deprivation of liberty "shall have as an essential aim the reform and social readaptation of the prisoners." The Convention does not give any guidance on how convicts must be treated in order to achieve this aim. It is highly probable that, first, there are many ways to do so and, second, that they change as the fields of criminal sociology and criminology develop. The Human Rights Committee has instructed States on this point, as there is a similar provision in the ICCPR, indicating that States must report to the Committee with "specific information concerning the measures taken to provide teaching, education and re-education, vocational guidance and training and also concerning work programmes for prisoners inside the penitentiary establishment as well as outside." The Committee also requires information on the existence or nonexistence of a post-incarceration support system.[203] The Inter-American Court has touched upon the subject in the case of Lori Berenson. In its judgment, it held that sometimes extremely harsh conditions of detention may become a form of cruel punishment and this is contrary to the "essential aim" of the penalty of imprisonment, as established in Article 5(6), "in other words 'the reform and social readaptation of the prisoners.' Judicial authorities must bear this in mind when applying or assessing the sanctions they establish."[204] There have been many cases where the condition of detention to serve a sentence are similar to those of Peru at the time, but the Court has not applied Article 5(6). In Pacheco Teruel, it also found that Honduras had "violated Article 5(6) of the Convention, by not allowing the inmates to carry out productive activities", because they considered them "to be members of the *Salvatrucha Mara*".[205]

In Mendoza *et al.*, examined above but from another point of view, the penalties of life imprisonment and perpetual reclusion applied to children "do not achieve the objective of the social reintegration of juveniles. Rather, this type of sentence entails the maximum exclusion of the child from society, so that it functions in a purely retributive sense, because the expectations of re-socialization are annulled to their highest degree". This was thus a violation of Article 5(6).[206]

Given the prison conditions in the region, it seems we are still far from full compliance with this provision.

---

203 HRC, General Comment No. 21, Article 10 (44th Period of Sessions, 1992, paras. 10 and11, reproduced in HRI/GEN /1/Rev.4, February 7, 2000, p. 133.

204 *Case of Lori Berenson v. Peru*, para. 101.

205 *Case of Pacheco Teruel v. Honduras*, para. 60. Salvatrucha Mara is one of the juvenile gangs in Honduras.

206 *Case of Mendoza et al. v. Argentina*, para. 167.

CHAPTER 5
RIGHT TO PERSONAL LIBERTY

Article 7. Right to Personal Liberty

1. *Every person has the right to personal liberty and security.*
2. *No one shall be deprived of his physical liberty except for the reasons and under the conditions established beforehand by the constitution of the State Party concerned or by a law established pursuant thereto.*
3. *No one shall be subject to arbitrary arrest or imprisonment.*
4. *Anyone who is detained shall be informed of the reasons for his detention and shall be promptly notified of the charge or charges against him.*
5. *Any person detained shall be brought promptly before a judge or other officer authorized by law to exercise judicial power and shall be entitled to trial within a reasonable time or to be released without prejudice to the continuation of the proceedings. His release may be subject to guarantees to assure his appearance for trial.*
6. *Anyone who is deprived of his liberty shall be entitled to recourse to a competent court, in order that the court may decide without delay on the lawfulness of his arrest or detention and order his release if the arrest or detention is unlawful. In States Parties whose laws provide that anyone who believes himself to be threatened with deprivation of his liberty is entitled to recourse to a competent court in order that it may decide on the lawfulness of such threat, this remedy may not be restricted or abolished. The interested party or another person in his behalf is entitled to seek these remedies.*
7. *No one shall be detained for debt. This principle shall not limit the orders of a competent judicial authority issued for nonfulfillment of duties of support.*

1. INTRODUCTION

1. Liberty of person is an important component for the region in the human rights catalogue. Its history reveals the States' misuse of their power to put a person in detention; the situation of imprisonment of people without cause, with no recourse to judicial review, reminds one of the need in the 17th century to pass the Petition of Rights in England. Some countries have had long periods

in a state of emergency that allowed all kinds of human rights violations, among which frequently that of the right to liberty of person. Even in times of democracy, the liberty of person was infringed continually. Criminal procedural laws did not comply with standards and judges did not fare better. The most frequent way of handling cases was to put the person allegedly having committed a crime in preventive detention, with absolute disregard for the presumption of innocence established in Article 8 and of the requirements of the Convention to order a detention. The Convention established a comprehensive set of rules and there was hope that these rules would be turned into domestic ones to put an end to abuse. However, while States were in the process of assimilating the changes, the increasing attention paid to safeguarding internal security, particularly in order to fight terrorism and drugs, has interfered with this aim. Because of this, in recent years the region has witnessed a social regression to the old forms of dealing with criminal offenses, forms that are incompatible with human rights in general and Article 7 in particular. This makes the firmness of the Court's jurisprudence on the matter an important element to counter the unwelcome effects of societies' unease.

2. The American Convention titles this right as the "right to personal liberty", but in its first paragraph it enshrines the right "to personal liberty *and security*". The concepts of both "liberty" and "security" can be understood more broadly than in the way that Article 7 of the Convention seems to suggest. The Court understands liberty in the following way: "[i]n its broadest sense, liberty is the ability to do or not do all that is lawfully allowed [...] the right of every person to organize his individual and social life in keeping with his own choices and beliefs, and in accordance with the law".[1] Liberty then is associated with the opportunity for self-determination – that is, for a person to live his or her life as he or she wishes, obviously as long as that person's actions are within the law. Liberty conceived thusly is the foundation of human rights; consequently it is associated with several human rights.[2] The concept of liberty that the Court handles is different. This is in agreement with Article 7 of the American Convention, which protects only one aspect of human liberty, the ability to move spatially without any limitations. Looking at it this way, the personal liberty found in Article 7 overlaps with the right enshrined in Article 22 of

1 *Case of Chaparro and Lapo v. Ecuador*, paras. 52–53.

2 As explained in Chapter 4, there is a close connection of liberty with Article 5 (personal integrity); in addition, there is a link with privacy, set forth in Article 11. See also how the Court links these concepts to formulate the right to identity, basing itself in Article 29 of the Convention. *Case of Contreras et al. v. El Salvador*, paras. 116–117. See also *Case of Atala v. Chile*, para. 162, where the Court states: "Thus, privacy includes the way in which the individual views himself and to what extent and how he decides to project this view to others". Actually, the catalogue of human rights constitutes specific protection of certain aspects of liberty such as for example the freedom to associate, to meet, and to express oneself.

the Convention: the right to move about the territory of a State in which one is legally present, as well as the right to freely leave any country, including one's own. No background helps draw the line between one right and the other. However, because Article 7 of the Convention puts practically all its emphasis on deprivation of liberty understood as imprisonment, one could conclude that the right protected in this provision is principally the right to not be confined to a space from where the person is prevented from leaving,[3] in principle like a prison.[4] However, even if it is not a small cell within a prison, the space should be limited, because – as said above – there are other ways of restricting personal liberty. Confinement within the limits of a city or village (*relegación*), for example, is a form of punishment established in criminal codes. This type of deprivation, in my view, would affect the right to move about in the territory of the State and thus be governed by Article 22. The Human Rights Committee's General Comment No. 35 also considers that "[d]eprivation of liberty involves more severe restriction of motion within a *narrower* space than mere interference with liberty of movement under article 12" (the equivalent of Article 22 of the Convention).[5]

That said, we must immediately make the caveat that the fact of its emphasis on prison does not mean that Article 7 of the Convention only protects against that type of deprivation of liberty. Any deprivation of liberty that involves the detention of a person in a limited space from which he or she cannot leave voluntarily falls within the realm of this right. In interpreting any human right, it is essential to look at its essence, the core that it protects, and not the conduct mentioned as possibly being in violation, as that conduct is only a reflection of what seemed likely to be in violation of the right at the time of drafting the catalogue. The interpretation of rights is dynamic. The wording of Article 7(2), which separates the right from the notion of "detention" or "imprisonment", reaffirms this position. The deprivations of liberty to which Article 7 would apply thus include every kind of confinement, whether for medical reasons, disciplinary reasons (including discipline within the armed forces), or others. Article 9 of the International Covenant on Civil and Political Rights (ICCPR),[6] which is a similar provision whose range of application was discussed during its drafting, has been interpreted in the same way, an interpretation that was later established by the Human Rights Committee. The Committee found that

---

3 The Human Rights Committee (HRC) interprets Article 9 of the ICCPR on personal freedom in a similar way. In its Unedited General Comment No. 35 (UGC 35) it states "[l]iberty of person concerns freedom from confinement of the body, not a general freedom of action" (para. I.3).

4 Manfred Nowak arrived at the same conclusion in his study on the rights found in the ICCPR. See M. Nowak, *U.N. Covenant on Civil and Political Rights. CCPR Commentary*, N.P. Engel Publisher, Kehl/Strasbourg/Arlington, 1993, p. 160.

5 HRC, UGC 35, para. 5.

6 International Covenant on Civil and Political Rights (ICCPR), adopted by General Assembly Resolution 2200A (XXI) of December 16, 1966. Entry into force on March 23, 1976.

Article 9 protects from "all deprivations of liberty, whether in criminal cases or in other cases such as, for example, mental illness, vagrancy, drug addiction, educational purposes, immigration control, etc."[7] Because of this position, the Committee has also recognized that the confinement of women to their homes and prohibiting them from leaving their homes without permission from their husbands, authorized by customary law in certain Muslim countries, falls under the umbrella of Article 9 of the ICCPR.[8]

Since Article 7(2) regulates deprivation of liberty in the context of a criminal proceeding, those who interpret and apply Article 7 to a different kind of deprivation of liberty should use the rules for criminal proceedings as a guide.[9]

3. The European Court holds that the right to personal security must be understood "in the context of physical liberty".[10] In the words of Fawcett, "liberty and security are the two sides of the same coin; if personal liberty spells actual freedom of the movement of the person, security is the condition of being protected by law in that freedom".[11] The European Court – although not in reference to legality but rather to arbitrariness – has also made the point when ruling that the right to personal security translates into a State obligation to prohibit arbitrary detentions and arrests.[12] In contrast, the Human Rights Committee has taken a different position. In the case of Delgado Páez v. Colombia, the victim alleged that he had been dismissed from his job due to his religious beliefs, and had later received death threats that forced him to leave the country. The Committee found that Colombia had violated the petitioner's right to personal security, rejecting the idea that the fact of the right to personal security being in the same paragraph as the right to personal liberty necessarily

7 The General Comment widens the examples as follows: police custody, "*arraigo*", remand detention, imprisonment after conviction, house arrest, administrative detention, involuntary hospitalization, institutional custody of children, and confinement to a restricted area of an airport, and also includes being involuntarily transported. In addition it mentions solitary confinement or physical restraining devices on a person already detained as falling in the field of Article 9. See HRC, UGC 35, *supra* n. 3, para. 5.

8 HRC, General Comment No. 28, (Article 3: Equality of rights between men and women), 68th Period of Sessions (2000), HRI/GEN/1/Rev.5, April 26, 2001, para. 14; *Concluding Observations: Sudan*, CCPR A/53/40 (1998), para. 125.

9 In the European system, see European Court of Human Rights, *Van der Leer v. the Netherlands*, A 170-A, para. 27, cited by D.J. Harris, M. O'Boyle and C. Warbrick, *Law of the European Convention on Human Rights*, Butterworths, London/Dublin/Edinburgh, 1995, p. 129. In the system of the ICCPR, see M. Nowak, *supra* n. 4, p. 174.

10 *Ibidem*, p. 103, citing the European Commission and the Committee of Ministers in the case of *East African Asians v. United Kingdom* (1973) 3 EHRR 76, p. 89. See also European Court of Human Rights, *Hajduová v. Slovakia*, Application No. 2660/03, judgment of November 30, 2010, para. 54.

11 J.E. Fawcett, *The application of the European Convention on Human Rights*, Clarendon Press, Oxford, 1987, p. 70.

12 D.J. Harris *et al.*, *supra* n. 9, p. 103, citing the *case of Bozano v. France*, A111, paras. 54 and 60 (1986).

meant that the right "arises only in the context of arrest and detention". The Committee added that:

> It cannot be the case that, as a matter of law, States can ignore known threats to the life of persons under their jurisdiction, just because he or she is not arrested or otherwise detained. Given that States parties are under an obligation to take reasonable and appropriate measures to protect them, an interpretation of article 9 which would allow a State party to ignore threats to the personal security of non-detained persons within its jurisdiction would render totally ineffective the guarantees of the Covenant.[13]

In its General Comment No. 35, the HRC limits security to protection "against intentional infliction of bodily or mental injury, regardless of whether the victim is detained or non-detained".[14] The reason for this may be that the ICCPR does not have in its catalogue a "right to personal integrity", as the American Convention does, but only the prohibition of torture and inhuman, cruel or degrading treatment or punishment.

In the inter-American system, the Convention's preparatory work does not shed any light on the scope of the concept of "security". In the Specialized Conference, the original text of this article only protected physical liberty.[15] In the discussion in Commission I, the delegate from Ecuador introduced the current wording, with no additional justification for it appearing in the minutes. That wording was approved without debate.[16] Later, as revealed in the final report on Commission I, a workgroup was formed that repeated Ecuador's idea in the sense that the right enshrined was a right to liberty and personal security.[17] This text remained in place until the end of the conference. The concept of security raises problems. To be "secure" means to be free from danger, free from risk; this meaning seems to place the right to security more in the area of humane treatment and life than that of personal liberty. In the American Declaration, Article I establishes that "[e]very human being has the right to life, liberty and the security of his person". This could be understood as the enshrinement of three different rights but seems to have been understood differently when

---

13 *W. Delgado Páez v. Colombia*, para. 5.5. This case law of the Committee has been repeated in several other cases: See HRC, *Peter Chiiko Bwalya v. Zambia*, Communication 314/1988, decision of July 14, 1993 (A/48/40 (Vol. II), 1993); *Angel N. Olo Bahamonde v. Equatorial Guinea*, Communication 468/1991, decision of October 1993 (A/49/40 (Vol. II), 1994); *Agnes N'Goya, on behalf of her husband, Katombe L. Eshishimbi v. Zaire*, Communication 542/1993, decision of March 25, 1996 (A/51/40 (Vol. I), 1997); *Carlos Dias and Carolina de Fatima da Silva v. Angola*, Communication 711/1996, decision of March 20, 2000 (A/55/40 (Vol. II), 2000); and *Rodger Chongwe v. Zambia*, Communication 821/1998, decision of October 25, 2000 (A/56/40 (Vol. II), 2001).

14 HRC, UGC 35, *supra* n. 3, para. 7.

15 See Inter-American Specialized Conference on Human Rights, San Jose, Costa Rica, November 7–22, 1969, *Minutes and Documents* (OEA/Ser.K/XVI/1.2), p. 16.

16 *Ibidem*, pp. 180 and 185.

17 *Ibidem*, p. 297.

reproduced in the American Convention.[18] Despite any issues with regard to its location, the right to personal security is set forth in Article 7 of the Convention together with the right to personal liberty. This raises the question of whether it is a right that is distinct from the right to personal liberty, and if so, if it is exclusively linked thereto – that is, if it should be understood only with regard to personal liberty. On the former question, rules of interpretation indicate that the interpreter must try to give an *effet utile* to a provision's content, for which reason one could suppose that the right to personal security ought to be different than the right to personal liberty.

The Court has connected personal security with personal liberty in the cases of Villagrán Morales *et al.* and Bámaca Velásquez, where it indicated that "by protecting personal liberty, a safeguard is also provided for both the physical liberty of the individual and his personal safety."[19] From this, one could perhaps infer that in speaking of personal security in the context of an absence of guarantees, that term is used only in reference to the physical integrity of those deprived of liberty. In the case of Chaparro and Lapo, as I explained, the Court had referred to the concept of liberty. Security was defined as "the absence of interferences that restrict or limit liberty beyond what is reasonable."[20] The Court adds in the following paragraph that "[s]ecurity should also be understood as protection against all unlawful or arbitrary interference with physical liberty."[21] This indicates that the Court will restrict itself to applying Article 7 with regard to security in the context of a deprivation of liberty. Even though this is the Court's position, Article 1 of the Convention directs States to protect threatened individuals from an imminent and real threat to the right to life, the right to humane treatment and the right to personal liberty.[22] I would affirm that a very broad concept of "safety" can be derived from the obligation to ensure, a concept that goes beyond the rights mentioned;[23] in light of the Court's case law concerning these rights, the existence of an autonomous right to security appears irrelevant.

---

18 Article 5 of the European Convention on Human Rights, adopted in 1950, likewise establishes that everyone has the right to liberty and personal security, and that Article 9 of the ICCPR, adopted in 1966, repeats that same wording. However, the source of both of these is Article 3 of the Universal Declaration of Human Rights, which also makes reference to three rights: life, liberty and security.

19 *Case of Villagrán Morales et al. v. Guatemala*, para. 135 and *Case of Bámaca Velásquez v. Guatemala*, para. 141.

20 *Case of Chaparro and Lapo v. Ecuador*, paras. 52–53.

21 *Ibidem*, para. 53.

22 See, for example, *Case of Cantoral Benavides v. Peru*, para. 102 and *Case of Hilaire, Benjamin, Constantine et al. v. Trinidad and Tobago*, paras. 167–169. More about this in Chapters 2 and 3.

23 The idea of a broad definition of security is reinforced historically with Article 8 of the Constitution of the Republic of France of June 24, 1793, cited by Nowak: "*La sûreté consiste dans la protection, acordée par la société à chacun de ses membres pour la conservation de sa personne, de ses droits et de ses propriétés.*" He argues that in the French Revolution, law had a horizontal effect. That is, the State was required to protect citizens from third-party interference in their rights (M. Nowak, *supra* n. 4, p. 162).

4. Article 7(1) sets forth a general right to personal liberty. The following paragraphs have the purpose of strictly regulating the possibility of restraining the right to personal freedom within a criminal proceeding. Like any restriction, the Convention requires a compatible aim, conduciveness to achieve the aim, absence of a less burdensome alternative, and proportionality. If the deprivation of liberty is due to a pending trial, there are two additional requirements: compliance with the principle of legality and presumption of innocence.[24]

I will examine the Convention's requirements to carry out an arrest, the act of apprehension itself, as well as to order preventive detention, that is keeping in detention a person who has been arrested. In a different section, I will deal with the application of Article 7 to children, migrants and migrant children, because their situation has deserved specific attention from the Court.

2. GENERAL REQUIREMENTS: LEGALITY AND ABSENCE OF ARBITRARINESS (ARTICLE 7(2) AND (3))

5. After laying out the rights that it enshrines, Article 7 of the American Convention establishes in paragraph 2 a general provision to the effect that no one shall be deprived of physical liberty except for the causes and conditions established beforehand by State constitutions or by laws put in place under those constitutions. The following paragraph stipulates that no one shall be subjected to arbitrary arrest or imprisonment. Thus from one paragraph to the next, the terminology changes. Paragraph 2 uses a broad expression – "deprived of [...] physical liberty" – indicating that any type of physical deprivation of liberty committed by any agent is covered by the provision; in contrast, paragraph 3 refers to "arrest or imprisonment". The minutes do not provide an explanation, but it is highly probable that the difference does not correspond to any fundamental reason but is simply stylistic. Obviously, it seems impossible to draw therefrom the conclusion that all physical deprivations of liberty require a basis in law, but that only arrest or imprisonment[25] are required to be carried out non-arbitrarily. No restriction on human rights – and the deprivation of liberty is a restriction – can be arbitrary. Consequently, the prohibition on arbitrariness applies to all forms of deprivation of liberty.[26] Article 7 does not clearly distinguish the requirements for an arrest from that for preventive detention. The Court usually does not make a separation. For this reason, I will treat them together and refer to one or the other specifically when needed.

---

24 *Case of López Alvarez v. Honduras*, paras. 67–68.

25 Nor are there elements for clarifying what is meant by "detention" and by "imprisonment".

26 The explanation might seem superfluous, but it is not far-fetched, if one examines the very literal and textual rules of interpretation taught in Latin American law schools.

2.1. LEGALITY

6. The requirements of legality imply the need for States to have regulations with the status of law[27] governing everything that has to do with deprivation of liberty, from the grounds permitting it, to the proceeding to which the action of depriving a person of liberty must be subject. The Court has clearly indicated that Article 7 has both a material and a formal aspect. The material aspect means that "no one shall be deprived of his physical liberty, except for reasons, cases or circumstances specifically established by law", while according to the formal aspect this deprivation can only be carried out "under strict conditions established beforehand by law".[28] The legal provisions are to be domestic and will be ruled in general by the legal order in each country, without prejudice to which they must meet the requirements established in other paragraphs of Article 7 of the Convention and therefore may be examined by the Court for compatibility with the Convention.

In order to carry out an arrest, the national law must contain the procedural aspects that make the arrest compatible with the Convention. The order to arrest must come from a judicial authority that has the competence to issue it. In several cases, the Court has held that a military judge or tribunal has no competence to try civilians and therefore cannot order arrest warrants.[29] A judicial process that is vitiated from the beginning, as in the case of Yvon Neptune which was initiated by a judge who was incompetent, makes the arrest and subsequent detention illegal.[30] This does not prevent a person from being arrested, if the domestic court so allows, when caught *in flagrante delicto* even if the other conditions for the procedure are not met, such as a requirement for an arrest warrant issued by a competent authority; that of course also has limitations. In general, notwithstanding differences in the domestic law of States, to detain *in flagrante delicto* means to catch a person in the very act of committing what at first sight is a criminal offense.[31] This requires a perception that is not always right. Cases of arbitrary arrest handled by the Court seem to have been blatant violations of the meaning of "flagrant". In the case of the Gómez Paquiyaury

---

27 Article 7 refers to the law both in its formal sense and its material sense, which agrees with the meaning that the Inter-American Court attributes the expression "law" in its Advisory Opinion 6, interpreting Article 30 of the American Convention. The Court found that law means "a general legal norm tied to the general welfare, passed by democratically elected legislative bodies established by the Constitution, and formulated according to the procedures set forth by the constitutions of the States Parties for that purpose" (*OC-6/86*, operative paragraphs).

28 *Case of Gangaram Panday v. Suriname*, para. 47; *Case of Bámaca Velásquez v. Guatemala*, para. 139; *Case of Durand and Ugarte v. Peru*, para. 85; *Case of Juan Humberto Sánchez v. Honduras*, para. 78; *Case of Maritza Urrutia v. Guatemala*, para. 65.

29 On military courts, see the Chapter 6 on due process.

30 *Case of Yvon Neptune v. Haiti*, paras. 99–100.

31 If domestic law extends the notion of flagrancy, it should be the Court's task to examine whether the definition falls within the requirements for the protection of personal liberty set forth in the Convention.

brothers, the Court found that they had been detained while walking along the street; in the case of García Asto and Urcesino Ramírez, one was arrested while waiting for the bus and the other when he was at home, sick.[32] The situation of these two victims is particular: they were subjected to trial before faceless judges and the trials were annulled, but their detention remained without any further judicial order until the new trials started, which took over a month for one and over two months for the other.[33] The reasons invoked for maintaining the detention were that they were presumed to be terrorists.[34] As international supervisory bodies do not in general have jurisdiction to interpret domestic laws, with this being a task normally left to domestic courts, it is for the latter to decide first whether a detention is legal. However, this does not prevent an international body from deciding in the case of a flagrant violation of domestic regulations that a detention was "illegal" – that is, did not take place in accordance with the regulations of the State in which it was carried out.[35]

Once before the Court, if a victim alleges that a detention was unlawful, the State must present evidence before the international body that, in contrast to what the alleged victim says, the person who carried out the detention was authorized by law to do so, or that the standard procedures for depriving someone of liberty were followed. Should the State fail to do so, it will be assumed that the action was not legal.[36]

7. A curious application by the Court of the requirement of legality of Article 7 is the case of Osorio Rivera and family. In spite of the arrest having been legal, the Court contended the legality. The Court considered that "the transfer of Mr. Osorio Rivera, deprived of liberty, to the Cajatambo Counter-subversive Base without being brought before the competent authority or his entry into the Base being registered evidently constituted an abuse of power" since the purpose was not to bring him to a tribunal "but to execute him or make him disappear".[37] The reference here to paragraph 124 of the judgment does not appear to me to be a justification for presuming the motive behind the arrest. There are other reasons to prove that this detention was the beginning of a disappearance.[38] The violation of Article 7 could also have been based on noncompliance with Article 7(5).

32 *Case of García Asto and Urcesino Ramírez v. Peru*, paras. 108 and 269.

33 *Case of García Asto and Urcesino Ramírez v. Peru*, paras. 97(90) and 97(91), 124 and 137. See also *Case of La Cantuta v. Peru*, para. 109 and *Case of Esué Zapata v. Colombia*, para. 86.

34 These two cases are an example of what happened in the time of Alberto Fujimori when many cases on terrorism or aggravated terrorism were carried out without granting any rights to the accused.

35 *Case of Castillo Páez v. Peru*, para. 56. See also *Case of Suárez Rosero v. Ecuador*, para. 44; *Case of Villagrán Morales et al. v. Guatemala*, para. 132; *Case of Juan Humberto Sánchez v. Honduras*, para. 79; and *Case of Cesti Hurtado v. Peru*, paras. 140–143.

36 *Case of Gangaram Panday v. Suriname*, paras. 50 and 51.

37 *Case of Osorio Rivera and family v. Peru*, para. 167.

38 See for example *ibidem*, para. 56.

2.2. ABSENCE OF ARBITRARINESS

8. Deprivation of liberty not only requires that the principle of legality be adhered to but also demands an absence of arbitrariness, both in the law regulating deprivation of liberty and in the conduct of the agents applying it. The concept of arbitrariness is assessed according to not only domestic law or considerations adapted solely to the national perception of "what is arbitrary", but also to the interpretation of the international supervisory body. The discussion of this condition during the drafting of the ICCPR, which contains a similar provision, led some of the drafters to equip arbitrariness with elements of injustice, unpredictability, lack of reasonability, capriciousness and lack of proportionality.[39] In the case of Van Alphen v. the Netherlands, the Committee found that a detention following a legal arrest must be reasonable and necessary under all circumstances, a condition not met in this case. It therefore declared that the Netherlands had violated Article 9 of the ICCPR.[40]

9. The Inter-American Court addressed arbitrariness in Gangaram Panday. It ruled that the provision preventing arbitrary detention or imprisonment implies that no one can be subjected to them "for reasons and by methods which, although classified as legal, could be deemed to be incompatible with the respect for the fundamental rights of the individual because, among other things, they are *unreasonable, unforeseeable or lacking in proportionality*".[41] In the case of Cantoral Benavides, the Court ruled that Article 7 of the American Convention had been violated because the State had subjected the victim to arbitrary preventive detention. It based this ruling on the fact that the victim remained in prison at the order of military judges – after the Special Tribunal of the Supreme Council of Military Justice had acquitted him definitively – in order for the petitioner to be brought to trial for the same facts, this time in a civilian court.[42] In the case of Juan Humberto Sánchez, the arbitrariness was derived from the fact that the detentions to which he had been subjected "come within the framework of abuse of power" corresponding to a pattern of human rights violations taking place at that time.[43] A thorough, detailed description of what the Court means by arbitrary is found in the case of Chaparro and Lapo, who were in preventive detention, by repeating the idea that all the requirements for

39 M. Nowak, *supra* n. 4, p. 172.

40 HRC, *Alphen v. the Netherlands*, No. 305/1988, cited by M. Nowak, *supra* n. 4, p. 173. See also: HRC, *Spakmo v. Norway*, No. 631/1995, A/55/40 vol. II (November 5, 1999) 22, para. 6.3; HRC, *Gorji-Dinka v. Cameroon*, No. 1134/2002, A/60/40 vol. II (March 17, 2005) 194, para. 5.1; and HRC, *Marques v. Angola*, No. 1128/2002, A/60/40 vol. II (March 29, 2005) 181, para 6.1.

41 *Case of Gangaram Panday v. Suriname*, para. 47 (emphasis added).

42 *Case of Cantoral Benavides v. Peru*, para. 75. A similar case is that of *Loayza Tamayo v. Peru*, para. 54.

43 *Case of Juan Humberto Sánchez v. Honduras*, para. 80.

any restriction of a right must be met. The principle on which it is based is that the sacrifice inherent in the restriction of the right to liberty is not exaggerated or excessive compared to the advantages obtained from this restriction and the achievement of the purpose sought.[44]

In short, a deprivation of liberty will be arbitrary when it does not comply with the requirements ordered by the Convention to make an interference with any right compatible with the treaty. In this case, the deprivation of liberty, carried out in accordance with the law, must seek to achieve an objective that is permitted by the Convention and must be "necessary in a democratic society". That is, it must be conducive to achieving the objective sought and be proportional,[45] and there must not be any other measure for achieving the objective than the deprivation of liberty. A lack of one of these elements would make a deprivation of liberty arbitrary. It will be shown below that arbitrariness usually results from the mistakes committed by the judiciary regarding the grounds invoked for arrest or preventive detention.

3. GROUNDS FOR ARRESTING AND FOR KEEPING A PERSON IN DETENTION (ARTICLE 7(2))

10. The reasons for which one can be deprived of liberty or be kept in prison must be established in the Constitution of each State or in laws enacted in accordance with the Constitution, meaning that they will be determined by the State. In the European Convention, states do not have this possibility, as Article 5 thereof establishes exhaustively the reasons for which a person can be detained.[46] Although States may decide the grounds for depriving a person of liberty, their power is not discretional, because deprivation of liberty may not be arbitrary.[47] To arrest, there must be a reasonable suspicion that the person detained has in one way or another participated in a criminal act. In the case of Chaparro and Lapo, the Court found the suspicion necessary to make an arrest has to be based on specific facts, not "mere conjectures or abstract intuitions". As a consequence,

---

44 *Case of Chaparro and Lapo v. Ecuador*, para. 93. In the same sense, see *Argúelles et al. v. Argentina*, para. 120.

45 Proportionality is emphasized, for example, in the *case of Palamara v Chile*, para. 67.

46 One attempt to establish specifically in the Convention the cases in which one could be deprived of liberty, put forward by the Brazilian delegation, did not receive support, with the more generic wording being preferred. (See Specialized Conference, *supra* n. 15, pp. 122–123 and 189–185).

47 For example, from this point of view, the so-called "detention for being suspicious" – that is, the detention of someone who without committing a crime and without an arrest warrant is detained because a police officer believes that the person may have "bad intentions", in the words of Article 260 of the Chilean Criminal Procedural Code prior to its reform, is not compatible with the Convention.

"the State should not detain someone to investigate him".[48] In Barreto Leiva the Court insists that an arrest order must be "based on sufficient circumstantial evidence".[49] In this sense a "hold" – "that is, a restriction of physical liberty" – of any individual whose criminal record "[may need] to be known [...] under circumstances that justify this", as the Argentinian law provides, does not comply with this requirement. The provision allows "the police to interfere with the physical liberty of persons in a way that is unpredictable and therefore arbitrary".[50]

11. Once the person arrested is brought before the judge, the judicial authority may decide to keep the person in detention during the proceedings. In order for the detention to be compatible with the Convention, specific reasons or grounds have to be invoked; the grounds derive from the text itself of paragraph 5 of the Article under analysis: liberty can "be subject to guarantees to assure his appearance for trial". Consequently, detention can be ordered when there is a risk that the person will not appear at the trial if released. Because one of the objectives of a criminal proceeding is to be able to investigate the facts without interference, it also seems possible to keep in detention a person who could be reasonably expected to go into hiding or alter the evidence of a crime if released – that is, generally block the judicial proceeding.[51] Pre-trial detention therefore cannot help but have procedural aims.[52] In Chaparro and Lapo the Court insists on this position. It clarifies that "deprivation of liberty of the accused cannot be based on general preventive or special preventive purposes, which could be attributed to the punishment, but [...] can only be based on a legitimate purpose, which is: to ensure that the accused does not prevent the proceedings from being conducted or elude the system of justice.[53] In the case of Argüelles *et al.*, the Court insists that the "procedural danger" cannot be presumed; it must be verified. Certainly, if there are several detainees, the conduct of one does not constitute a reason to keep the rest in detention.[54] Similar to arrest, an order of preventive detention, or pre-trial detention, cannot be given without a

---

48 *Case of Chaparro and Lapo v. Ecuador*, para. 103.

49 *Barreto Leiva v. Venezuela*, para. 115.

50 *Case of Torres Millacura et al. v. Argentina*, para. 79.

51 Regarding interference with justice, see D.J. Harris *et al.*, *supra* n. 9, p. 140. In the context of the ICCPR, see, *inter alia*, HRC, *A. v. Australia*, Communication 560/93, decision of April 3, 1997, A/52/40 (Vol. II), Annex VI, sect. L (pp. 125–146), para. 9(2); *W.E.B. v. the Netherlands*, Communication 432/90, decision on inadmissibility of October 23, 1992, para. 6(3); and *Hill and Hill v. Spain*, Communication 526/93, decision of April 2, 1997, A/52/40 (Vol. II), Annex VI, sect. B (pp. 5–21), para. 12(3).

52 A. Bovino, "El encarcelamiento preventivo en los tratados de derechos humanos", in M. Abregú and C. Courtis (eds.), *La aplicación de los tratados sobre derechos humanos por los tribunales locales*, Centro de Estudios Legales y Sociales (CELS), 1997, pp. 442–445.

53 *Case of Chaparro and Lapo v. Ecuador*, para. 103. See also *Case of Barreto Leiva v. Venezuela*, para. 111.

54 *Case of Argüelles et al. v. Argentina*, para. 127.

clear statement of the reasons the judge is invoking to issue it. If there are no grounds given for ordering preventive detention, there will be arbitrariness; this was made clear in the cases of Palamara and of López Alvarez. In the first, the Court held that "in order for the presumption of innocence not to be disregarded when issuing measures that restrict personal liberty, it is necessary for the State to provide grounds therefor and evidence that the applicable requirements under the Convention are met in each specific case."[55] In the second, the Court found there was a requirement "that the preventive detention be justified in each specific case, through the elements that concurred in the same".[56] Of course, the mere mention of the provision in the Code of Criminal Procedure authorizing detention will not be enough.[57]

The reasons to keep a person in detention are limited. In the case of Barreto Leiva the Court held that the only reasons to keep a person in detention were "to ensure that he will not impede the efficient development of an investigation and that he will not evade justice".[58] The European Court has accepted other reasons for keeping a person in detention, such as the necessity of preventing crime and preserving the public order.[59] This seems highly doubtful as far as its compatibility with international law goes: judges are not placed in the State apparatus to prevent crime but to decide whether an action constitutes a criminal offense.

Given that liberty is the general rule, the risk of absconding or altering the evidence must be imminent and real. Elements for deciding whether there is a risk of escape can include, for example, whether the accused has a stable work relationship in the country, a family, or property, or other similar considerations. Should it be proven that the risk exists, it must also be proven that it is not possible to counteract that risk in any way other than deprivation of liberty. Therefore, when assessing whether there is a risk of flight, the first alternative the judge must examine is the possibility of ensuring appearance at trial through another kind of guarantee. This could include bail or, for example, confining the person within the country – which constitutes a limitation that is less burdensome than deprivation of liberty and that is permitted by Article 22(3) of the Convention. It is possible to require other elements in order to prevent manipulation of evidence. These other elements would depend on the type of evidence whose protection is sought. The Court had the opportunity to examine this issue again in the case of Norín *et al.*, as in Chile domestic law allows preventive detention when the detainee presents "a risk for the security of society". The Court considered that this formulation

55 *Case of Palamara v Chile*, para 198.

56 *Case of López Alvarez v. Honduras*, para. 82.

57 *Case of Palamara v. Chile*, para. 205.

58 *Case of Barreto Leiva v. Venezuela*, para. 121. See also *López Alvarez v. Honduras*, paras. 60 and 81.

59 D.J. Harris *et al.*, *supra* n. 9, pp. 140–142.

could have various interpretations that could be used for legitimate aims or for non-precautionary aims. If it were to be interpreted in the latter sense, the Court insists that preventive detention is exceptional, temporal, must be proportional and possible to order only under strict necessity in order to secure the success of the proceedings and cannot become a penalty in advance of the conviction. This would contravene the presumption of innocence.[60] The Court considered the declaration of a Chilean expert in this regard, who explained that the Chilean courts as a rule interpreted the provision as it had done in Norín *et al.* and the circumstances that judges invoked to order the preventive detention were the seriousness of the penalty assigned to the offense and the nature thereof. However, the Court considered that the provision did not prevent the judge from using other criteria that would allow him to apply the provision for procedural aims and consequently, the national law in itself did not violate the Convention. It was the tribunal applying the law committed the violation of Article 7 but not the Chilean legislation,[61] because the fact that the provision was always interpreted and applied for non-procedural measures was insufficient justification.[62] I find this a peculiar decision.

4. PROCEDURAL REQUIREMENTS FOR AN ARREST OR FOR PREVENTIVE DETENTION

12. The importance of the right to personal freedom and the serious effects of deprivation of that personal freedom have led to the emergence of numerous declarations or resolutions from the United Nations developing the basic rights established in treaties to which the Court resorts for its decisions. Among them are the Minimum Rules for the Treatment of Prisoners,[63] the Body of Principles for the Protection of All Persons under Any Form of Detention or Imprisonment,[64] and the Rules of the United Nations for the Protection of Minors Deprived of Their Liberty.[65] These principles and rules attempt to construct the rights with precision, and international supervisory bodies are incorporating obligations arising therefrom as they interpret the corresponding provisions on deprivation of liberty.

---

60 *Case of Norín et al. v. Chile*, para. 361.

61 *Ibidem*, paras. 362–364.

62 *Ibidem*, para. 352.

63 Adopted by the First United Nations Congress on the Prevention of Crime and the Treatment of Offenders, held at Geneva in 1955, and approved by the Economic and Social Council by its Resolutions 663 C (XXIV) of July 31, 1957 and 2076 (LXII) of May 13, 1977.

64 Adopted by the UN General Assembly in Resolution 43/173 of December 9, 1988.

65 Adopted by the UN General Assembly in Resolution 45/113 of December 14, 1990.

13. Paragraphs 4 and 5 of Article 7 of the Convention establish the procedural requirements for carrying out a detention or a *retention*. The preparatory work does not explain the possible differences between these two forms of deprivation of liberty; it only mentions that the word "retained" was added to paragraphs 4 and 5 of Articles 7 during the first full session of the Conference, but it does not indicate the origin of the amendment nor the reasons for it.[66] This means that one can only speculate as to the meaning of each of these concepts, with the additional complication that the terms "detention" (*detención*), "prison", "imprisonment", "retention" (*retención*) and others used throughout Article 7 of the Convention have different meanings in the legal language of the different States Parties.[67] The variety of nomenclature makes any attempt to specify the meaning of the two concepts found in paragraph 4 useless. The addition of the word "retained" in this paragraph can only be understood as an attempt to broaden the protection to another form of deprivation of liberty, likely derived from the drafters' knowledge of the variety of the language used in this field.[68] This interpretation is backed by a request from the Panama delegation that the record show that it understands the word "detention" to be a synonym for deprivation of liberty; and finds that the remedy for demanding the right to freedom should include the case of those who have been convicted should that conviction have been illegal. Protection should also be given to those who have been convicted without the guarantee of due process.[69] No one objected to Panama's position, thus it should be understood that all forms of deprivation of liberty, including deprivation of liberty through a domestic court judgment not compatible with the Convention (which was what seemed to have been that delegation's concern) is included in the concepts of detention and retention.

There are various procedural requirements. Although one could argue that conditions for arrest procedures are clear, careful examination shows that interpretive work in order to specify them point by point is indispensable. The purpose of these requirements is to protect individuals from arrest and later illegal or arbitrary preventive detention. Thus, their interpretation must take this idea as a guiding principle. From what has been said, it is clear that arrests and detention must be individualized. Mass detention[70] or collective detention or

66 Specialized Conference, *supra* n. 15, p. 442.

67 For a comparison of legislation, see *Question of human rights of all persons under any form of detention or imprisonment. Report of Working Group on Arbitrary Detention*, E/CN.4/1997/4, December 17, 1996, section 4.

68 See in *ibidem* the considerations of the Work Group on Arbitrary Detention addressing the problem of deciding on which elements could distinguish between the terms "detention" and "imprisonment".

69 Specialized Conference, *supra* n. 15, p. 443 (emphasis added).

70 Such as in the case of Bulacio, arrested with many others at a disco, or in the case of Torres Millacura, disappeared. See *Case of Bulacio v. Argentina*, para. 137 and *Case of Torres Millacura v. Argentina*, para. 76.

arrest,[71] apparently made for purposes of identification, do not comply with the Convention.

14. The obligations established for States in Article 7 of the Convention can be suspended during an emergency, given that this provision is not included in Article 27(2) of the American Convention. Without prejudice to this, the Court has reiterated that with regard to this right, as with others, the suspension of obligations must not go beyond what is strictly necessary, given that:

> [t]he limits imposed upon the actions of a State come from "the general requirement that in any state of emergency there be appropriate means to control the measures taken, so that they are proportionate to the needs and do not exceed the strict limits imposed by the Convention or derived from it".[72]

This means that although Article 7 of the Convention does not fully apply during an emergency, legislation must exist establishing a detainee's right to be put at the disposal of a judicial authority. The Court had an opportunity to rule on the appropriateness of periods in the context of an emergency in the case of Castillo Petruzzi. The arrests of Castillo Petruzzi and other accused individuals took place during a time of "great disturbance of the public peace". The emergency law in Peru allowed individuals presumably implicated in the crime of treason to be held in detention without judicial intervention for 15 days, extendable for another similar period.[73] The State's defense in this case consisted of arguing that Peru had adopted emergency measures that included the suspension of Article 7 of the Convention. In its judgment, the Court reminded Peru that no measures adopted during an emergency situation may go beyond what is strictly necessary and concluded that Peruvian law itself contradicts Article 7(5) of the Convention. It also ruled that, since the facts had taken place during a period of approximately 36 days from the detention to the date on which the accused were put at the disposal of a judge, the period was obviously excessive.[74] In the case of Ms. J., the Court affirmed that the meaning of "promptly" had to be examined according to the particularities of each case. It admitted that terrorism had to be considered when analyzing if the presentation before the judge had been prompt, but it found 15 days were excessive, particularly because there were in the files no reasons for the delay.[75]

---

71 *Case of Servellón García v. Honduras*, paras. 90–93.

72 *Case of Castillo Petruzzi v. Peru*, para. 109.

73 *Ibidem*. However, this reasoning did not make it clear whether the Court felt that 15 days was an excessive period for the state of emergency or if the expression "promptly" found in Article 7(5) should always be applied, whether in normal times or in states of emergency. The Court reiterated this in the *Case of Cantoral Benavides v. Peru*, para. 73. In the same sense, see *Case of Loayza Tamayo v. Peru*, paras. 49–50.

74 *Ibidem*, para. 111.

75 *Case of J. v Peru*, para. 144.

4.1. RIGHT TO BE INFORMED OF THE REASONS FOR ARREST (ARTICLE 7(4))

15. The first requirement is the obligation for the person making the arrest to inform the person arrested[76] of the reasons for the arrest. This information should also be given, as well as the notification of the charges, to those arrested *in flagrante delicto*.[77] Even though the Convention is not specific, it seems obvious that this information must be provided immediately;[78] any State interference with human rights requires an explanation of the action, as this allows the person to have an opportunity to react with arguments that could perhaps lead the agent to desist. At this stage, no charges have been made. This is simply a reasonable explanation of why the action is taking place that must go further than just indicating, for example, the legal provision authorizing the arrest. Rather it must contain a summary description of the facts invoked as grounds for the arrest.[79] Of course, the grounds for the arrest must be previously established by law and be compatible with the Convention.

The Court had the opportunity to examine this point in the case of Gangaram Panday. The case examined several aspects of Article 7 of the Convention: the alleged failure to inform the victim of the reasons for the detention, the illegality of the detention and the detention's possible arbitrariness. Regarding the first point, which is the one at issue here, the Inter-American Court found that there was not sufficient evidence to conclude that the victim and the victim's family had been unaware of the reasons for the detention. The case file showed that the victim himself, when he was detained at the airport, said to his relatives: "I've got problems". It also mentioned that "in the early hours of the day following the abovementioned detention, the victim's brother [...] was informed by the Military Police that the reason for the detention was the fact that [the victim] had been expelled from Holland and, furthermore, that the latter had told the guard at the shelter 'that he had been expelled from Holland, even though he had of his own free will reported to the Immigration Police'".[80] Possibly because it ruled definitively that the detention was illegal, the Court did not elaborate further on this point. That would have been very useful for elucidating its opinion on whether: (i) knowing that one "has problems" is sufficient to conclude that a person was informed "of the reason for his detention"; and (ii) reporting

76 I use the expressions "the person making the arrest" and "the person arrested" to draw a distinction between the moment of the apprehension and the maintaining of the detention by a judge.

77 *Case López Alvarez v. Honduras*, para. 83.

78 The Convention used both the European Convention and the ICCPR as precedents for its drafting, but Article 7 seems to have been guided principally by the latter. The ICCPR explicitly establishes in its Article 9(2) that the first information must be provided "at the time of the arrest and the charge must be notified promptly". The Convention failed to do so.

79 *Case of Chaparro and Lapo v. Ecuador*, para. 71.

80 *Case of Gangaram Panday v. Suriname*, para. 44.

the reasons to the relatives can exempt the State from its obligation to inform the person being arrested at the time of his arrest. Nor did the Court rule on the possible arbitrariness of the detention; it would have been interesting to know its opinion on whether the fact of having been deported from the Netherlands is a ground for detention of a citizen of a State, compatible with the Convention. The obligation to inform properly has been stated in later rulings, explaining its objective by indicating that the information "is a mechanism to avoid illegal or arbitrary detentions, from the very moment when a person is deprived of his or her liberty. It also ensures the right to defense of the detainee."[81] In the case of children and adolescents, the information must also be provided to those representing them – that is, their legal guardians.[82] In the case of Espinoza Gonzales, the victim was only told that she was being detained in order to clarify a crime of terrorism. The Court found this notice did not comply with the requirement of telling the detainee the conducts she had incurred to be detained, nor was the subsequent lack of notification of the charges compatible with Article 7(4).[83]

As soon as a person is arrested, it is an obligation that the arrest be registered in a record stating its reasons, who carried it out, the time it took place and the time of release, to prevent the possibility of the disappearance of the detainee, as it happened to Mr. Torres Millacura.[84] Failure to register the detention is a violation of Article 7(2).[85]

4.2. RIGHT TO BE NOTIFIED OF THE CHARGES WITHOUT DELAY (ARTICLE 7(4))

16. The wording of Article 7(4) of the Convention allows for the assumption that the requirement that a detainee be notified without delay of the charge or charges being brought against him or her comes at a stage that can be subsequent to the act of apprehension itself.[86] The content of this notification is more formal and will require a description of the legal charges on which a person has been detained, empowering that person to be able to eventually challenge the detention.[87] As has been seen above, the identification of the charges must contain the facts and the alleged criminal provision that could be infringed, in a reasoned decision. Otherwise, it will lead to an arbitrary detention. In the case

[81] *Case of Juan Humberto Sánchez v. Honduras*, para. 82; *Case of Bulacio v. Argentina*, para. 128.
[82] *Case of Bulacio v. Argentina*, para. 128.
[83] *Case of Espinoza Gonzales v. Peru*, paras. 127 and 128.
[84] *Case of Torres Millacura et al. v. Argentina*, para. 76.
[85] *Case of Espinoza Gonzales v. Peru*, para. 123.
[86] One reason for not immediately providing notification of the charges could be, for example, a lack of training of the person making the arrest on how to properly articulate the charges.
[87] See in this regard a similar provision in the ICCPR, M. Nowak, *supra* n. 4, p. 175.

of Ms. J., the Court stated that this notification had to be in writing and found a violation because there was "no record in the case file that she was notified of the facts, causes and reasons that had led the State to make this accusation."[88] There is nothing to indicate the criteria that the court must consider to decide whether this notification was made "without delay". As will also be seen in other situations, such as in the interpretation of Article 8(1) of the Convention, the Court must rule on each case on its individual merits, taking into consideration that according to the wording of the paragraph itself, the period must be very short.

4.3. RIGHT TO BE BROUGHT PROMPTLY BEFORE A JUDICIAL AUTHORITY (ARTICLE 7(5))

17. The third requirement is that all individuals deprived of liberty must be brought promptly before a judge or other officer authorized by law to exercise judicial power. This official may be the one who informs the detainee of the charges against him or her. At this point, the individual ceases to be under police custody,[89] and if the person is not set free or released provisionally on bail or with other alternative measures, the person will be in preventive detention pursuant to the orders of a court authority. The involvement of a judge or official authorized to exercise judicial power ensures the rectitude and legality of preventive detention. This measure avoids a detention becoming arbitrary and illegal.[90] In the case of Cabrera García and Montiel Flores, the Court reiterated that "in areas of significant presence, where the members of the military institution take control of the internal security, the transfer without delay before the judicial authorities is more important in order to minimize any risk of violation of the rights of the person".[91]

It seems clear that the State official who does not have the title of judge must have judicial authority and at least hold a position that is independent of other State bodies, as independence is the minimum guarantee for protecting individuals' personal liberty and – eventually – personal integrity. In the case of Cantoral Benavides, the Court found that Peru had violated Article 8(1) of the Convention because the accused had been prosecuted by a military criminal judge who was not the "competent, independent and impartial judge" required by that provision. This constituted a violation by Peru of Article 7(5) of the Convention, as it had put the victim at the disposal of a military criminal

88 *Case of J. v. Peru*, para. 198.
89 I use the expression "police custody" in the sense of the Spanish expression "*custodia policial*" and the French expression "*garde à vue*".
90 *Case of Bulacio v. Argentina*, para. 129.
91 *Case of Cabrera García and Montiel Flores v. Mexico*, para. 102.

judge.[92] With this, the Court asserts that not just any authority has the judicial power to examine the legality and reasonableness of a detention. Rather, only those who do not violate the principle of the judge with rightful jurisdiction can do so.[93] In the case of Palamara, the Court said that the Prosecutor who had ordered the preventive detention, although "vested with the exercise of judicial functions under the domestic laws", could not control the legality of its own decision.[94] Nor was it accepted by the Court when the person before whom the detainee appeared was a mayor of the town.[95] In the case of Chaparro and Lapo, the Court stated that the obligation to bring the person promptly before the judge was not complied with when the judge was only present when the detentions were carried out. Article 7(5) required the judge to hear the detainee and assess his statement.[96]

The placing of the detainee at the disposal of the judicial authority must be carried out "promptly". The Court, in my opinion without fully realizing the meaning and consequences of the statement, has spoken in some judgments of "immediate judicial oversight",[97] which could lend itself to an erroneous interpretation of the Convention. Clearly, this obligation cannot be imposed on the State, as it is often physically impossible to comply with it. The term "promptly" must be interpreted on a case-by-case basis. Often, domestic legislation itself indicates the time periods for these purposes, which normally range between 24 and 48 hours; these time periods can serve as a basis for a ruling of the Court on a possible violation of the provision, but they are not decisive. The Inter-American Commission has opined that a tolerable delay is "that which is necessary for preparing the transfer", which seems to be a good standard for examining each situation.[98] The Court has found this provision to have been violated several times after States failed to put detainees at the disposal of a judicial authority, particularly but not exclusively[99] in the case of disappearances[100] and summary executions.[101] In these cases, the delay in

---

92 *Case of Cantoral Benavides v. Peru*, paras. 75 and 76.

93 Regarding the "*juez natural*", which is the wording in Spanish, see Chapter 6 on due process.

94 *Case of Palamara v. Chile*, para. 223.

95 *Case of Chaparro and Lapo v. Ecuador*, para. 128.

96 *Case of Chaparro and Lapo v. Ecuador*, para. 85. See also *Case of Tibi v. Ecuador*, paras. 118–119; *Case of Acosta Calderón v. Ecuador*, para. 80.

97 *Case of Bulacio v. Argentina*, para. 129; *Case of Maritza Urrutia v. Guatemala*, para. 66.

98 *Case of Castillo Petruzzi v. Peru*, para. 105(a), citing the Commission.

99 In the case of Suárez Rosero, a detention that took place in the context of a proceeding related with drug trafficking, the Court found that the petitioner had never been brought before a judicial authority (*Case of Suárez Rosero v Ecuador*, para. 56). See also *Case of Maritza Urrutia v. Guatemala*, para. 74.

100 *Case of Velásquez Rodríguez v. Honduras*, para. 155; *Case of Castillo Páez v. Peru*, paras. 57–58; *Case of Bámaca Velásquez v. Guatemala*, paras. 142–143.

101 *Case of Paniagua Morales et al. v. Guatemala*, para. 166; *Case of Villagrán Morales et al. v. Guatemala*, paras. 133–135; *Case of Juan Humberto Sánchez v. Honduras*, para. 83.

placing the detainee in front of a judge clearly exceeded all possible length that one could consider to constitute "promptly".

The Court finds that Article 7(5) establishes "a real control mechanism in the face of unlawful and arbitrary detention" and thus protects the presumption of innocence. In the case of Bayarri, this was not done; the judge receiving Bayarri's statement did not examine the entirety of his statement and "did not order a medical appraisal to determine the causes of the alleged victim's state of health, even though he showed signs of severe traumatism". Furthermore, he ordered the transferal of Bayarri to a "penitentiary center without ordering pre-trial detention, as established in the Code of Criminal Procedure" of Argentina. These facts constituted a violation of Article 7(5).[102]

4.4. RIGHT TO BE BROUGHT TO TRIAL WITHIN A REASONABLE TIME OR TO BE RELEASED (ARTICLE 7(5))

18. In Article 7(5), the American Convention, like other human rights treaties regulating the right to personal liberty, establishes the right of a detainee to be brought to trial within a reasonable time or to be released. The rule follows the principle that detention while awaiting trial – or preventative detention – cannot be the general norm but rather must be the exception, as it is a restriction on a human right and restrictions are always exceptional.[103] The right to be brought to trial within a reasonable time or to be released is the basis of frequent complaints before international supervisory bodies. It is regularly violated in Latin America; there is a clear tendency to transform pre-trial detention into the norm and freedom into the exception, with the consequence that a significant number of those held in prison are accused but not convicted, transforming preventive detention into a penalty.[104] In the case of Nadege Dorzema *et al.*, of Haitian nationality, the Court noted that the victims had been detained by the military inside the country, but had not been brought to a judicial authority. Instead, they were expelled from the Dominican Republic territory within a few hours of their detention. The Court found a violation of Article 7(5).[105]

The Convention does not establish the duration of the reasonable period; domestic legislation can (and often does) establish specific maximum periods for detention or preventative detention. As with the periods mentioned in the previous section, domestic periods can be an element to take into consideration in cases in which a violation of this right found in the Convention is alleged,

---

102 *Case of Bayarri v. Argentina*, para. 69.

103 The idea of the exceptionality of detention is explicitly included in the text of Article 9(3) of the ICCPR.

104 See A. Bovino, *supra* n. 52, p. 430.

105 *Case of Nadege Dorzema et al. v. Dominican Republic*, para. 143.

but they are not decisive for the international supervisory body's ruling. It is important to indicate here that this right is different from the one established in Article 8(1) of the Convention, which establishes that a person has a right to a "hearing, with due guarantees and within a reasonable time [...] in the substantiation of any accusation of a criminal nature made against him." The period found in Article 7 has to do with the duration of detention, while that found in Article 8 refers to the duration of the judicial proceedings, whether or not those involved are subjected to pre-trial detention. A situation is possible in which the period of detention is not reasonable – in which circumstance the individual must be released under penalty of the State's action being found to be in violation of the Convention – while the duration of the trial is found to be reasonable, in which case no violation will have taken place on that point.

It should likewise be emphasized that the right to be freed after a reasonable time is not the same as the right of an individual to be released due to lack of grounds for keeping him or her in detention. In the case of Palamara, for example, the Court found the purpose invoked by the judge to maintain Palamara in detention – that steps in the proceedings had yet to be taken – was not valid, as the steps could be taken while the accused was released.[106] In that case, the detention must cease immediately without considering its duration. In order to have any effect, Article 7(5) of the Convention must be interpreted in the sense that even though there may in principle be reasons for keeping an individual detained, that person must be released if the period of detention has been unreasonably exceeded.

19. The European Court has emphasized an interpretation according to which the key element for understanding Article 5(3) of the European Convention – the equivalent to Article 7(5) of the American Convention – is recalling that it forms part of the guarantee of personal liberty, for which reason

> it is the provisional detention of accused persons which must not, according to Article 5 (3) (art. 5-3), be prolonged beyond a reasonable time. The purpose of supervisory bodies is to determine whether the time that has elapsed, for whatever reason, before judgment is passed on the accused has at some stage exceeded reasonable limit, that is to say imposed a greater sacrifice than could, in the circumstances of the case, reasonably be expected of a person presumed to be innocent.[107]

---

106 *Case of Palamara v. Chile*, para. 211.

107 European Court of Human Rights, *Wemhoff Case*, judgment of June 27, 1968, para 5, Publ. Court A, Vol. 7 p. 22, and *Matznetter Case*, para. 12, reproduced in Council of Europe, *Digest of Strasbourg Case-Law relating to the European Convention of Human Rights*, Vol. 1 (Articles 1–5), Carl Heymanns-Verlag KG Köln, Berlin/BonnMunich, 1984, p. 505. See also *Letellier v. France*, A. 207, para. 35 (1991), cited by D.J. Harris *et al.*, *supra* n. 9, p. 137. *McKay v. United Kingdom*, Application No. 543/03, judgment of October 3, 2006, para. 43 and *Krikunov v. Russia*, Application No. 13991/05, judgment of December 4, 2014, para. 37.

In the Stögmüller case, the European Court indicated that it does not agree with a distinction proposed by the Austrian government arguing that, on examining the duration of a detention, the reasons invoked for it need not be examined because they are irrelevant.[108] The European Court finds that a *sine qua non* condition for the validity of maintaining a detention is that reasonable suspicion persists with regard to whether the detainee has committed a crime. However, in order to decide on whether to prolong a detention, the reasonableness of the grounds that persuaded the judicial authority to decide to break so seriously from the rules on personal liberty and the presumption of innocence must be examined. The grounds must demonstrate that there are "good reasons in the public interest" for maintaining the detention that persuaded the judicial authority to veer so seriously from the rules that order respect for personal liberty and for the presumption of innocence.[109] This is correct, because if there are no reasons for keeping a person in detention that are compatible with the Convention, that person must be freed. What the European Court expresses is that in order to keep a person detained beyond a reasonable time, more powerful reasons are required than the ones that would allow the initial detention. However, this does not clarify the problem of deciding how to determine what that reasonable period is. The European Court's position seems to be contrary to the very idea of the right to not be detained "beyond a reasonable time", because it would suggest that if there are "good reasons in the public interest", the detention would be legitimate even if it is for many years, which would completely annul the right being interpreted. In addition, the European Court finds that the Convention would also be violated should the investigation and the trial itself be carried out over a longer period than what could be reasonably expected.[110] Under its second approach, the supervisory body's examination would be similar to the one made with regard to Article 6(1) of the European Convention, equivalent of Article 8(1) of the American Convention.

The only criteria that seems salvageable from the European Court judgment under examination is the criteria that weighs whether prolonging the detention has "imposed a greater sacrifice than could, in the circumstances of the case, reasonably be expected of a person presumed to be innocent".

20. The Inter-American Court does not have yet a clear interpretation of this issue. The subject was raised in the case of Suárez Rosero and, in my opinion, in that judgment the Court was not careful about the distinction between the period mentioned in Article 7(5) and the one mentioned in Article 8(1), both from the American Convention. In part of its reasoning, the Inter-American Court indicates

---

108 European Court of Human Rights, *Stögmüller Case*, judgment of November 10, 1969, para. 4, Publ. Court A Vol. 9 pp. 39–40, reproduced in *ibidem*, pp. 505–506.

109 European Court of Human Rights, *Wemhoff Case*, judgment of June 27, 1968, paras. 16–17, pp. 25–26.

110 *Ibidem*.

that the purpose of the reasonable time referred to in these two articles "is to prevent accused persons from remaining in that situation for a protracted period and to ensure that the charge is promptly disposed of."[111] This, however, is the purpose of the period mentioned in Article 8(1), not of that found in Article 7(5), whose objective is to protect the personal liberty of the accused.[112] In the same case, the Inter-American Court examined a domestic law that ordered individuals to be released who had remained in detention without their cases having received an order to dismiss or open a plenary action for a period equal to or greater than a third of the length of the maximum punishment for the crime. This provision was not applicable to individuals charged with crimes punished under the Narcotic and Psychotropic Substances Act. Unfortunately, the Inter-American Court did not analyze the law itself but only the laws on equal protection of those being put on trial for consumption or distribution of drugs. A jurisdictional ruling on the compatibility of that provision with Article 7, which enshrines the idea that pre-trial detention should not exceed a reasonable time, would have been interesting.[113]

In later judgments, the Court has not fared much better in finding a suitable interpretation of Article 7(5). In the case of Bayarri, it was clear that the period of his detention had grossly exceeded what was reasonable: he had been in prison for around 13 years, subsequently being acquitted of all charges.[114] Bayarri had requested his release several times, but his petitions were always rejected based on the "characteristics of the offense of which Mr. Bayarri was accused, his personal situation as a sergeant of the Argentine Federal Police and the punishment requested in order to presume, with justification, that, if he was granted his liberty, [...] he would evade the action of justice".[115] In the judgment, the Court stated that Article 7(5) "imposes temporal limits on the duration of pre-trial detention and, consequently, on the State's power to protect the purpose of the proceedings by using this type of precautionary measure". It added that "[w]hen the duration of pre-trial detention exceeds a reasonable time, the State can restrict the liberty of the accused by other measures that are less harmful than deprivation of liberty by imprisonment and yet ensure his presence at the trial".[116] Following this idea, it also said that, "even when there are reasons for keeping a person in preventive detention, Article 7(5) guarantees that he will be released if the detention period has exceeded a reasonable time".[117] However, this trend of reasoning stopped there because the Court decided that, since Argentine law established a maximum period of three years after which it was

111 *Case of Suárez Rosero v. Ecuador*, para. 70.

112 For the pertinent examination of the Court's position on the reasonable delay in Article 8, set forth in its judgment in *Suárez Rosero*, see Chapter 6.

113 *Case of Suárez Rosero v. Ecuador*, paras. 95–99.

114 *Case of Bayarri v. Argentina*, para. 73.

115 *Ibidem*, para. 73.

116 *Ibidem*, paras. 69–70.

117 *Ibidem*, para 74.

not possible to continue depriving the accused of his liberty", it was obvious "that Mr. Bayarri's detention could not exceed this timeframe".[118]

In the case of Barreto Leiva the Court did attempt to separate Article 7(5) from Article 8(1). Mr. Barreto Leiva had been in preventive detention for 16 days longer than the penalty he was finally given. The Court considered that:

> it is necessary to make a distinction between this provision [article 7(5)] regarding the duration of the pre-trial detention as precautionary measure and the provision contained in Article 8(1) that relates to the term for the substantiation of the proceeding. Even when they refer to different issues, both rules have the same purpose: to limit, as much as possible, the abridgement of rights of an individual.[119]

It continued its reasoning stating that when preventive detention "exceeds a reasonable time, the State can restrict the liberty of the accused by other measures that are less harmful than deprivation of liberty by imprisonment".[120] It insisted that the only reasons to keep a person in detention were not to "impede the efficient development of an investigation" and preventing the accused to evade justice, as "[p]reventive detention is [...] a precautionary rather than a punitive measure".[121] After those considerations, the Court deviates to the requirement of absence of arbitrariness, particularly the need for proportionality by affirming that preventive detention is limited by the principle of proportionality,[122] by virtue of which a person that is presumed innocent cannot be treated equal to or worse than a convicted person. The State must avoid the measure of procedural coercion being equally or more harmful to the defendant than the punishment in the event of conviction. This means that it should not be appropriate to authorize preventive detention in cases where it is not possible to impose a prison term.[123] The principle of proportionality also implies a rational relationship between the precautionary measure and the purpose sought, so that the sacrifice inherent in the restriction of the right to liberty is not exaggerated or excessive compared to the advantages obtained from this restriction and the achievement of the purpose sought. After these considerations, it concluded that there had been a violation of Article 7(5) *and of Article 8(2)* "insofar as the pre-trial detention of Mr. Barreto Leiva exceeded the temporal, reasonable and proportional limits to which it should have been subjected".[124]

Unfortunately, the most recent judgments have not shed much light on the issue.

---

118 *Ibidem.*

119 *Case of Barreto Leiva v. Venezuela*, para. 119.

120 *Ibidem*, para. 120.

121 *Ibidem*, para. 121.

122 Ibidem, para. 122. There, the Court quotes several cases: *Case of the "Juvenile Reeducation Institute" v. Paraguay*, judgment of reparations and costs, para. 228; *Case of López Álvarez v. Honduras*, para. 67; and *Case of Chaparro and Lapo v. Ecuador*, para. 93.

123 *Ibidem.*

124 *Ibidem.*

21. From all that has been said, one can appreciate the difficulty of establishing the scope and content of this right to be brought to trial within a reasonable time or released. Without presuming to solve the problem, but rather to contribute toward shedding some light on reasoning out this point, it seems useful and necessary to establish certain basic premises from which to start in order to attempt to find the meaning of paragraph 5 of Article 7 of the Convention. The first is that the interpretation should give Article 7(5) a content that is different from that of Article 8(1) of the Convention; otherwise, the right found in Article 7(5) is useless because it lacks its own content. The second is that this differentiated content must come from the fact that this paragraph protects personal liberty, in contrast to Article 8(1), which protects the notion of "a due process" or a just process. The latter has the purpose, for example, of preventing damage from being done to a person as a result of spending a long time in a situation of uncertainty with regard to his or her situation in a criminal proceeding. The purpose could also be preventing damage to the defense, among other things because the passage of time blurs the memories of witnesses or makes it difficult for them to appear at trial to testify. As a consequence of this, the time period indicated in Article 7 of the Convention must have to do with the duration of the period of detention, while the time period mentioned in Article 8 of the Convention refers to the duration of the trial, whether or not the persons on trial are in detention. It is thus possible to conceive of the existence of a violation of Article 7(5) of the Convention for an excessive period of detention without a violation of Article 8(1), because the period of the trial is reasonable. The third is that the need for its own content implies that the right established in Article 7(5) cannot be equivalent to finding that an individual must be released because the grounds for keeping the individual detained no longer apply. In that case, I would reiterate, the detention must cease immediately and without considering its duration. Otherwise, it would be arbitrary and in violation of Article 7(3). In order to have any effect, Article 7(5) of the Convention must be interpreted in the sense that even when reasons exist in principle for keeping a person detained, that person must be released if the period of detention has exceeded a reasonable period of time. The fourth is that this period cannot be determined in the abstract, but rather on a case-by-case basis and according to the circumstances of each case. This raises the problem of determining what elements must be considered for deciding when a period ceases to be reasonable.

What are the possible options for interpretation? One – which seems to be the option pursued by both the European Court and the Inter-American Commission – is to argue that the right established in Article 7(5) of the Convention is related to the persistence of *strong* reasons for keeping a person in detention and that the reasonable period of time is, in reality, the period of the trial itself. Therefore, when strong reasons exist for depriving someone of liberty, one must examine whether the investigation and trial have been carried out with the necessary swiftness, taking into consideration that a person is involved who has been accused and is deprived of liberty. This would imply that Article 8(1) could be differentiated from Article 7(5) in that when there is an accused individual deprived of liberty, the period should probably be shorter than when not. This is despite the fact that in our examination of due process, we will see that an element to take into consideration when deciding whether the period is reasonable or not – for the sake of Article 8 – is how much the duration of the trial affects the accused. For this reason, the same result can be obtained without the existence of Article 7(5) of the Convention. The second option is perhaps to argue that what should be examined is only whether the duration of the detention is excessive, and that this examination must be carried out through an attempt to balance the public interest against the burden that the deprivation of liberty places on each accused individual. There has not yet been any case law toward determining the elements to consider when making this measurement. In Barreto Leiva, the Court attempts to set some criteria by stating, "the pre-trial detention of Mr. Barreto Leiva exceeded the temporal, reasonable and proportional limits to which it should have been subjected."[125] This however does not solve the problem of which criteria is to be used to decide on these factors. It is up to the Inter-American Court to make an authorized interpretation of this subject or conclude that the provision in Article 7(5) is the same as that of Article 8(1) and that it only reinforces the need for a more speedy trial when the accused is in prison.

22. Another problem arises in determining how to measure the period that must be examined in order to decide whether Article 7(5) of the Convention has been violated. The start date is simple, as that is determined by the moment at which the individual was deprived of liberty. It is more difficult to decide on the date of conclusion because there is a substantial difference between the Anglo-Saxon system and the continental system. In the Anglo-Saxon system,[126] pre-trial detention generally ends with the handing down of a judgment at the conclusion of an oral trial. If the ruling imposes a sentence of deprivation of liberty, the person begins serving that sentence as of that moment and is no longer considered to be in preventative detention, even if the ruling itself is not final and there are remedies pending. In contrast, in the continental system, deprivation of liberty is considered preventative detention as long as a judgment is not final and there is no *res judicata*, although often the time during which the person is subjected to preventative detention is counted after sentencing as time served. The job of the supervisory body, however, is to transcend specific legal systems and establish

125 *Case of Barreto Leiva v. Venezuela*, para. 123.

126 Since most of the cases refer to American States with a continental system, it is probable that the problem will not present itself. Nevertheless, as the Court has jurisdiction over Barbados, a State with a common law legal system, this should be taken into account.

law that applies to all individuals in common. I would argue that if the reason for the existence of the right to be brought to trial within a reasonable time or be released is to not cause harm unjustly by depriving a presumably innocent person of liberty, then that reasoning works as long as there is a possibility that the accused will be declared innocent.[127] Thus, it would seem fair to apply the continental legal system. The Court has not elaborated this issue in depth with regard to preventive detention. It has done so when examining Article 8(2); from that examination, the Court follows the continental interpretation.[128]

4.5. WRIT OF *HABEAS CORPUS* (ARTICLE 7(6))

23. Paragraph 6 of Article 7 of the Convention sets forth the right of all persons deprived of liberty to have "recourse to a competent court, in order that the court may decide without delay on the lawfulness of [their] arrest or detention and order [their] release if [an] arrest or detention is unlawful". This right to a remedy is violated if the remedy does not exist at all or if it exists but is not granted "without delay", even if the detention itself is legal. The Inter-American Court has connected *habeas corpus* with the general right found in Article 25 of the Convention to a simple and quick remedy for protecting rights recognized by that international instrument, as well as the rights recognized by the constitutions and domestic legislation of States Parties.[129] *Habeas corpus* is the way in which this right found in Article 25 of the Convention is expressed when protecting personal liberty.[130]

According to case law, *habeas corpus* is "the suitable means to ensure liberty, to control respect for life and the right to humane treatment [of the person], and to impede [... its] disappearance or non-determination of [its ...] place of detention."[131] As the remedy protects not only liberty but also personal integrity, the Court has found that *habeas corpus* requires that the detainee be brought in person before a judge or court that is competent to examine the legality of the detention.[132]

---

127 The European Court found a conflicting solution, but the provision of Article 5(1) on which the Court based its conclusion is different from that found in Article 7, such that it is not an appropriate reference (See D.J. Harris *et al.*, *supra* n. 9, pp. 137–138).

128 *Case of Tibi v. Ecuador*, para. 169, where the Court finds that the term starts from the moment of detention and ends "when an unappealable [sic] judgment is issued on the matter, which exhausts the jurisdiction, and that, especially regarding criminal matters, said term must include the whole proceeding, including the appeals that may be filed."

129 *Case of Suárez Rosero v. Ecuador*, para. 64.

130 *OC-8/87*, paras. 32 and 34.

131 *Case of Juan Humberto Sánchez v. Honduras*, para. 122; *Case of Maritza Urrutia v. Guatemala*, para. 111; and *Case of "La Cantuta v. Peru*, para. 111.

132 *OC-8/87*, para. 35. On this point, see C. Riego, "El sistema procesal penal chileno frente a las normas internacionales de derechos humanos", in M. Abregú and C. Courtis (eds.), *supra* n. 52, pp. 296–299.

The remedy is available for all deprivations of liberty and not only detentions carried out by the police or ordered by a court. It also applies to individuals in solitary confinement[133] and even during periods of constitutional emergency, as it is one of the non-derogable guarantees pursuant to Article 27 of the Convention and the Court's interpretation of it.[134] The Convention is also violated when the suspension is not explicit but rather implicit.[135] This remedy cannot be eliminated based on the type of crime for which a person has been detained. In the case of Loayza Tamayo, the Inter-American Court ruled that Peru had violated Article 7(6) on establishing by law that actions for guaranteeing the rights of detainees could never be granted with regard to crimes of treason, those actions including *habeas corpus*.[136]

Habeas corpus should be compatible with other ordinary proceedings that may be initiated by the detainee. An ordinary proceeding will never fulfill the purpose that the former has: to examine the release of the detainee in a simple and fast procedure.[137] Equally, the Court has reiterated that the principles of due process of law cannot be suspended in a situation of emergency, particularly with regard to *habeas corpus*. Due process is indispensable for the protection of all non-derogable rights.[138]

Petitioners should be able to exercise the remedy at reasonable intervals, given that pre-trial detention requires the persistence of circumstances that make detention indispensable. The importance of the right to liberty is in the emphasis placed by the Court on a periodical revision of detention, even if the detainee has not requested it. In the case of Barreto Leiva, it affirmed that:

> the judge does not have to wait until he hands down an acquittal for the detained person to recover his liberty, but should periodically assess whether the reasons and need for the measure and its proportionality are maintained, and whether the duration of the detention has exceeded the limits established by law and reasonableness.[139]

The decision on the *habeas corpus* must not exceed a reasonable time,[140] and this period must be brief, as it seeks to review whether the legal provisions protecting

---

133 *Case of Suárez Rosero v. Ecuador*, para. 59; *Case of Cesti Hurtado v. Peru*, para. 123.

134 *OC-8/87*, paras. 35–36 and 42–43. See also *Case of Castillo Petruzzi et al. v. Peru*, paras. 109 and 186.

135 *Case of Neira Alegría et al. v. Peru*. Therein, the Court found that the Armed Forces' control and jurisdiction over the San Juan Bautista Prison had the effect of implicitly suspending *habeas corpus*, in violation of the Convention (paras. 84–85).

136 *Case of Loayza Tamayo v. Peru*, paras. 51–55; *Case of Castillo Petruzzi et al. v. Peru*, para. 182; *Case of Cantoral Benavides v. Peru*, para. 165.

137 *Case of Anzualdo Castro v. Peru*, para. 73.

138 *OC-9/87*, para. 30.

139 *Case of Barreto Leiva v. Colombia*, para. 76. See also *Case of Chaparro and Lapo v. Ecuador*, para. 107 and *Case of Ivon Neptune v Haiti*, para. 108.

140 The European Court ruled that 15 months was not a reasonable period and that one month could be reasonable (see *Herczegfalvy Case*, judgment of September 24, 1992, A.244,

liberty have been violated. In the case of Mr. Bayarri, the procedure established by the law gave 48 hours for appealing the mayor's decision to enabling a hearing by a judge and then another 48 hours to send the appeal to the Constitutional Court. In the Court's consideration, this procedure, which should be simple and fast, is detrimental to the detainee and consequently incompatible with the Convention.[141] As for the meaning of the expression "promptly", the Court has not established general criteria for determining whether a remedy complies with Article 7(6) of the Convention; it only found that a period of 14 months for a *habeas corpus* ruling was obviously excessive.[142] Given that *habeas corpus* is one of the species of the general remedy created by Article 25 of the Convention, it must also be effective; remedies that turn out to be illusory because of the general conditions in a country or specific conditions of a case do not comply with the provision of Article 7(6) under analysis.[143] The writ of *habeas corpus* is the first remedy filed in cases of disappearance, as it is the most appropriate in terms of duration and simplicity. Invariably, in those cases the remedy is not effective. In the case of Blanco Romero, the Court ordered Venezuela to have legislation that makes *habeas corpus* effective in cases of disappearances. In doing this, the State must take into account the scope of this remedy in international law "in the sense that such writ represents the effective means to ensure that people's life and physical integrity are respected, and to prevent their disappearance or the uncertainty about their place of detention".[144] In the case of Rochac Hernández *et al.* v El Salvador, a case of disappearances, the Court found a violation of Article 7(6) because the domestic court had placed an excessive burden of proof on those who presented the claim[145] and because the domestic court had rendered *habeas corpus* ineffective.[146]

5. OTHER STATE OBLIGATIONS WITH REGARD TO DEPRIVATION OF LIBERTY

24. As stated previously, other declarations or bodies of principles and the development of international case law complement the provisions of Article 7 of the Convention. One initial important development is set forth in Advisory

pp. 24–25 and *Bezicheri Case*, judgment on October 25, 1989, A.164, both cited in P. Van Dijk and G.J.H. Van Hoof, *Theory and Practice of the European Convention on Human Rights*, 3rd edition, SIM, Kluwer Law International, The Hague/London/Boston, 1998, p. 468.

141 *Case of Bayarri v. Argentina*, paras. 76–77.

142 *Ibidem*, para. 64.

143 *Case of Cesti Hurtado v. Peru*, para. 125.

144 *Case of Blanco Romero et al. v. Venezuela*, para. 104.

145 *Case of Rochac Hernández v. El Salvador*, paras. 165 and 167.

146 *Ibidem*, para. 168.

Opinion 16/99[147] with regard to the right to legal aid in the context of the Vienna Convention on Consular Relations. In this opinion, the Court ruled that in the case of deprivation of liberty of a foreign national, the receiving State must inform the detainee of his or her rights "without delay". This implies that the notification must be made "at the time the accused is deprived of his freedom, or at least before he makes his first statement before the authorities". The purpose of the notification is to guarantee due process, and particularly the right to a defense.[148] Among the rights of detainees is the right to know that they can notify a third party that they are in State custody; for example, the detainee could notify a relative, an attorney and/or legal counsel, as may be the case, at the time of deprivation of liberty.[149] The mention of the right to notify an attorney relates to Principle 17 of the Body of Principles. The provision establishes that the individual must be informed of the right to assistance from an attorney "at the time the accused is imprisoned" and that the State must facilitate adequate means for exercising that right. It also establishes that should it be required in the interest of justice, the individual under arrest will have the right for a judge or authority to assign him or her an attorney, free of charge should that person lack sufficient means to pay the attorney.[150] When detention affects a child, the States must comply with any domestic rule that protects its personal liberty. This was not the situation in the case of the Landaeta brothers, since according to Venezuelan law, if the special Juvenile Judge was not involved, his parents or his guardian, or the Juvenile Attorney or the National Institute for Juveniles could have requested its participation. This did not happen and therefore there was a violation of Article 7.[151]

The Human Rights Committee has been clear in stating that the presence of an attorney from the moment of the detention itself is a right held by the detainee.[152] In the European system, the Court has approached the subject from a different angle. It indicates that – if according to the domestic legal system consequences are attached to the attitude of an accused at the initial stages of police interrogation, which are decisive for the prospects of the defense in any subsequent criminal proceedings – an attorney must be present in order to comply with the demands of due process.[153] In the case of Salduz v. Turkey, the European Court reaffirmed its earlier case law but clarified further:

> Article 6 §1 requires that, as a rule, access to a lawyer should be provided as from the first interrogation of a suspect by the police, unless it is demonstrated in the light

147 *OC-16/99*, para. 106.
148 *Ibidem*, paras. 86–87.
149 *Case of Bulacio v. Argentina*, para. 130.
150 Also see Principle 18.
151 *Case of the Landaeta brothers v. Venezuela*, paras. 160 and 164.
152 HRC, Case of *Kelly v. Jamaica*, para. 9.2.
153 P. Van Dijk and G.J.H. van Hoof, *supra* n. 140, p. 468, commenting on the Court's ruling in John Murray, of February 8, 1996 (Reports 1996-I, Vol. I, para. 63).

> of the particular circumstances of each case that there are compelling reasons to restrict this right. Even where compelling reasons may exceptionally justify denial of access to a lawyer, such restriction – whatever its justification – must not unduly prejudice the rights of the accused under Article 6 [...]. The rights of the defence will in principle be irretrievably prejudiced when incriminating statements made during police interrogation without access to a lawyer are used for a conviction.[154]

In the case of Vélez Romero, the Court stated the three essential obligations of the State with respect to a detained person. The first was "the right to be informed of his rights under the Vienna Convention"; the second, "the right to have effective access to communication with the consular official"; and the third, "the right to the assistance itself".[155] As will be seen in Chapter 6, these obligations are closely related to Article 8 on due process.

25. Another important State obligation arises from Advisory Opinion 16/99: the obligation to identify the detainee, among other things, serves several purposes and is required particularly for the prevention of disappearances; it also allows the detainee's age to be established and ensures treatment appropriate to his or her circumstances.[156] In one case, the Court ordered Honduras in the reparations section of a ruling to set up "a record of detainees to enable control of legality of the detentions, which must therefore include identification of the detainees, the reason for their detention, the competent authority, the day and time of admission and of release, and information on the arrest warrant."[157] A later judgment broadened this by ruling that the record required at least:

> identification of the detainees, cause for detention, notification to the competent authority, and to those representing them, exercising custody or acting as defence counsel, if applicable, and the visits they have paid to the detainee, the date and time of entry and release, information given to the minor and to other persons regarding the rights and guarantees of the detainee, record of signs of beating or mental illness, transfers of the detainee, and meal schedule. The detainee must also sign and, if he or she does not, there must be an explanation of the lack of signature.[158]

Deprivation of liberty causes the person arrested or detained to be vulnerable. Experience in the region with regard to the treatment of those deprived of liberty bears this out.[159] It is no coincidence that Article 5 of the American

---

154 European Court of Human Rights, *Case of Salduz v. Turkey*, Application No. 36391/02, judgment of November 27, 2008, para. 55.

155 *Case of Vélez Romero v. Panama*, para. 153.

156 *OC-16/99*, para. 94.

157 *Case of Juan Humberto Sánchez v. Honduras*, para. 189.

158 *Case of Bulacio v. Argentina*, para. 132.

159 This has been a subject that has caught the attention of the Inter-American Commission on Human Rights, which in 1995 created a Work Group on the conditions of persons deprived of liberty (see: Annual Report 1995, OEA/Ser.L/V/II.91 Doc. 7 rev., February 28, 1996, pp. 233–235). See also, IACHR, Report on the Human Rights of persons deprived of liberty in

Convention requires States to treat persons deprived of liberty with the respect due to the dignity inherent in the human being.[160] Nor is it just by chance that the Inter-American Court has linked the right to *habeas corpus* with the protection of physical integrity of persons.[161] Along with this, the Human Rights Committee indicated in its General Comment on Article 7 of the ICCPR that "the protection of the detainee [...] requires that prompt and regular access be given to doctors".[162] Principle 24 of the Body of Principles mentioned previously establishes that all persons imprisoned or under detention shall be provided with proper medical examinations within the shortest time possible following their entry into the place of detention.[163] The Inter-American Court has ruled in the same sense in more detail. It indicates that, preferably, a physician chosen by the victim should carry out the medical care privately; the results should be "delivered to the judge, the detainee and his attorney, or to him and whoever exercises custody or representation of the minor according to the law".[164]

26. Deprivation of liberty necessarily affects the enjoyment of other human rights. As the rule for every restriction is that it must lead to, and be proportional for, achieving its objective, it is important to try to limit as much as possible the effects – which we could perhaps call collateral damage – that deprivation of liberty has on other human rights. This is established in the Standard Minimum Rules for the Treatment of Prisoners.[165] A right that will necessarily be affected is the right to privacy and non-interference with the family life of the detainee; another that could be affected would be freedom of expression, particularly with regard to the right to be informed by any medium and to communicate privately with persons. There is also a possibility that the right to participate in government might be affected, as well as the right to assembly. However, the idea that deprivation of liberty necessarily brings with it restrictions that are implicit or inherent to it must be rejected. It is essential that the eventual restriction

the Americas, OEA/Ser.L/V/II.Doc.64, December 31, 2011, and Report on the use of pre-trial detention in the Americas, OEA/Ser.L/V/II. Doc. 46/13, December 30, 2013.

160 On this, see Chapter 4 of this book.

161 *OC-8/87*, paras. 35–36.

162 HRC, General Comment No. 20, 44th Period of Sessions (1992), HRI/GEN/1/Rev.5, April 26, 2001, para. 11.

163 Also see Principles 25 and 26.

164 *Case of Bulacio v. Argentina*, para. 131.

165 Imprisonment and other measures which result in cutting off an offender from the outside world are afflictive by the very fact of taking from the person the right of self-determination by depriving him of his liberty. Therefore the prison system shall not, except as incidental to justifiable segregation or the maintenance of discipline, aggravate the suffering inherent in such a situation." (*Standard Minimum Rules for the Treatment of Prisoners*, adopted by the First United Nations Congress on the Prevention of Crime and the Treatment of Offenders, held at Geneva in 1955, and approved by the Economic and Social Council by its Resolutions 663C (XXIV) of July 31, 1957 and 2076 (LXII) of May 13, 1977. *Ibidem*. para. 57 citing para. 10 of the Rules).

of these rights go through an examination of their necessity in a democratic society according to the standards on restricting each one of the rights. From this point of view, detainees' contact with family and with the world has tended to progressively broaden, and what seemed impossible before – such as conjugal visits – is now a right in a significant number of States. Nor does the elimination of the right to vote in some countries seem at all justified for people accused of crimes punishable by relatively harsh sentences, if this is done not in application of a sentence but as a consequence of the status of the accused.

The Inter-American Court ruled on the rights of persons deprived of liberty on a provisional measure requested by the Commission with regard to inmates in the Urso Branco Prison in Brazil. In that measure, handed down in August 2002, the Court found that the State had a special obligation to ensure the rights of inmates and, in particular, to make the Minimum Rules for the Treatment of Prisoners[166] applicable, rules which in this way have been incorporated into inter-American case law.

6. PROHIBITION ON DETENTION FOR DEBTS (ARTICLE 7(7))

27. The right not to be detained for debts, established in Article 7(7) of the Convention, is also set forth in Article 11 of the ICCPR. The Convention does not differentiate between the origins of the debt for the application of this provision. From this, one could argue that in principle, whatever the source of the debt, a failure to pay it cannot result in deprivation of liberty. In drafting this paragraph during the Specialized Conference, there was some debate over the concept of "debts" arising from the question of whether this would exclude deprivation of liberty for failing to pay support for a spouse and children. The delegate from Brazil indicated that the legal concept of debt in the civil law world was as broad as possible, for which reason he could not accept that wording. The delegate from Colombia clarified that he would understand the concept as it is understood in Colombia's constitution, which is to say that it refers to purely civil debts or obligations "save for a special judicial form of deprivation of liberty" (*arraigo judicial*). The discussion did not conclude with a common interpretation of the concept, but rather with the addition of a sentence that left "orders of a competent judicial authority issued for nonfulfillment of duties of family support"[167] out of the prohibition.

The Inter-American Court has not yet had any opportunity to rule on this prohibition.

---

166 IACtHR, Provisional measures regarding the Federal Republic of Brazil, Urso Branco Prison, decision of August 29, 2002, para. 6.

167 Specialized Conference, *supra* n. 15, pp. 188–190.

7. DEPRIVATION OF LIBERTY OF CHILDREN AND ADOLESCENTS

28. The adoption and entry into force of the International Convention on the Rights of the Child[168] has had important consequences for the interpretation of the American Convention as regards children. The Inter-American Commission requested the Court's opinion "with the aim of determining whether the special measures set forth in Article 19[169] of that same Convention establish 'limits to the good judgment and discretion of the States' with respect to children."[170] Although the consultation was made with regard to Articles 8 and 25 of the American Convention, the opinion has important implications for the right to personal liberty that must be taken into consideration. For one thing, it uses the International Convention on the Rights of the Child, the United Nations Standard Minimum Rules for the Administration of Juvenile Justice (Beijing Rules), the Directives of the United Nations for the Prevention of Juvenile Delinquency (Riad Directives), and the Standard Minimum Rules for Non-custodial Measures (Tokyo Rules) as bases for its assertions. This means legitimating all these instruments for use in the interpretation of the provisions of the American Convention.

The Advisory Opinion is enriched by contributions made by Costa Rica and the United Mexican States, the Inter-American Children's Institute, the United Nations Latin American Institute for the Prevention of Crime and the Treatment of Offenders (ILANUD) and various nongovernmental organizations. One can derive from these contributions a common vision of ways to protect children who are abandoned or who enter the justice system due to their actions. The Court accepts in this consultation that it refers to individuals who have not reached 18 years of age.[171] This implies, as expressed by Judge García Ramírez, that the age of 18 is a precise borderline between two ages that involve two distinctive situations in the ambit of this Opinion: one, regarding those who find themselves outside the subjective validity of normal criminal rules, and the other pertaining to those who are subject to them.[172] Therefore, children must have their own statute that is different in certain aspects from that of adults, although this does not mean that they do not enjoy the safeguards of international human rights law as regards their own human rights.

---

168 The International Convention on the Rights of the Child. Adopted on November 20, 1989. Entry into force on September 2, 1990. All Latin American States are party to this Convention.

169 Article 19 of the American Convention estipulate: "Every minor child has the right to the measures of protection required by his condition as a minor on the part of his family, society, and the state".

170 *OC-17/2002*, para. 1.

171 *Ibidem*, para. 42.

172 *Ibidem*, concurring opinion of Judge Sergio García Ramírez, para. 5.

The reason for the consultation is clear. At least in Latin America, the doctrine of "minors in an irregular situation",[173] meaning children and adolescents who have not infringed the law but live on the streets, is applied generally, with the result that they are not recognized as rights holders and can be deprived of liberty without any kind of safeguards.[174] In addition, it also seems necessary to examine which additional safeguards children must have due to their situation of greater vulnerability compared to that of adults.[175] With regard to personal liberty, the Commission consulted the Court on the following hypothetical practice:

> The deprivation of liberty of minors by internment in guardianship or custodial institutions on the basis of a determination that they have been abandoned or are prone to fall into situations of risk or illegality, motives which should not be considered of a criminal nature, but, rather, as the result of personal or circumstantial vicissitudes.[176]

The Court establishes the basic premise that the interpretation and application of the provisions of the Convention must be carried out taking "the best interests of the child" as a guide.[177] A logical consequence is that the institutions that protect children and take part in their care or protection must provide "appropriate staff, adequate facilities, suitable means and proven experience in this type of tasks."[178] This implies that places of detention and State agents that take part in depriving children of liberty must comply with these requirements.

The Advisory Opinion cited finds likewise with regard to jurisdictional bodies.[179] Additionally, it refers to the impossibility of comparing the situation of children alleged to be in conflict with criminal laws to those who have not engaged in conduct defined by law as a crime, but who are at risk or endangered due to destitution, abandonment, extreme poverty or disease. Even less so do they include others who simply behave differently from how the majority does, those who differ from the generally accepted patterns of behavior, who are involved in conflicts regarding adaptation to the family, school, or social milieu generally, or who alienate themselves from the customs and values of their society. The concept of crime committed by children or juvenile crime can only be applied to those who fall under the first aforementioned situation, that is, those who engage in conduct legally defined as a crime.[180]

---

173 On this point, see E. García Méndez, *Derecho de la Infancia y Adolescencia en América Latina: de la situación irregular a la protección integral*, Forum Pacis, Bogotá, 1994. Also see Inter-American Children's Institute, OAS and Inter-American Court, *Juridical Condition and Human Rights of the Child*, Annex II, pp. 196–197.

174 *OC-17/2002*, para. 2.

175 An excellent explanation of this can be found in the concurring opinion of Judge García Ramírez to Advisory Opinion 17.

176 *OC-17/2002*, para. 18.

177 *Ibidem*, paras. 56–61.

178 *Ibidem*, para. 78.

179 *Ibidem*, para. 109.

180 *Ibidem*, para. 110.

As deprivation of liberty is only possible in general with the purpose of subjecting a person to a criminal proceeding, this means that deprivation of liberty is not justified for the children to which this paragraph of the Opinion refers. In its conclusion, the Court finds that the State can only intervene when the child's conduct is described in criminal law, and that cases of "abandonment, destitution, risk or disease, must be dealt with in a different manner from procedures applicable to those who commit criminal offenses."[181] With wording that is unmistakable, the Inter-American Children's Institute also opines that internment of youths who are in situations of social risk, applying the principles of the doctrine of the "irregular situation" that views them as objects of protection rather than subjects of rights, involves applying an undefined sanction. That breaches the principle of lawfulness of punishment, aggravated by the fact that generally this is ordered without defining its duration. It is also contrary to the rules of due process.[182]

In the case of children, certainly preventive detention must have as main aim the superior interest of the child. In the case of Panchito López, the Court emphasizes that preventive detention must be used when there is no other alternative and its duration must be as short as possible. The Court mentioned in the judgment other possible measures, such as strict supervision, foster care, counselling and vocational training programs.[183] In the case of Mendoza *et al.*, where several children were convicted to life imprisonment or reclusion for life, the Court alluded to Article 37 of the Convention on the Rights of the Child, which establishes the basic principles that regulate deprivation of liberty of children: *ultima ratio* and shortest time possible, temporal determination and periodic review of the measure of deprivation of that right. The latter means that the State must also provide early release programs in its legal order. The Court found that the penalty imposed on the victims in this case did not comply with any of the principles and thus amounted to an arbitrary deprivation of liberty and consequently violated Article 7(3).[184]

The obligation to determine identity and age was addressed by the Court in the case of the Landaeta brothers, a case in which Article 7 had been violated on several counts. Eduardo Landaeta was under 18 but the arrest information said that he was 18. The Court clarified that to identify age when no official document existed the State had to resort to scientific criteria – physical and psychological – for this determination and that, in case of doubt, the benefit of the doubt had to be given to the detainee.[185] The Court found that, as the State had not complied with this obligation *ex officio*, Eduardo had not been sent to the corresponding

181 *Ibidem*, para. 137.
182 *Ibidem*, para. 15. In the same sense, see Costa Rica (*idem*).
183 *Case of "Panchito López" v. Paraguay*, paras. 225–226, 230–231.
184 *Case of Mendoza et al. v. Argentina*, paras. 163–164.
185 *Case of Landaeta brothers v. Venezuela*, paras. 172–173.

authority who dealt with children and had not been given any special protection because he was underage. That constituted a violation of the Convention.

8. DEPRIVATION OF LIBERTY OF MIGRANTS

29. Similar to women and children, the case of migrants is another example of the need to explain repeatedly that every human being is entitled to all human rights. Migrants are human beings and yet the Court was requested by the Government of Mexico to produce an Opinion with regard to their human rights, because of its profound concern about "the incompatibility with the OAS human rights system of the interpretations, practices and enactment of laws by some States in the region".[186] Mexico was referring of course to the violation of the principle of equality between migrants and non-migrants, particularly in respect to the labor rights of the former.[187] Among the various questions, it is worth mentioning question 3 asking for the compatibility of domestic laws that subordinate or condition human rights of migrants "to achieving migration policy goals" in spite of international law norms that "have an *erga omnes* character".[188]

The Court noted that the international community had recognized the need to adopt special measures to ensure the protection of the human rights of migrants. It gave its Opinion agreeing with the reasons provided by the State and by many *amici curia* concluding that the State could have a different treatment only with respect to *undocumented* migrants, "provided that this differential treatment is reasonable, objective, proportionate and does not harm human rights". It was also of the opinion that "States may also establish mechanisms to control the entry into and departure from their territory of undocumented migrants, which must always be applied with strict regard for the guarantees of due process and respect for human dignity."[189]

This opinion was the basis for developing the issue of the treatment of migrants in the case of Vélez Loor, which deals primarily with the deprivation of liberty of the alleged victim, an Ecuadorian man who was caught entering Panama without documents after having been expelled from that country some years before due to a lack of appropriate documents.[190] According to the Court,

---

186 Advisory Opinion, *OC-18/03* of September 17, 2003.

187 *Ibidem*, para. 3. Mexico requested the Court to interpret the following norms: Articles 3(1) and 17 of the Charter of the Organization of American States; Article II of the American Declaration on the Rights and Duties of Man; Articles 1(1), 2 and 24 of the American Convention; Articles 1, 2(1) and 7 of the Universal Declaration on Human Rights, and Articles 2(1), 2(2), 5(2) and 26 of the International Covenant on Civil and Political Rights.

188 *Ibidem*, para. 4.

189 *Ibidem*, para. 119.

190 *Case of Vélez Loor v. Panama*, paras. 2 and 94.

"the measures restricting the personal liberty applied to Mr. Vélez Loor were not related to the commission of a criminal crime, but responded to an irregular immigration status for having entered Panama through an unauthorized area, without the necessary documents and in violation of a prior deportation order".[191] Deprivation of liberty of undocumented migrants must comply with all the requirements of any other type of detention. Nevertheless, the Court was aware of the *de facto* situation of migrants in the region and of the fact that it had not referred before to detention outside the framework of a criminal procedure. It was necessary then to examine the general requirements to specify what they meant when they were to be applied to detentions of this kind.

Examining the grounds and requirements to order the detention of an irregular migrant, the Court found that in Panama "the arrest warrant of irregular immigrants was automatically issued after the initial arrest", without any mention of the reasons that justified the particular arrest of each person.[192] On a similar point, the Court stated that since "States have the authority to control and regulate the entrance and stay of foreign persons in their territory" this could constitute "a lawful purpose according to the Convention". The Court added that "the application of preventive custody may be suitable to regulate and control the irregular immigration in order to ensure that the individual appears before the immigration proceeding or, in addition, to guarantee the application of an order for deportation."[193] What was not suitable was the use of deprivation of liberty as a punitive measure. Mr. Vélez Loor was detained to punish him for having entered Panama without appropriate documents after a prior deportation ordered some years before. The undocumented migrant was not only arrested but also submitted to an administrative procedure, without due process, that concluded in a punitive penalty of two years' imprisonment. The Court, aside from finding violations of Article 8 of the Convention, found – on the basis of the views of the Working Group on Arbitrary Disappearance[194] and of two reports of the UN Rapporteur on the Human Rights of Migrants[195] – that "the detention of people for non-compliance with immigration laws should never involve punitive purposes. Hence, a custodial measure should only be applied when it is necessary and proportionate in the specific case to the purposes mentioned *supra* and only for the shortest period of time."[196]

---

191 *Ibidem*, para. 106.

192 *Ibidem*, paras. 118 and 116.

193 *Ibidem*, para. 169.

194 Working Group on Arbitrary Detention, Group Report, A/HRC/7/4, January 10, 2008, para. 53.

195 United Nations, "Specific Groups and Individuals: Migrant Workers. Human Rights of Migrants", Report of the Special Rapporteur, Ms. Gabriela Rodriguez Pizarro, submitted pursuant to Order 2002/62 of the Human Rights Commission, E/CN.4/2003/85, December 30, 2002, para. 73.

196 *Case of Vélez Loor v.* Panama, paras. 169–171.

A different matter was the real access to justice of these people. The Court emphasized the importance of legal aid, given the persons affected are aliens without any knowledge of the legal system that will be applied to them.[197] It even mentioned that, in this case, there was no evidence that "free legal representation provided by Court appointed counsel or by any other free legal counsel provided by the State" had been offered to Mr. Vélez Loor. It said also that the Office of Immigration did not have court appointed counsel to assist those who did not have financial means to hire this assistance.[198]

The Court also reaffirmed the obligation that migrants be assisted by the consul of the State of which they are nationals, stating that there were "three essential components of the right due to the person by a State Party", provided they had previously requested international protection. The first was "the right to be informed of his right under the Vienna Convention"; the second, to have an *effective* access to communication with the consul; and the third, interestingly, "the right to the assistance itself".[199] This third right is referred to in a later paragraph, where the Court states that the right to seek consular assistance binds the State of which the detainee is a national.[200] The task of the consul is, for example, "granting or hiring legal counsel, obtaining evidence in the country of origin, corroborating the conditions under which legal assistance is provided, and observing the situation of the accused while he or she is in prison", so that the task guarantees and enforces "the rights to personal liberty, humane treatment, and defense".[201]

Irregular migrants are, according to the Court, particularly vulnerable when they are held in penitentiary centers together with persons undergoing a criminal trial or serving time for the commission of a criminal offense, where it is probable that they be subjected to abusive treatment. Consequently, migrants "must be held in facilities specifically destined for that purpose, according to their legal situation and not in common prisons, the purpose of which is incompatible with the nature of the possible detention of a person for her or his immigration status". The State's obligation is then to "provide public establishments specifically designed for that purpose", and in their absence, other premises specially assigned for them, with material conditions and a regime "appropriate to their legal situation and staffed by suitably-qualified personnel".[202]

---

197 *Ibidem*, para. 32.

198 *Ibidem*, para. 136.

199 *Ibidem*, para. 153.

200 *Ibidem*, para. 158.

201 *Ibidem*, para. 154.

202 *Ibidem*, paras. 208–209. In a similar position, the Court cites here the European Court of Human Rights, *Ha You ZHU v. United Kingdom*, Application No. 36790/97, Admissibility of September 12, 2000, folio 6 and the United Nations, Working Group on Arbitrary Detention, Group Report, Civil and Political Rights, in particular the issues related to torture and detention, E/CN.4/2004/3/Add.3, December 23, 2003, Recommendation 75.

9. DEPRIVATION OF LIBERTY OF MIGRANT CHILDREN

30. Late in 2014, the Court issued an Advisory Opinion on the issue of the obligations of States "in relation to the possible measures to be adopted regarding children, their immigration status or the status of their parents". This Opinion focuses on migrant children. The request was made in relation to several articles of the Convention, among which Article 7 on deprivation of liberty, several articles of the American Declaration and Article 13 of the Inter-American Torture Convention.[203] In Latin America, this is a matter of the utmost importance, explained by the Court in a section entitled "General Considerations". There, it gives information on the number of migrants in this region and the reasons they or their parents have to leave their own country. The Court analyzes the phenomenon of migration and the human rights aspects that need consideration by the States in order to comply with international law. It affirms that the only way to ensure protection complying with international law is "by admitting a potential asylum applicant into a safe country, by guaranteeing the right to seek and receive asylum, and by respecting the principle of *non-refoulement*, among other rights, until achieving a durable solution".[204] This is in tune with Latin American tradition. Article 22(7) of the American Convention sets forth the right of every person "to seek and be granted asylum in a foreign territory, in accordance with the legislation of the state and international conventions, in the event he is being pursued for political offenses or related common crimes". States must design their immigration policies with a human rights approach and using as a guide the special protection granted to children.[205]

The Opinion deals in detail with the right to personal freedom, as the request specifically consults "on the interpretation that should be given to the *ultima ratio* (last resort) principle of detention [...] in the context of immigration proceedings". In its Opinion, the Court uses the expression "deprivation of liberty" in a broad meaning.[206] It understands "that restriction of personal liberty is any measure that involves impairment of this right, either through total deprivation by reclusion in a closed place or any other lesser restriction that, owing to its form, duration, effects and method of implementation, entails interference in the right of everyone to personal liberty".[207] Subsequently, the

---

203 Advisory Opinion, *OC-21/2014*, requested by the Argentine Republic, the Federative Republic of Brazil, the Republic of Paraguay and the Oriental Republic of Uruguay, of August 19, 2014, Rights and guarantees of children in the context of migration and/or in need of international protection.

204 *Ibidem*, para. 38.

205 *Ibidem*, para. 41.

206 *Ibidem*, para. 145.

207 *Ibidem*, para. 187. This definition is based on European case law mentioned in the paragraph, as well as on the United Nations High Commissioner for Refugees (UNHCR), *Guidelines*

Court states that the difference between deprivation and restriction of liberty depends on "the level of intensity of the measure", but it is not one of nature or substance; both are covered by the protection of Article 7.[208] The Court emphasizes, following the UN High Commissioner for Refugees, that the element to put Article 7 in operation, "regardless of the specific name it is given at the local level, is the fact that the person, in this case the child, cannot or is unable to leave or abandon at will the place or establishment where she or he has been placed".[209] Deprivation of liberty of migrants may affect asylum seekers, refugees, stateless persons and irregular migrants. However, the Court limits the scope of the Opinion to some cases. One relates "specifically to children in an irregular migratory status". The other relates to children "seeking asylum who have not obtained the recognition of refugee status based on being unable to fulfill the elements necessary to qualify and who are submitted to a judicial process that can end in an expulsion or deportation order to the country of origin or, in the alternative, an order that allows the child to stay". It leaves aside deprivation of liberty as a penalty or punitive sanction; for the Court, as was already mentioned above, this is an arbitrary action, incompatible with the Convention, as found in the case of Vélez Loor.[210]

The two premises on which the consultation is based are the principle of *ultima ratio* and the need to provide the grounds justifying the measure of deprivation of liberty. Quoting the Committee on the Rights of the Child, the Court affirms that the principle of *ultima ratio* is a principle of international human rights law, "since the purpose of criminal proceedings in the case of children is fundamentally pedagogical".[211] This principle should also be applied to detention on remand.[212] The Court reflects that offenses related to entry or stay in a country are not comparable to criminal ones, and so the consequences should also be different. In addition, migration and criminal proceedings have different procedural purposes; therefore, the principle of *ultima ratio* of the imprisonment of children is also outside the scope of the consultation.[213]

The Opinion conducts its analysis and evaluates the situation using the four elements that a restriction must comply to restrict a right: the objectivity of the measure, its conduciveness, the necessity to order it in a democratic society, and its proportionality.[214] Using these parameters, the Court deems that the deprivation of liberty of a child migrant in an irregular situation, on this basis

on the Applicable Criteria and Standards relating to the Detention of Asylum-Seekers and Alternatives to Detention, published in 2012.

208 *Ibidem*. Also based on European case law mentioned in the same paragraph.

209 *Ibidem*, para. 145.

210 *Ibidem*, paras. 148 and 151.

211 *Ibidem*, para. 149.

212 *Ibidem*.

213 *Ibidem*, para. 150.

214 *Ibidem*, para. 153.

alone, is arbitrary and incompatible with the Convention and the American Declaration.[215] According to the Court, the State should use as a parameter "the prevalence of the best interest of the child migrant and the guiding principle of respect for the child's right to life, survival, and development by [... taking] measures adapted to the child's needs".[216] The measures will be different depending on whether the child is alone or accompanied by his or her parents. Unaccompanied children are more vulnerable and thus should have special care, since they are directly under the responsibility of the State.[217] In this case, deprivation of liberty is inappropriate.[218] Accompanied children, stresses the Court, have a right to live with their families, but this right cannot justify putting the children in prison with the parents; therefore, the State has an obligation to seek alternative measures for the parents so as not to divide the family.[219]

On concluding this part of its analysis, the Court deems that deprivation of liberty of children, unaccompanied or accompanied by their parents, should not be used as a precautionary measure in immigration proceedings; the State should establish "other less harmful alternatives".[220] If the child has perpetrated a criminal offense, the principle of *ultima ratio* applies and detention should be "for the shortest time possible.[221]

The Opinion then addresses the characteristics of the measures mentioned above and the guarantees for their application. As to the characteristics, the Court explains that ontologically the measures "must be conceived precisely by opposition to "deprivation of liberty" and must result "in a lower level of harmfulness", giving as examples reporting to authorities at regular intervals or staying in open centers or at a designated place.[222] After saying this, the Court reaffirms that there is a general principle of non-deprivation of liberty, so accordingly voluntary measures "should not be conceived as alternatives to detention". The measures should be for "priority implementation" with the objective of giving the child personalized full protection of his or her rights.[223] Rights that must be specially protected would be health, adequate nutrition, education and recreation. The aims of the measures should be the satisfaction of basic material, physical and educational needs, emotional care and protection against any type of abuse.[224] For indigenous children, measures must consider their cultural context.[225]

---

215 *Ibidem*, para. 154.
216 *Ibidem*, para. 155.
217 *Ibidem*, para. 156.
218 *Ibidem*, para. 157.
219 *Ibidem*, para. 158.
220 *Ibidem*, para. 160.
221 *Ibidem*, para. 159.
222 *Ibidem*, para. 162. It is not clear to me whether the word "place" refers to a designated locality.
223 *Ibidem*, para. 163.
224 *Ibidem*, para. 164.
225 *Ibidem*, para. 168.

The State consequently has obligations to achieve these aims. Measures should be established in domestic law, taking care that child protection systems prevail over immigration control institutions.[226] There must exist a competent administrative or judicial authority and the right to a review of an unfavorable decision. Children must be heard and their views must be taken into account. The best interests of the child must be the primary consideration.[227] The Court ends this section of the Opinion concerning the right to personal liberty of migrant children by reiterating that States must have in their domestic law

> a set of non-custodial measures to be ordered and implemented while the immigration proceedings are held that promote, above all, the comprehensive protection of the rights of the child, in keeping with the characteristics described above, with strict respect for their human rights and the principle of legality.[228]

The Court applies in this section the same principles used for the former section. The Court admits the possibility that there could be circumstances in which the States need "to resort to such measures as placing children in a shelter or accommodation, either for a short period or for as long as necessary to resolve the immigration status". This requires evidence of "an exceptional, inevitable, and imperative need for precautionary measures" and that no less harmful alternative exists "than placing the child in a center where the child can coexist with her or his family". In the case of unaccompanied children, when "there is no possibility of accommodating the child in a family or community environment". In such a situation, children may be placed in an institutionalized center, a custodial measure, where children must nevertheless remain separated from those accused or convicted of criminal offenses, and the center must be specifically intended to accommodate migrants.[229]

The Court examines as well the characteristics of basic accommodation for children.[230] It analyzes three points: (i) the principle of separation and right to family unity; (ii) open accommodation centers; and (iii) material conditions and an adequate regime that ensure the comprehensive protection of rights. Concerning the first, the Court says that there are two dimensions of separation: "(i) unaccompanied or separated children should be lodged in places apart from those for adults, and (ii) accompanied children should be lodged with their family members, unless it is more appropriate to separate them in application of the principle of the child's best interest". It adds that the age of unaccompanied children should be considered to divide the children according to the specific

---

226 *Ibidem*, paras. 166, 165, 167 and 169.

227 *Ibidem*, para. 169.

228 *Ibidem*, para. 170.

229 *Ibidem*, para. 173. These sentences have been checked against the Spanish version, to clarify the difficult English translation. See also *Case of Vélez Loor v. Panama*, para. 208.

230 *Ibidem*, paras. 171 through 184.

needs of particular age groups.[231] As to the other two points, they follow the logical path set by the principles already mentioned above.

31. The following section addresses another question of the consultation: the guarantees of due process in immigration proceedings involving children and adolescents when their personal liberty is restricted. The Court explains again that the "difference between deprivation of liberty and restriction of liberty stems from the level of intensity of the measure". The consequence that follows from this assertion is that "in certain circumstances, a 'delay,' even merely to identify the person, may constitute a deprivation of physical liberty".[232] The Court states that all guarantees in Article 7 are applicable to migrants, and the special protection that should be given to children must result in a careful application of these guarantees to migrant children.[233] There are specific points that should be mentioned. The language to be used to arrest and in further proceedings should be one that the migrant child understands, adapted to his or her maturity and age, and the unaccompanied child must be informed of the right to have a guardian adopted.[234] In addition, the child should be notified of his or her right to consular assistance and effective access to communicate with the consul should be provided.[235] Obviously, this is not necessary when the migrant is an asylum seeker, refugee, or is the beneficiary of international protection for other reasons.[236]

The Opinion contains more analysis that is not pertinent to examine here. One should conclude that the treatment of migrant children, as analyzed by the Court, reaffirms the fact that children migrants are human beings and thus holders of human rights. The Court's task here has been to detail for States what the obligation to ensure entails for them.[237]

32. A few days after the last Advisory Opinion was issued, the Court pronounced on a case of the expulsion of persons of Haitian origin from the Dominican Republic.[238] Some of the people expelled were Dominicans, whose nationality was in the process of being annulled, according to a new law passed years after they had obtained their documents; others had never been able to obtain their documents since not even their birth had been registered due to the many obstacles placed in their way by the authorities. There were massive expulsions and in order to carry them out, detentions infringed all provisions

---

231 *Ibidem*, paras. 178 and 179.
232 *Ibidem*, para. 187.
233 *Ibidem*, paras. 188, 189 and 190.
234 *Ibidem*, para. 197.
235 *Ibidem*, para. 202.
236 *Ibidem*, para. 203.
237 On this, see Chapter 1.
238 *Case of Expelled Dominican and Haitian Persons v. Dominican Republic.*

set forth in domestic law: there were no arrest orders and they were not given the time to come before a court or to present an injunction for their liberty. Many of the victims in this case were children. In their case, the State had not taken any special measures of protection.[239] The judgment relied heavily on its own Opinion to find violations of Articles 7 and 19 of the Convention. The thrust of this case, however, is the examination of Article 22, which, as said before, while being close to Article 7, operates in a different area.

239 *Ibidem*, para. 344.

CHAPTER 6
RIGHT TO DUE PROCESS*

Article 8. Right to a Fair Trial

1. *Every person has the right to a hearing, with due guarantees and within a reasonable time, by a competent, independent, and impartial tribunal, previously established by law, in the substantiation of any accusation of a criminal nature made against him or for the determination of his rights and obligations of a civil, labor, fiscal, or any other nature.*
2. *Every person accused of a criminal offense has the right to be presumed innocent so long as his guilt has not been proven according to law. During the proceedings, every person is entitled, with full equality, to the following minimum guarantees:*
   a. *the right of the accused to be assisted without charge by a translator or interpreter, if he does not understand or does not speak the language of the tribunal or court;*
   b. *prior notification in detail to the accused of the charges against him;*
   c. *adequate time and means for the preparation of his defense;*
   d. *the right of the accused to defend himself personally or to be assisted by legal counsel of his own choosing, and to communicate freely and privately with his counsel;*
   e. *the inalienable right to be assisted by counsel provided by the state, paid or not as the domestic law provides, if the accused does not defend himself personally or engage his own counsel within the time period established by law;*
   f. *the right of the defense to examine witnesses present in the court and to obtain the appearance, as witnesses, of experts or other persons who may throw light on the facts;*
   g. *the right not to be compelled to be a witness against himself or to plead guilty; and*
   h. *the right to appeal the judgment to a higher court.*

---

* An excellent compilation of international and Inter-American case law on "due process" with comments can be found in *El Debido Proceso Legal. Análisis desde el Sistema Interamericano y Universal de Derechos Humanos*, Ministerio Público Fiscal de la Ciudad Autónoma de Buenos Aires, Argentina, 2013.

3. *A confession of guilt by the accused shall be valid only if it is made without coercion of any kind.*
4. *An accused person acquitted by a no appealable judgment shall not be subjected to a new trial for the same cause.*
5. *Criminal proceedings shall be public, except insofar as may be necessary to protect the interests of justice.*

1. INTRODUCTION

1. The importance of the existence of an international right to a fair trial in Latin America cannot be underestimated. A look at all the judgments on the merits from the first judgment of the Court in 2004[1] to the last judgment examined by this book in November 2014,[2] shows that the vast majority of them find a violation of the right to a fair trial. Most of the remaining cases approach due process under Articles 25 (right of judicial protection)[3] or 13 (freedom of expression and its judicial guarantees)[4] or find that there was no violation of Article 8.[5] Just two of them deal with questions where Article 8 does not play a part.[6] This is not at all surprising.[7] Latin American countries have gone from an inquisitorial criminal system to an adversarial one in the last two decades. The changes have been progressive and have faced obstacles of a political nature (lack of adequate support), of a financial nature, or of a cultural nature among those who are supposed to carry them out, one of which, for example, is the abundant use of preventive detention, deprivation of liberty also having due process components.[8] The reform of the system still does not seem to be complete and is highly dependent on a change of behavior, mainly of judges and prosecutors, but also of society. Nor is this surprising if we realize that due process of law is the cornerstone of the human rights protection system; it is, par excellence, the

1 *Case of Massacre Plan de Sanchez v. Guatemala.*
2 *Case of Espinoza Gonzáles v. Peru.*
3 *Case of the Saramaka people v. Suriname; Acevedo Buendía et al. v. Peru*; and *Abril Alosilla et al. v. Peru.*
4 *Cases of Ríos et al.* and *Perozo et al.*, both v. Venezuela.
5 For example, *case of Grande v. Argentina.*
6 *Case of Castañeda v. Mexico* on political rights and *case of Artavia Murillo et al. v. Costa Rica* on in vitro fertilization.
7 See in this regard paragraph 3 of the concurrent vote of Judge García-Sayán in the *case of Barbani Duarte v. Uruguay.* He stated: "When this judgment was adopted, in October 2011, the Court had declared a violation of Article 8 of the Convention in more than 95% of the cases it had heard and had referred to the content and requirements of this article in 50% of its advisory opinions. Thus, the issue of due process of law has been and continues to be present permanently in the cases submitted to the Inter-American Court."
8 See C. Riego, "Nuevas tendencias de las reformas procesales penales en América Latina", in CEJA, Reformas procesales penales en América Latina: Resultados del Proyecto de Seguimiento, IV etapa at www.cejamericas.org.

guarantor of all human rights and a *sine qua non* requirement for the existence of the rule of law. It is protected both in Article 6 of the European Convention and in Article 14 of the International Covenant on Civil and Political Rights (ICCPR).[9] It is not difficult to imagine the enormous problems the Court has had to face in dealing with issues of Article 8 when the cases presented came from countries where there had been no rule of law for so long or from countries where due process was usually applied only lightly.

2. Article 8 of the Convention, which according to its heading enshrines the right to a "fair trial", establishes what is known in international human rights law as the right to "due process". The right to due process is based on the principle of equality – both parties to a case have what is called usually equality of arms – and on the principle that the process shall be held with due guarantees publically and before a competent, independent and impartial tribunal. These are the basic notions that guide the interpretation of Article 8 by the Inter-American Court.

3. In the Convention, the right to a fair trial is very broad. On the one hand, it seeks to protect the rights of the parties to a conflict and to have the conflict be resolved in as just a manner as possible. This is so whether those conflicts are, on the one hand, between private parties or State bodies or whether or not they deal with issues of human rights. On the other hand, it regulates the requirements of criminal proceedings that determine the guilt or innocence of a person.[10] As the Court holds, Article 8 "is not limited strictly to judicial remedies,[11] 'but to a series of requirements that must be observed by the procedural bodies' so that a person may defend himself adequately against any act of the State that could affect his rights."[12] As an example of this broad scope Article 8 covers, *inter alia*, individual clemency petitions, which in the case of Hilaire, Constantine and Benjamín *et al.*, had been characterized by "a lack of transparency, lack of available information and lack of participation by the victims".[13]

The Convention establishes general requirements that must be met by all proceedings. In addition – because in criminal cases the accused is particularly vulnerable to State power and because these proceedings always affect the reputation of persons and bring with them at least the risk that another human right (the right to personal liberty) be limited – Article 8(2) of the Convention

9 The International Covenant on Civil and Political Rights (ICCPR), adopted and opened for signature, ratification and accession by General Assembly Resolution 2200A (XXI) of December 16, 1966. Entry into force March 23, 1976.

10 See M. Melgar Adalid, "El derecho humano de acceso a la justicia", in Inter-American Court, *Líber Amicorum Héctor Fix-Zamudio*, Vol. I, San Jose, Costa Rica, 1998, pp. 1035–1048 (1045–1040).

11 The title of this right in Spanish is *Garantías Judiciales* (judicial guarantees). Hence this clarification by the Court.

12 *Case of Ivcher Bronstein v. Peru*, para. 108.

13 *Case of Hilaire, Benjamin, Constantine et al. v. Trinidad and Tobago*, paras. 186, 188 and. 189.

contains the minimum guarantees for ensuring due process for the accused. These guarantees are contained in Article 8(1) under the concept of "due guarantees" but Article 8(2) specifies some of them for criminal proceedings to emphasize for judges the need to always have these present in this type of case. Their existence does not depend on the decision of a judge. On the other hand, in criminal proceedings, there may be other guarantees besides those of paragraph 2, because this paragraph does not replace the general guarantees contained in paragraph 1 but rather specifies them. Consequently, in a criminal trial it is possible that guarantees other than those in Article 8(2) may be necessary for a particular criminal proceeding to be compatible with the demands of due process, in accordance with the provisions of Article 8(1).

In the eyes of the Court, the position of due process is paramount, because it constitutes the safeguard of all the rights in the Convention.[14] Its importance is such that the Court has considered that due process, *habeas corpus* and the right to judicial protection constitute the judicial guarantees that cannot be suspended in a state of emergency.[15] The Court has stated that the general principles of due process of law could not be suspended in situations of martial law, as those principles establish the conditions necessary for the procedural instruments regulated by the Convention to be considered as judicial guarantees.[16]

4. As already indicated, Article 8 of the Convention contains in its paragraph 1 a general rule that applies to all proceedings, while its paragraph 2 contains the minimum guarantees enjoyed by the accused in criminal proceedings. This chapter will examine the various guarantees set forth in Article 8 mainly in the order they are placed in the Convention, with some minor alterations. Later, it will address other aspects: the requirement for a confession to be accepted, the principle of *non bis in idem*, and the characteristics of a trial compatible with the Convention. However, there is one issue that should be examined first, the issue of the fourth instance, to clarify the extent and scope of the Court's jurisdiction in the application of Article 8.

2. THE ISSUE OF THE FOURTH INSTANCE

5. Before the specific analysis of the different aspects contained in Article 8, there is an issue that deserves attention in the application of this provision by the Court: the so-called fourth instance. It refers to the fact that the Court cannot in principle interfere with the domestic judiciary, so limits have to be drawn to monitor States Parties' compliance with the rules of due process. The

14 *Case of Vargas Areco v. Paraguay*, para. 73.
15 I refer to Article 27 of the Convention on suspension of guarantees.
16 *OC/9/87*, para. 30.

examination of this type of case often places the Commission and the Court in the situation of ruling on matters on which one or more domestic courts have already ruled. A decision has to be made as to how far the Court may go. As a product of the incipient development of international human rights law in our countries, the States' natural reaction to Court's revisions is one of rejection. The argument employed is that once domestic courts have ruled definitively on a case, resulting in the corresponding *res judicata*, it is not up to an international body to alter that ruling. States remark that national courts have heard the case and weighed the evidence at the time it was presented, and it would seem unlikely that an international body with *a posteriori* involvement that did not participate directly and personally in collecting the evidence would be able to re-examine and judge the case anew. This is known as "the fourth instance doctrine".

In fact, no international supervisory body – be it the European Court, the Human Rights Committee or the Inter-American Commission or Court – has ever attempted to replace domestic courts with its rulings on cases. A proceeding before an international body does not infringe on the principle of *res judicata* because a domestic proceeding that can lead to a violation of Article 8 of the Convention deals with different parties, a different substance of the claim (*eadem res*) and a different reason for the claim (*eadem causa petendi*). When a case of this kind reaches the supervisory body – in the case of the Inter-American system, the Commission and eventually the Court – the body examines the national judiciary's compliance with the obligations imposed by Article 8 of the Convention. The Commission and the Court do not examine anew the evidence of the trial in question in order to find, for example, that a defendant in a criminal trial is innocent and not guilty. Instead, they examine whether domestic courts have respected the obligation, *inter alia*, to grant adequate time and opportunity for the defense and give the party a fair chance to challenge the evidence presented against him or her. In sum, it decides whether there has been a violation of the basic procedural rules established in Article 8 of the Convention. If any of these requirements have not been met during the domestic trial, the supervisory body will find that this provision has been violated. Thus, none of these bodies exercises its powers as if it were an appeals court (fourth instance). One must insist on this point, as it would not be appropriate for an international body to cease rigorously supervising compliance with the demands of due process – a pillar of human rights guarantees – due to a fear of becoming a "fourth instance", particularly regarding States that have, in general, a noticeable deficiency in this area.

6. The Court has addressed this problem. In the case of Villagrán Morales, it found Guatemala's courts had not carried out "an adequate investigation and judicial proceeding that would lead to the punishment of those responsible".[17]

17 *Case of Villagrán Morales et al. v. Guatemala*, para. 229.

The State had completely failed to investigate the details of the kidnapping and torture of the victims (some of them minors) and "evidence that could have been very important for the due clarification of the homicides was not ordered, practiced or evaluated."[18] With regard to the weighing of the evidence, the Court stated that: "If we consider how those judges proceeded as a whole, it is evident that they fragmented the probative material and then endeavored to weaken the significance of each and every one of the elements that proved the responsibility of the defendants, item by item."[19]

Examining the case law of the Court on this point, a superficial analysis might lead one to think that the Court reaches quite far in its review of the establishment of the facts and the evidence by domestic courts, and in doing so, transforms itself into a fourth instance court. However, this is not so. One should take into consideration that the case law on the Court's jurisdiction regarding facts and evidence is often established in cases of disappearance or summary executions at the hands of State agents. In those cases, domestic courts commonly do not wish or are not able to comply with any of the rules of due process, which makes it necessary to review the proceedings in a way that makes it possible to ascertain whether the right to due process has been observed. The Inter-American Court has expressed this clearly. In the same case of Villagrán Morales, it indicated that: "In order to clarify whether the State has violated its international obligations owing to the acts of its judicial organs, the Court may have to examine the respective domestic proceedings."[20] Later, citing the European Court, it stated that "the function of the international court is to determine if all the proceedings, and the way in which the evidence was produced, were fair."[21] Insisting on the scope of its jurisdiction, the Court added that it "has attributions, not to investigate and punish individual conduct of State agents that may have participated in these violations, but to establish the international responsibility of States as a result of human rights violations".[22] In the case of Genie Lacayo, it also observed:

> All [the Court] is empowered to do in this case is call attention to the procedural violations of the rights enshrined in the Convention which have injured Mr. Raymond Genie-Peñalba, the interested party in the matter; however, it lacks jurisdiction to remedy those violations in the domestic arena, a task, as has been pointed out before, that falls to the Supreme Court of Justice of Nicaragua when it disposes of the application for judicial review which is yet to be resolved.[23]

---

18 *Ibidem*, para. 230. Translator's version. This paragraph and those following it in the judgment include the details supporting this general assertion.

19 *Ibidem*, para. 233. This is the official version.

20 *Ibidem*, para. 222.

21 *Ibidem*.

22 *Ibidem*, para. 223.

23 *Case of Genie Lacayo v. Nicaragua*, para. 94.

In later cases, such as the case of the Massacre of Mapiripán, the Court insisted that the substance of the dispute in the national courts is irrelevant for the Court; what is relevant is "whether the domestic proceedings enabled protection of true access to justice in accordance with the standards set forth in the American Convention."[24] In the case of González Medina and family, concerning a disappearance, the State presented a preliminary objection because the Court "would act as a fourth judicial instance, in violation of the [Convention]."[25] The Court rejected the objection because the issue in the case was not to review "assessment of the evidence, the facts, or domestic law", but to decide if there had been a violation of the Convention by the domestic court's judgment.[26] In the case of Cabrera García and Montiel Flores, the State objected to the competence of the Court when the domestic courts have exercised "effectively the *ex officio* 'conventionality control' that must prevail for a fourth instance exception to be applicable", alluding to the fact that it would constitute a "fourth instance".[27] The Court rejected this preliminary objection since the Court's role is precisely to see if in the application of the Convention to a domestic case the State has not violated it.[28]

7. There is a fine line to be drawn regarding what the Court can do when the failure is at the stage of the investigation. The Court said in Nogueira de Carvalho *et al.* that "[i]t is not the responsibility of this Court to replace the domestic jurisdiction by ordering concrete methods or forms for investigating and judging a specific case in order to obtain a better or more effective outcome; instead, its role is to find whether or not, in the steps actually taken domestically, the State's international obligations embodied in Articles 8 and 25 of the American Convention have been violated".[29] In the case of Castillo González, the Court rejected the arguments of the Commission as to the lack of some concrete measures of investigation. It stated that it would only accept those measures that had been ordered by the authorities, because, in principle, it is not within the Court's competence to decide whether certain specific, concrete measures of investigation are warranted or useful, "*unless the omission of carrying them out is* contrary *to objective rules or is manifestly unreasonable*".[30] In another case, it insisted that "the Court is unable to 'settle the disagreements between the parties concerning specific implications of the evidence or the application of domestic

24 *Case of the Massacre of Mariripan v. Colombia*, para. 211. Quotes of European case law are also given; see paras. 212–213.

25 *Case of González Medina v. Dominican Republic*, para. 36. Sea also *Mejía Idrovo v. Ecuador*, para. 18.

26 *Ibidem*, paras. 40–41. See also *Case of Massacre of Mapiripán v. Colombia*, para. 211.

27 *Case of Cabrera García and Montiel Flores v. Mexico*, para. 13.

28 *Ibidem*, paras. 16–22.

29 *Case of Nogueira de Carvhalo et al. v. Brazil*, para. 80.

30 *Case of Castillo González et al. v. Venezuela*, para. 153 (judgment only in Spanish) (emphasis added; author's own translation).

law on aspects that are not directly related to compliance with international human rights obligations'".[31] On the contrary, in the case of Myrna Mack Chang, the Court did pronounce on the investigation and the lack of evidence finding that "elements had been omitted that were fundamental to the proper course of the judicial investigation, including failures to take blood samples and to examine the victim's clothing". In this case the omission was unreasonable and the measures indicated by the Court were warranted.[32] The same position was taken in other cases, such as González *et al.* ("Cotton Field") v. Mexico, as will be seen later on and the case of Landaeta brothers *et al.*[33]

The standard for the Court seems to be then that during the investigative stage any action contrary to objective rules or manifestly unreasonable falls within the supervisory jurisdiction of the Court and does not constitute a fourth instance review.

3. RIGHT TO A HEARING OR ACCESS TO JUSTICE

8. In this section, I will analyze the first paragraph of Article 8, which establishes the due process requirements that are applicable to all cases – whether criminal or not. Covered by this paragraph are matters of a criminal, civil, labor, fiscal, or any other nature. The Court has consistently found that this paragraph must be given a broad interpretation based on both the letter and the spirit of this provision derived from a representative, democratic form of government.[34]

9. The obligation for the determination of rights or obligations and a ruling on the guilt or innocence of a person to be made in accordance with due process obviously implies that every individual has the right to appear before a court for such purposes. The guarantee of the exercise of this right implies in turn a State obligation to establish agencies and proceedings that meet the requirements of Article 8, as well as to provide individuals with the minimum means for accessing them. There are consequently positive State obligations to comply with Article 8.

All individuals are entitled to the right to a hearing, without discrimination. To deny access for reasons of a person's status is forbidden. In Advisory Opinion 18/03 on the human rights of migrants and particularly on the right to due process, the Court concluded "[t]hat the general obligation to respect

---

31 *Case of Palma Mendoza et al. v. Ecuador*, para. 102. See also, in this same sense, *Case of the Afro-descendant communities displaced from the Cacarica river basin (Operation Genesis) v. Colombia*, para. 225.

32 *Case of Myrna Mack Chang v. Guatemala*, paras. 166–167.

33 *Case of the Landaeta brothers et al. v. Venezuela*, paras. 220 and following.

34 Case *of Blake v. Guatemala*, para. 96. See also, for example, *Case of Durand and Ugarte v. Peru*, para. 128.

and guarantee human rights binds States, regardless of any circumstance or consideration, including the migratory status of a person".[35] This is the consequence of the universality of human rights and of the State obligation to respect and ensure human rights for "all persons subject to [its] jurisdiction", established in Article 1 of the Convention. Consequently, the Court found "[t]hat the right to due process of law must be recognized as one of the minimum guarantees that should be offered to any migrant, irrespective of his migratory status. The broad scope of the preservation of due process encompasses all matters and all persons, without any discrimination".[36] A similar position has been held with regard to aliens ordered to be expelled or deported. There must be due process for the decision. This means that "(a) an alien can only be expelled in compliance with a decision reached in accordance with the law, and (b) the alien must be empowered with the means to: (i) provide arguments against the expulsion (ii) submit his or her case before by the competent authority, and (ii) be heard and represented for such purpose before the competent authority".[37] The expulsion may only be carried out when each person who will be deported has had the opportunity to explain his or her situation. Consequently, there can be no collective expulsion. Collective expulsion, furthermore, is prohibited by the Convention itself.[38] The Court took the same position in the case of the Pacheco Tineo family with regard to the expulsion procedure. In that case, it also applied the same criterion to decide on the alien's refugee status or to apply the rule of *non-refoulement*.[39] Finally, the asylum request must be handled as well with the guarantees of due process.[40] A 2014 case on the expulsion of Haitian and Dominican persons of Haitian origin from the Dominican Republic also found that the standards on proceedings of expulsion included the application of Article 8.[41]

10. It is a violation of the Convention to impede the access to justice by any form. In the case of Aguado-Alfaro *et al.* (Dismissed Congressional Employees), the Court affirmed the incompatibility of Article 8 with a prohibition on contesting the effects of a decree-law. The prohibition applied to the dismissed individuals prevented those affected by it from contesting *ab initio* any effect they deemed prejudicial to their interests and therefore it was a violation of Article 8. Such a norm was not "a valid limitation of the right of those affected by

---

35 *OC-18/03*, para. 173.

36 *Ibidem*. Also, see separate concurring opinion of Judge Sergio Garcia Ramírez, particularly paras. 35–39.

37 *Case of Nadege Dorzema et al. v. Dominican Republic*, para. 161.

38 *Ibidem*, para. 175. Article 22(9) of the American Convention forbids collective expulsion.

39 *Case of the Pacheco Tineo family v. Estado Plurinacional de Bolivia*, section B.1 of the Considerations of the Court, paras. 128–136 and section B.2, paras. 137–150.

40 *Ibidem*, paras. 154–160.

41 *Case of Expelled Dominican and Haitian Persons v. Dominican Republic*, para. 407.

the decree to a genuine and effective access to justice, which cannot be arbitrarily restricted, reduced or annulled".[42] Furthermore, there was in the State a "climate of legal uncertainty promoted by the norms that restricted complaints against the evaluation procedure and the eventual dismissal of the alleged victims"; this meant that those affected by the situation "had no certainty about the proceeding they should or could use to claim the rights they considered violated, whether this was administrative, under administrative law, or by an action for *amparo*".[43]

11. The existence of courts and proceedings necessary for a State to comply with due process must be accompanied by a real opportunity for the corresponding individual judges or courts to exercise the judicial powers assigned to them. In cases that have come before the Inter-American Court, situations are not uncommon in which judges cannot materially exercise their authority due to obstacles put in their way by other State agents. In the case of Genie Lacayo, the Court ruled that it had been proven that "certain military authorities had blocked the judge's work to the point where that court was constrained to contact the President of the Republic [...] to intercede with the military authorities for them to afford the facilities needed for the inspection of Military Unit 003, its weapons, vehicles and weapons log".[44] One case that is typical of violations of access to justice for these reasons is that of Myrna Mack Chang. The Court analyzed the alleged violation of Article 8 of the Convention, organizing its examination according to subjects that show the degree to which the obstruction of the exercise to the right to due process can reach. The Court ruled that it had been proven, *inter alia*: (i) that the highest police authority, at that time a member of the Army, covered up and manipulated the official version of the investigation;[45] (ii) that the President's staff and the National Ministry of Defence submitted "manipulated documents with the intention of concealing information that was important for elucidation of the facts";[46] (iii) that the National Ministry of Defence invoked secrecy in order to avoid turning over documents or in order to provide judicial authorities with only vague information;[47] and (iv) that an investigator was murdered and that other police

42 *Case of the Dismissed Congressional Employees v. Peru*, para. 119.

43 *Ibidem*, para. 129.

44 *Case of Genie Lacayo v. Nicaragua*, para. 76 (translator's version). See *case of Bámaca Velásquez v. Guatemala*, para. 200 and *case of Las Palmeras v. Colombia*, para. 57, in which the Court indicates, among other obstructive actions, the following: the changing of the garments the victims were wearing and their later destruction, the absence of an official document registering the collection of the bodies at the place of death, the failure to collect evidence, intimidation and threats toward relatives and witnesses, and the spread of distorted information with regard to the activities of the victims.

45 *Ibidem*, paras. 168–172.

46 *Ibidem*, para. 173.

47 *Ibidem*, paras. 175–182.

investigators, witnesses and several individuals connected with the investigation into the case were harassed.[48] All these actions constituted, according to the Court, a violation of Article 8 of the Convention.

12. The lack of certain guarantees may prevent access to justice absolutely. In the case of Fernández, Ms. Fernández, an indigenous woman, could not present a complaint because she did not speak Spanish and had no access to an interpreter.[49] Another instance of preventing access to justice happened in the case of Ibsen Cárdenas and Ibsen Pena. In the national criminal proceedings, which lasted nine years, approximately 111 different judges of different levels and jurisdiction tendered abstentions, some of which delayed the trial for almost a year.[50]

In many cases of violations perpetrated by State agents, particularly the military, one finds various other ways to impede the right to a hearing. In the case of "Las Dos Erres" Massacre v. Guatemala, aside from a number of refusals of State agents to provide information, there had been an abuse by the accused – probably in connivance with authorities – of resorting to the Court only to delay the trial: "between April 2000 and March 2003 the accused filed: at least 33 appeals for legal protection, 19 appeals for reversal, 19 claims for remedy, 2 motions for amendment, and one constitutional motion."[51] The Court found that even when there are legal recourses, the accused could abuse them to tire out the alleged victims and prevent the course of justice and it was for the domestic courts to put a stop to this abuse. Otherwise, this constituted a violation of the right in Article 8.

13. The Inter-American Court examined another method of hindering access to justice in a judgment in the case of Cantos. Some of the case's facts are important for the Court's ruling, so they deserve a brief explanation. First, on July 15, 1982, prior to Argentina's ratification of the American Convention, Mr. Cantos and the governor of the province of Santiago del Estero allegedly signed an agreement according to which the latter granted the former an indemnity for damages suffered as a result of confiscations made by the province. Mr. Cantos began to demand that the province comply with this agreement on March 24, 1986 and received no response. He then brought a lawsuit against the province and the federal State before the Supreme Court of Justice. In order to pursue the litigation, the victim had to pay a "court filing fee", which he felt should be the minimum as the amount of damages at issue in the trial had not been determined. After a series of procedural issues, the

48 *Ibidem*, paras. 183–196.
49 *Case of Fernández Ortega et al. v. Mexico*, para. 201.
50 *Case of Ibsen Cárdenas and Ibsen Peña v. Bolivia*, para. 180.
51 *Case of "Las Dos Erres" Massacre v. Guatemala*, para. 100.

Court found that the amount of damages at issue in the trial was established. As a consequence of this determination, a court fee of 83.4 million Argentine pesos (equivalent to the same amount in US dollars) had to be paid on pain of incurring a fine equivalent to 50% of the amount should the payment not be made within five days.[52] Mr. Cantos did not pay the filing fee in time and the aforementioned fine was thus levied.[53] The case was suspended due to the failure to pay the filing fee, but it apparently continued until the final judgment was handed down on September 3, 1996. Finally, because of the failure to pay the court filing fee, on October 9, 1996, the National First Instance Adversarial Administrative Court placed a "general injunction" on him to prevent him from carrying out his economic activity.[54] The question brought before the Inter-American Court was on whether a court filing fee of that amount is compatible with Articles 8 and 25 of the Convention. The Court found that the amount set in the form of filing fees and the corresponding fine ordered in this case constituted an obstruction to access to the courts. They were unreasonable, even though in mathematical terms it was proportional to the amount being claimed.[55] In addition, it stated that the limitations the State places on access to justice must maintain a correlation between the means employed and the purpose sought and cannot themselves become a denial of the right.[56] Finally, the Court reasoned that:

> [t]he fact that a proceeding concludes with a definitive court ruling is not sufficient to satisfy the right of access to the courts. Those participating in the proceeding must be able to do so without fear of being forced to pay disproportionate or excessive sums because they turned to the courts. The problem of excessive or disproportionate filing fees [becomes still more serious] when, in order to force payment, the authorities attach the debtor's property or deny him the opportunity to do business.[57]

The Court also found that the fact that the Argentine Supreme Court ordered Mr. Cantos to pay the amount of 6.4 million Argentine pesos in honoraria to the attorneys representing Mr. Cantos, the State, the province, the State's technical advisor, and the expert witnesses was an obstruction to access to justice.[58]

14. Indigenous populations have also been the concern of the Court with regard to access to justice. The Court, making reference to Article 14(3) of ILO

---

52 Mr. Canto's claim was in the amount of 2,780,015,303.44 Argentine pesos, and the court filing fee was equivalent to 3% of the total value of the suit, with no upper limit (See *Case of Cantos v. Argentina*, para. 53).

53 *Ibidem*, para. 43, letters k–n.

54 *Ibidem*, para. 43, letter t.

55 *Ibidem*, para. 54. The English version has been corrected to match the Spanish one.

56 *Ibidem*.

57 *Ibidem*, para. 55. See also paras. 56, 60 and 62.

58 *Ibidem*, paras. 43, letters q–s and para. 56.

Convention No. 169, incorporated into Paraguayan domestic legislation by Law No. 234/93, found:

> [t]his international provision, in combination with Articles 8 and 25 of the American Convention, places the State under the obligation to provide an effective means with due process guarantees to the members of the indigenous communities for them to claim traditional lands, as a guarantee of their right to communal property.[59]

In Tiu Tojin, it asserted that "in order to guarantee the members of indigenous communities access to justice, 'it is necessary that the States grant an effective protection taking into account their specific features, economic and social characteristics, as well as their special situation of vulnerability, their common law, values, uses and customs'".[60] In sum, "[a]ny regulation or practice of the domestic order that makes individual access to the courts difficult and is not justified by the reasonable needs of the administration of justice itself shall be understood as contrary to the previously mentioned Article 8(1) of the Convention".[61]

The Court has thus developed the Convention provisions and given more detailed content to the general rule that every person has a right to a hearing without discrimination.

4. DETERMINATION OF RIGHTS AND OBLIGATIONS AND CRIMINAL CHARGES

15. The right to be heard raises the question of what kind of proceedings it applies to. Article 8(1) of the Convention answers this question in principle in its own wording, where it indicates that every person has the right to a hearing for "the determination of his rights and obligations of a civil, labor, fiscal, or any other nature" and in "the substantiation of any accusation of a criminal nature made against him." As has already been noted, for this latter case, the Convention adds another special provision to this general one in the article's second paragraph, establishing what are known as "minimum guarantees for the accused".

16. Regarding the determination of rights or obligations of any kind, the broad wording of the American Convention's provision makes it unnecessary to examine the nature and characteristics of required noncriminal due process, given that in principle all determinations of rights and obligations are covered

---

59 *Case of the Indigenous Community Yakye Axa v. Paraguay*, para. 96.

60 *Case of Tiu Tojin v. Guatemala*, para. 96. See also *Case of Saramaka v. Suriname*, para. 168. See also the *Case of the Indigenous Peoples Kuna de Madungandí and Emberá de Bayano and their members v. Panama*, para. 166.

61 *Ibidem*, para. 95.

by the guarantees. This is different from what happens in the European system where, given the restrictive wording of Article 6 of the European Convention which only enshrines the existence of due process for the determination of civil rights and obligations, the idea of an autonomous concept of "civil rights and obligations" had to be developed and determined by the international supervisory body.[62] The creative interpretation of this provision in Europe was crucial for preventing legal systems from avoiding the requirements of due process by transferring matters to administrative venues. In the ICCPR, the wording is different as Article 14 speaks of "the determination of rights and obligations in a suit at law". The last General Comment issued by the Human Rights Committee on Article 14,[63] after verifying the different authentic languages in which the ICCPR is written, decided to indicate what the concept of "a suit at law" encompasses:

- judicial procedures aimed at determining rights and obligations pertaining to the areas of contract, property and torts in the area of private law, as well as
- equivalent notions in the area of administrative law such as the termination of employment of civil servants for other than disciplinary reasons,
- the determination of social security benefits or the pension rights of soldiers, or procedures regarding the use of public land or the taking of private property.
- In addition, it may cover other procedures which, however, must be assessed on a case by case basis in the light of the nature of the right in question.[64]

This description reflects approximately the meaning of "determination of rights or obligations" in Article 8 of the Convention, but the concept does not apply to extradition, expulsion and deportation procedures.[65] All the relevant guarantees of Article 14, however, apply where expulsion takes the form of a penal sanction or where violations of expulsion orders are punished under criminal law.[66]

17. The Court has examined with some frequency the application of Article 8(1) with regard to administrative and political procedures, that is, to procedures that are not conducted before an ordinary judge or court. Two different issues are important with regard to the range of Article 8. The first refers to the classification of a situation as an "administrative or political procedure"; the second is whether these procedures will be handled according to paragraph 1 or to paragraphs 1 and 2 of Article 8. The first issue appeared in the Court in the case of Claude Reyes.[67] The facts of the case were (i) the refusal of the Director

---

62 On this, see P. van Dijk *et al.* (eds.), *Theory and Practice of the European Convention on Human Rights*, 4th edition, Intersentia, Antwerp/Oxford, 2006, pp. 524–539.

63 HRC, General Comment No. 32, Article 14: Right to equality before courts and tribunals and to a fair trial (CCPR/C/GC/32, August 23, 2007).

64 *Ibidem*, para. 16. The reference to the individual cases quoted has been omitted.

65 *Ibidem*.

66 *Ibidem*, para. 62.

67 *Case of Claude Reyes et al. v. Chile.*

of a State office to provide information to some people who wished to contest the authorization of that agency of an investment program on grounds of its negative effects on the environment; and (ii) the hearing of an unsuccessful *amparo* remedy before a national court. The majority of the Court decided that there had been a violation of Article 8 both in the rejection of the petition by the Director of the Agency and the judicial process started by the victims to complain about this negative decision to provide information. According to the Court, Article 8 applied "to all the requirements that must be observed by procedural instances, whatsoever their nature, to ensure that the individual may defend himself adequately with regard to any act of the State that may *affect* his rights."[68] A partial dissenting opinion[69] questioned the classification of a "process" given to the petition to a State agent that had been denied. In the view of the dissenters, a simple request rejected is not "a process". What the rejection does is to create a dispute and to decide the dispute one may go to a jurisdictional organ where the right to a hearing may be invoked, which did happen in this case. I believe the mistake made by the Court was to quote Article 8 incorrectly: not every act of the State that *affects* human rights must be carried out in a procedure governed by "due process"; one speaks of "a process" if through that proceeding a human right or obligation is "*determined*", that is to say, decided. One would never say that if one goes to a window in a public office and is not given a document that has been requested there has been a process. If one were to require that, life would become very cumbersome.

The case of Barbani *et al.* v. Uruguay poses a somewhat similar problem. It deals with a complicated issue of the situation of the Banco de Montevideo in the context of a banking crisis in the country. The Uruguayan Central Bank had ordered the dissolution and liquidation of the Montevideo Bank "due to its negative net worth".[70] A domestic law, 17.613, passed to strengthen the financing system, contained a provision authorizing the Central Bank to grant depositors of the Montevideo Bank and another Bank "whose deposits have been transferred to other institutions without their consent, the same rights enjoyed by other depositors of these Banks".[71] The Central Bank was to establish a commission that would function for an extendible period of sixty days in order to decide by a well-founded resolution who would benefit from this provision. The commission was to advise the Board of the Central Bank of the decisions it took "insofar as the legislator granted the latter the authority to determine the status as depositor of the *Banco de Montevideo S.A.* (in liquidation) and *Banco La Caja Obrera S.A.* (in liquidation), in the conditions established in the first paragraph of [Article 31 of Law 17.613]." The commission's decisions

68 *Ibidem*, para. 119.
69 *Ibidem*. Dissenting opinion signed by Judge Abreu and myself.
70 *Barbani et al. v. Uruguay*, para. 68.
71 Article 31 of Law 17.613.

were not binding for the Board, "which could diverge from them for well-founded reasons".[72] The commission's functioning was prolonged more than once, but since it was "a special mission nature" it dissolved when the mission was accomplished.[73] In the application of the provision by the commission a problem arose regarding one of the requirements to grant the benefits of Article 32 of Law 17.613, the consent of the interested party. A considerable number of persons were challenging the fact that the commission and the Board had decided to establish a presumption of consent. According to the procedure, the decisions of the Board could be the object of an appeal for annulment before the Contentious-Administrative Tribunal, a jurisdictional body, not part of the judiciary but "independent of the three branches of the State".[74] In examining the case, the Court applied Article 8 of the Convention to both the procedure before the Commission finally decided by the Board of the Central Bank and to the procedure followed before the Contentious Administrative Tribunal. Three concurring votes maintained that the Court had applied in this case the consistent jurisprudence of the Court that administrative procedures that determined rights should comply with Article 8.[75] One judge dissented.[76] The dissent, in the part relevant to this issue, partially invokes the dissenting opinion in the case of Claude Reyes mentioned above. Briefly, Judge Vío's position was that what happened at the stage of the national commission and the Board of the Uruguayan Central Bank is not a judicial process, a suit at law in the words of the Human Rights Committee, and therefore Article 8(1) should not have been applied. The judicial process only happened before the Contentious-Administrative Tribunal. However, the commission reporting to the Central Bank did contain the possibility of an exchange of views and there was the possibility to have a type of contentious exchange, which made this case not as clear-cut as I believe was the situation in Claude Reyes. I was not a judge in this case and therefore I did not benefit from the debate and arguments of the judges, but in principle I might tend to agree with this dissenting vote. I believe the Court has not perceived this position as being strictly contesting the notion of "suit at law" or "process" and not as objecting that this was an administrative process, regarding which there is no difference with the Court's majority decision.

18. Other proceedings, in my view, have been properly classified as administrative by the Court. The case of Yatama is an example. The subject of the case was the refusal by the authorities to register the candidates of Yatama,

72 *Ibidem*, para. 79.

73 *Ibidem*, para. 81.

74 *Ibidem*, para. 101.

75 *Ibidem*, concurring votes of Judges Diego García-Sayán, Margarette May Macaulay and Rhadys Abreu Blondet.

76 *Ibidem*, Judge Eduardo Vío Grossi.

an indigenous organization, for the municipal elections that were to take place at the time. The court found that the decisions on this matter "may affect the enjoyment of political rights" and therefore Article 8 had to be observed. This assertion implied that Article 8(1) was being applied and that the domestic legal order should have a particular type of procedure to decide on electoral matters. One understands that the particular proceeding had to take into consideration that promptness and simplicity were to be considered for designing it.[77] In my view, in the case of López Mendoza on the issue of elections, the Court also correctly applied Article 8(1).[78]

The Court reiterates the idea of special administrative procedures with regard to members of indigenous peoples. It expresses that "it is essential for the States to grant effective protection that takes into account their specificities, their economic and social characteristics, as well as their situation of special vulnerability, their customary law, values, and customs."[79] Reading Articles 8 and 25 of the American Convention in conjunction with Article 14(3) of ILO Convention No. 169, incorporated into Paraguayan domestic legislation by Law No. 234/93, it also asserted that, in order to guarantee members of indigenous peoples their right to communal property, States must establish "an effective means with due process guarantees [...] for them to claim traditional lands as a guarantee of their right to communal property".[80]

19. There is a different type of administrative or political procedure to that which only determines a right or an obligation: the one that applies a sanction. In the Human Rights Committee this type of procedure is not covered by the concept of "suit at law", but – as explained below – it falls under the notion of criminal charge. The Court has sometimes applied Article 8(2) to processes that are mainly administrative ones, but end with the imposition of a sanction. I will explain here why I think this is the wrong formulation of the Court and I do not think that it reflects what that body actually does. Article 8(2) sets forth the minimum guarantees for those accused of a criminal offense. The concept of "criminal offense" does not appear in the Convention, and neither does the Inter-American Court seem to have had a chance to examine the subject in cases that have come before it. In its General Comment No. 32, the Human Rights Committee defines criminal charges, in principle, as those "acts declared to be punishable under domestic criminal law". It adds that the concept "may also extend to acts that are criminal in nature with sanctions that, regardless of their qualification in domestic law, must be regarded as penal because of their

---

77 *Case of Yatama v. Nicaragua*, para. 150.

78 *Case of López Mendoza v. Venezuela*, on disqualification of the victim from holding public office. See section VI of the judgment.

79 *Case of the Indigenous Community Yakye Axa v. Paraguay*, para. 63.

80 *Ibidem*, para. 96. See also *Case of Saramaka v. Suriname*, para. 168.

purpose, character or severity".[81] In the case of the European Court, the Court found first that the concept of "criminal offense" was, like all civil rights and obligations, an autonomous concept that transcended domestic legal systems. It thus falls to the international supervisory body to rule on whether a criminal offense is involved in each specific case that it hears. Second, the European Court found that the concept should be interpreted broadly, arguing that a restrictive interpretation does not fit with the objective and purpose of Article 6 of the European Convention establishing the right to due process.[82] Finally, in the case of Engel v. the Netherlands, the European Court established three criteria for determining whether a charge was criminal in the sense of Article 6 of the European Convention: the classification of the offense by domestic law; the nature of the offense; and the level of severity of its possible punishment. If the State itself classifies the offense as criminal, that is sufficient for the Court to consider it so; if the State does not place the offense in the category of criminal offenses, the two other criteria come into play.[83]

From the Convention, it is clear that Article 8(2) refers only to the minimum guarantees of the accused. As said before, the protection of an individual subject to a criminal trial requires that the Convention spells out some guarantees that can be found in Article 8(1) and that, by omission or decision of a court, are not applied in a particular case. In my opinion, the case law of the Inter-American Court has not been clear in making this distinction and has unnecessarily broadened the scope of the application of Article 8(2). It is in this respect that administrative procedures may mingle with criminal procedures. A couple of cases will clarify the problem.

One is the case of the three members of the Constitutional Tribunal of Peru who were dismissed during the government of Alberto Fujimori as a consequence of an impeachment proceeding that took place in the Congress of Peru. The dismissal was in response to a decision made by the Constitutional Tribunal that ruled Law 26.657 – which interpreted the law to allow Mr. Fujimori to be re-elected president – was inapplicable. The Inter-American Commission, the body that brought the case before the Court, did not address the problem from the point of view of whether this proceeding determined civil, labor, fiscal or any other kind of rights or obligations. It rather argued that the magistrates of the Constitutional Tribunal should enjoy the guarantees of independence and impartiality enjoyed by all judges, adding that Article 8(1) of the Convention implicitly guarantees the permanence of judges. For this reason, the procedure

---

81 HRC, General Comment No. 32, Article 14: Right to equality before courts and tribunals and to a fair trial (CCPR/C/GC/32, August 23, 2007), para 15.

82 European Court of Human Rights, *Deweer Case*, judgment of January 17, 1970 (A. 11, p. 15), cited in P. Van Dijk *et al.*, *supra* n. 62, p. 540. See also European Court of Human Rights, *Case of Adolf v. Austria*, Application No. 8269/78, judgment of March 26, 1982, para. 30.

83 D.J. Harris, M. O'Boyle and C. Warbrick, *Law of the European Convention on Human Rights*, Butterworths, London/Dublin/Edinburgh, 1995, p. 167.

to remove judges must be established in the Constitution and must enjoy "all due judicial guarantees" – that is, a fair trial – a requirement that had not been met in this case.[84] The Court began its examination by indicating that: (i) a political trial constitutes an exercise of the State's power to impose sanctions to the person being tried; (ii) this power not only presupposes that authorities act with total respect for the legal order, but also implies that *the minimum guarantees* of due process will be granted to all persons subject to its jurisdiction under the requirements established in the Convention;[85] and (iii) therefore, every individual subject to a trial before any kind of State body must be provided with the guarantee that the body is competent, independent and impartial and acting pursuant to procedures established in law for hearing and ruling on cases brought before it. Thus far, the reasoning matches the idea of the European Court and of the Human Rights Committee. Unfortunately the Court added:

> [A]lthough [... Article 8(1)] does not establish minimum guarantees in matters relating to the determination of rights and obligations of a civil, labor, fiscal or any other nature, the full range of minimum guarantees stipulated in the second paragraph of this article are also applicable in those areas and, therefore, in this type of matter, the individual also has the overall right to the due process applicable in criminal matters.[86]

The formulation seems to imply that paragraph 1 of Article 8 could never be read as containing any of the minimum guarantees mentioned in paragraph 2. This would have as a consequence, for instance, that in noncriminal cases there is no right to have an interpreter or a translator provided by the court "if [the accused] does not understand or does not speak the language of the tribunal or court". An absence of such a right might deny access to court at least to indigenous groups wishing to have their rights determined, which is contrary to any reasonable interpretation of the guarantees granted in the Convention.

The second case in which the Court examined the extension of Article 8(2) to noncriminal cases was Ricardo Baena *et al.* v. Panama, a case on the dismissal of 270 State employees through an alleged improper procedure. The executive branch fired the workers using the powers granted to it by Law 25 to dismiss public servants who had participated in various types of action that allegedly threatened democracy and constitutional order. The law authorized the Cabinet Council to determine which actions would be placed in that category. The State argued that Article 8 of the Convention – that is to say, due process requirements – was not applicable to this case because dismissals are administrative and not criminal sanctions.[87] In the Baena case, the Court started on the right track

84 *Case of the Constitutional Court v. Peru*, para. 64.

85 *Ibidem*, para. 68.

86 *Ibidem*, paras. 69–70. The Court had said the same in the *case of Paniagua Morales et al.* and in Advisory Opinion 11.

87 *Case of Baena Ricardo et al. v. Panama*, para. 129.

when stating that Article 8 contains the collection of requirements that must be met by procedural instances "in order for all persons to be able to defend their rights adequately vis-à-vis any type of State action that could affect them." From that it follows that "due process of law must be respected in any act or omission on the part of the State bodies in a proceeding, whether of a punitive, administrative, or of a judicial nature".[88] Following that line of reasoning, the Court found a difference between exercising administrative discretion that allows for freely naming and removing public officials, and removing a worker through administrative sanctions. Discretionary removal of an official is obviously not subject to due process; removal as a result of a sanction, in contrast, does require due process.[89] The Court cites for support the ruling of the European Court to the effect that:

> the principles stipulated in paragraph 2 (art. 6–2) and 3 (to wit, sections |a, b and d) [... of the European Convention of Human Rights] are applied *mutatis mutandis* to the disciplinary proceedings to which section 1 refers (art. 6–1), in the same manner in which they are applied to cases where a person is charged with an offence of a penal nature.[90]

This latter point seems to indicate that the Court examined the administrative disciplinary proceeding as if it were criminal, something that is coherent with the European Court's judgment, given that the European Court is applying the criteria developed in the Engels case, where it found that the proceeding itself *was* a criminal one. However, the Inter-American Court finds that given that Article 8(1) applies in the determination of civil, labor, fiscal or any other rights and obligations, and thus it is broad in scope, "the individual has the right to the due process as construed under the terms of Articles 8(1) *and 8(2)* in both, penal matters, as in all of these other domains".[91] Here, the Court seems not to understand the reasoning of the European Court and reiterates the same mistake made in the former case. Subsequently, the Court states that it is obvious that Law 25 is not of a criminal nature as it does not describe an offense and does not contain a penalty, but deals with an administrative or labor matter. It then adds: "It is for this Court, consequently, to determine the scope of the application of Article 8 and, particularly, if this is applicable only to criminal matters",[92] while it is obvious that Article 8 applies to all types of processes.

Curiously, when the Court examines the possible violation of Article 9 of the Convention, it compares administrative sanctions to penal ones, stating that at

88 *Ibidem*, para. 124.
89 *Ibidem*, paras. 131 and 134.
90 *Ibidem*, para. 128.
91 *Ibidem*, para. 125 (emphasis added).
92 Ibidem, para 123. This is not an official translation; the Court's version is unclear and does not represent the sense of this paragraph's wording. The Court repeats this idea in para. 127.

times they can be "similar in nature", admitting then that these sanctions may be criminal *in nature*.[93]

The third case in which the Court ruled in the area of the application of Article 8(2) is that of Ivcher Bronstein. That case addressed the problem of a proceeding to nullify the Peruvian nationality acquired by the victim. Peru's General Directorate of Immigration and Naturalization was the authority that handed down the resolution in question. In its judgment the Court insisted that Article 8 is applicable "in situations in which a public rather than a judicial authority issues resolutions that affect the determination of such rights".[94] Subsequently, the Court indicated that although this article does not stipulate minimum guarantees in matters which concern the determination of the rights and obligations of a civil, labor, fiscal or any other nature, the minimum guarantees established in paragraph 2 of the article should also apply to those categories. Therefore, in that respect, a person has the right to due process in the terms recognized for criminal matters, to the extent that it is applicable to the respective procedure.[95]

The Court had already held that same position in its Advisory Opinion 11/90 where it stated that Article 8(1) does not specify minimum guarantees like Article 8(2) does, but it provides due guarantees.[96] This should have been enough, but then it added "consequently, the individual here also has the right to the fair hearing provided for in criminal cases".[97] In the case of the Pacheco Tineo family,[98] the Court again made the same error. It found that "the State cannot decide punitive administrative or judicial decisions without respecting certain minimum guarantees, the content of which is substantially the same as those established in paragraph 2 of Article 8 of the Convention".[99]

In the recent cases of Quintana Coello *et al.* and Camba Campos *et al.*, the Court skirted the issue by deciding that since a violation of Article 8 had been found, there was no need to decide about other arguments related to that article. In the former, a case concerning the dismissal of members of the Constitutional Court, Electoral Tribunal and Supreme Court justices in Ecuador, the Court had found that the body carrying out the process was not competent and therefore that was enough to find the violation; on the other hand, "given the effects on

93 *Ibidem*, paras. 106–115.

94 *Case of Ivcher Bronstein v. Peru*, para. 105.

95 *Ibidem*, para. 103.

96 *OC-11/90*, para. 28. The Court also repeated this in the *case of Paniagua Morales*, para. 148. Paragraph 70 of the judgment in the *case of the Constitutional Tribunal* reiterated this, but clarified it with the idea that "in this type of matter, the individual also has the *overall* right to the due process applicable in criminal matters" (emphasis added).

97 *OC-11/90*, para. 28.

98 For the *case of Pacheco Tineo family*, see Chapter 5, section on migrants.

99 *Case of the Pacheco Tineo family v. Plurinational State of Bolivia*, para. 132. See also *Case of Dominican and Haitian persons expelled from the Dominican Republic v. Dominican Republic*, paras. 355 and 356.

the separation of powers and the arbitrary nature of the action by Congress, the Court considers it unnecessary to analyze in detail the arguments of the parties as to whether or not the decision to dismiss the judges was an action of a punitive nature, and therefore it will not examine its alleged effects on Article 8(2) of the Convention".[100] In the case of Camba Campos *et al.*, regarding the arbitrary termination in office of eight members of the Constitutional Tribunal of Ecuador by a decision of the National Congress of November 25, 2004, the Court decided on the same terms as in the case of the Constitutional Court v. Peru and the case of Baena *et al.* v. Panama.[101] It also repeated what had been said in Quintana Coello *et al.*, concerning the issue of the guarantees that should have been applied.

In my view, the reasoning of the Court in these cases is not right. Again, the judgments suggest the idea that the application of Article 8(1) to administrative procedures is debatable and therefore it must be "deduced" from Article 8(1), while this is stated clearly in the text of the provision itself. Second, the need of the Court to resort to Article 8(2) to grant the minimum guarantees for the accused to individuals that are not qualified by the Court as "accused" diminishes the potential of Article 8(1). This is done by inducing the reader to believe that Article 8(1) is not sufficient to apply all "*due* guarantees" in every process so that in certain cases guarantees have to be borrowed from Article 8(2). However, Article 8(1) is the general rule and it does not contain a list of the guarantees that must be applied; on the contrary, it is open and wide: *due guarantees* – depending of the circumstances in each case – must be granted to the parties in noncriminal trials. The Court's interpretation narrows its contents. Third, it does not seem clear for the Court that the qualification of a trial as criminal or not depends on the Court. It seems erroneous – inconveniently so – to derive guarantees for all proceedings by making Article 8(2) applicable to all noncriminal cases. An interpretation of this nature reads too much into the wording and, in addition, requires States to establish *all* minimum guarantees for accused persons in *all* types of proceedings. This would at times appear to be excessive. I believe that the requirements that should inform all proceedings can and should be derived from Article 8(1), given that Article 8(1) is the generic rule. It establishes that persons shall be heard "with due guarantees", an expression that should be interpreted in the sense that it includes the application of whichever guarantee is necessary for a given case to make the process fair.[102] This will of course contain the principle of equality and the adversarial

---

100 *Case of Quintana Coello et al. v. Ecuador*, para. 181.

101 *Camba Campos et al. v. Ecuador*, paras. 166–167 and 180.

102 See, for example, the case of *Airey v. Ireland* before the European Court, where this organ held that sometimes it was necessary in a civil case to have free legal aid, although there was no free legal aid in the European Convention for civil cases. The basic reason of the Court was that without free legal aid, Ms. Airey would not be able to present her case before the High Court without a lawyer, as the proceedings were too complicated and she had no

principle,[103] and this in turn allows for the establishment of the need for equality of arms, the right to defense, and other rights. There is no need to turn to paragraph 2 of the article. The Court has the power to consider a procedure not labelled as a criminal procedure by the national legal order differently. For this, it should develop criteria to make the expression "accusation of a criminal nature" an autonomous concept. This would allow the Court to decide when an "accusation of a criminal nature" is at issue and to legitimately apply the specific guarantees found in Article 8(2). This, as mentioned before, is what the Court did in the Baena case, although by analyzing not the violation of Article 8 but rather the violation of Article 9 of the Convention.[104]

20. There is one further point in this analysis.[105] If the Court qualifies an administrative or political procedure as criminal when handling it, it is necessary to consider how minimum guarantees should be managed by the Court. One thing that strikes me as difficult is the application of the criminal law principle of legality in certain of these processes. For example, the cause for impeachment in many countries of the region, applicable to judges, is "serious dereliction of duties". This description is ambiguous and would not pass the test of the principle of legality of criminal law. In addition, Congress does not pass the test of being impartial to function as a jury that decides an individual has engaged in impeachable conduct. On the other hand, the Court is right to insist that this type of proceeding leading to sanctions must comply with Article 8(1) and (2). If one follows this line of thought, it leads to a conclusion that may be shocking to the political culture prevailing in all the countries of the region. There is an incompatibility between some of these political or administrative trials and Article 8 and therefore new legislation should design a new system to process these cases with full compliance with due process, taking into account that there are a variety of administrative and political situations that might need a variety of solutions to achieve compatibility with the Convention.

---

money to hire a private counsel. Judgment of October 9, 1979, paras. 20–28 and 31–33 of the reasons. In the same case of *Airey v. Ireland* as well as in other rulings, the Court has stated that the question whether or not Article 6 requires the provision of legal representation to an individual litigant will depend upon the specific circumstances of the case. *Case of Airey v. Ireland,* para. 26; *Case of McVicar v. United Kingdom,* Application No. 46311/99, judgment of May 7, 2002, para. 48; *Case of Steel and Morris v. United Kingdom,* Application No. 68416/01, judgment of February 15, 2005, para. 61.

103 See in this sense, United Nations Human Rights Committee, *Case of Yves Morael v. France,* decision of July 28, 1989, para. 9.3, in A/44/40 (1989) Annex X sect. E (pp. 210–221).

104 On this point, see Chapter 7, where the Court's examination of the violation of Article 9 in this case is addressed in detail.

105 I wish to thank Oscar Parra for his incisive questions in this regard.

5. COMPETENT, INDEPENDENT AND IMPARTIAL TRIBUNAL, PREVIOUSLY ESTABLISHED BY LAW

5.1. THE CONCEPT OF A TRIBUNAL

21. The right to a hearing requires that a competent, independent and impartial tribunal, previously established by law, makes the determination of rights and obligations or of a person's guilt or innocence. Inter-American case law clearly indicates that for the Court, a body is classified as a "tribunal" based on the type of functions it carries out and not on the name assigned to it; if its function allows it to make decisive rulings that determine the rights or obligations of persons, Article 8 will be applied.[106] Once its function has been established, the body must comply with the requirements of competence, independence and impartiality even if national legislation does not classify that body as a "judge or tribunal". The Court's position on this subject has been consistent. In the case of the Constitutional Court, it indicated that:

> when the Convention refers to the right of everyone to be heard by a competent judge or court to "determine his rights", this expression refers to any public authority, whether administrative, legislative or judicial, which, through its decisions determines individual rights and obligations.[107]

It complemented this position by adding that therefore "any State organ that exercises functions of a materially jurisdictional nature has the obligation to adopt decisions that are in consonance with the guarantees of due legal process in the terms of Article 8 of the American Convention."[108] In the Baena case, the Court insisted – in my opinion correctly – that the titles of those who make the determination of a right are unimportant. It is, however, essential that the rulings they make *determine* the rights or obligations of persons.[109] In the Yatama case, the Court reiterated this by stating that all organs of a jurisdictional nature must apply Article 8 to their proceedings. The requirement of competence "is also applicable in situations in which a public rather than a judicial authority issues decisions that affect the determination of such rights".[110] In the case of Claude Reyes, the Court reaffirms this rule by establishing that "Article 8(1) of

106 The Court's concept of a tribunal is similar to the one contained in General Comment No. 32 of the Human Rights Committee. The Committee states in in paragraph 18 of its Comment: The notion of a "tribunal" in Article 14(1) designates a body, regardless of its denomination, that is established by law, is independent of the executive and legislative branches of government or enjoys in specific cases judicial independence in deciding legal matters in proceedings that are judicial in nature.

107 *Case of the Constitutional Court v. Peru*, para. 71.

108 *Ibidem.*

109 *Case of Baena Ricardo et al. v. Panama*, para. 130. The authorities who had ordered the dismissals were general directors and the boards of directors of the State enterprises.

110 *Case of Yatama v. Nicaragua*, para. 149.

the Convention does not apply merely to judges and judicial courts", as the States sometimes empower "administrative, collegiate, and uni-personal authorities to adopt decisions that determine rights." It moderates this powerful assertion by stating that although "the guarantees inherent in a jurisdictional body are not required of him, he must comply with the guarantees designed to ensure that his decision is not arbitrary".[111] This assertion requires further elaboration. The Court is undoubtedly referring to the fact that the authority does not need to be a part of the judiciary. In addition, the notion of independence and impartiality may vary in administrative cases. For example, no such strict requirements may be needed to consider an administrative court to possess these qualifications. Probably that will depend on the type of administrative procedure. Since what is required are "due guarantees", the Court may decide that there is independence and impartiality accordingly. This complements what has been said above regarding the need to adjust the procedures to make them compatible with Article 8.

5.2. TRIBUNAL PREVIOUSLY ESTABLISHED BY LAW

22. An essential requirement is that the Tribunal be established by law in order to ensure that the legislature is the body that decides on the organization and jurisdiction of a State's tribunals or other bodies that exercise jurisdictional powers, all prior to the date on which the facts being judged took place. The purpose of the provision is double. First to ensure the independence and impartiality of the body making the determination and second to prevent *ad hoc* tribunals, which distort these qualities essential for and inherent to all bodies that hold court.

The Inter-American Court refers to this due process requirement in the case of Ivcher Bronstein. A few weeks before issuing a resolution to take away Mr. Bronstein's naturalized Peruvian nationality, the Executive Commission of the Peruvian Judicial Branch changed the composition of the chamber of the Supreme Court. The change consisted in giving that chamber the authority to create temporary Superior Chambers and Specialized Public Law Courts, as well as to appoint and/or ratify their members. The chamber created the First Specialized Temporary Corporate Public Law Court and named its judge. That judge heard several of the remedies sought by Mr. Bronstein in his defense. The Inter-American Court found that these facts did not guarantee the petitioner his right to be heard by judges or courts previously established by law.[112] In the case of Castillo Petruzzi *et al.*, the Court also referred to the same point, adding the need for the law to establish a tribunal's jurisdiction, as this was an element that

111 *Case of Claude Reyes v. Chile*, paras. 118–119.
112 *Case of Ivcher Bronstein v. Peru*, paras. 113–114.

would ensure independence. Thus it held, "a basic principle of the independence of the judiciary is that every person has the right to be heard by regular courts, following procedures previously established by law." Then it added, "States are not to create '[t]ribunals that do not use the duly established procedures of the legal process [...] to displace the jurisdiction belonging to the ordinary courts or judicial tribunals.'"[113]

5.3. COMPETENT, INDEPENDENT AND IMPARTIAL TRIBUNAL

23. The requirement that the court providing the hearing be competent is intimately related to the previous requirement. The spatial, temporal, material and personal areas in which a court can exercise its jurisdictional authority must be established by law in general terms and be independent of the specific case, a requirement whose purpose is also to ensure the independence and impartiality of the judge. This means that on establishing the court and assigning it jurisdiction, the State must respect the ban in Article 1(1) on discrimination with respect to those subjected to the jurisdiction.[114] This concept requires not only that courts be established by statute, but also that in assigning competence the statute must respect certain principles.

24. Because of the application of the doctrine of separation of powers, the foundation of a democratic system, a tribunal's independence relates to its autonomy from any other State agency to exercise its jurisdictional functions. Impartiality, for its part, means that in order to be able to make a fair ruling in a particular case, a court must be free from prejudice or bias as regards the court's relationship with the parties in a given proceeding.[115] While a lack of independence also frequently means a lack of impartiality, it is useful to maintain a distinction between the two concepts.

---

113 *Case of Castillo Petruzzi et al. v. Peru*, para. 129. The citation in the considering paragraph is from the Basic Principles on the Independence of the Judiciary. The Principles were adopted in the seventh United Nations Congress on the Prevention of Crime and the Treatment of Offenders (Milan, Italy, from August 26 to September 6, 1985) and confirmed by the General Assembly in its Resolutions 40/32 of November 29, 1985, and 40/146 of December 13, 1985.

114 This idea is behind the concept of "judge with the rightful jurisdiction" (*juez natural* in Spanish) which is a very well developed doctrine in Latin America. On natural judges in criminal proceedings, see A. Binder, *Introducción al derecho procesal penal*, 2nd updated and expanded edition, Ad-Hoc publishing house, Buenos Aires, 2000, pp. 141–148; J. Maier, *Derecho procesal penal argentino, Fundamentos,* Editorial Hammurabi S.R.L., 1989, pp. 487–497.

115 For an analysis of different aspects of judicial independence, see L.P. Mora Mora, "La independencia del Juez como derecho humano", in *Liber Amicorum Héctor Fix Zamudio, supra* n. 10, pp. 1079–1096.

25. Independence requires the application of certain principles with regard to the appointment of judges, the duration of their terms, the conditions governing their promotions, transfers and removal from duties, and even their remuneration.[116] As to appointment, there is no one single solution for designing a system of appointments and the related promotions and transfers of judges that fully ensures their independence. There are States in which the appointment rests exclusively on the executive branch; in others, the system involves a second body that could be the judicial branch or Congress; further developed models create an independent body to handle these tasks; finally, there are States in which the election of judges is by popular vote. All of these methods have advantages and disadvantages but the Court has not pronounced on them. Regarding appointments, popular election clearly raises the risk of politicization and can therefore have a considerable impact on independence. One could argue that mechanisms that involve more than one agency ensure independence better than those involving just one. In addition, it should be considered that the participation of political bodies such as Congress would tend to politicize judicial appointments.[117] Perhaps the best system is to have an independent body to assume this task, but even that could have disadvantages depending on the composition of the body and the appointment of the members thereof. If we look at the duration of the term, a short term certainly makes it difficult for judges to interpret the law and apply it to the facts of a case regarding which the body that decides their reappointments may have an interest or opinion. Therefore, should the appointments not be for life, ending only under certain circumstances such as misconduct, illness, or others of that kind, it is advisable that the term at least be a long one. There is also an argument that independence can only be achieved when a judicial system controls its own finances (as opposed to having the executive or Congress control its budget), and the remuneration of judges allows them a standard of living similar to that of other high-level professionals. In sum, it is vital that extreme care be taken in designing the mechanism, taking into consideration the difficulties and dilemmas mentioned which obviously does not make it an easy endeavor.

26. As far as impartiality is concerned, the case law is persistent in holding that it must be both subjective and objective.[118] The European Court has used this wording in many cases, establishing that subjective impartiality has

116 On the independence of courts in the European system, see *ibidem*, pp. 231–234 and P. van Dijk *et al.*, *supra* n. 62, pp. 613–614. For the system under the ICCPR, see S. Joseph, J. Schulz and M. Castan, *The International Covenant on Civil and Political Rights. Cases, Materials, and Commentary*, Oxford University Press, Oxford, 2000, pp. 287–288. See also HRC, General Comment No. 32.

117 This is the case in Chile regarding the appointment of judges to the Supreme Court.

118 See S. Stavoros, *The guarantees for Accused Persons under Article 6 of the European Convention on Human Rights*, Martinus Nijhoff, London, 1993.

to do with the personal convictions of a particular judge in a particular case, while objective impartiality means that the judge should give a reasonable impression of impartiality to the individual being judged so as to pre-empt legitimate doubts.[119] The European Court has found that, "[w]hat is at stake is the confidence which the courts in a democratic society must inspire in the public and, above all, as far as criminal proceedings are concerned, in the accused."[120] The importance of impartiality is seen in numerous cases heard by the European system. That Court held, for example, that a judge who ruled on the pre-trial detention of an accused person based on his conviction that there was a reasonable suspicion of the accused's guilt, could not later form part of the tribunal that would rule on that person's innocence or guilt.[121]

27. The Inter-American Court has on several occasions made reference to competence, independence and impartiality, but generally does not differentiate between the concepts. A case clearly dealing with competence was the case of Barreto Leiva. Competence was challenged before the Court on the basis of the privilege of certain authorities of being tried in a higher court of a different level than would usually be the case and the fact that those connected to the offense but not being authorities had to follow the privileged court of the authorities, in this case a former President. The alleged victim argued that this situation violated the right to be judged by the "natural judge" (*juez natural*). The Court did not accept the argument, holding that in the case of a connection such as this, there was no conflict because the rule was a legal one and not a decision of the executive or of the judiciary itself.[122] Whenever there is an allegation that the judge handling a case is not the "natural judge", what is being discussed is always competence.

28. The majority of the judgments of the Court analyze the problem of competence together with independence and/or impartiality in proceedings before military courts. Case law has varied. In the case of Genie Lacayo, an old case, the Commission argued that "to prosecute ordinary crimes as though they were military crimes simply because they had been committed by members of the military breached the guarantee of an independent and impartial tribunal".[123] The victim's allegations were similar, stating that a military court lacked both

119 The first judgment establishing this distinction was the *Case of Piersack v. Belgium* (European Court of Human Rights, judgment of October 1, 1982, paras. 30–32, A, Vol. 53, pp. 14–16, reproduced in Council of Europe, *Digest of Strasbourg Case-Law relating to the European Convention on Human Rights*, Vol. 2 (Article 6), Carl Heymanns-Verlag KG Köln/Berlin, Bonn/München, 1984, pp. 672–674). See also, European Court of Human Rights, *Case of Micallef v. Malta*, Application No. 17056/06, judgment of October 10, 2009, para. 93.

120 D.J. Harris *et al.*, *supra* n. 83, p. 235, citing *Fey v. Austria* (A 255-A para. 30 (1993)).

121 See *ibidem*, p. 237.

122 *Case of Barreto Leiva v. Venezuela*, paras. 77 and 81.

123 *Ibidem*, para. 53.

requirements. The victim added a second violation; the judgment invoked the "Sandinista legal conscience" and that denoted a bias as well. The Court found that "the fact that it involves a military court does not *per se* signify that the human rights guaranteed the accusing party by the Convention are being violated",[124] not really addressing the first argument of the victim; with regard to the second one, it found that the legal provision mentioning a "Sandinista conscience" had not been applied and consequently there was no violation.[125] The Court also found that using a provision that called for the application of "Sandinista's legality" in the proceeding was not a violation of independence and impartiality; the expression made reference to guidelines that "are common to general military criminal law regardless of the political orientation of the State in question."[126] Later on, the Court's case law evolved to the point of concluding in the case of Castillo Petruzzi *et al.* that Peru had violated Article 8. It found that:

> "[t]ransferring jurisdiction from civilian courts to military courts, thus allowing military courts to try civilians accused of treason, means that the competent, independent and impartial tribunal previously established by law is precluded from hearing these cases" given that the military courts were created to maintain order and discipline within the armed forces and civilians "cannot engage in behaviors that violate military duties".[127]

In the case of Durand and Ugarte, the Court insisted that in a democratic State, "criminal military jurisdiction must have a restrictive and exceptional scope" and operate to protect "special juridical interests related to the functions assigned by law to the armed forces". If this was the rule, only military personnel could "be judged for the commission of crimes or offenses that by nature threaten the legal rights of the military".[128] The Court introduced as elements to decide on jurisdiction the status of the persons to be tried and the nature of the offenses that fell within military jurisdiction, thus defining the military court's competence more narrowly.

An important case in terms of the lack of competence of military courts is the case of Palamara, where a military court judged Mr. Palamara, a former Navy officer who left the institution and later went to work there as a civilian. The question of the status of Palamara had been also addressed and resolved by the Court in the case of Cesti Hurtado: "a person having [had] military status and having filed an application for retirement from active duty could not be tried

124 *Case of Genie Lacayo v. Nicaragua*, para. 84.

125 *Ibidem*, para. 86.

126 *Ibidem*, para. 87.

127 *Case of Castillo Petruzzi et al. v. Peru*, paras. 128 and 132. The Court reiterated this in the *case of Cantoral Benavides v. Peru*, para. 112 and, in the *Case of Las Palmeras v. Colombia*, para. 51.

128 *Case of Durand and Ugarte v. Peru*, paras. 117–118 (translator's version). In the same sense, *Case of Cesti Hurtado v. Peru*, para. 151.

by the military courts".[129] In Palamara, the Court reiterated that the right to be judged by ordinary tribunals is a basic principle of due process. The ordinary criminal judge is the "natural judge", so:

> military criminal regulations must clearly set forth without any ambiguities whatsoever, which persons are deemed to be military members – the only perpetrators of military criminal offenses –, which criminal offenses fall within the specific military scope, and the illegal nature of criminal offenses by means of a description of the injury to or endangerment of military legal interests which have been seriously attacked, which may justify the exercise of punitive military power, as well as establish the appropriate sanction.[130]

Finally, in this judgment the Court made clear that only military personnel can commit military offenses, "while performing specific duties related to the defense and external security of a State." In times of peace, military criminal courts, when not eliminated, should reduce their jurisdiction "to the minimum and be inspired in the principles and guarantees prevailing in modern criminal law".[131] A good example to show what this means is the case of Fernández Ortega, where the Court held that "[i]n no case does the rape of someone by military personnel bear a relationship to the military discipline or mission". Therefore, the military courts have no jurisdiction to try such a case, not even to conduct the preliminary investigations.[132]

The Court also dealt with the issue of military courts and the competent tribunal in the case of Vélez Restrepo. Colombia argued that up to the 2009 judgment in Radilla Pacheco v. Mexico, the applicable standard "to determine whether a conduct should be heard by the ordinary jurisdiction, was the extreme gravity of the human rights violations" and that "other human rights violations examined by military courts would not be *per se* violations of the American Convention".[133] The State added that when Vélez's personal integrity had been affected "the military criminal jurisdiction had the status of the natural judge". The pronouncements of the Court over criminal tribunals had "undergone 'important changes between 1996 and 2006'". It invoked in its argument the judgment in Genie Lacayo v. Nicaragua in 1997 where there had been no pronouncement on military jurisdiction. The State also maintained that to apply these changes to the case "would be against the principle of the non-

---

129 *Case of Cesti-Hurtado v. Peru*, para. 151.

130 *Case of Palamara v. Chile*, para. 126.

131 *Ibidem*, para. 132. See also a clear explanation of the Court's position in the concurring vote of Judge Garcia Ramírez.

132 *Fernández Ortega v. Mexico*, para. 177. See also *Case of Nadege Dorzema et al. v. Dominican Republic*, para. 198, where the Court reiterates that just the investigation carried out by a military court is incompatible with the Convention, because it constitutes the initiation and the necessary presumption for the subsequent intervention of an incompetent court.

133 *Case of Vélez Restrepo v. Colombia*, para. 237.

retroactive nature of obligations in international law".[134] The Court reiterated its consistent case law in the sense that "only soldiers on active duty who have committed crimes or misdemeanors that, owing to their nature, harm juridical rights of a military nature, can be tried by the military justice system".[135] It also mentioned that around the time of the Court's judgment in Genie Lacayo, there had been other judgments containing the ruling against military justice trying human rights violation cases. This is true: the Court had started to change its interpretation a long time before the judgment in Vélez Restrepo.[136] The Court also noted that although it interpreted the obligations of the Convention authoritatively, "the obligation not to investigate and prosecute human rights violations under the military criminal jurisdiction is a guarantee of due process derived from the obligations contained in Article 8(1) of the American Convention and does not depend solely on what this Court has reaffirmed in its case law."[137] It is clear that the Court changed its position after Genie Lacayo – which is acceptable and in my view faithful to the reading of Article 8 – but did not explain the reasons for the change immediately that the change occurred. In Vélez Restrepo – that is, several years after – it conceded that "it has been able to construct the restrictive jurisprudential criterion, which it is currently developing fully, through the analysis of the different contentious cases that have been submitted to its consideration."[138] Even though a change of jurisprudence cannot be invoked as if this has created a retroactive obligation, I find it is convenient for the Court to announce any such change and to explain the reasons for so doing.

It is possible that the military initiate a disciplinary procedure to investigate the responsibilities of an alleged perpetrator among its rank, but this will not eliminate the obligation for the State to start a judicial process. In the case of La Rochela, the Court stated that disciplinary procedures complement "but [do] not entirely substitute the function of the criminal courts in cases of grave human rights violations."[139] One notices that in La Rochela the Court again returns to the wording that grave violations fall outside the jurisdiction of the military courts. In Vélez Restrepo, where Peru repeated Colombia's argument regarding the change in the interpretation of Article 8, the Court settles the subject, stating that "the criteria to investigate and prosecute human rights violations before the ordinary jurisdiction reside not on the gravity of the violations, but rather on

---

134 *Ibidem*.

135 *Ibidem*, para. 240.

136 See, for example the *Case of Castillo Petruzzi at al. v. Peru*, para. 128, where the Court held that military jurisdiction is not "naturally" applicable to civilians.

137 *Case of Vélez Restrepo v. Colombia*, para. 241.

138 *Ibidem*, para. 243.

139 *Case of the Massacre of La Rochela v. Colombia*, para. 215. See also the cases of the *Ituango Massacres*, para. 333 and of the *Püeblo Bello Massacre*, para. 203, quoted by the Court.

their very nature and on that of the protected juridical right".[140] In the case of Rosendo Cantú, the State argued that "the rights to judicial guarantees and to judicial protection have not been violated because the investigations remain at the ministerial (investigative) stage." The Court does not accept this argument and stresses that in particular it must "examine the measures that relate to and constitute the grounds for judicial proceedings, particularly the investigation procedure, the results of which the opening and progress of said proceedings depend".[141]

29. A case that placed the Court before illicit conduct different from those this chapter has examined made the Court revisit the issue of the independence and impartiality of military courts. In Argüelles *et al.* v. Argentina, the Court dealt with alleged victims who had been submitted to a military court accused of irregularly having assigned to themselves credits of the Argentinean Air Force; the personal appropriation of other funds of the Air Force; and the falsification of documents for those purposes.[142] The alleged victims attempted to benefit from the Court's case law, as applied to cases of disappearance and others of the kind. However, even before presenting the case in the inter-American system, Argentina had changed the extent of the jurisdiction of the military courts and had ordered a review of the cases decided by those courts, including the case of Argüelles and his other co-accused. This review complied with all the requirements of due process. Consequently, the Court did not find a violation of Article 8(1) regarding independence of the domestic court that had finally decided on the case.[143]

30. As said above, the Inter-American Court has on several occasions made reference to the requirements of independence and impartiality of courts, but generally does not differentiate between the concepts. However, in the case of Apitz *et al.*, the Court did point out the difference between the two concepts. The Court stated that the purpose of independence is to prevent "the Judicial System in general and its members in particular, from finding themselves subjected to possible undue limitations in the exercise of their functions, by bodies alien to the Judiciary or even by those judges with review or appellate functions". Impartiality, on the other hand, "demands that the judge acting in a specific dispute approach the facts of the case subjectively free of all prejudice and also offer sufficient objective guarantees to exclude any doubt the parties or the community might entertain as to his or her lack of impartiality".[144] Impartiality

---

140 *Case of Vélez Restrepo and family members v. Colombia*, para. 244. See also *Case of Osorio Rivera and family v. Peru*, para. 190.

141 *Case of Rosendo Cantú v. Mexico*, para. 159.

142 *Case of Argüelles et al. v. Argentina*, para. 1.

143 *Ibidem*, para. 166.

144 *Case of Apitz et al. v. Venezuela*, paras. 55–56. Sea also *Case of Barreto Leiva v. Venezuela*, para. 98.

comes together with the right of the parties or of the accused to challenge a judge, as this "works as a guarantee for the parties to the proceedings, and on the other hand, it aims at providing credibility to the role performed by the Jurisdiction."[145] The Court dealt with the suspension or removal of a judge in relation to independence, finding that:

> judges cannot be removed on the sole ground that one of their decisions has been overturned on appeal or review by a higher judicial body. This safeguards the independence of judges internally, since they should not feel compelled to avoid dissenting with the reviewing body that, basically, only plays a distinct judicial role that is limited to dealing with the issues raised on appeal by a party who is dissatisfied with the original decision.[146]

In the case of Reverón Trujillo, the Court summed up most of what constituted its case law on independence. It states that "one of the main objectives of the separation of the public powers is the guarantee of the judges' independence." Independence had to be guaranteed by the State "both in its institutional aspect, that is, with regard to the Judicial Power as a system, as well as in connection with its individual aspect, that is, with regard to the specific judge as an individual." An appearance of independence of the judiciary should also exist so that the public finds it is legitimate and can be trusted.[147] Based on the Basic Principles of the United Nations on the Independence of the Judiciary, its own jurisprudence and that of the European Court, it found that the guarantee should encompass three aspects concerning judges: (i) an adequate appointment process; (ii) the tenure in the position; and (iii) the guarantee against external pressures.[148] As to the first aspect, it is required for judges to be appointed and later promoted "based on objective criteria, namely the judge's personal merits, his qualifications, integrity, ability, and efficiency, all of which are the preponderant elements to be considered".[149] Equal opportunity also has to be ensured.[150] Concerning tenure, it does not pronounce on the length of the mandate. Rather it adopts the position of the Basic Principles. The first is that "[j]udges, whether appointed or elected, shall have guaranteed tenure until a mandatory retirement age or the expiry of their term of office, where such exists". In addition they "shall be subject to suspension or removal only for reasons of incapacity or behavior that renders them unfit to discharge their duties". Finally, "[a]ll disciplinary, suspension or removal proceedings shall be determined in accordance with established standards of judicial conduct".[151] The Court had already stated that "the free removal of judges foments an objective

145 *Ibidem*, paras. 63–63.
146 *Ibidem*, para. 84.
147 *Case of Reverón Trujillo v. Venezuela*, para. 68.
148 *Ibidem*, para. 70.
149 *Ibidem*, para. 71.
150 *Ibidem*, paras. 72–73.
151 *Ibidem*, paras. 75–78.

doubt in the observer regarding the effective possibility they may have to decide specific controversies without fearing the retaliation".[152] Finally, there must be a guarantee against external pressures, such as "improper influences, inducements, pressures, threats or interferences, direct or indirect, from any quarter or for any reason".[153] In the case, the Court found that Ms. Reverón, a provisional judge, was denied reinstatement without an appropriate justification. It gave as examples of appropriate causes: "i) that the court or tribunal for which the service was offered no longer exist; ii) that the court or tribunal to which it offered her service be made up by titular judges appointed pursuant with the law; and iii) that the dismissed judge has lost her physical or mental capacity to exercise the position".[154] The Court reiterates in Apitz that judges who are appointed on a provisional basis must have certain stability and permanence in their functions to ensure independence and impartiality.[155]

31. In the 2013 case of Quintana *et al.*, the Court made a review of its case law on independence, specifying certain aspects that had been developed in Reverón. It stated that judicial independence relates not only to the person under trial; judges also must have certain guarantees to safeguard their attributes. Among them, judges require job tenure[156] and stability to be truly independent.[157] The Court adds that the autonomous exercise of the judicial function must be guaranteed in its institutional aspect, that is regarding the judiciary as a system, as well as its individual aspect, in which the person of the judge must be guaranteed independence. With respect to the first aspect, the objective dimension transcends the judge and affects society in its entirety.[158] The Court noted that in 14 days the Ecuadorian Congress dismissed all the members of the Supreme Court, the Constitutional Court and the Electoral Tribunal, and that there was evidence of the existence of a political alliance to prevent the continuation of criminal trials opened against the President and the former President of the Republic. The Court found that this was a clear violation of Article 8 of the Convention.[159] In the case of Camba Campos *et al.* (case of the Constitutional Tribunal), also against Ecuador, the Court dealt with a similar situation. The victims were members of the Constitutional Court. First, Congress dismissed the members of the Constitutional Court due to the alleged illegality of their nominations.[160] Congress decided this without notifying the members

152 *Ibidem*, para. 78 quoting the *case of Apitz v. Venezuela*.
153 *Ibidem*, para. 80.
154 *Case of Reverón Trujillo v. Venezuela*, para. 134.
155 *Ibidem*, para. 67.
156 There is no exact equivalent in English of "*inamovilidad*", the Spanish word used by the Court. Basically it refers to job security.
157 *Case of Quintana et al. v. Ecuador*, para. 153.
158 *Ibidem*, para. 154.
159 *Ibidem*, paras. 175–177.
160 *Case of Camba et al. v. Ecuador*, para. 61.

of the Constitutional Court and without a hearing.[161] In addition and after the cessation of their functions, Congress started impeachment proceedings. The reasons invoked for the impeachment were two decisions of the Constitutional Court with which some Congressmen did not agree. The vote on the impeachment occurred on December 1, 2004 and Congress rejected the various motion of impeachment; thus the process ended.[162] On December 8, 2004, the President of the Republic convened Congress to vote again on the same motions. Among objections from some Congressmen that the issue had been decided and was *res judicata*, the session took place and one motion for the impeachment of five members was approved.[163] In Camba Campos *et al.*, the Inter-American Court resorted to its case law in Constitutional Tribunal v. Peru[164] and Quintana Campos *et al.* v. Ecuador and *mutatis mutandis* followed the reasoning and decisions in those two judgments, finding a violation of Article 8.[165]

In these two cases, the Court gave the issue of independence a different dimension. In Quintana, it specified that "the institutional guarantee of judicial independence is directly related to a judge's right to remain in his post, as a consequence of the guarantee of tenure in office." The Court quotes a case in the Human Rights Committee where the Committee decided that the dismissal procedure of a judge was not carried out with due process and did not provide him with "the necessary guarantees to which he was entitled in his capacity as a judge, *thus constituting an attack on the independence of the judiciary*".[166] For this reason the Committee found a violation of Article 25 (equal access to public functions) in conjunction with Article 14(1) of the ICCPR. After this quotation, the Court set out the following reasoning: (i) respect for judicial guarantees implies respect for judicial independence; (ii) the scope of judicial independence translates into a judge's subjective right to be dismissed from his position exclusively for the reasons permitted by law; and (iii) when a judge's tenure is affected in an arbitrary manner, the right to judicial independence enshrined in Article 8(1) of the American Convention is violated.[167] This is in conjunction with the right to access and remain in public office, on general terms of equality, established in Article 23(1) of the American Convention. The Court does not specifically say to whose detriment the right is violated. It is fair to conclude that the Court believed, although it did not explicitly say, that it was also the judge's right to have independence, since the lack thereof would prejudice his or her performance as a judge and this would affect his dignity because it would

161 *Ibidem*, para. 65.
162 *Ibidem*, para. 88.
163 *Ibidem*, para. 94.
164 *Case of the Constitutional Tribunal v. Peru*.
165 *Case of Camba et al. v. Ecuador*, para. 222.
166 HRC, Communication No. 1376/2005, *Soratha Bandaranayake v. Sri Lanka*, CCPR/C/93/D/1376/2005, para. 7.2.
167 *Case of Quintana et al. v. Ecuador*, para. 155.

impede him or her from acting as a judge in the way a judge ought to act in a trial. Camba *et al.* is similar in this respect.

In the case Norín *et al.*, the Court added a new explanation to its position in the two cases mentioned above. It found that independence had two facets: an external one, alluding to the protection of the judiciary as a system; and an internal one, when the State provides protection to the person of a specific judge. Now including impartiality, the Court considers both as a right in favor of the person submitted to trial but also as a guarantee for the judges themselves, so they can comply with their duties. The aim of protection is to avoid the judiciary in general and each judge in particular being subject to undue pressures while performing their function, either by other organs or even by members of the judiciary who exercise functions of review or appeals.[168]

I hesitate to find solid reasons for this interpretation. I do not quite understand how one can go from premises (i) and (ii) to premise (iii) in the case of Quintana *et al.* In principle, one could affirm that to have an independent judge try the case is the right of the person appearing before the judge. If a judge is denied stability in the role (just one element of independence), to which judges are entitled, the judge would have the right to complain that he or she has been denied without due process his or her right to stay in office. This could allow the judge to request justice in a due process of law and probably invoke Article 25,[169] but not, as the Court reasons, argue that his or her independence has been violated.

32. The true importance of the requirement of a court's independence lies in the fact that it is a fundamental guarantee for the individual participating in a suit of law or a trial. A relatively recent judgment of the Court casts doubt on whether what has been advanced so far for the protection of this guarantee of due process will be reversed. The case of Brewer Carias v. Venezuela, undoubtedly with political overtones, deals with the attempt to depose President Hugo Chávez in 2002, in which Mr. Brewer Carias was allegedly involved as a main participant, among several others. At the start of the domestic proceedings, the victim alleged the lack of independence and impartiality of the domestic courts and of the Prosecutor,[170] requesting the annulment of the actions carried out.[171]

---

168 *Case of Norín et al. v. Chile*, paras. 13–16.

169 My thanks to Oscar Parra for bringing this issue to my attention and to Oswaldo Ruiz for discussing it with me.

170 The General Prosecutor had published a book where he had referred that there had been versions accusing the alleged victim as being the author of the "Carmona Decree", a key element of the accusations against Mr. Brewer Carias. See *Case of Brewer Carias v. Venezuela*, para. 59. As to the judges, there was a situation of provisional judged that left them completely dependent on the Executive.

171 It is appropriate to mention here that the case law of the Court requires independence and impartiality not only of judges. It extends these requirements "to the non-judicial bodies responsible for the investigation prior to the judicial proceedings, conducted to determine

Up to the end of the proceedings before the Court, this petition had not been answered. The evidence in the Court's files shows that on several occasions decisions that directly or indirectly favored Mr. Brewer Carias had been quashed and the judges or courts that took them had been suspended or had been ceased in their functions.[172] The Court, in my view departing radically from its case law, accepted the preliminary exceptions invoked by Venezuela of non-exhaustion of domestic remedies. The Court found that the failure to exhaust remedies was based correctly on the fact that the criminal trial against the alleged victim had not yet ended and there were domestic stages at which to discuss the alleged irregularities and there were remedies that could be presented within the criminal process.[173] The second point put forward by the Court, I would say repeating the same idea, was that it was not possible to pronounce on the alleged violation of the judicial guarantees since there was not yet certitude as to how the proceedings would continue and there had not been "at least" a first instance decision.[174] The alleged victim's representatives argued that the Convention exempted the complainant from exhausting domestic remedies when "the domestic legislation of the state concerned does not afford due process of law for the protection of the right or rights that have allegedly been violated".[175] The Court did not agree with the argument and decided that given the "early stage of the trial" Mr. Brewer Carias could only come before the inter-American system at a later stage. Finally, the Court considered that an alleged context of the provisional status of the judiciary – something that had been proved in previous cases against Venezuela – did not allow the application of this provision as that would imply accepting an "argument of a general nature".[176]

As mentioned above, the Court has dealt before with cases regarding the situation of the judiciary in Venezuela. There has for long time been a phenomenon of provisional or temporary judges, as well as provisional prosecutors, and this makes the judicial operators dependent on the executive. The Court has always found that this amounts to a violation of Article 8. The history of the Venezuelan cases is mentioned in the Brewer Carias case, but the Court does not seem to see fit to apply this precedent here, first because at the procedural stage of the case (no first instance decision) a *prima facie* conclusion on the impact of the quality of provisional of judges on the guarantee of judicial

---

the circumstances of a death and the existence of sufficient evidence". The reason is that an effective and well-conducted investigation is essential for the Court to conduct a trial complying with due process. See *Case of Cantoral Huamani et al. v. Peru*, para. 133. See also *Case of J. v. Peru*, para. 293, where the Court found that due guarantees were violated when the Prosecutor only considers the incriminating elements of the evidence and not those that could vindicate the accused.

172 *Ibidem*, paras. 50, 54 and 56.

173 *Ibidem*, para. 81.

174 *Ibidem*, para. 88.

175 ACHR, Article 46(2)(a).

176 *Case of Brewer Carias v. Venezuela*, para. 105.

independence is not possible, and second, astonishingly, because in those cases the victims were the judges themselves.

There is a strong and well-founded dissenting opinion of two judges of the Court that should be read to understand the extent to which the Court has deviated from its previous case law,[177] to the detriment of the victim's right to be tried by an independent and impartial court.

33. To sum up, the Court has clarified the notion of competence particularly with regard to military courts, concluding that they are not competent to try either civilians or the military when they perpetrate human rights violations. The competence of the military jurisdiction is granted only to deal with special "legal interests related to the functions assigned by law to the armed forces", thus they should have only disciplinary jurisdiction. This interpretation is the application to jurisdiction of the doctrine of the "natural judge" or judge with the rightful jurisdiction. Behind this is the idea that in principle there must be an imperative need to deviate from the rule that the judge should belong to the ordinary jurisdiction and not to a special one. The Court often deals with independence and impartiality together, but it can be concluded that concerning independence the Court follows the case law of Europe that examines the elements of appointment, tenure and guarantee against pressure from other State agents. Provisional judges, mainly in Venezuela, are assessed against these parameters and are found wanting, usually because they can be freely removed without cause. The Court has also decided that independence has two facets: an external and an internal one; the internal facet, according to the Court, creates a right for the judges that is violated, for example, if they are removed without cause. The principle of impartiality, in its turn, is examined with regard to the participation in proceedings of faceless judges and to the presence of judges in more than one stage of the proceedings; both are found to be violations of impartiality.

6. DUE GUARANTEES

34. The expression "due guarantees" alludes to the Anglo-Saxon legal concept of "fair trial". Both concepts are undefined, as they do not determine the elements comprising them. Therefore, it is necessary to examine each individual process in order to assess whether it is a "due or just process"[178] on the basis of the Convention and the Court's case law. In the case of Vargas Areco, a 15-year-old

[177] *Ibidem*. Dissenting opinion of Judges Manuel Ventura Robles and Eduardo Ferrer MacGregor Poisot.

[178] On "fair hearing", see D.J. Harris *et al.*, *supra* n. 83, pp. 202–203.

child who was drafted by the Army and subsequently killed for trying to escape, the Court held that:

> [g]iven its close connection to other specific rights, the duty to safeguard the right to fair trial may be fulfilled in different manners; therefore, whether the State has said duty to safeguard the right to fair trial will depend on the specific right at stake and the circumstances of the case.[179]

One could say *grosso modo* that due guarantees have to do with certain minimum requirements for conducting a trial. It is not enough that a competent, independent and impartial tribunal carries out the trial; it is also necessary for the tribunal to give the parties the opportunity to present their cases without unjustified constraints. This means the presence of a defender in all types of trials should the complainant so wishes; time and opportunity to present the evidence in support of their pleadings; a reasonable evaluation of the evidence; and reasoned rulings from the tribunal, all based on the principle of equality. The guarantees due in a trial may vary depending on the circumstances of the case. The Convention, however, imposes some principles to guide the decisions on which guarantees should be applied.

35. In the case of the Dismissed Congressional Employees (Aguado-Alfaro *et al.*), the Court had to decide:

> whether in the historical context mentioned above and according to the norms under which they were dismissed, the alleged victims could determine with legal certainty the proceeding to which they could and should resort to claim the rights they considered had been violated and whether they were guaranteed real and effective access to justice.[180]

This issue led the Court to hold that "in any proceeding or process that exists under the State's domestic system there should be extensive judicial guarantees, which should include the formalities that must be observed in order to guarantee access to these guarantees". It was the domestic courts' duty to verify "the procedural criteria relating to the admissibility and legitimacy of the specific recourse filed" before going into the merits.[181]

6.1. PRINCIPLES OF *AUDI ALTERAM PARTEM* AND EQUALITY

36. Due guarantees include the idea of the principle of *audi alteram partem*. As with every human right, the right to due process must be enjoyed by all,

179 *Case of Vargas Areco v. Paraguay*, para. 73.

180 *Case of the Dismissed Congressional Employees v. Peru*, para. 110.

181 *Ibidem*, para. 126.

without discrimination. The principle of equality therefore underlies this right, as it does all other human rights found in the Convention, and is reflected in the principle of *audi alteram partem*. In terms of a proceeding, it means that the court must behave without fear or favor toward all parties to a proceeding and that the parties must have the same rights, both to present petitions, pleadings and evidence and to challenge the petitions and evidence presented by the other party. This also includes the notion that the wording of the rules of procedure must be such that they do not place one party at a disadvantage with regard to the other.

The Court has clarified in the case of López Mendoza that the establishment in domestic law of certain steps within the proceedings that cannot be subject to objections "is not *per se* contrary to the American Convention". According to the Court, there is no violation of the principle of equality if the impossibility to challenge certain aspects of the proceeding does not show that it prevented overall the due defense regarding the fines that were imposed on the alleged victim.[182]

37. In a criminal proceeding, the principle of *audi alteram partem* "consists of a real opportunity for the defense for maximum rebuttal of the accusations"[183] and constitutes a guarantee for the accused. As far as the principle of equality goes, during the debate over the draft Convention, the inclusion of a letter (b) under Article 8(2) was suggested, establishing that "due process in criminal proceedings will include the following minimum guarantees: [...] b) Equality of rights and duties of the parties during the trial." The suggestion was rejected and replaced with the current wording of paragraph 2, which grants minimum guarantees only to the accused, in full equality, abandoning the idea of equality of the parties.[184] This means that due process is a right of individuals before the State and cannot be invoked by the State before itself. As Maier says, criminal procedural law can grant authority to the Public Prosecutor's Office to exercise the State's power of criminal prosecution; however, it cannot provide guarantees to that office.[185] It seems clear that at the adoption of the American Convention there was no trace of the idea that "bilateralism of the hearing" between the accused and the accuser applied in criminal proceedings.[186] Nor is there the idea

---

182 *Case of López Mendoza v. Venezuela*, para. 120.

183 M.I. Horvitz and J. López, *Derecho Procesal Penal Chileno*, Vol. II, Chapter X, section 3.3. (author's translation).

184 Inter-American Specialized Conference on Human Rights, San Jose, Costa Rica, November 7–22, 1969, *Minutes and Documents*, General Secretariat, OAS, Washington DC, OEA/Ser.K/XVI/1.2, pp. 59, 105 and 190.

185 J. Maier, *supra* n. 114, pp. 543–44, cited in M.I. Horvitz, "Estatus de la Víctima en el Proceso Penal. Comentario a dos fallos de la Corte Suprema" (2003) 3 *Revista de Estudios de la Justicia* 135.

186 This does not imply that the prosecutor will not have the right to present evidence or be able to object to the evidence presented by the accused.

that there could be "bilateralism" and "equality" between the defendants or the accused and the next of kin of certain victims. However, in certain cases[187] the Court gives equal rights to them. In a case that is not recent – Genie Lacayo – applying not Article 8 but rather Article 24 of the Convention, the Court ruled that:

> it has not been proven that Mr. Raymond Genie-Peñalba [father of the victim] found himself in a *clear situation of inferiority* in relation to the defendants or the military judges when he appeared as the accusing party before the military courts; consequently, there was no violation of the right to equal protection of the law.[188]

The judgment speaks here of the right of the victim or the victim's relatives and seems to use European case law meant for the accused when requiring the possible situation of inferiority to be clear. In the case of Kaufman v. Belgium, the European Commission found that "everyone who is a party to such proceedings [referring to both criminal and noncriminal cases] shall have a reasonable opportunity of presenting his case to the court under conditions which do not place him at *substantial* disadvantage vis-à-vis his opponent".[189] The same decision appears in the case of Dombo Beheer B.V. decided by the European Court.[190] The principle was also invoked by the Inter-American Court in support of its finding in the case of Radilla Pacheco. In that case, the Court found that the refusal of the State to provide "copies of the investigation to the victims constitutes a disproportionate burden in their detriment, not compatible with their right to participate in the preliminary inquiry". This information is "not subject to reservations of confidentiality, since it refers to the investigation of crimes that constitute grave violations to human rights, such as the forced disappearance of Mr. Rosendo Radilla-Pacheco".[191]

6.2. RIGHT TO BE REPRESENTED BY AN ATTORNEY

38. An important guarantee is the access to legal assistance in court. If the accused is a person of means, Article 8 is enough to ensure that person legal representation. If the person lacks financial means, Article 8 is not enough as it does not establish a State obligation to provide this legal assistance for free to people without financial means either in criminal or noncriminal proceedings. With regard to criminal cases, the wording of letter (e) of Article 8(2) is somewhat strange: it establishes "the inalienable right to be assisted by counsel" but then leaves to the State the decision of whether to provide this counsel for

---

187 See Chapter 2, section 4.2.
188 *Case of Genie Lacayo v. Nicaragua*, para. 88 (emphasis added).
189 Quoted in D.J. Harris *et al.*, *supra* n. 83, p. 207.
190 Quoted in P. van Dijk *et al.*, *supra* n. 62, p. 580.
191 *Case of Radilla Pacheco v. Mexico*, paras. 256–259.

free. Thus, according to the American Convention, due process can be complied with simply by allowing the person without means to present his or her case before the court personally. However, an individual's lack of sufficient education together with a lack of means can be a great obstacle to justice. Although the Convention does not make this obligation for the State explicit, the principle of due process could require the State to provide at some point this kind of assistance in certain criminal or even noncriminal trials – for example, when the proceeding is not simple enough to make having or not having legal assistance irrelevant.[192] Of course, if the domestic legal system does not allow a person to litigate on his or her own behalf, as is the case in some States, the State should be required to provide free legal assistance to those persons lacking sufficient financial means.

The Inter-American Court has established the groundwork for developing the idea of free legal aid, both in an advisory opinion and in several judgments. In response to a consultation from the Inter-American Commission on exceptions to exhaustion of domestic remedies, the Court opined that:

> [e]ven in those cases in which the accused is forced to defend him or herself because he or she cannot afford legal counsel, a violation of Article 8 of the Convention could be said to exist if it can be proved that the lack of legal counsel affected the right to a fair hearing to which the person is entitled under that Article.[193]

It added that in noncriminal cases "the concept of "due guarantees" applies also to these orders; consequently, on these issues the individual also has the right to the due process that applies in criminal cases. "It is important to note here that the circumstances of a particular case or proceeding – its significance, its legal character, and its context in a particular legal system – are among the factors that have a bearing on the determination of whether legal representation is or is not necessary for a fair hearing".[194]

6.3. REASONABLE TIME

39. Article 8(1) establishes a person's right to a *hearing* "within a reasonable time". The notion of a reasonable time was examined in some detail in the prior chapter concerning the provision contained in Article 7(5) of the Convention on the reasonable time to keep a person in *preventive detention*. In Article 8(1) of the Convention, the purpose of the requirement of a reasonable time for the completion of the proceedings is clear. In criminal proceedings, it seeks to prevent the accused from remaining in a situation of uncertainty for a long

---

192 See *supra* n. 102 on the European Court's case of *Airey v. Ireland*.

193 *OC-11/90* of August 10, 1990, para. 27. See the debate on the interpretation of Article 8 with regard to free legal assistance in criminal cases, *infra*.

194 *Ibidem*, para. 28.

time, given that such situation undoubtedly affects the enjoyment of certain of their human rights. In civil proceedings, the purpose is as quick as possible a determination of rights or obligations in order for the one whose right is recognized to be able to begin its enjoyment, and the one whose obligation is established to be relieved of the uncertainty of not knowing whether he or she has an obligation to fulfill.[195]

Due to the peculiarities of the inter-American system, the reader will see that predominantly the Court has used the concept of reasonable time to deal with courts that refused to carry out investigations on disappearances, summary executions or other crimes occurred in a State when there was an absence of the rule of law. This was made possible by the Court deciding that the next of kin of victims of those gross violations had the right to demand access to a criminal trial and to participate in it. Consequently, most of the case law on the concept of reasonable time addresses this delay, prejudicial to the next of kin and one of the main consequences of those crimes remaining in impunity.

6.3.1. Factors to Decide on the Reasonableness of a Delay

40. The Convention does not set forth criteria for guiding those who apply these provisions in establishing this reasonable period, but there is enough case law, particularly European, indicating the factors to be considered to determine the reasonableness of the period. In short, the factors that allow a finding on this issue of the time of duration of the trial are, in principle: (i) the complexity of the matter; (ii) the judicial activity of the interested party; and (iii) the behavior of the judicial authorities. The concept is applicable both to criminal and noncriminal trials.

In the case of La Cantuta on the kidnapping and disappearance of a professor and several students of a Peruvian university in the time of President Fujimori, the trial of which had lasted 14 years when the Court issued its judgment, the Court held:

> [T]he right to justice is not limited to the formal institution of domestic proceedings, but it also involves the assurance within reasonable time of the right of alleged victims or their relatives to have every necessary step taken to know the truth and punish those responsible for the events.[196]

The Court then added that "the State's duty to wholly serve the purposes of justice prevails over the guarantee of reasonable time". This means that the right of the victims or the next of kin to have the violation investigated and the authors prosecuted and convicted prevail over the guarantee of reasonable delay in favor of the accused.[197] The same position was taken in the case of Anzualdo Castro.[198]

---

[195] *Case of Yvon Neptune v. Haiti*, para. 81.

[196] *Case of La Cantuta v. Peru*, para. 149.

[197] *Ibidem.*

[198] *Case of Anzualdo Castro v. Peru*, para. 156.

41. The Court used the three factors mentioned above in resolving the case of Genie Lacayo. In its judgment, it ruled that in order to decide on the reasonableness of the period in a proceeding, the three elements mentioned above must be taken into account.[199] The complexity of the matter could arise from different sources, for example the fact that a proceeding has many parties; or the fact that many difficult expert witness reports must be prepared; or the fact that part of the investigation must be carried out through requests for judicial assistance from other courts. The procedural activity of the interested party is also analyzed from the point of view of the good faith with which the actions are carried out. In principle, the use of all remedies that the law itself provides for cannot by themselves cause a delay; on the contrary, it is the State's responsibility to prevent the rules of procedure themselves from causing the delay.[200] The conduct of judicial authorities is a particularly important factor:[201] any delay must have a justification, and an excessive amount of work faced by the court cannot be one of them. This, I would reiterate, is because the responsibility for due process "within a reasonable time" fully belongs to the State, which has the obligation to organize a justice system that functions properly. In the case of Juan Humberto Sánchez, which also examined a criminal proceeding, the Court found that the case had no complexity that could justify a preliminary investigation stage that was still pending after ten years.[202] The Court did not spell out its reasoning, noting in an examination of the Court's case file that the delays were clearly attributable to State agencies. First, there was evidence that the judicial authorities had not been diligent in processing the case; an example of this was the fact that the court carried out the collection of evidence between 1992 and 1998, with long periods of inactivity. Second, other State agents had been negligent in performing their duties, for example the armed forces, which did not respond to the courts' requests for several years.[203] Nor did the Court accept the State's defense that the relatives were responsible for taking action to move the proceeding forward. The Court reiterated here that it is the State's responsibility to investigate, something that must be done *ex officio*.[204] For this reason, one must conclude that the criterion for assessing a party's activity in a criminal proceeding refers to the accused and not to the victim or the victim's next of kin. This is another illustration of the complexity of the Court's position granting the relatives of a victim a role in a criminal proceeding.

Following the same path, in the case of Bulacio, the Court referred to the subject of judicial neglect and abuse of procedural remedies – this latter in

199 *Case of Genie Lacayo v. Nicaragua*, para. 77; *Case of Juan Humberto Sánchez v. Honduras*, para. 129.

200 *Case of Genie Lacayo v. Nicaragua*, para. 79.

201 *Ibidem*, para. 80.

202 *Case of Juan Humberto Sánchez v. Honduras*, para. 130.

203 *Ibidem*, paras. 130–131.

204 *Ibidem*, para. 132.

direct reference to the activities of the accused – as a basis for finding the period to have been unreasonable. It argued that in the domestic proceeding, "the defense counsel for the accused filed a large number of diverse legal questions and remedies [...] which have not allowed the proceedings to progress toward their natural culmination."[205] This has been tolerated by acting judicial bodies forgetting that their function is not exhausted by enabling due process that guarantees defense at a trial, but that they must also ensure, within a reasonable time, the right of the victim or his or her next of kin to learn the truth about what happened and have those responsible punished.[206] In this type of criminal proceeding, the Court rejected the consequence sought with these delays, which is to allow the accused to object to the criminal action on grounds of the statute of limitations.[207] In the case of Myrna Mack Chang, the Court made an examination of the collection of judicial actions and reached the conclusion that there had been a "lack of diligence and will on the part of the courts to move the criminal proceeding forward."[208] Although it admitted that one reason for the delay was the existence of rules of procedure that required writs of *amparo* requested by the accused to be processed even when they were manifestly inadmissible, it found that the judges had exceeded legal deadlines, paralyzing the criminal proceeding. As it did in the Bulacio case, the Court warned the State that a court must balance the guarantee of defense in the trial with the right of the victim or the victim's relatives to know the truth within a reasonable time. It stated that: "The right to effective judicial protection therefore requires that the judges direct the proceeding in such a way as to avoid undue delays and obstructions that lead to impunity, thus frustrating due judicial protection of human rights."[209]

In the case of Tibi on long and arbitrary preventive detention and torture, the concept of reasonable time operated in favor of the accused. Mr. Tibi had been in prison for almost nine years and then was granted a provisional dismissal, in spite of which he was not released. The Court held that the alleged complexity of the case, the characteristics of the matter object of the investigation and the factual possibilities of the State to carry out the proceedings more speedily were insufficient to justify the delay. Nor had Mr. Tibi obstructed the procedure. There was, consequently, a violation of this requirement of due process.[210] In the case of the Yakye Axa Community, a final decision was not made on the land demands of the Community in an administrative procedure lasting 12 years.

---

205 *Case of Bulacio v. Argentina*, para. 113.

206 *Ibidem*, para. 114. In the same sense, separate opinion of *ad hoc* Judge Ricardo Gil, para. 4, where he contrasts the guarantees found in Article 8 with Article 25's protection of the victim.

207 *Ibidem*, para. 116. See also the *Case of Barrios Altos v. Peru*, para. 41.

208 *Case of Myrna Mack Chang v. Guatemala*, para. 203.

209 *Ibidem*.

210 *Case of Tibi v. Ecuador*, para. 176.

The Court stated that such a delay "constitutes in itself a violation of the right to a fair trial" since the State could not prove "that the delay is directly related to the complexity of the case or to the conduct of the parties involved".[211] In Sawhoyamaxa, the administrative proceedings for a similar case were also not finished for around 12 years.[212] In the case of García Asto and Urcesino Ramírez, a criminal case, the Court decided that a delay of eight years in the trial amounted to a violation of the right to be heard within a reasonable time.[213] In the case of the Guerrilha do Araguaia, the procedure of an Ordinary Action – aimed at obtaining information on the military operations with regard to the Guerrilha in order to find when persons had disappeared and where the bodies were – took 21 years to produce its first instance judgment. This extraordinarily long time could not be justified by the delay for the judge to gain access to official documents on the military operations against the Guerrilha do Araguaia. Furthermore the violation was graver since it took more than six years for the State to initiate execution of the judgment and the execution itself was finally ordered 11 years later.[214]

In noncriminal cases, the judge must see to it that the procedure is not unnecessary long. The judge is, in this sense, "a director of the proceedings". A delay of fifteen years to process "a civil proceeding for damages of a summary nature, based on a criminal sentence for the offense of defamation" is unreasonable, particularly if there is "a general injunction to sell or encumber property" in force.[215]

42. To the three elements that we have examined, a fourth should be added that, in fact, the case law takes into account: the seriousness of the consequences of the procedural delay for the party.[216] It seems reasonable to think that in general criminal proceedings must be resolved in less time than noncriminal proceedings. In criminal cases, the accused in detention is an important element to consider for increasing the swiftness of the case, but there can be other factors. Take as an example the case of an accused person in an abnormal state of mental health for whom the burden of waiting for a ruling on guilt or innocence would be greater than for an average person. These kinds of special circumstances may also play a role in noncriminal cases. For instance, a civil lawsuit deciding on alimony for a minor could in principle be a proceeding that must always be resolved urgently. In other trials, it would depend on their particular

---

211 *Case of the Yakye Axa Community v. Paraguay*, paras. 85–80 and 98.

212 *Case of Sawhoyamaxa v. Paraguay*, para. 95.

213 *Case of García Asto and Urcesino Ramírez v. Peru*, para. 162.

214 *Case of the Guerrilha do Araguaia v. Brazil*, paras. 219 and 224.

215 *Case of Mémoli v. Argentina*, para. 183.

216 *Case of Valle Jaramillo v. Colombia*, para. 155. See also, as examples, *Case of Anzualdo Castro v. Peru*, para. 156; *Case of Díaz Peña v. Venezuela*, para. 49; and *Case of Uzcátegui v. Venezuela*, paras. 232–236.

circumstances. This type of reasoning constitutes a legitimate argument that the defender of an affected party would have the right to raise under Article 8(1) of the Convention. In the case of Kawas Fernández, a criminal trial, the Court said again that in order to decide on a reasonable time it was necessary to consider the impact the trial has on the individual's situation.[217] Swiftness of the procedure is also necessary when the crime has caused harm that should be repaired and the obtention of the reparation by means of a civil action is dependent on the completion of the criminal proceedings.[218] The Court has also taken into consideration the fact that the person affected by the trial was both a child and disabled. In Furlan, a civil suit, it gave attention to a detailed analysis of all the elements to decide on the reasonability of the delay, particularly the effect of the delay on the victim, reaching the conclusion that the delay was a violation of which the State was responsible.[219] It recalls Article 13(1) of the Convention on the Rights of Persons with Disability in asserting that:

> when vulnerable persons are involved, as in the case of a person with disabilities, it is imperative to take the pertinent actions, such as ordering the authorities to give priority to addressing and settling such cases, in order to avoid delays in their processing so as to ensure a prompt decision and execution thereof.[220]

43. Most of the case law and doctrine refer to a maximum period when examining the State's obligation to conclude a proceeding "within a reasonable time". This does not mean that the idea of reasonableness of the period must not apply when determining a minimum one. The parties must have the opportunity to present their evidence and to contest the evidence of the opposing party. The judge also needs the opportunity to study the case and find the basis for his or her ruling. In noncriminal cases, the problem is closely related to the concept of "due guarantees" and the principle of *audi alteram partem*. In criminal cases, it has to do with one of the minimum guarantees of the accused: that of adequate time and means for defense.[221] The Inter-American Court refers to the brevity of the period in the case of Las Palmeras, in which it analyzed the possible violations of rights found in the Convention perpetrated during an operation that had resulted in the deaths of several people. The proceeding that was the subject of study was an investigation into the responsibility of police officers in that operation, but the ruling that the time was not reasonable because of its brevity intended to safeguard the right of the relatives of the dead individuals to a serious investigation. In that judgment, the Court ruled that a disciplinary proceeding that lasted only five days "prevented the presentation of evidence"[222]

---

217 *Case of Kawas Fernández v. Honduras*, para. 115.

218 *Case of Castro Castro v. Peru*, para. 395; *Case of Suárez Peralta v. Ecuador*, para. 103.

219 *Case of Furlan v. Argentina*, paras. 156–159, 164–186, 187–190.

220 *Ibidem*, paras. 194–196.

221 See *infra* section 8.4.

222 *Case of Las Palmeras v. Colombia*, para. 49.

without making it clear if that consideration in itself was enough for finding a violation of Article 8(1) of the Convention, which I think it is.

44. It is apparent from what has been said that reasonable time is an open and indeterminate concept and that a specific period to be applied generally in cases, although of a similar nature, cannot be established. Only on a case-by-case basis can the delicate equilibrium that must exist between the swiftness of the ruling, the opportunity for the parties to develop their defenses, and the chance for the judge to have the necessary time to carefully examine the pleadings and evidence be assessed. Domestically, there are often rules of procedure that establish a standard time for the different types of proceedings. This is positive in principle, but normally the rules also allow a court to justify having missed the deadline. These periods in domestic legal systems can serve as a reference for international bodies when deciding on reasonability, but for the reasons already stated they have to be tested with the specific situation under review.

6.3.2. Burden of Proof

45. The right to a proceeding within a reasonable time raises the problem of determining with whom the burden of proof rests: should the affected party prove that the period was not reasonable, or should the State prove that it was reasonable? In order to answer the question, however, a supervisory body needs an initial baseline, which can be found, I believe, in the case law and practice of the Human Rights Committee. It is important to have an estimate of the minimum time generally needed to carry out a proceeding adequately. If at the time the lack of reasonableness of the period is alleged, this minimum, abstract and general period of time, determined *prima facie,* has not passed, the supervisory body will rule that there has been no violation unless the petitioner making the complaint provides reasons as to why that period of time, although apparently brief, is not reasonable. On the other hand, if the period of time presumed theoretically reasonable has passed, a violation will have taken place unless the State justifies, based on the aforementioned criteria, that the time period is reasonable, even if long. Of course, this abstract period will vary depending on the type of proceeding under examination, and the decision of what that period is will be made based on the experience of the members of the supervisory body.[223]

223 For example, see HRC, *Allen v. Jamaica,* Communication 332/1988, decision of March 31, 1994, in which the duration of a criminal trial seemed to be brief and the petitioner did not provide evidence of negligence, and *Fillastre and Bizouarn v. Bolivia,* Communication 336/1988, decision of November 5, 1991, in which the duration of a criminal trial was four years (para. 6.6) and *Rouse v. the Philippines,* Communication 1089/2002, decision of July 25, 2005 in which the Committee observed that there was a delay of two years and eight months between the last appeal brief and the Supreme Court's judgment. Altogether, there was a delay

The Inter-American Commission used this reasoning in its pleadings in the case of Hilaire, Constantine and Benjamín *et al.*, arguing that "in cases of unacceptable delay, the burden of proof falls on the State to justify the delay".[224] The Inter-American Court has also placed the burden of proof on the State when the period clearly appears to be excessive. The Court ruled thusly in the case of Las Palmeras, in which it rejected an objection raised by the State of a failure to exhaust domestic remedies, finding that the facts of the case originated in January 1991 and the State had not given "a satisfactory explanation regarding the procedural measures between that date and the beginning of 1998." During that period, the case had not gone beyond the preliminary investigation stage.[225] The Court reiterated its position in the judgment on the merits on finding a violation of Article 8(1) for the same reason.[226] It did the same in the case of Hilaire, Constantine and Benjamín *et al.*[227] However, in the case of Genie Lacayo, the Court ruled that a period of five years from the moment the court order was issued to open the proceeding with no final judgment was not reasonable, yet it did not address whether the State had provided any explanation.[228] This could lead to the conclusion that when a period is beyond any reasonability, the Court will not ask the State to justify the delay. The delay will be per se a violation of due process, as was held by the Court in the case of Tibi mentioned above or in the case of García Lucero, where Chile started a criminal investigation of the torture and other ill treatment to which the victim had been submitted, almost 17 years after the facts took place.[229]

6.3.3. *Start and End of the Period to be Counted*

46. For the purposes of Article 8(1), the moment at which one begins counting the period depends on the type of trial. In criminal matters, the period must be counted from the date on which an individual is first exposed to the criminal court system as a suspect. In the case of Suárez Rosero, for example, the Inter-American Court found that "the first act of the proceeding was Mr. Suárez Rosero's arrest on June 23, 1992, and, therefore, the time must be calculated from that moment".[230] On the other hand, in the case of Genie Lacayo, as the claimant was the father of the victim and not the accused, the Court found that it should count the period as from the date on which the first instance judge

of six and a half years between the author's arrest and the judgment of the Supreme Court. The Committee concluded that this delay could not be attributed to the author's appeal and that without any pertinent explanation from the State, the delay was not reasonable.

224 *Case of Hilaire, Constantine and Benjamin et al. v. Trinidad and Tobago*, para. 122.
225 *Case of Las Palmeras v. Colombia*, judgment on preliminary objections, para. 38.
226 *Ibidem*, para. 62.
227 *Case of Hilaire, Constantine and Benjamin et al. v. Trinidad and Tobago*, para. 145.
228 *Case of Genie Lacayo v. Nicaragua*, para. 81.
229 *Case of García Lucero v. Chile*, para. 127.
230 *Case of Suárez Rosero v. Ecuador*, para. 70.

issued the order to open the proceeding.[231] In the case of Caesar v. Trinidad and Tobago, the Court came up with a different rule in a situation where the trial started before the State had recognized the Court's jurisdiction. In that case, it was decided that the period could only be counted from the moment of the recognition and not from the date when the trial had in fact started, concluding then that the delay had been reasonable.[232] In criminal trials, the period is counted generally until there is a final judgment in the proceeding. This is what the Inter-American Court found in the case of Genie Lacayo[233] and in the case of Suárez Rosero. In this latter case, the Court clearly expressed that "the time must cover the entire proceeding, including any appeals that may be filed."[234] The same has been decided in the case of López Alvarez[235] and in Acosta Calderón.[236]

47. In noncriminal proceedings, the period must be counted from the first action taken to initiate it; the standards that are often applied by national procedural law to decide when a lawsuit begins cannot be used here. For the complainant, for example, it is his or her complaint that puts the legal system in motion and it is at that moment that the State is called on to act. As to deciding the end of the process, the Court has also determined that the procedure to execute a judgment awarding compensation to the winning party should also be considered when deciding if a delay has been reasonable.[237]

6.3.4. Is the Trial an Indivisible Unit for Purposes of Jurisdiction?

48. In cases where the Court acquired jurisdiction after the case has begun but the judicial procedure is still pending, the Court will count the period to decide on "reasonable time" from the moment the State recognized its competence. This has been constantly used,[238] but not exclusively,[239] to examine cases where the Court will not have jurisdiction on the substantive violations but only on those of a procedural nature, as has been explained when examining the phenomenon of disappearances. This position has been employed by the Court to deal not only with disappearances but also with summary executions and other serious

231 *Case of Genie Lacayo v. Nicaragua*, para. 81.
232 *Case of Caesar v. Trinidad and Tobago*, paras. 111–112.
233 *Ibidem.*
234 *Case of Suárez Rosero v. Nicaragua*, para. 71. In the same sense, *Case of Hilaire, Constantine and Benjamin et al. v. Trinidad and Tobago*, para. 142.
235 *Case of López Alvarez v. Honduras*, paras. 129–130.
236 *Case of Acosta Calderón v. Ecuador*, paras. 104–106.
237 *Case of Furlan v. Argentina*, paras. 149–151.
238 See, for example, *Cases of Blake v. Guatemala*, para. 40 and *Case of Serrano Cruz sisters v. El Salvador*, para. 55.
239 *Case of Caesar v. Trinidad and Tobago*, para. 11.

violations. The principle behind it is that if a trial is open, there can be a violation of Article 8 in the proceedings after the Court acquired jurisdiction.

In the case of Almonacid, Chile presented a preliminary objection to the Court's competence to hear the case. Chile's recognition of competence – which was similar to that of El Salvador examined in the case of the Serrano Cruz sisters – said:

> the State of Chile expresses that its recognition of the jurisdiction of the Court refers only to events which were subsequent to the date on which this Instrument of Ratification was deposited or, in any case, to events which *started* after March 11, 1990.

Accordingly it stressed that the judicial proceeding of Almonacid's execution was a criminal investigation started in September 1973 and characterized it by stating that:

> c) It is a judicial proceeding which started in September 1973 and since then has been dismissed time and time again. The proceeding cannot be partitioned, divided, separated or disassociated, not even materially or formally, for it is and has always invariably and permanently been a single proceeding, the processing of which has been ongoing, as has the numbering of the case file under which it was started, and that
> d) the judicial actions started by the victim's next of kin after 1990 are not "independent events," a characteristic which is far from the material, formal, and legal reality.[240]

The Court found that it indeed had no jurisdiction on the execution itself – following its position in the Serrano Cruz sisters – but that it had jurisdiction to deal with the violations of Article 8 perpetrated by Chile after it had recognized the Court's jurisdiction. The Court found that during a procedure there may be separate facts, each of which can potentially be a violation of Article 8. It gives several examples: preventing counsel for the defense from participating; preventing counsel from meeting privately with his or her client; challenging incriminating evidence; and others of a similar nature.[241] All these facts fall under the jurisdiction of the Court. The Court found as well that it was competent to deal with the decree-law on amnesty for crimes committed within the period that the execution of Mr. Almonacid had occurred. The obligation of the State "to adapt its domestic legislation" started when Chile "bound itself to adapt its domestic legislation to the provisions of the Convention, that is, at the moment the State ratified the Convention."[242] The Court has maintained this position constantly.[243]

---

240 *Case of Almonacid v. Chile*, para. 39.
241 *Ibidem*, para. 48.
242 *Ibidem*, para. 50.
243 See, for example, *Case of García Lucero v. Chile*, paras. 35, 38.

6.3.5. *How to Measure the Period*

49. Finally, it is important to determine what periods are relevant in deciding whether the duration of a process is reasonable, and whether that decision is to be made by taking into consideration the trial as a whole or by examining each of the trial's proceedings individually. Concerning the former, the task of the supervisory body is to add up the time that the court has spent on the case – subtracting possible unjustified delays that are the responsibility of the party in question – in order to be able to conclude whether the State has violated the obligation found in Article 8(1) of the Convention. The subtraction of the delays attributable to the interested party will only be done when there has been an abuse of the procedure by that person. It has to be considered that it is the State's responsibility to move the procedures forward. If, for example, the witnesses have been threatened, as was the case in the Massacre of Mapiripán, such a subtraction cannot take place.[244]

With regard to the second point, one possibility would be to follow European case law as set forth in Harris *et al.* The European Court first examines the total duration of the case; if it seems excessive on its face, the proceeding is then examined in detail and the burden of proof falls to the State. Some authors, with whom I agree, argue that this method can be detrimental to the injured party. If followed, there is a possibility the European Court would overlook unnecessary delays should it find that as a whole the proceeding has concluded within a reasonable period, thus basing its ruling on an abstract criteria on how long a trial of a particular nature should last and not on the specific characteristics of the case under examination.[245] Thus the focus of the Human Rights Committee – explained above with regard to the burden of proof – seems more appropriate, as it combines an examination of the period as a whole with an examination of each individual delay.

The Court has sometimes applied the European approach. In the case of Genie Lacayo, the Court decided to carry out an analysis of the overall proceeding, using the European Court's focus.[246] It repeated this approach in the Cantos case, a noncriminal case, allowing us to observe the problem raised previously, although the judgment on this point also intermixes with other elements.[247] In the latter, it was shown that a period of ten years had passed between the moment Mr. Cantos filed his complaint before the Supreme Court of Justice and the moment that court issued its judgment. Based on this, the victim argued that there had been unreasonable delay. The Inter-American Court agreed that ten years was in principle excessive, but nevertheless found

---

244 *Case of the Massacre of Mapiripán v. Colombia*, paras. 217–219.

245 D.J. Harris *et al.*, *supra* n. 83, p. 229.

246 *Case of Genie Lacayo v. Nicaragua*, para. 81.

247 See paragraph 12 of this chapter.

that "both the State and the plaintiff engaged in behaviors that, either by action or omission, served to prolong the proceedings in the domestic courts. If the plaintiff's own conduct somehow helped to prolong the proceedings, then it is hard to make the case that it is the State that has violated the 'reasonable time' clause".[248] Without commenting on the result, this reasoning should be criticized. The problem of the delays that may arise in the proceedings due to the actions or omissions of a plaintiff is related to the periods that can be added up in order to decide whether the period was reasonable. Periods of delay attributable to actions of the plaintiff must be subtracted from the final total, but they should not serve to cancel out the State's neglect.[249] Nevertheless, the Court ruled in the end that "taking into account the complexity of the matter and the lack of interest on the part of the plaintiff, among other factors, the total duration of the litigation is not sufficiently significant for declaring a violation" of Article 8(1).[250] Thus it is not precisely known whether the ruling was based solely on the neglect of the plaintiff or if considerations of the complexity of the matter had an influence. Furthermore, it somehow contradicts what the Court always asserts: even in civil trials the legislature and the judge have a task to fulfill, which is to design and apply the law in a manner that avoids long delays.

Without rejecting its position, in the recent case of Tarazona Arrieta *et al.* the Court deviates from its position regarding the determination of the reasonable delay, stating that in certain specific situations it may be pertinent a specific assessment of the various stages of the proceedings.[251]

6.4. RIGHT TO A REASONED RULING

50. Article 8(1) does not establish that a ruling in a case must have a legal and factual basis upon which it is based. However, due process guarantees could be annulled if a court is not required to offer explicit legal and factual considerations in its rulings. The absence of reasoning blocks the parties' right to formulate their own reasoned appeal, as appropriate. The Court stated this in the case of Yatama, holding that "[d]ecisions adopted by domestic bodies that could affect human rights, such as the right to political participation should be duly [based on reason]; otherwise, they would be arbitrary decisions".[252] The Court's position was similar in the Apitz case.[253] In the case of López Alvarez, the Court

248 *Case of Cantos v. Argentina*, para. 57.

249 In addition, a reading of the judgment in this specific case indicates that it is possible that many of the applicant's actions that delayed the proceedings had to do with the fact that the Argentine courts were requiring him to pay an exorbitant court filing fee something he was unable to do.

250 *Case of Cantos v. Argentina*, para. 57.

251 *Case of Tarazona Arrieta et al. v. Peru*, para. 100.

252 *Case of Yatama v. Nicaragua*, para. 152. The word in Spanish in the text is *fundamentada*.

253 *Case of Apitz et al. v. Venezuela*, para. 78. See also *Case of Escher v. Brazil*, paras. 208–209.

applied this rationale to the rulings regarding pre-trial detention, holding that the legality of this detention "cannot be reduced to a mere formality, instead it must examine the reasons invoked by the claimant and make express statements regarding the same, according to the parameters established by the American Convention".[254]

6.5. RIGHT FOR THE RULING TO BE ENFORCED

51. This right is not explicitly set forth in Article 8 of the Convention, but if individuals can demand that their civil rights and obligations – or their guilt or innocence – be determined by a court that meets a series of requirements in a proceeding that also meets international standards, the State will not have complied with its obligations until the final judgment is carried out. In my view, a failure to comply with a final judgment constitutes a violation of due process, as the ultimate purpose of due process is the final resolution of a problem.

The Inter-American Court did not accept the right for the ruling to be enforced as part of the right to due process. In the case of the Five Pensioners, it declined to rule on the possible violation of Article 8 of the Convention, despite the fact that the State administration's failure to execute a court ruling was part of the basis for the claim. The Court agreed with the Commission that Article 25 was violated "by not executing the judgments of the Constitutional and Social Law Chamber of the Supreme Court of Justice of Peru until almost eight years after they had been delivered".[255] *A contrario sensu*, this implies that the Court considers that Article 8 does not contain the obligation of the State to enforce the judgments of a national court and there is a need to resort to Article 25 to find a violation. The Court took the same position in the case of Mejía Idrovo, asserting: "Given that the lack of implementation of the judgment of the Constitutional Tribunal is directly linked to effective judicial protection of the execution of domestic rulings, this Court will carry out its analysis in the section on Article 25(2) of the American Convention".[256] In the case of Furlan, it took the same stand, quoting Mejía Idrovo, but adding that it "considers that the analysis of the enforcement phase of judgments can also be addressed in accounting for the duration of proceedings, in order to determine its impact on prolonging the reasonable term of the proceedings".[257] I will deal with Article 25 in another chapter but I stress here that there would be no point at all in having a right to due process that would not cover the duty to enforce its result, so the Court should revisit its interpretation of what due process is.

---

254 *Case of López Álvarez v. Honduras*, para. 96.

255 *Case of the "Five Pensioners" v. Peru*, paras. 138, 141 and 122.i.

256 *Case of Mejía Idrovo v. Ecuador*, para. 84.

257 *Case of Furlan and family v. Argentina*, para. 149.

7. INVESTIGATION, DUE DILIGENCE AND RIGHT TO THE TRUTH

7.1. INVESTIGATION

52. This book has so far referred in an incidental manner to the duty of States to investigate and the need to do it with "due diligence". This duty is an important part of the Court's pronouncements regarding Article 8. Jurisprudence mainly addresses judges' activities but also refers to officers who work in the investigative part of trials including personnel dealing with autopsies and other scientific work necessary for a good investigation. The most significant negative feature of the judiciary with regard to criminal trials in the region is the lack of rigor of the courts and investigation officers in searching for the persons responsible for criminal actions, the tardiness with which steps are taken and sometimes the lack of instruments to help their task. Of course, during the period of dictatorships affecting one or another state intermittently, the cause of all this was, to put it mildly, the lack of political will of the rulers of the moment to do differently, but, after those periods, adjustments to a different system have been slow. To change the *modus operandi* of the judiciary system in a way implies a change of culture, a change in how State organs approach the judicial task, independent of other organs, and in how it is understood that those that resort to the Courts are individuals exercising their human rights. Any radical remodeling usually takes a significant amount of time. The Court contributes to this endeavor by detailing in each case what it expects from the State for the faithful compliance with its conventional obligations. Some of the Court's positions regarding compliance with Article 8 appear in the considerations on the merits; many others appear in the section on reparations of the judgment.

So far, it has been explained that the obligation to investigate emerges from the obligation to ensure human rights.[258] With respect to certain human rights violations – disappearances, summary executions, torture and perhaps long illegal deprivation of freedom, usually occurring in times when the rule of law does not prevail – the obligation is absolute to the point that it trumps statutes of limitations, amnesties and other instruments of the kind. Other human rights violations are not susceptible to investigation; as I have said before,[259] a violation committed by the very provisions of domestic law will not cause the Court to order an investigation, but just an amendment or derogation of the incompatible law.

What will be examined here is not when a State should investigate a human rights violation but what the Court has said on *what* and *how* to investigate certain types of violations.

---

[258] See Chapter 1.

[259] See Chapter 1, para. 30.

53. Many of the cases that reach the Court are not isolated violations, but instances of massive and systematic ones or violations perpetrated in a context of lack of democratic institutions or due to situations of structural discrimination. In these cases, the Court never leaves "the context" aside and expects the national investigators to act in like manner. Instances of the first sort of situations abound. They are found in cases against Central American countries,[260] Southern Cone countries[261] and others[262] that happened during situations of internal conflicts or of dictatorship. The context refers to the quantity and the egregiousness of the violations plus the impunity that followed them. If there are problems of jurisdiction with respect to certain aspects of the case the Court may use and has used context to address them. The Court held in the case of Radilla Pacheco that "the principle of non-retroactivity and the optional clause of acknowledgement of this Court's contentious jurisdiction does not imply that an act that occurred prior to the same shall be excluded of all consideration when it can be relevant for the determination of what occurred". In addition, it observed that "the political and historical surroundings are determining factors in the determination of the juridical consequences in the case".[263] In the case of Goiburu, who was part of Operation Cóndor,[264] the Court explains that "the context in which the facts took place permeates and conditions the State's international responsibility" regarding its obligations emerging from Articles 4, 5, 7, 8 and 25 of the Convention.[265] In the case of Contreras, the Court ruled that in order to guarantee its effectiveness, the investigation had to take into account the fact that the violations "took place in the context of the Armed Force's counterinsurgency operations".[266]

54. In cases of massacres or extra judicial executions, for example, the Court has ordered specifically that the provisions in the United Nations Manual on the Effective Prevention and Investigation of Extra-Legal, Arbitrary and Summary Executions should guide the investigations on death. The State authorities in charge of an investigation must seek, at the least, *inter alia*: (i) to identify the

260 See, for example, *Cases of Blake, Massacre of Plan de Sánchez, Molina Theissen, Massacre of the Two Rs, Massacre of Rio Negro*, all v. Guatemala; *Case of Massacres of El Mozote and nearby places v El Salvador*; *Cases of Velásquez Rodríguez, Juan Humberto Sánchez and Pacheco Teruel*, all v. Honduras.

261 *Case of Almonacid Arellano v. Chile; Case of Torres Millatura v. Argentina; Case of Juan Gelman v. Uruguay.*

262 *Case of Goiburú v. Paraguay; Case of La Rochela Massacre v. Colombia.*

263 *Case of Radilla Pacheco v. Mexico*, para. 116.

264 Operation Condor was "a code name given to the alliance of the security forces and intelligence services of the Southern Cone dictatorships in their repression of and fight against individuals designated 'subversive elements.' The activities deployed as part of this Operation were coordinated basically by the military personnel of the countries involved". Operation Condor took place when Stroessner was the dictator of Paraguay (1954–1989). *Case of Goiburu v. Paraguay*, paras. 61–66.

265 *Case of Goiburu v. Paraguay*, para. 63.

266 *Case of Contreras et al. v. El Salvador*, para. 146.

victim; (ii) to obtain and preserve evidence regarding the death, so as to aid any potential criminal investigation regarding those responsible; (iii) to identify possible witnesses and receive their statements regarding the death under investigation; (iv) establish the cause, manner, place and time of death, as well as any pattern or practice that may have caused the death; and (v) differentiate between natural death, accidental death, suicide, and homicide. It is also necessary to investigate exhaustively the crime scene. With respect to autopsies, competent professionals, applying the most appropriate procedures, must conduct analyses of human remains rigorously.[267]

55. In the second type of situation, where there is a structural problem, the Court has given detailed guidance on taking the context of the violations into consideration to carry out a proper investigation. The best instance of this type of guidance is the case of Campo Algodonero, where the problem of the prevalence of violence against women in Ciudad Juárez, Mexico, was discussed based on a complaint filed on behalf of three young victims whose bodies were discovered some time after their disappearance. At the reparations stage, the Court stated impunity for violations that amount to a criminal offense in the domestic legal order, "constitutes a source of additional suffering and anguish for the victims, who have the right to know the truth about what happened." This right requires "a determination of the collective patterns of action".[268] The fact that the context is taken into consideration has the consequence that investigations and reparations have to be conducted not only with the purpose of redressing the individual victim of the case but also of alleviating and eventually eliminating the structural discrimination. With regard to the investigation itself, the Court analyzes and sets forth measures on custody of the crime scene, collection and handling of evidence, autopsies, and identification and return of the victims' remains.[269] Of the other directives, a very important one is that the investigation "shall include a gender perspective; undertake specific lines of inquiry concerning sexual assault, which must involve lines of inquiry into the corresponding patterns in the area; be conducted in accordance with protocols and manuals that comply with the directives set out in this judgment; […] the investigation shall be carried out by officials who are highly trained in similar cases and in dealing with victims of discrimination and gender-based violence". The Court adds that the State must provide the necessary human and material resources "and those who take part in the investigations shall be given due guarantees for their safety", and "[t]he results of the proceedings shall be published so that Mexican society is aware of the facts that are the purpose of the instant case".[270]

267 *Case of the Mapiripan Massacre v. Colombia*, para. 224. See also *Case of the Pueblo Bello Massacre v. Colombia*, para. 117.

268 *Case of Gonzalez et al. ("Cotton Fields") v. Mexico*, para. 454.

269 *Ibidem*, paras. 296–312. See also *Case of Fernández Ortega v. Mexico*, para. 194.

270 *Ibidem*.

Aside from these directives, in the case of J. the Court explained further that a criminal investigation into sexual violence requires a proper location to take the victim's statement and the recording thereof. After examination by a doctor, the victim should be provided with physical and psychological health care that follows a treatment protocol designed to reduce the consequences of the rape and have access to free legal assistance.[271] The Court also makes use of the Inter-American Torture Convention to recall that the State's obligation to investigate emerges when a complaint is filed or when there is a well-founded reason to believe that an act of torture has been committed within the sphere of the State's jurisdiction. This is not a discretionary power of the State. This should have been done in J.'s case, as she indicated forms of ill-treatment.[272] The State argued that rape could not be investigated *ex officio* because it was subject to private right of action, but the Court did not accept this argument based on the fact that, as investigating was an international obligation, it could not be disregarded or made subject to conditions by domestic law.[273] I would add that in this case the victim had mentioned ill-treatment and the violation consisting in the rape was perpetrated when she was in the hands of her captors, who were State agents. In the case of Espinoza González, the Court dealt at length with the issue of investigation and due diligence in cases of sexual violence against women in a situation of internal conflict.[274]

7.2. DUE DILIGENCE

56. One could say that due diligence refers to the reasonable care a State should have when fulfilling an international obligation. The problem which the State faces – and the Court ruling on a case – is to decide what is reasonable. Of course, the decision should be taken on a case-by-case basis, but the standards that are established should be consistent. Due diligence in investigation, which is where the Court has mainly applied the concept, is always required. However, how "diligent" diligence must be? Is due diligence required when the Court deems that the lack thereof has not jeopardized the case?

In the case of Castillo González, the Court appears to be particularly careful when stating that the investigation must be assessed in its entirety, taking into account that the obligation is one of means and not of results and that in this case the intervention of the State in the homicide had not been proven.[275] The Court adds that there have been omissions and delays during the trial, but that they do not have the magnitude or graveness needed to merit the international

271 *Case of J. v. Peru*, para. 344.
272 *Ibidem*, para. 347.
273 *Ibidem*, para. 350.
274 On this case see Chapter 4.
275 *Case of Castillo González v. Venezuela*, para. 161.

responsibility of the State.[276] I wonder if this points to the fact that the diligence should have been stricter had it been the State the author of the homicide. This would mean that the State has a lesser responsibility when the violation is one of omission instead of one of action. I do not find any basis to sustain such a position, unless it is the magnitude of the omission that makes the difference. In the case of Luna López v. Honduras, a case following Castillo González, the Court notes the existence of "certain omissions as regards cordoning off the area, the collection of evidence, the procedure to remove the body and the respective autopsy". However, it reiterates that the investigation should be assessed as a whole, considering that it is an obligation of means and not of results and "bearing in mind that it is not up to the Court, in principle, to decide on the admissibility of investigative measures". It is also necessary "to consider whether the occurrence of certain omissions or delays is sufficient to constitute international responsibility by the State", adding that the State's role in the assassination had not been proven.[277] Here the Court refers directly to the type of omissions that would make the State incur responsibility. If one compares these considerations with, for example, those of the case of Gutiérrez and family v. Argentina, which follows together with many others the traditional case law of the Court, a difference is noted. The Court seems to be giving more room to States in the judicial process, which could be right if the States had changed their attitude and laws on due process. I am not certain that this has been the case yet and therefore it could be submitted that this careful approach by the Court may put victims in a weaker position to be able to obtain a fair investigation.

7.3. THE RIGHT TO THE TRUTH

57. As has been said before, the treatment of disappearances generated a significant impact on the way the Court has handled other violations. One of the most relevant is the creation of what is called "the right to the truth", intimately linked with the obligation to investigate violations. In disappearances, as well as in other particularly egregious violations, the right to the truth emerged as an essential demand of the next of kin of the victims of those violations.[278] The demand and its arguments led the Court to find that the next of kin had a right that amounted to knowing the truth of what had happened to their relative. The right emerged from the various judgments concerning the State's obligation to investigate, prosecute and eventually punish the perpetrators of disappearances. The Commission used this notion for the first time in the case of Castillo Páez, stating that the next of kin had a right to the truth and to information about

276 *Ibidem*, para. 162.

277 *Case of Luna López v. Honduras*, para. 165.

278 See Chapters 3 and 5 for more on this.

what had happened to the disappeared person.[279] The Court responded to this pleading by arguing that the right "does not exist in the American Convention, although it may correspond to a concept that is being developed in doctrine and case law",[280] but emphasized that "the victim's family still have the right to know what happened to him and, if appropriate, where his remains are located".[281]

In later cases, the Court went a step further and did use the expression "right to the truth", identifying it as the right of the next of kin to have a disappearance investigated and the perpetrators eventually prosecuted and punished, stating that Articles 8 and 25 of the Convention were the source of the right so described. In the case of Durand and Ugarte, it used the wording put forward by the Commission in the case of Castillo Páez. There it speaks of the "right to truth", explaining that:

> Article 8(1) of the American Convention, in connection with Article 25(1) thereof, confers on victims' relatives the right to investigate their disappearance and death by State authorities, to carry out a process against the liable parties of unlawful acts, to impose the corresponding sanctions, and to compensate damages suffered by their relatives.[282]

In the case of Juan Gelman, the Court invoked in support of this proposition the recognition of this right "in various instruments of the United Nations and by the General Assembly of the Organization of American States". The contents of this right, especially in disappearances, is part of the "right of the next of kin to know the fate of the victims, and where possible, the location of their remains". Consequently, the right is "encompassed in the right to access to justice and the obligation to investigate – forms of reparation to know the truth in the specific case".[283] In the case of Blanco Romero *et al.*, the State took responsibility for the facts and violations complained of by the representatives of the victim, who had also invoked Article 13 of the Convention (freedom of thought and expression) as a basis for the right. The Court firmly declared that it did not consider "the right to know the truth to be a separate right enshrined in Articles 8, 13,[284] 25 and 1(1) of the Convention [...] and, accordingly, it cannot find acceptable the State's acknowledgement of responsibility on this point".[285]

279 *Case of Castillo Páez v. Peru*, para. 85.
280 *Ibidem*, para. 86.
281 *Ibidem*, para. 90.
282 *Case of Durand and Ugarte v. Peru*, para. 130. This same position appears in several of the Court's judgments: see *Case of Bámaca Velásquez v. Guatemala*, para. 201; *Case of Barrios Altos v. Peru*, para. 48; and *Case of Juan Humberto Sánchez v. Honduras*, para. 136.
283 *Case of Juan Gelman v. Uruguay*, para. 243.
284 There has been one instance in which the Court also found that Article 13, on freedom of expression and access to information had been violated, but this was the result of the fact that the State had accepted responsibility in that regard and the next of kin had indeed invoked that article in the local proceedings. See *Case of Gómez Lund et al. (Guerrilha do Araguaia) v. Brazil*, paras. 196–202.
285 *Case of Blanco Romero et al. v. Venezuela*, para. 62.

The Court thus refused to find yet another right forming part of the description of what was called "right to the truth". In the case of Gudiel Alvarez, the Court was requested to find a violation of Article 13 in a disappearance case because of the refusal of the Ministry of Defense to provide information to judicial and other authorities, which amounted to noncompliance with the right to the truth. The Court, however, deemed that the failure to inform prevented the domestic court from shedding light on the facts of the case and as such had been assessed under the violation of Articles 8 and 25 and also when handling the violation of Article 7.[286] This positions the right to the truth as a positive aspect of the obligation to investigate, whose holders are the victim and, in the case of disappearances or deprivations of life, the victim's next of kin. As said above, the right derives from the rights recognized in Articles 8 and 25 of the Convention.

The Court reiterated this position in the recent case of Rodríguez Vera *et al.* v. Colombia,[287] which was rebutted in a concurring vote of Judge Ferrer MacGregor.[288] Judge Ferrer advocated for the Court to recognize the right to know the truth as an autonomous right and to find in this case a specific violation of this right. He argued that this would clarify "the contents, dimensions and real scope of the right".[289] According to Judge Vío, an autonomous right to know the truth could be invoked before authorities other than judiciary and, if those were to respect it, it might prevent the victims from having to come before an international body.[290] Judge Ventura stated that the lack of a declaration of an autonomous right to the truth had prevented the possibility of determining whether civil agents of the executive branch or members of the legislative branch had breached the international obligations of the State.[291] I do not see that the lack of this "autonomous" right had the consequences that the three judges mention. In the first place, the decision of the Court that an investigation should be carried out addresses the State, not only the judiciary; it is implicit that the Court requires all the State's authorities to do their bit to comply with a mandatory judgment. Besides, it is highly unlikely in the type of cases where the right to the truth is at issue that executive agents or legislative members that have not complied with the local judicial authorities to provide information will provide it when directly requested to do so by the victims.

58. Although the right to demand from the State its obligation to investigate, try and punish apparently belongs to the next of kin, the Court has found that

286 *Case of Gudiel Álvarez et al. ("Diario Militar") v. Guatemala*, para. 269.
287 *Case of Rodríguez Vera et al. v. Colombia*, para. 511.
288 *Ibidem*, concurring vote of Judge Eduardo Ferrer MacGregor Poisot, also subscribed by Judges Manuel Ventura Robles and Jorge Vío Grossi. The vote has a good summing up of the Court's case law on the right to the truth.
289 *Ibidem*, para. 25 of the vote.
290 *Ibidem*, para. 5 of Judge Vio's statements.
291 *Ibidem*, para. 8 of Judge Ventura's statements.

a failure to comply with this obligation hurts society as a whole. This seems to be in harmony with the idea that the creation of a code of conduct for States interests the whole community. The Court asserted this in its judgment in the case of Juan Humberto Sánchez, in which it ordered the State to release to the public the results of a judicial inquiry into the extrajudicial execution of the victim "for Honduran society to know the truth".[292] In Anzualdo Castro, the Court sets forth the importance of the right to the truth beyond those closely linked with the victims of the case. It deems that the right to know the truth "represents a necessary effect for it is important that a society knows the truth about the facts of serious human rights violations". This would also satisfy a fair expectation that the State will investigate.[293] The Court used similar wording in the case of Gómez Palominos and stated that knowing the truth allows Peruvian society to explore new avenues for prevention; this means that it serves as a guarantee for non-repetition.[294]

59. The obligation to investigate does not prevent a State from establishing Truth Commissions, although they do not replace judicial investigation. They "can contribute to build and safeguard historical memory, to clarify the events and to determine institutional, social and political responsibilities in certain periods of time of a society".[295]

60. The right to the truth, finally, involves other obligations for States. In the case of La Rochela, the Court stated, for example, that in cases of grave violations "the adoption of institutional structures that permit this right to be fulfilled in the most suitable, participatory, and complete way" is necessary. The Court also emphasized that the satisfaction of the collective dimension of the right to truth requires a legal analysis of the most complete historical record possible. This determination must include a description of the patterns of joint action and should identify all those who participated in various ways in the violations and their corresponding responsibilities.[296]

61. It was previously noted how difficult it is to identify the nature of the various measures that a State must take to comply with the Convention, but sometimes this identification is necessary. Even though the obligation to investigate and the closely related right to the truth are normally identified by the Court with the duty to prevent, the Court has ruled differently on at least two occasions. On those occasions, the Court said that "the possibility of the victim's next of kin knowing what happened to the victim and, if that be the case, the

---

292 *Case of Juan Humberto Sánchez v.* Honduras, para. 186.
293 *Case of Anzualdo Castro v. Peru*, para. 119.
294 *Case of Gómez Palominos v. Peru*, para. 78.
295 *Ibidem*. See also *Case of González Medina and family v. Dominican Republic*, para. 263.
296 *Case of the La Rochela Massacre v. Colombia*, para. 195.

whereabouts of the victim's mortal remains, is a means of reparation, and therefore an expectation regarding which the State must satisfy the next of kin of the victims and society as a whole".[297] From the testimonies given by the next of kin in these types of cases one learns that the family's first and strong desire is to find out everything related to the disappeared person, and their second desire is that the States ensure that there will be no repetition for them and for others of these abhorrent violations. Every single member of the families of disappeared or the tortured persons proclaims "*nunca más*" (never again) before the Court. I think that anyone who has had any experience with the phenomenon of disappearances would agree that knowing the truth is a very important part of reparations. However, conceiving the right for the State to investigate only as a form of reparation has consequences that the Court had perhaps not foreseen in this judgment. An important consequence was expressed in the judgment in the case of Garrido and Baigorria, where the Court changed its position. The Court found that the obligation to ensure – which carries with it the obligation to investigate – is not a form of reparation. The victim of a human rights violation can decline reparations (in this case the reparation being identified as pecuniary indemnity), while the victim's forgiveness cannot excuse the State from complying with its obligation to mete out punishment to the perpetrators of the disappearance and therefore investigate them beforehand. In the Court's words, "the purpose of that obligation is that every State party ensure, within its legal system, the rights and freedoms recognized in the Convention".[298] Later, in the case of González and family, the Court reconciled its position, finding that the right to the truth – subsumed in the rights of Article 8 and 25 of the Convention – "also constitutes a form of reparation".[299]

The previous considerations lead one to conclude that the obligation to investigate disappearances serves two purposes: prevention, and satisfaction – a form of reparation – through prevention. To investigate is a State obligation derived from the right violated as interpreted in light of Article 1(1) and, as the Court has said, the so-called "right to the truth" is established not only for the benefit of the victim and the victim's relatives but also for society as a whole. Preventive measures and those against recidivism begin by revealing and recognizing the atrocities of the past, as was ordered by the Court in its judgment in Bámaca Velásquez. Society has the right to know the truth regarding such crimes, in order to be able to prevent them in the future.[300]

---

297 *Case of Bámaca Velásquez v. Guatemala*, judgment on reparations, para. 76. See also *Case of Trujillo Oroza v. Bolivia*, judgment on reparations, para. 114 and *Case of Gómez Palomino v. Peru*, para. 78.

298 *Case of Garrido and Baigorria v. Argentina*, para. 72.

299 *Case of González Medina and family v. Dominican Republic*, para. 263.

300 *Case of Bámaca Velásquez v. Guatemala*, judgment on reparations, para. 77. In the same sense, see *Case of the Caracazo v. Venezuela*, judgment on reparations, paras. 117 and 118.

8. SPECIAL GUARANTEES FOR THE ACCUSED

62. As stated previously, Article 8(2) of the Convention establishes certain special guarantees for the accused. These guarantees coexist with the general guarantees found in the first paragraph of that article. They intend to set forth specific protection for people subjected to a criminal trial given the effect that this type of trial may have on certain human rights, such as the right to personal freedom and the honor of the person subjected to the proceeding.[301] Although it is up to the State to prove the guilt of the accused, the accused must enjoy the appropriate conditions to be able to contest the evidence on which the State bases its accusation.

The Inter-American Court has heard cases in which possible violations of these guarantees were alleged; an examination of its case law reveals the precarious situation that the accused has faced in several jurisdictions on the issue of guarantees of their rights and how much further the region must advance to make its legislation and judicial practices compatible with its international obligations. In general and until now, the kinds of violations that have been brought before the Court with regard to these guarantees are so flagrant that the Court has not had an opportunity to bring the content of these rights into sharp focus. This confirms the slow advancement of the judiciary, and of democracy, in Latin American States. We must await progress in this area and hope that other types of cases begin arriving in the system that allow for the development – through international case law – of these guarantees that are so important for the defense of persons subjected to criminal proceedings.

8.1. PRESUMPTION OF INNOCENCE

63. Article 8(2) sets forth that any person accused of a crime has "the right to be presumed innocent so long as his guilt has not been proven according to law". The presumption of innocence establishes explicitly that the State cannot affect any human right without a justification for doing so. Given that one consequence of a criminal conviction is a significant diminishing of a person's capacity to exercise and enjoy a number of human rights, it seems appropriate that as long as a person's guilt has not been demonstrated, that person should not suffer any consequences. On first sight, the principle seems to mean both that the person must be treated as innocent until found guilty in a court ruling, and that nobody can be convicted unless the State proves to the reasonable satisfaction of the court that the person is guilty of what he or she is accused of.

---

301 In general, with regard to criminal due process, see V.M. Rodríguez Rescia, "El debido proceso legal y la Convención Americana sobre Derechos Humanos", in *Liber Amicorum Héctor Fix-Zamudio*, *supra* n. 10, pp. 1295–1328 (1306 and following).

The judge hearing the matter is the one directly and most fundamentally bound by the presumption of innocence.

64. Because of the position it takes with regard to several of these points, one interesting ruling is the judgment on the merits in the case of Cantoral Benavides, in which the Court ruled that this presumption had been violated. The apparent basis for the Court's decision was that the sentence to convict had been handed down before any clear evidence had been established of the guilt of the accused. This was demonstrated by the existence of a pardon benefiting the accused, granted "to persons who have been convicted of terrorism or treason against the fatherland on the basis of insufficient evidence."[302] This consideration was in itself enough to find a violation of the presumption of innocence. However, the Court added another consideration in the section examining the violation of the principle, a consideration that is worth analyzing even though it is not clear that it was decisive for finding a violation. The Court indicates in the judgment that the petitioner was "paraded before the media, dressed in defamatory clothing, as the perpetrator of the crime of treason against the fatherland, before he had been legally tried or convicted."[303] The Court's consideration that Mr. Cantoral Benavides had been paraded before the media before he was brought to trial or convicted broadens the principle's field of action and removes it from the narrow realm of the procedural. This minimum guarantee that innocence must be presumed, along with others, must be respected from the moment a person is exposed to the justice system. This interpretation also takes into consideration the fact that the term "accused" can have different meanings in the different legal systems of the States Parties to the Convention, and that in order to properly read the guarantee its objective and purpose have to be taken into account. Another point that should be noted is that parading Mr. Cantoral Benavides before the media was not ordered by the judge in the case but rather by the government of Peru. The Court's position is thus that the principle goes beyond the framework of the actions of the court during a criminal proceeding and binds other State bodies aside from the court hearing the matter. This would coincide with the position of the United Nations Human Rights Committee, which has ruled as much on stating in its General Comment on Article 14 of the ICCPR that "the presumption of innocence implies a right to be treated in accordance with this principle. It is, therefore, a duty for all public authorities to refrain from prejudging the outcome of a trial".[304] The Court clearly stated this in the case of Lori Berenson. It said, quoting the European Court, that the right to the presumption of innocence could be violated not only by a judge or a court, but also by any public authority. Lori Berenson had been exhibited before the

302 *Case of Cantoral Benavides v Peru*, paras. 120–122.
303 *Ibidem*, para. 119.
304 HRC, General Comment No. 13 (1984) in A/39/40 (1984) Annex VI (pp. 143–147).

press by a section of the police called Dirección Nacional contra el Terrorismo (DINCOTE), as the perpetrator of the crime of treason against the Fatherland.[305] Other agents, such as the press, should respect the presumption of innocence because they shape public opinion.[306]

In the case of J. v. Peru, brought to the Court many years after the facts had occurred, the Court repeats most of what it had found in previous Peruvian cases from the time of Fujimori's rule.[307] Ms. J. was exonerated of the accusation of terrorism in June 1993, following which she left Peru. After the acquittal, the Supreme Court of Peru – composed of faceless judges – ordered a new trial, still pending at the time the case reached the Court. There was an international warrant issued for her arrest. The Court begins by stating that "the irrefutable proof of guilt constitutes an essential requirement for imposing criminal punishment; hence, the burden of proof lies with the accuser and not with the accused".[308] Then it refers to the presumption of innocence in several parts of the judgment. One part concerns the long and arbitrary length of preventive detention; another, the failure of the Supreme Court to provide a reasoning for its ruling on the acquittal. The third refers to several statements of State officials concerning J.'s guilt and the fact that there was evidence presented that had been illegally obtained. One of the examples given is a video presented on television, without sound, that shows Ms. J. defending herself "indignantly from the accusation of the Minister of the Interior", while the State explained her behavior as that of a "'typical terrorist' [...]with quite energetic and aggressive behavior", and said that she had "come out waving Shining Path banners".[309] In the case, the Court insists that there is an obligation of particularly special care "in situation of great social conflict, disturbance of public order, and social or political polarization – such as the counter-terrorism struggle in Peru – precisely due to the series of risk that this may entail for certain persons or groups at a given moment". It adds that a balance must be maintained between keeping society informed and the discretion necessary to guarantee the presumption of innocence.[310]

---

305 *Case of Lori Berenson v. Peru*, paras. 158–161.

306 *Ibidem*, para. 160.

307 As the Court states in this judgment: "In previous cases, this Court has recognized that the said armed conflict intensified and included a systematic practice of human rights violations, including extrajudicial executions and forced disappearances of persons suspected of belonging to illegal armed groups, such as the Peruvian Communist Party – Sendero Luminoso ('Shining Path') and the Túpac Amaru Revolutionary Movement (MRTA). These actions were carried out by State agents following the orders of senior military and police officers". The reference is to the *cases of Castillo Páez, La Cantuta and Miguel Castro Castro*, all v. Peru. See *Case of J. v. Peru*, para. 59.

308 *Ibidem*, para. 233. See also HRC, General Comment No. 32, para. 30.

309 *Ibidem*, paras. 238 and following.

310 *Ibidem*, para. 245.

65. From another perspective, the Court also established that there could be a violation of the presumption of innocence when a person remains in detention for an extended period.[311] The link between an excessive length of deprivation of liberty and the presumption of innocence is constant jurisprudence of the Court. In Chaparro and Lapo, the Court held

> that there would be a violation of the Convention if individuals whose criminal responsibility has not been established are deprived of their liberty for a disproportionate length of time, because this would be tantamount to anticipating a sentence, which is at odds with universally recognized general principles of law.[312]

In the case of López Alvarez, the deprivation of the victim's liberty for six years, without justification, violated his right to the presumption of innocence.[313] The presumption of innocence was also violated when razzias (mass detentions carried out by the police in Argentina) were carried out.[314] In the case of Ricardo Canese, the Court found two violations of this right. The first, because the law itself put on the accused the burden of proving that it had had no intent to defame the complainant with an article he had published in the press. The second, because the Court – as a precautionary measure – had prevented the accused from leaving the country for more than eight years.[315] In the case of García Asto and Urcesino Ramírez, the Court held that "[w]hen presuming the guilt of Urcesino Ramírez-Rojas and requesting, in turn, that Urcesino Ramírez-Rojas himself show his innocence", Peru had violated the right to presumption of innocence as enshrined in Article 8(2) of the Convention, in relation to Article 1(1) thereof.[316] In the case of Norín *et al.*, the presumption of innocence was violated because in the description of the terrorist conduct the law presumed the intent to cause terror when the action was perpetrated by certain means, such as fire.[317]

8.2. RIGHT TO A TRANSLATOR OR INTERPRETER

66. It seems obvious that "the right of the accused to be assisted without charge by a translator or interpreter, if he does not understand or does not speak the language of the tribunal or court", contained in Article 8(2)(a) of the Convention,

---

311 *Case of Suárez Rosero v. Ecuador*, paras. 77–78. In that case, detention pending resolution of the case had lasted for almost four years.

312 *Case of Chaparro and Lapo v. Ecuador*, para. 146.

313 *Case of López Álvarez v. Honduras*, para. 144.

314 *Case of Bulacio v. Argentina*, para. 137. See also *Case of Servellón García et al. v. Honduras*, paras. 93–96 and *Case of Dominicans and Haitians expelled from Dominican Republic v. Dominican Republic*, para. 348.

315 *Case of Canese v. Costa Rica*, paras. 161–162.

316 *Case of García Asto and Urcesino Ramírez v. Peru*, para. 160.

317 *Case of Norín et al. v. Chile*, para. 171.

must exist. In order to defend themselves, the accused must be able to understand what they are accused of. It is possible that the problem of how much an accused person must understand in order to make an interpreter unnecessary will arise in the future. For example, I would point to the region's indigenous populations and the difficulty that many of their members may have in fully expressing their thoughts, despite the fact that they speak Spanish. Inadequate language skills is a significant disadvantage, particularly in trials that must be oral. The Court has pronounced on this point in the case of Rosendo Cantú, stating that Ms. Cantú, who was an indigenous woman, did not speak fluent Spanish; she did not have an interpreter and had to rely on her husband. The Court found this "inappropriate to: respect her cultural diversity; ensure the quality of the contents of the statement, and duly protect the confidentiality of the complaint." Particularly unfitting was that Ms. Cantú "had to turn to her husband to narrate the facts of the rape".[318] In addition, in the case of Fernández, another indigenous woman, the Court found a violation of this provision because the alleged victim did not have "a translator provided by the State in order for her to present her initial claim and the subsequent expansion of the claim". In addition, she did not receive information in her language about the actions taken in her case. These facts implied discrimination in the access to justice.[319]

67. Interpretation of the text suggests at least one question that the Court must eventually resolve: Article 8(2) refers to the "proceedings", a term that can include both oral and written actions. This raises the question of whether assistance for the accused refers only to that person's ability to communicate orally with the court or if it extends to the reading of trial documents. One can base a restrictive interpretation on the use of the conjunction "or" in Article 8(2)(a), which could indicate that the drafters of the Convention felt that the words were synonyms. A broad interpretation could be based on the meaning assigned to these words. In Spanish, the word "translator" applies to someone who puts in one language something written in another language, while "interpreter [...] is used for a person who explains to others, in a language that they understand, what is being said in another language which is unknown to them".[320] In deference to the broader interpretation, one could argue that in addition to the interpretation of the literal meaning of the provision, it must be taken into consideration that the objective and purpose of the right is to allow people to understand the charges and the evidence brought against them. The financial costs of covering translations for every single document of the proceedings make it advisable that the domestic court be the one to decide which instruments of the

318 *Case of Rosendo Cantú et al. v. Mexico*, para. 179(iv). See also *Case of Tiu Tojin et al. v. Guatemala*, para. 100.

319 *Case of Fernández Ortega v. Mexico*, para. 201.

320 See *Diccionario de la Lengua Española*, Real Academia Española, 22nd edition, 2001, Vol. II, pp. 2205 and 1293, respectively.

proceedings in each case the accused needs to be able to understand in order to mount an adequate defense, or if on the contrary it is enough that the accused's defense attorney understands their content. Naturally, an oversight body would have jurisdiction to review whether the State fully complied with this obligation.

68. The word "accused" in this provision must also be understood broadly, as the right must exist from the moment it becomes necessary for the person who has come in contact with the justice system to communicate with the authority in question. For example, even though Article 7(4) does not establish the right to an interpreter when persons are informed of the reasons for their detention and of the charge or charges brought against them in a language that they understand, it is clear that the State must provide an interpreter should it become aware that a detainee does not understand what is being said.

8.3. RIGHT TO BE INFORMED OF THE ACCUSATION

69. According to Article 8(2)(b), once formal charges have been filed, a "prior and detailed" notification of them must be made to the accused. The word "prior" would indicate a moment preceding the beginning of the oral trial and answers to the idea that the accused must have the information available for an amount of time sufficient for preparing a defense. This relates closely with the guarantees found in Article 8(2)(c) which grants the accused the right to have adequate time and means for the preparation of their defense. The word "detailed" seems to indicate the difference between this communication and the communication with the detainee intended to comply with the obligations of Article 7(4) of the Convention. The one ordered by Article 7(4) can be more general, given that the obligation must be complied with "without delay", preventing the kind of exhaustive analysis that would allow for the formulation of precise charges. The goal sought by Article 8(2)(b) here is to provide the accused with all the elements of fact and law on which the charges are based so that they may defend themselves properly.

In the case of Barreto Leiva the Court found that Article 8(2)(b) implied notification of the charges, the reasons and the evidence for the charges and the legal definition of the facts.[321] As this is an essential instrument for a defense, the rationale behind it is that there should be no step during the proceedings that is unknown to the accused and could be used against him.[322] In the case of J., the Court found that the vagueness of the description of the criminal conduct of which she was being tried, also impinged upon the accused's right to a defense.[323]

321 *Case of Barreto Leiva v. Venezuela*, para. 28.
322 *Ibidem*, paras. 29–30.
323 *Case of J. v. Peru*, para. 294.

8.4. RIGHT TO DEFENSE OF THE ACCUSED

70. In subparagraph (c), Article 8(2) establishes that the accused has a right to adequate time and means to prepare a defense. According to the Court, the right to defense "must be necessarily exercised as from the moment a person is accused of being the perpetrator or participant of an illegal act and ends when the jurisdiction thereby ceases, including, where applicable, the enforcement phase". Otherwise, the investigative powers of the State are magnified "to the detriment of the fundamental rights of the person under investigation".[324]

Decisions regarding adequate time and means must be made on a case-by-case basis. In the case of Castillo Petruzzi *et al.*, the Court ruled that Peru had violated this right. In conformity with Peruvian law, after filing the charges, the defense was given 12 hours to study the court documents, a period of time that is clearly not sufficient to prepare a defense adequately.[325] In addition, there were numerous restrictions for a defense attorney to prepare the defense.[326] In the case of Fermín Ramírez, a case involving the imposition of the death penalty, the Court invoked Article 8(2)(b) and (c). The issue was the determination in criminal proceedings of "the nature and content of the so called 'principle of coherence or correlation between the indictment and the verdict'" in the light of the judicial guarantees in Article 8 of the Convention. The Court examined the consequences of the criminal judge giving the illicit act a legal classification different to the one established in the indictment, or the inclusion of "facts not included in the latter, all in relation with the defendant's right to a defense".[327] The Court was of the view that it was necessary to consider the role of the indictment *vis-à-vis* the right to a defense when it applied Article 8(2). It found that, although the legal classification of the facts might change after the indictment, "the so-called 'principle of coherence or correlation between the indictment and the conviction' implies that the judgment may fall only upon the facts or circumstances included in the indictment".[328] In the case of Fermín Ramírez, new facts were included in the proceedings before the judgment without the possibility for the accused to give a new statement in their regard. The Court found that "[t]hese omissions deprived the defense of a certainty regarding the facts imputed (Article 8(2)(b) of the Convention) and, therefore, represented an obstacle for an adequate preparation of the defense, in the terms of Article 8(2)(c) of the Convention".[329]

---

324 *Ibidem*, para. 30. See also *Case of López Mendoza v. Venezuela*, para. 117.

325 *Case of Castillo Petruzzi et al. v. Peru*, paras. 138 and 141.

326 See, for example, *ibidem*, para. 86.16.

327 *Case of Fermín Ramírez v. Mexico*, para. 64.

328 *Ibidem*, para. 67.

329 *Ibidem*, paras. 68 and 73. The Inter-American Court quotes here case law from the European Court (*Pélissier and Sassi v. France and several others*).

71. Subparagraph (d) of Article 8(2) allows the accused to either defend himself personally or be assisted by legal counsel of his own choosing, and to communicate with that legal counsel freely and privately. Subparagraph (e) establishes "the inalienable right to be assisted by counsel provided by the state, paid or not as the domestic law provides, if the accused does not defend himself personally or engage his own counsel within the time period established by law".

The Court has examined subparagraph (d) in different cases. In Peru, Decree-Law 25.475 on the crime of terrorism contained a provision banning defense attorneys from assisting more than one accused individual simultaneously, even when they were not co-defendants.[330] The Court found that although this law limited choice, it was not *per se* a violation of Article 8(2)(d) of the Convention.[331] I disagree with this finding. It can be argued that counsel should not represent more than one defendant when there is a possibility of conflict of interest; in such cases, the provision is justified. But a general prohibition of the kind included in the law, which does not answer to a clear and legitimate need is in itself incompatible with Article 8. The ruling of the Court does not appear to me to have examined the reasoning behind that prohibition, nor does it take into consideration the situation of those accused of terrorism in Peru. During the time these trials took place, obtaining legal assistance for the accused was difficult: on the one hand, attorneys feared consequences for defending one of these people; on the other, the accused were normally individuals without money who could not hire private attorneys. For this reason, they often turned to *pro bono* services, which were always scarce and almost non-existent if an attorney could only defend one client at a time. Consequently, the prohibition seriously affected an accused person's ability to obtain legal assistance not appointed by the military court itself – as that court was frequently the one with jurisdiction in these cases. Naturally, this brought with it a serious risk that the accused would have a poor defense.

In the case of Yakye Axa, Article 8(2)(d) was violated because the Community was not allowed to appoint a defense attorney in a criminal trial.[332]

72. The Court has also examined the right of the accused to communicate freely and privately with his or her defender. In the case of Castillo Petruzzi *et al.*, the Court used clause eight of the Basic Principles on the Role of Lawyers[333] as a parameter for measuring compliance with this provision. That clause establishes

330 See expert witness report from attorney Bazán Chacón in the judgment in *Case of Loayza Tamayo v. Peru*, para. 45(g).

331 *Case of Castillo Petruzzi et al. v. Peru*, para. 147.

332 *Case of Yakye Axa v. Paraguay*, paras. 106, 118–119.

333 *Basic Principles on the Role of Lawyers*, adopted by the Eighth Congress of the United Nations Congress on the Prevention of Crime and the Treatment of Offenders, Havana, Cuba, August 27–September 7, 1990.

that "[a]ll arrested, detained or imprisoned persons shall be provided with adequate opportunities, time and facilities to be visited by and to communicate and consult with a lawyer, without delay, interception or censorship and in full confidentiality", with only visual supervision being allowed during attorney-client meetings.[334] The Court found that in this case, it was not legally possible to have counsel from the time of their detention and until after they had testified before DINCOTE. After testifying they were assigned court-appointed attorneys. Thus, Article 8(2)(d) had been violated.[335] In the case of Cantoral Benavides, the Court also found a violation of this provision because the State had impeded the victim from having free and private communication with his defender.[336]

73. Article 8(2)(e) establishes the right to legal counsel provided by the Court as an inalienable right. It could be debated from the point of view of human rights whether it is appropriate for a court to always have the authority to name a defender for an accused individual who refuses to have one or whether it is only required to appoint one in the interests of justice, as suggested in Article 14 of the ICCPR. The preparatory work of the Convention does not shed much light on this point. The delegate from the United States called attention to this draft Article 8(2)(e), arguing that it conflicted with the article's previous subparagraph. However, the Presidency clarified that in the legal system of Latin American States, the accused must always have counsel even if they do not wish to mount a defense. If they refuse to appoint counsel, the State will provide one even against the wishes of the accused.[337] The rule therefore intends to maintain this aspect of the region's continental legal system. Nevertheless, one might wonder what reasoning is appropriate, for example, to give a court the authority to assign an attorney when the accused considers this Court incompetent and biased. This would block the accused from expressing repudiation by refusing to defend themselves and entering into the public record that they did not do it, nor did they allow counsel to defend them. This latter issue deserves more reflection since this is not a far-fetched possibility in Latin American countries.

The expression "paid or not as the domestic law provides" also led to a discussion during the Specialized Conference, a discussion that did not reach a clear conclusion. The delegate from Trinidad and Tobago argued that it was not possible to impose such a financial burden on the State, while the delegate from Uruguay suggested that the Convention states expressly that legal counsel would be free for the accused. A workgroup was set up to settle the dispute. However,

---

334 *Case of Castillo Petruzzi et al. v. Peru*, para. 139.

335 *Ibidem*, para. 146.

336 *Case of Cantoral Benavides v. Peru*, para. 127.

337 Specialized Conference, *supra* n. 184, p. 201.

the minutes of its meetings are not on the record, and the only fact recorded is the approval of the paragraph as it is found in the Convention along with a comment from the delegate from Uruguay to the effect that:

> This paragraph was subjected to very careful consideration and [...] the fact that a final text has been produced speaks very favorably of the goodwill of the delegations from the representatives of the Anglo-Saxon legal system, who with spirit of conciliation sought to understand our reasoning, as we did theirs.[338]

One could understand from the quote that the Convention allows for the possibility that States can decide on remuneration. The report from the Rapporteur of Commission I, in which this part of the Convention was discussed, indicates: "the advisability of specifying terminology with regard to the courts, legal defence for the accused, and providing those legal defence services for free was considered".[339] Barbados and Dominica seem to have understood the provisions of Article 8(2)(e) to mean that the State is required to provide free legal defense, as both of them made a reservation on this provision.[340]

74. In its Advisory Opinion 11/90 in response to the Commission's request for interpretation of Article 46(2) of the Convention containing exceptions to the obligation to exhaust domestic remedies, the Court took a position on this point, stating that since the Convention "does not stipulate that legal counsel be provided free of charge when required, an indigent would suffer discrimination for reason of his economic status if, when in need of legal counsel, the state were not to provide it to him free of charge".[341] The Court found that although the Convention did not require free legal counsel to be provided, the necessity of legal counsel for ensuring due process took precedence. It was possible to violate Article 8 "if it can be proved that the lack of legal counsel affected the right to a fair hearing to which he is entitled under that Article".[342] The Court added that this situation could also arise in matters concerning the determination of civil, labor and other rights and obligations and the obligation to provide legal counsel would exist.[343] While I agree with this latter argument, I would argue that the Court's interpretation is not correct with regard to criminal trials. Human rights must be interpreted *pro persona*, and grounds can be found in the preparatory work to resolve the unclear points of the provision in a different way so that States would be bound to provide legal counsel free in some cases. Additionally,

338 *Ibidem*, p. 224.
339 *Ibidem*, p. 297.
340 Barbados submitted its reservation on ratifying the Convention on November 5, 1981; Dominica submitted its reservation on ratifying the Convention on June 3, 1993.
341 *OC-11/90*, para. 25.
342 *Ibidem*, para. 27.
343 *Ibidem*, paras. 27 and 28.

one should always remember that for the reasons stated previously, criminal trials deserve greater guarantees.

The Court emphasized in the case of Vélez Loor the importance of legal aid counsel and decided that in certain cases the State must provide it free of charge. Vélez Loor was an individual who was submitted to an administrative trial that could have resulted in his deportation, expulsion or imprisonment. The Court found that "free legal representation is an imperative for the interests of justice".[344] The Court added that this right had to be provided from the moment the investigation begins onwards[345] and could not be replaced by the equivalent to an Ombudsman (*Defensor del Pueblo*).[346] A similar case was that of Barreto Leiva, where the Court found that the Office of the Public Prosecutor could not replace the counsel to which the accused had a right for his defense.[347]

If the State provides a public defender, it has the obligation to make certain that the defense is acceptable and reaches a minimum level of professionalism. In the case of Chaparro and Lapo, when Mr. Lapo made his pre-trial statement, his legal aid counsel was present only at the moment he began his statement and at the moment he had to sign, being absent during the rest of the proceeding.[348] The Court found this attitude "clearly incompatible with the State's obligation to provide an acceptable defense lawyer to anyone who is unable to defend himself or appoint a private defense lawyer".[349] In another case, the Court gave an example of what would not constitute an unacceptable defense. In Dacosta Cadogan it stated that "[t]he Court considers that there were a number of available defenses that the state-appointed defense counsel could have pursued at trial. However, his failure to pursue a defense of diminished responsibility and his decision to choose instead other available defenses certainly did not amount to gross incompetence".[350] No violation was found.

75. Article 8(2)(f) refers to the principle of *audi alteram partem*[351] – to which I have already made reference – by stating that the accused has the right to use all evidentiary measures at his or her disposal and can object to all the evidentiary measures brought before the court by the State. However, its wording

---

344 *Case of Vélez Loor v. Panama*, para. 146. The Court quotes here the *Case of Benham v. United Kingdom*, judgment June 10, 1996, paras. 61 and 64.

345 *Ibidem*, para. 132.

346 *Ibidem*, para. 133.

347 *Case of Barreto Leiva v. Venezuela*, para. 64.

348 *Chaparro and Lapo v. Ecuador*, para. 156.

349 *Ibidem*, para. 159. In the same sense see *Case of Tibi v. Ecuador*, para. 184.

350 *Case of Dacosta Cadogan v. Barbados*, para. 93. See also *Case of Yakye Axa v. Paraguay*, para. 166.

351 See HRC, General Comment No. 32, Article 14: Right to equality before courts and tribunals and to a fair trial (CCPR/C/GC/32, 23 August 2007, paras 13–14).

is unfortunate, as it does not allude to all the aspects of the principle.[352] However, regardless of the wording, there is no doubt that those aspects can be drawn from a correct reading of Article 8(1) of the Convention.

The Court has found violations of this provision on several occasions. In the case of Castillo Petruzzi, it found that the defense had not been able to interrogate the DINCOTE agents – the police officers who participated in the investigation phase of the case and on the basis of whose testimony the accused were convicted. In addition, one of the accused had been convicted by the highest court "based on new evidence that his defense attorney had not seen and consequently could not rebut."[353] As found by the Court, the fact that a defense attorney was not involved from the time the accused was exposed to the justice system up to the moment in which he was allowed to testify meant that it was impossible to challenge the evidence collected and placed in the police affidavit, resulting in a violation of Article 8(2)(f). The same violation resulted from "restrictions imposed on the victims' defense attorneys", restrictions that came, *inter alia*, from the laws governing the proceeding, as attorneys were given 12 hours to examine the case file and the ruling was issued the following day.[354] In the case of Cantoral Benavides, the Court found that the violation had been proven because "the victim's lawyer was unsuccessful in presenting certain evidence crucial to the defense." These procedures included interrogation of DINCOTE members and the cross-examining of an expert witness.[355]

In the case of Barreto Leiva, the Court found that there was a violation of the right to defense in the secrecy of all investigative actions including the supporting documents when the person was not under arrest. This resulted in the subordination of the defense to the prosecutor, without the court having any possibility of analyzing the particular circumstances of the case.[356]

76. An interesting case regarding the right of defense is the recent trial against Norín *et al.*, members of the Mapuche people. The Mapuche people are undergoing an unsettling social situation as a consequence of their claim for devolution of their ancestral territories and for respect of the use and enjoyment of that land and their natural resources. The protests have grown after the increase of the forest exploitation by various nonindigenous persons and corporations resulting in the enclosement of the communal property of

---

352 In the *Case of Loayza Tamayo v. Peru*, the Court found a clear violation of the principle of *audi alteram partem*, as "the defendants were not allowed [by law] to challenge or examine the evidence" (*Case of Loayza Tamayo v. Peru*, para. 62).

353 *Case of Castillo Petruzzi et al. v. Peru*, paras. 138 and 140. See also *Case of García Asto and Urcesino Ramírez v. Peru*, para. 153.

354 *Ibidem*, paras. 138, 140–141, 153 and 155.

355 *Case of Cantoral Benavides v. Peru*, para. 127.

356 *Case of Barreto Leiva v. Venezuela*, para. 56.

the Mapuche, who were left surrounded by private properties.[357] The accused were charged and convicted, some of arson of land estates or threats to commit arson, and others of arson of trucks. Some of the accused were tried within the framework of the old inquisitive procedure and some with the new adversarial procedure. This in itself could have meant, if examined, the finding of other violations, but the Court did not enter into that discussion.[358] The issue in the case was the use of unidentified witnesses in convicting the accused, which prevented the defense from inquiring about possible enmities or biases.[359] The witnesses declared behind a screen with a device which altered their voice and the lawyer for the defense was only allowed to interrogate them under these circumstances. The trial was annulled and in the second trial the lawyers for the defense were permitted to know the identity of the witnesses, under the prohibition to transmit the information to the accused. They refused.[360] In addition, in the case of one of the accused, Mr. Ancalef Llaupe, the defense did not have access to all the evidence as the court maintained certain evidence secret, in what is called "reserved files", without expressing any reason therefor, except the legal provision being applied in the taking of the measure.[361] There were no measures to counteract the damage that the secrecy could cause on the witnesses. The Court found that in such a case, the domestic court had to play an important part in protecting the rights of the accused, and the lawyers for the defense had to have the opportunity to get to know the behavior of the witness to assess its credibility.[362] Furthermore, the conviction could not be based solely or in a significant part on this type of declaration.[363] The anti-terrorist law in Chile did not comply with the requirements specified by the Court.[364] This judgment may be an important precedent for the treatment of offenses classified as terrorist activities.

8.5. PLEADING OF GUILT, CONFESSION AND COERCION

77. Article 8(2)(g) grants the accused the right not to be compelled to be a witness against himself or not to plead guilty. This guarantee emphasizes the idea that it is the State's burden to prove a person's guilt and is fundamentally associated with the prohibition of torture and cruel, inhuman or degrading

[357] *Case of Norín Catrimán et al. (leaders, members and activists of the Indigenous Mapuche people) v. Chile*, paras. 79–80.
[358] *Ibidem*, para. 193.
[359] *Ibidem*, para. 242.
[360] *Ibidem*, para. 234.
[361] *Ibidem*, para. 236.
[362] *Ibidem*, para. 246.
[363] *Ibidem*, para. 247.
[364] *Ibidem*, paras. 249, 251, 252, 254 and 260.

treatment.[365] This being the case, it leads to the necessary conclusion that a confession dragged out of a person using this type of treatment is not valid as evidence. The Convention reiterates this by establishing in Article 8(3) that "[a] confession of guilt by the accused shall be valid only if it is made without coercion of any kind." It is the State's responsibility to investigate all allegations of this type of treatment. The person making the allegations has neither the responsibility to take the initiative nor the burden of proof of the existence of the alleged torture or cruel, inhuman or degrading treatment.[366]

78. The Court found a violation of Articles 8(2)(g) and (3) of the Convention in the case of Cantoral Benavides, on finding it proven that the victim was subjected to torture and forced to confess to certain criminal conduct.[367] In contrast, in the case of Castillo Petruzzi *et al.*, the Court found that merely demanding that the accused tell the truth did not constitute a violation of Article 8(3), as "nothing in the record suggests that any punishment or other adverse legal consequence was threatened if they did not tell the truth." Nor was there evidence that the national court had asked the accused to give a sworn statement or make any promises to tell the truth. The Court found that, had this been the case, it would have been a violation of "their right to choose between testifying and not testifying".[368] The *travaux préparatoires* of the Convention do not contain any discussion of Article 8(3).

In the case of Cabrera García, two Mexicans who could not read and write, the Court reiterated the universal recognition of the norm of exclusion from judicial proceedings of all evidence obtained under torture or through cruel or inhumane treatment and expressed that this rule is "absolute and irrevocable".[369] It added that Article 8(3) of the Convention indicates that "the defendant's confession is only valid if made without duress of any kind" and thus it is "not limited to the factual situation of torture or cruel treatment, but extends to any form of duress".[370] When the confession is not valid due to coercion, it invalidates as well the evidence derived from it.[371] Finally, the Court rejected the possibility of a second confession be admitted as valid, since the cruel treatment suffered by the victims was performed in order to break down their psychological resistance and force them to incriminate themselves or confess to certain illegal activities.[372]

---

365 This guarantee was added to the text of the Convention at the last minute, as a similar prior provision had not been approved before. See Specialized Conference, *supra* n. 184, pp. 203 (motion of Paraguay) and 443.

366 On the State's responsibility to investigate torture, see Chapter 4 of this book.

367 *Case of Cantoral Benavides v. Peru*, paras. 132–133.

368 *Case of Castillo Petruzzi et al. v. Peru*, para. 167.

369 *Case of Cabrera García and Mantiel v. Mexico*, para. 165.

370 *Ibidem*, para. 166.

371 *Ibidem*, para. 167.

372 *Ibidem*, para. 175.

8.6. RIGHT TO APPEAL THE JUDGMENT TO A HIGHER COURT

79. The American Convention sets forth that in criminal trials, it is a minimum guarantee of the accused to appeal the ruling to a higher court.[373] A second instance appeal is a means to impugn before a higher court a decision of a lower court, where the higher court has competence to review the facts and the application of the law by the lower court and issue a new decision. The replacement of a second instance appeal with the possibility of annulling the judgment in certain cases, given certain limited grounds, is part of domestic law in many Latin American countries. The aim of the change is to shorten the time for criminal trials, which is in general extremely long. Furthermore, the annulment of the judgment pays attention to the principle of immediacy. That principle allows judges to form their own impressions of evidence and allows the evidence to be presented in a public trial in the presence of a judge; these constitute guarantees for the accused and are an important aspect of the trustworthiness of the factual basis of a judgment. A full review of a judgment by a second instance court does not occur in the new model.

The Human Rights Committee caused apparently a first stir in Latin American States when dealing with a Spanish case, Cesario Gómez Vásquez.[374] The Committee found that Spain's law had a very limited review of the case and did not allow a review of any fact, except in very extreme circumstances, "the review having been limited to the formal or legal aspects of the conviction". The Committee stated that whichever remedy the State sets forth and whichever name it takes must comply with the requirements of Article 14(5) of the ICCPR.[375] The Committee has also pointed out that the expression "according to law" only allows discretion in deciding the modalities with which the higher court will review the decision but cannot prevent "a second review" thereof.[376]

The Inter-American Court has dealt with this same issue several times. In the case of Herrera Ulloa the Court, quoting from Castillo Petruzzi, held that "the right to appeal a judgment, recognized in the Convention, is not satisfied merely because there is a higher court than the one that tried and convicted the accused and to which the latter has or may have recourse." It pointed out that the Convention required "the higher court to have jurisdictional authority to take

373 In Spanish, to appeal (*apelar*) has a legal definition, meaning actually a second trial in the Appeals Court. The Spanish word in the Convention is *recurrir* instead of *apelar* at the suggestion of a delegate who said that in some countries there could be three instances. *Recurrir* is the general word used to mean various ways to challenge a decision, not necessarily through an appeal.

374 The ICCPR sets forth that "[e]veryone convicted of a crime shall have the right to his conviction and sentence being reviewed by a higher tribunal according to law".

375 *Case of Cesario Gómez Vásquez v. Spain*, Communication 701/1996, Views of July 20, 2000.

376 HRC, *Case of Gomariz v. Spain*, Communication 1095/2002, July 22, 2005, para. 7.1; *Case of Terrón v. Spain*, Communication 1073/2002, November 5, 2004, para. 7.4.

up the particular case in question" and stressed that a criminal proceeding is "a *single* procedure in various stages including the processing of the ordinary challenges filed against the judgment."[377] Then it affirmed that "the remedy contemplated in Article 8(2)(h) of the Convention must be an effective, ordinary remedy" and, although "States have a margin of discretion" to regulate it, it is not possible to establish restrictions or requirements inimical to the very essence to the right to appeal the judgment."[378] In the Herrera Ulloa case, there was only a right to cassation, where the assessment of facts could not be reviewed allowing only a review of the applicable law. In a concurring vote, Judge Sergio García Ramírez stressed that the aim of the review by a higher court was "to allow that higher court or judge to get into the merits of the case, examine the facts alleged, the defense's counter-arguments, the evidence taken, the weighing of that evidence, the laws invoked and their application".[379] In the case of Barreto Leiva, the Court insisted that the accused had the right to a full review of the condemnatory judgment.[380] The Court had a similar position in the case of Vélez Loor.[381] In the case of Mendoza *et al.* v. Argentina, the Court reiterated that compliance with Article 8(2)(h) required that the appeal constitute "an appropriate means of obtaining the rectification of a wrongful conviction". There must be an examination of the facts, evidence and law on which the contested judgment was based; they are all interdependent.[382] Argentinian legislation, on the contrary, only allowed cassation when there was an erroneous application of the substantive law or a violation of a procedural rule.[383]

In the case of Mohamed, a case of manslaughter allegedly committed by a bus driver and decided at the end of 2012, one of the allegations was the violation of the right in Article 8(2)(h). The issue was a first conviction applied to Mr. Mohamed at the second instance of the trial, he having been acquitted on first instance. According to Argentinian law "the only remedy was the special appeal" or review, and that "did not provide a timely, accessible and effective review in accordance with" the Convention standards. The scope of the review is restricted to "matters of patent unconstitutionality and arbitrariness". It is also possible for the Supreme Court to reject this appeal "without [...] examining the merits of the matter."[384] The State invoked as an argument[385] Article 2(2) of Protocol 7 of the European Convention on Human Rights.[386] The Court rejected

377 *Case of Herrera Ulloa v. Costa Rica*, para. 159.
378 *Ibidem*, para. 161.
379 *Ibidem*, vote of Judge Sergio García Ramírez, para. 31.
380 *Case of Barreto Leiva v. Venezuela*, para. 131.
381 *Case of Vélez Loor v. Panama*, para. 179.
382 *Case of Mendoza et al. v. Argentina*, para. 245.
383 *Ibidem*, para. 253.
384 *Case of Mohamed v. Argentina*, para. 66.
385 *Ibidem*, para. 90.
386 Article 2(2) states: "This right [to have his conviction or sentence reviewed by a higher tribunal] may be subject to exceptions in regard to offences of a minor character, as

that argument on the basis that in Europe there is a conventional provision allowing this, but it was not the situation in the American Convention. As to the issue itself, it found:

> It is contrary to the purpose of that particular right that it should not be guaranteed to someone who is convicted in a judgment that overturns an acquittal. To interpret it otherwise would leave the convicted person without the right to an appeal against the conviction. This involves a guarantee to the individual against the State and is not merely a guide for the design of appeal systems within the domestic legal systems of the States Parties to the Convention.[387]

Argentina had argued that Mr. Mohamed did not pursue the special remedy of review. The Court examined this remedy and heard experts on Argentinian law, reaching the conclusion that "it is possible to confirm that this special federal recourse is not a remedy under criminal procedure to challenge a conviction, but an exceptional recourse regulated by the Code of Civil and Commercial Procedure".[388] In the case of Herrera Ulloa, the Court had stated that "[t]he right to file an appeal against a judgment must be guaranteed before the judgment becomes *res judicata.* The aim is to protect the right of defense by creating a remedy to prevent a flawed ruling, containing errors unduly prejudicial to a person's interests, from becoming final".[389] In the Mohamed case, it reiterated this idea,[390] and as a consequence there was a violation of Article 8(2)(h). In the case of Mendoza *et al.* v. Argentina, the Court repeated the examination and analysis carried out in the case of Mohamed. Argentina argued here that there was a special remedy to review certain final judgments, which the victims had used successfully. The Court found that this remedy of review was not an ordinary remedy and that it only operated after the judgment was *res judicata*; therefore it was not the remedy of Article 8(2)(h) as it did not fulfill its requirements.[391] Therefore, it found a violation of the Convention's provision.[392]

In the case of Norín Catrimán *et al.*, filed by leaders, members and activists of the indigenous Mapuche people, the Court dealt in depth with the right to review of a conviction, called annulment in Chile. It affirmed that this remedy had to be an ordinary one, accessible to all convicted persons, and effective. It should allow an integral examination and review of the judgment, making it

---

prescribed by law, or in cases in which the person concerned was tried in the first instance by the highest tribunal or was convicted following an appeal against acquittal." Protocol 7 of the European Convention for the Protection of Human Rights and Fundamental Freedoms (http://conventions.coe.int/Treaty/en/Treaties/Html/117.htm).

387 *Case of Mohamed v. Argentina*, para. 93.

388 *Ibidem*, paras. 105–113.

389 *Case of Herrera Ulloa v. Costa Rica*, para. 158.

390 *Case of Mohamed v. Argentina*, para. 100.

391 *Case of Mendoza et al. v. Argentina*, para. 261.

392 *Ibidem*, para. 262.

possible to analyze the facts, evidence and law on which the judgment was based. The grounds to be invoked by the person convicted must allow all this.[393] In the case of one of the accused, the national court that dealt with the remedy of annulment of the first instance judgment had not examined the facts or given the legal considerations necessary to find if the conduct of the accused fitted the description of the offense.[394] In the case of another, the Temuco Court of Appeals clarified that the remedy to nullify the first judgment must restrict itself to assessing whether that judgment is enough on its own; it added that it is not the Court of Appeals' function to review the facts determined in the first instance judgment.[395] The Inter-American Court established that the higher tribunal must ensure that the lower tribunal fulfills its duty to present an assessment of the evidence both for and against the accused. This had not been done in the case and therefore it had violated Article 8(2)(h) of the Convention.[396]

The Court seems to understand that it is rather the old model, the one in accordance with the Convention, which seems logical, since at the time the Convention was drafted and then ratified, this was the system in many if not all Latin American States. This will be a difficult point to resolve if States wish to pursue modernization of the criminal procedural rules.

The right to review is also applicable with regard to criminal trials with special proceedings, such as trials in which a higher court acts as the first instance court due to the privileged forum assigned to the accused. In the case of Mohamed v. Argentina, mentioned above, the Court had concluded that the right to review would be applicable even if the highest court operates as a court of first instance and it would be the State's duty to design a system to make this possible.[397] In the case Liakat Alibux, the Court found that the lack of an appeal of judgments pronounced directly by the highest court of the State, something that the Surinamese legislation did not allow, was a violation of Article 8(2)(h). The Court suggested various ways in which to deal with this situation, such as having the plenary handle the appeal and a chamber handle the judgment to review the appeal. The Court also affirmed that this solution and others have been the practice of some States in the region.[398] The State should organize itself "in a manner that it deems appropriate in order to guarantee the corresponding right to appeal the judgment of high ranking public officials".[399]

---

393 *Case of Norín Catrimán et al. (leaders, members and activists of the Indigenous Mapuche people) v. Chile*, para. 270.

394 *Ibidem*, para. 278.

395 *Ibidem*, para. 283.

396 *Ibidem*, para. 289.

397 *Case of Mohamed v. Argentina*, para. 93.

398 *Case of Liakat Ali Alibux v. Suriname*, para. 105.

399 *Ibidem*, para. 105.

8.7. PRINCIPLE OF *NON BIS IN IDEM*

80. Article 8(4) of the Convention holds that "[a]n accused person acquitted by a non-appealable judgment shall not be subjected to a new trial for the same cause." The principle does not apply in the case of a possible review of the conviction based on the appearance of new facts indicating the person's innocence. The wording of the Convention differs from that of the ICCPR, which does not refer to "the same cause", but to the "same crime", something that has moved the Inter-American Court to indicate that the Convention is more favorable for the victim than the ICCPR.[400]

In the case of Loayza Tamayo,[401] an ordinary court tried and acquitted the victim for the crime of treason (also called aggravated terrorism). However, Ms. Loayza underwent a second criminal proceeding for the crime of terrorism. The Court found that this violated Article 8(4) of the Convention. On the one hand, the description of crimes contained in various decree-laws "refer to actions not strictly defined, so that they may be interpreted similarly within both crimes by the Ministry of the Interior, the corresponding judges and, in the case under consideration, by the 'Police (DINCOTE) itself'".[402] On the other hand, the case constituted a violation because the second proceeding was based on the same expanded police report used before the Special Navy Court that had acquitted Ms. Loayza Tamayo.[403] In the case of Cantoral Benavides, the Court handled the issue in a different manner. The facts of the case are similar, as Cantoral Benavides was put on trial for treason before a military court and was acquitted. The military court then forwarded all the trial material to a civilian court for a new trial, and this second proceeding culminated in a conviction and a sentence of twenty years in prison. Later, the victim submitted a request for a pardon, which was granted.[404] However, the Court ruled that based on the fact that the first trial was carried out before a military court that was not competent, not independent, and not impartial, "the actions and decisions taken by the authorities of the exclusive military jurisdiction in the matter of [the victim] do not constitute the type of proceeding called for in Article 8(4) of the Convention."[405] Thus, "the alleged infraction of Article 8(4) of the Convention

---

400 *Case of Loayza Tamay v. Peru*, para. 66. In reality, I would argue that notwithstanding the wording of Article 14(7) of the ICCPR, an interpretation that allows someone to be tried again based on the same facts but changing the type of crime would not be acceptable, as this would make the provision irrelevant.

401 On the principle of *non bis in idem* in the *case of Loayza Tamayo v. Peru*, see D. Acevedo, "La decisión de la Corte Interamericana de Derechos Humanos sobre enjuiciamiento penal múltiple (*non bis in idem*) en el caso Loayza Tamayo", in *Liber Amicorum Héctor Fix Zamudio, supra* n. 10, pp. 279–300.

402 *Case of Loayza Tamayo v. Peru*, para. 68.

403 *Ibidem*, paras. 74–75.

404 *Case of Cantoral Benavides v. Peru*, para. 63, subparagraphs ll., ñ., o. and r.

405 *Ibidem*, paras. 137–138.

is included in the violation of Article 8(1) of same."[406] What the Court is saying is that there is no *non bis in idem* when the first trial is invalid in the eyes of the Court.

It is interesting to note that the Court has pointed out that the principle of *non bis in idem* is not absolute and admits exceptions so as not to prevent the investigation of gross human rights violations.[407] This was further elaborated in the case of Almonacid Castro with examples. The Court said that the principle should not be applied: (i) when a court had dismissed the case or acquitted an alleged author in order to shield the accused party from criminal responsibility; (ii) when the proceedings "were not conducted independently or impartially in accordance with due procedural guarantees"; and (iii) when "there was no real intent to bring those responsible to justice. The Court found that in these cases there was "an "apparent" or "fraudulent" *res judicata* case.[408] The expression had been used in Carpio Nicole. The Court finally found that if a new fact or evidence was presented and it showed that the perpetrators were not those convicted, the case can be reopened, "even if the case ended in an acquittal with the authority of a final judgment, since [...] the spirit and the wording of the American Convention supersedes the protection of the *ne bis in idem* principle".[409] I agree with the decision but do not share its wording. It is not a question of "superseding" the principle, but that in these cases the principle cannot be applied because there cannot be *res judicata* in such a situation. This is what the Court labels "fraudulent *res judicata*". The Court stated in that judgment that fraudulent *res judicata* resulted "from a trial in which the rules of due process have not been respected, or when judges have not acted with independence and impartiality".[410] This was the case in Almonacid, because the military court that tried the victim was neither the "natural" judge not independent and impartial and the application of a decree-law prevented those allegedly responsible from being brought to trial.[411] In the case of Gutiérrez and family, the Court also found that the principle was not applicable if "the judicial proceedings were not in keeping with the guarantees of "due process" established in the said Article 8 and, consequently, "did not produce the 'non-appealable judgment' mentioned in paragraph 4 of this article".[412]

In the case of J. v Peru, the Court stated that there would be a violation of Article 8(4) when in the first trial (i) the accused had been acquitted; (ii) the

406 *Ibidem*, para. 140.

407 As was the case in *Case of Barrios Altos v. Peru*, judgment on the merits, para. 41; *Case of Massacres of El Mozote and nearby places v. El Salvador*, para. 319; and others.

408 *Case of Almonacid v. Chile*, para. 154. See also *Case of Nadege Dorzema et al. v. Dominican Republic*, paras. 195 and 197.

409 *Ibidem*, para. 155.

410 *Case of Carpio Nicole et al. v. Guatemala*, para. 131. See also *Case of Gutiérrez v. Colombia*, para. 98.

411 *Case of Almonacid v. Chile*, para. 155.

412 *Case of Gutiérrez and family v. Argentina*, para. 129.

acquittal was the result of a final judgment, and (iii) the new trial was based on the same facts that were the grounds for the first trial.[413] After a complicated review of the facts, the Court reached the conclusion that the acquittal had not been final and therefore the *non bis in idem* principle had not been violated with the new trial.[414]

8.8. PUBLIC TRIAL, ORAL TRIALS, AND RULINGS OPEN TO THE PUBLIC

81. Article 8(5) establishes that "criminal proceedings shall be public, except insofar as may be necessary to protect the interests of justice." In contrast to the provisions of Article 14(1) of the ICCPR, the Convention's requirement that proceedings be public only applies to criminal proceedings.[415] This is a formal requirement intending to ensure transparency in the justice system by allowing the presence of third parties when the trial takes place. The State therefore has an obligation to make it possible in fact and law for the public to have access to the trial. In addition to protecting the accused, requiring a trial to be public is also a community right, as everyone should be able to supervise, through their own presence, the way in which justice is served in a democratic society.

82. The right to a public trial means that it must be oral, as a written proceeding does not allow for this sort of democratic supervision.[416] The Human Rights Committee has already addressed this to the effect that the requirement for a public trial implies that its oral nature forms part of the concept of "due process" in international law.[417] In principle, it does not seem necessary for everything that takes place during the proceeding to be conducted orally given that the purpose of this requirement is to allow the accused and the judge to get a direct impression of the evidence, and for the accused to be able to hear that evidence directly and contest it. Thus, a cassation proceeding, in which the court of cassation discusses only questions of law, would not need to be carried out orally. The public nature of the proceedings also covers the reading of the ruling,

---

413 *Case of J. v. Peru*, para. 262.

414 *Ibidem*, para. 267.

415 Notwithstanding this, given that all States Parties to the Convention are also parties to the ICCPR, noncriminal proceedings are also required to be public in all these countries.

416 In addition, it does not seem possible to ensure the accused's minimum guarantees or the principle of immediacy in a written trial.

417 Article 14(3)(d) of the ICCPR does not call for proceedings to be oral, but there is consensus that this is implicit in the requirement found in Article 14(1) that all trials, whether criminal or not, must be public (See M. Nowak, *U.N. Covenant on Civil and Political Rights. CCPR Commentary*, N.P. Engel Publisher, Kehl/Strasbourg/Arlington, 1993, p. 249). For oral proceedings in the European system, see P. van Dijk *et al.*, *supra* n. 62, pp. 589–581.

as the American Convention states that the "proceedings" must be public, and the ruling is the culmination of the proceedings.

The Inter-American Court found violations of the requirement that trials must be public in the case of Castillo Petruzzi *et al.* There, anonymous military judges and prosecutors carried out the proceedings, in secret and in isolation.[418] The same situation occurred in the case of Cantoral Benavides, whose trial proceedings before civilian courts included several hearings that took place inside prison facilities.[419] In the case of Palamara, the Court found that Chile's Military Justice Code violated Article 8(5) because the summary stage of the proceedings was secret. The Court considered these provisions "oppose the right to defense of the accused, as they prevent access to the record of the case and to the evidence gathered against him, which, in turn, prevents him from defending himself adequately", in violation of the provisions set forth in Article 8(2). The proceedings of the Code of Military Justice were, of course, in accordance with the inquisitorial system existing not only in that Code, but in the Code of Criminal Procedure as well. This meant that it suffered from other weaknesses, such as being a written procedure, which made obtaining knowledge of the non-secret parts of the proceedings very difficult. The Court also found this to be incompatible with the Convention.[420] Concerning the lack of publicity, the Court considered it as an obstacle to access by the parties to all the steps taken during such procedural stage that could not be justified as "a strategy to temporarily protect sensitive information which may affect the course of the investigation".[421]

The Convention authorizes closing a proceeding to the public. However, it does not specify the cases in which it allows this, thus giving the judge a great degree of discretion to decide when the need to preserve the interests of justice requires a closed proceeding. The expression "the interests of justice" does not clearly cover certain situations in which closing a proceeding to the public is intended rather to protect the parties, such as in criminal cases in which the accused is a child or an adolescent. However, a contextual interpretation of the Convention should include such situations as a legitimate exception to publicity.

9. POSSIBILITY OF OTHER GUARANTEES NOT INDICATED IN ARTICLE 8

83. The thrust of minimum guarantees for the accused and due process guarantees in general is to subject the process to rules that ensure the individuals

418 *Case of Castillo Petruzzi et al. v. Peru*, paras. 172–173.
419 *Case of Cantoral Benavides v. Peru*, paras. 146–147.
420 *Case of Palamara v. Chile*, paras. 169–170.
421 *Ibidem*, para. 174.

affected to be able to mount a good defense and be treated fairly. It is therefore possible that other guarantees are necessary that are not explicit in the Convention but are normally implicit in the correct interpretation of the general provision. For example, a person can only be brought to trial if he or she has the mental capacity to understand the charges and provide the background information necessary for mounting a defense. If this is not the case, the trial cannot take place on pain of violating Article 8, as it would be impossible in such a case for the accused to make use of the rights granted him or her by this provision.

84. The right to be present at the trial is one of the most classical guarantees not set forth explicitly in the Convention. This right undoubtedly derives from – among other rights – the right of the accused to defend themselves personally and to object to evidence submitted against them. In the region, as said above, trials were always carried out in a written form so it is probable that the courts applying the oral procedures will learn from the case law of European states.

The rights to defense and to be present at the trial mean that, in principle, *in absentia* trials are not compatible with international law. However, in my view, there can be exceptions to this rule. The purpose of a trial is to determine the guilt or innocence of a person – but also, if the court finds that the accused is guilty, to apply the criminal punishment deserved. Therefore, it does not seem fair for the accused to be able to prevent justice to operate by choosing not to appear at trial. However, nor does it seem fair that a person who is not attempting to evade justice be tried *in absentia*. Additionally, waiting for the accused to appear can harm the process of collecting evidence for the case. To make those interests compatible, *in absentia* trial should be allowed once all possible actions have been taken to inform an individual that he or she will be subject to the proceeding, as long as the person in question is given the opportunity to defend him or herself should he or she later appear.[422] The Court has not ruled on this point, but Venezuela made a reservation to Article 8(1) because *in absentia* trials are practiced in that country.[423] This points to the idea that in principle this type of trial is not compatible with the Convention.

85. The Court made an important ruling on the minimum guarantees of the accused, broadening on the previously mentioned approaches.[424] This was the result of an Advisory Opinion requested by Mexico on the individual's right to information on consular assistance established in Article 36(1)(b) of the Vienna Convention on Consular Relations. To reach its conclusion, the Court reasoned

---

422 In the European system, a new trial is often not allowed if the accused has fled to escape justice (D.J. Harris *et al.*, *supra* n. 82, p. 205).

423 Venezuela made its reservation on ratifying the Convention on August 9, 1977.

424 *OC-16/99*, para. 117.

that one objective of due process is "to protect, to ensure, or to assert the entitlement to a right or the exercise thereof" and indicated that its requirements are "the prerequisites necessary to ensure the adequate protection of those persons whose rights or obligations are pending judicial determination."[425] With this being the general principle, all other guarantees required for responding to needs arising from special circumstances or that are the result of greater development and refinement of the idea of due process will be part of the minimum guarantees set forth in Article 8. The idea regarding special circumstances led the Court to advance the interpretation of the principle of equality that informs due process, arguing that "to accomplish its objectives, the judicial process must recognize and correct any real disadvantages that those brought before the bar might have".[426] In doing this, the Court affirmed that the State must adopt "countervailing measures that help to reduce or eliminate the obstacles and deficiencies that impair or diminish an effective defense of one's interests."[427] In the case of this Advisory Opinion, which addresses the right of a foreign national being subjected to legal proceeding to information on consular assistance, the Court indicated that "the real situation of the foreign nationals facing criminal proceedings must be considered".[428]

Taking all these concepts into consideration, and in order to establish its jurisdiction pursuant to Article 64 of the Convention, the Court decided that Article 36 of the Vienna Convention on Consular Relations enshrines a true individual right to information on consular assistance. This right "concerns the protection of the rights of a national of the sending State and is part of the body of international human rights law."[429] International law includes for these purposes Article 14 of the ICCPR, which for its part addresses the protection of human rights "in the American States".[430] Next, the Court added that this right to be informed "allows the right to due process of law recognized in Article 14 of the ICCPR to have practical effects in concrete cases". It added that this provision "establishes minimum guarantees that can be amplified in the light of other international instruments such as the Vienna Convention on Consular Relations, which expand the scope of the protection afforded to the accused."[431] A logical consequence of all this is that the State has the obligation to provide that information, and a failure to comply with that obligation would constitute a violation of due process leading to the State's international responsibility and reparations.[432] Regarding the specific consultation, a case that could end up

425 *Ibidem*, paras. 117 and 118.
426 *Ibidem*, para. 119.
427 *Ibidem*.
428 *Ibidem*, para. 121.
429 *Ibidem*, paras. 141(1) and 141(2).
430 *Ibidem*, paras. 141(4) and 141(5).
431 *Ibidem*, para. 141(6).
432 *Ibidem*, para. 141(7).

with the application of the death penalty, the Court went further. The failure to comply with this obligation led the Court to hold that, in such a case, in addition to a violation of due process, there would be a violation of Article 4 of the American Convention and Article 6 of the ICCPR.[433]

86. The Court has invariably applied this guarantee of the right of foreigners to be informed of the possibility to contact his or her consul. In the Tibi case, concerning a Frenchman detained in Ecuador, the Court noted the absence of information given to Mr. Tibi on his right to communicate with his consul and found a violation of his right to defense along the lines of Advisory Opinion 16. In the case of Acosta Calderón, a Colombian detained in Ecuador, the information about his right to access the consul was also lacking. The Court insisted that:

> the consul may assist the detainee in different acts of defense, such as the granting or hiring of legal representation, the obtainment of evidence in the country of origin, the verification of the conditions in which the legal assistance is exercised, and the observation of the defendant's situation while he is imprisoned, therefore it must be considered within the framework of the minimum guarantees of article 8.[434]

The Court found the same violation in the cases of Bueno Alves[435] and Vélez Loor.[436]

10. DUE AND SPECIAL GUARANTEES FOR CHILDREN[437]

87. The rights of children[438] to justice have exceptional characteristics. Article 19 of the Convention protects children, setting forth: "[e]very minor child has the right to the measures of protection required by his condition as a minor on the part of his family, society, and the state." In addition, Article 5(5) of the Convention establishes that "[m]inors while subject to criminal proceedings shall be separated from adults and brought before specialized tribunals, as speedily as possible, so that they may be treated in accordance with their status as minors."[439]

433 *Ibidem.*
434 *Case of Acosta Calderón v. Ecuador*, para. 125.
435 *Case of Bueno Alves v. Argentina*, para. 116.
436 *Case of Vélez Loor v. Panama*, paras. 158–159.
437 For a comprehensive study of human rights of children, see IACHR, Report on Juvenile justice and human rights in the Americas (pdf version), OEASer.L/V/II. Doc. 78, July 13, 2011.
438 For the Court, "child" refers to any person who has not yet turned 18 years of age. See Advisory Opinion No. 17, para. 42.
439 See in this regard Chapter 4.

88. The situation of children in Latin America has been and still is deplorable. In 1999, the Court pronounced a judgment in the case of Villagrán Morales *et al.* ("Street Children"), victims in this occasion. The State itself had "acknowledged that 84 children had been murdered in the first three months of 1996 and that, according to available information, there had only been seven [convictions]".[440] Some of the children had committed criminal offenses. This prompted the Court to reflect on various aspects of the situation of children regarding the justice system, realizing that what was happening in Guatemala was not an isolated occurrence. The reflections were expressed in an Advisory Opinion on the Juridical Condition and Human Rights of the Child requested by the Inter-American Commission.[441] The request was based in the "various legal frameworks and practices of countries of the Americas" and in certain premises that the States applied. First, since minors are incapable of full discernment, their participation in proceedings to deal with them is "reduced or annulled". Second, the judicial or administrative officials presume this lack of discernment and, invoking the best interest of the child, attach little importance to procedural guarantees. Third, the child's family milieu, such as economic situation and family cohesion, the family's lack of material resources, educational situation and others, are key decision-making factors with respect to treatment when a child or adolescent is placed under criminal or administrative jurisdiction. These premises are the basis "to decide on his or her responsibility and situation in connection with an alleged offense, or to determine measures that affect rights such as the right to a family, right of abode, or right to liberty". The Commission is speaking of children who find themselves in an "irregular situation". This means that they have been abandoned, have dropped out of school, live in a family without financial resources or other similar situations.[442] Such treatment prevents the effective exercise of the rights and guarantees recognized by Articles 8 and 25 of the American Convention and it involves abridgment or restriction of their right to fair trial and to judicial protection. It may also affect the children's rights to humane treatment, to personal liberty, to privacy, and the rights of the family, and may justify the application of measures proper in the punishment of crimes.[443]

89. Most of the Court's Advisory Opinion deals with judicial and administrative proceedings involving children. The Court makes use of other international instruments for its conclusions, the most important being the Convention on the Rights of the Child.[444] It makes clear that the special

---

440 *Case of Street Children v. Guatemala*, para. 183.

441 Advisory Opinion *OC-17/2002* of August 28, 2002.

442 *Ibidem*, para. 3.

443 *Ibidem*, paras. 2 and 3.

444 The Convention on the Rights of the Child (Children's Convention) was adopted and opened for signature in GA Resolution 44/25 of November 20, 1989. It entered into force on September 2, 1990.

measures that States should take would be the same for every child; the difference in age only required a flexible degree of participation.[445]

With regard to administrative procedures, the Court aims at having rules of due process in order to reduce and limit the discretion for the decision-maker, setting thus a few guidelines. It states that protection measures should comply with the law and have as objective to "seek continuation of the child's ties with his or her family group, if this is possible and reasonable". Those participating in decision-making process must have professional competence "to identify advisable measures from the standpoint of the child's interests". The objective must be the re-education and re-socialization of the child. Measures involving deprivation of liberty must be exceptional.[446]

The Opinion addresses judicial procedure in more detail. First, regarding the capacity to be subjected to criminal procedures, the Court notes that "[i]t is generally accepted that children under a certain age lack that capacity. This is a generic legal assessment, one that does not examine the specific conditions of the minors on a case by case basis, but rather excludes them completely from the sphere of criminal justice."[447] Those who may be charged with a crime enjoy the full guarantee of Article 9, that is, there can be no crime and no penalty without a law that precedes the action for which a State decides to try a child.[448] There must be special procedures and special courts to try children, vested with the necessary expertise.[449]

The Court rules out the possibility of subjecting children to procedures of a similar nature when they have not committed any crime but are at risk or endangered, as it was permitted in all Latin American countries until recently (and in some countries even as I write). According to the Court, children may be at risk or endangered "due to destitution, abandonment, extreme poverty or disease"; others because they differ from the generally accepted patterns of behavior. These children do not pass immediately to the "dominion of the State" and its absolute discretion and there must be legislation not allowing this to happen.[450]

90. Guidelines regarding due process follow the rules set forth "mainly but not exclusively, in the Children's Convention, the Beijing Rules, the Tokyo Rules, and the Riyadh Guidelines".[451] They will apply to all judicial and "other proceedings conducted by the State, or under its supervision".[452]

---

445 *Ibidem*, para. 101.
446 *Ibidem*, para. 103.
447 *Ibidem*, para. 105.
448 *Ibidem*, para. 108.
449 *Ibidem*, paras. 109 and 120.
450 *Ibidem*, paras. 110–113.
451 *Ibidem*, para. 116.
452 *Ibidem*, paras. 116–117.

In principle, children enjoy all the guarantees of due process examined in this chapter. However, the court trying a child must consider that "due to his or her age or other circumstances, the child may not be able to critically judge or to reproduce the facts on which he or she is rendering testimony and the consequences of his or her statement, and in this case the judge can and must be especially careful when assessing the statement."[453] The Court follows the Convention on the Rights of the Child when recognizing that the basis of all decisions with respect to children is "the best interest of the child". The Court declares that the phrase "entails that children's development and full enjoyment of their rights must be considered the guiding principles to establish and apply provisions pertaining to all aspects of children's lives".[454]

With this request and the Court's Opinion, children are recognized as holders of human rights instead of objects of protection by the State.[455] However, these acknowledged "holders" need special measures from the State to deal with their problems. The Court finds, to support this conclusion, that:

> There are certain factual inequalities that may be legitimately translated into inequalities of juridical treatment, without this being contrary to justice. Furthermore, said distinctions may be an instrument for the protection of those who must be protected, taking into consideration the situation of greater or lesser weakness or helplessness in which they find themselves.[456]

It is the state's obligation "to adopt all positive measures required to ensure protection of children against mistreatment, whether in their relations with public authorities, or in relations among individuals or with non-governmental entities".[457]

91. The Court has made ample use of its opinion in cases that have come under its jurisdiction. One of them was the case of "Panchito López".[458] Panchito López was a Juvenile Reeducation Institute in Paraguay where children and very young adults were kept to be "re-educated". The premises had been the house of the head of the prison and had grown up in height to allow hundreds of young people. It had undergone two fires and the case was brought to the system after a third one. In Panchito López there was torture and inhuman, cruel and degrading treatment. Most of the children at the Center came from marginal sectors of society. There was overcrowding, children coexisted with adults, and children in preventive detention were mixed with convicts, even adults. In its judgment, the Court often invoked the Opinion it had delivered

453 *Ibidem*, para. 130.
454 *Ibidem*, para. 137.2.
455 *Ibidem*, para. 95.
456 *Ibidem*, para. 46.
457 *Ibidem*, para. 87.
458 *Case of the Juvenile Reeducation Institute "Panchito López" v. Paraguay.*

in 2002, but elaborated on the specifics. It stated that laws and procedure for accused children should have several features, and an important one was the existence of measures to deal "with such children without resorting to judicial procedures". In judicial proceedings, the court should be able "to order a variety of measures, such as psychological counseling for the child while on trial, control over the way the child's testimony is taken, and regulation of the public nature of the proceedings". There should be a margin of discretion throughout the proceedings and those dealing with the case "should be specially qualified or trained in the human rights of the child and child psychology".[459]

92. Judgments in the last decade have stressed the rights of children to access to justice. In the case of Atala Riffo, where the issue was discrimination against a lesbian mother by refusing to give her guardianship over her children, the Court emphasized that children are bearers of human rights and therefore have the right to have a voice in proceedings in which their rights are determined, in the light of Article 12 of the Convention on the Right of the Child.[460] The Committee of that treaty sets forth several points in this regard that are taken up by the Court:

- States cannot assume that a child is incapable of expressing his or her own views;
- it is enough that the child has "sufficient understanding" to enable the child to appropriately form his or her views on the matter;
- the child must have the right to decide whether he or she wants to exercise this right without pressure;
- the exercise of this right requires the child to be informed about "the matters, options and possible decisions to be taken and their consequences by those who are responsible for hearing the child, and by the child's parents or guardian";
- "the capacity of the child [...] has to be assessed in order to give due weight to her or his views, or to communicate to the child the way in which those views have influenced the outcome of the process";
- "children's levels of understanding are not uniformly linked to their biological age", for which reason the maturity of the child must be determined based on "the capacity [...] to express their views on issues in a reasonable and independent manner";[461]
- if the child's capacity shows reasonability and independence, "the decision maker must consider the child's views as a significant factor in the settlement of the issue".[462]

459 *Ibidem*, para. 211.
460 *Case of Atala Riffo v. Chile*, paras. 196–200.
461 *Ibidem*, para. 198, quoting the Committee on the Rights of the Child, General Comment No. 12, The Right to be Heard (CRC/C/GC/1220 July 2009, 25–30).
462 *Ibidem*, para. 200.

In the instant case, the Court also stated that the child may concur with an opinion either directly or through a representative, but "where a conflict of interests arises between the mother and the father, the State must guarantee, as far as possible, that the child's interests are represented by someone outside said conflict".[463] The Court found against the State of Chile because the Chilean Supreme Court had failed to take into consideration "the statements and preferences expressed by the girls and included in the case file" and had not explained the reasons why it had disregarded their wishes. On the contrary, the Supreme Court simply based its decision on the alleged best interest of the three minors.[464] The Court here asserted the right of children to be heard in any proceeding that might affect them.

93. Some relatively recent cases show other facets of the need to protect the child during judicial procedures, such as in the Fornerón case, where the matter of the trial was the guardianship and visiting rights over the daughter of the victim. The mother had surrendered her daughter to a family not complying with the requirements of Argentine law. In addition, the father, who was the victim in this case, had not been consulted. The father requested his daughter's guardianship when she was nine months old.[465] The Court considered that administrative and judicial procedures concerning the protection of the human rights of the child, particularly those legal proceedings related to adoption, guardianship and custody of boys and girls in early childhood, should be handled by the authorities with exceptional diligence and celerity.[466] The Court determined that there was a violation of the reasonable time for trial and a lack of due diligence, as the guardianship trial had lasted three years and the visiting rights trial more than ten.[467] What was important for the Court was that this delay was "a determinant factor for the Superior Court of Justice of the province of Entre Ríos to rule, arguing the best interests of the child, that the legal guardianship of M should be awarded to the couple B-Z", as it was not possible to alter the long-standing *de facto* situation of the child.[468]

In December 1988, Salvador Furlan, a 14-year-old who lived in a poor neighborhood, fell down when attempting to hang from a crossbeam in the grounds of an abandoned military training circuit belonging to the State. The field was not enclosed and it was used by children to play and exercise.[469] The beam, weighing approximately 45–50 kilograms, fell on Salvador's head and knocked him out. The child's father filed suit in a civil court to claim

---

463 *Ibidem*, para. 199.
464 *Ibidem*, para. 208.
465 *Case of Fornerón and daughter v. Argentina*, paras. 79–86.
466 *Ibidem*, para. 51.
467 *Ibidem*, paras. 77 and 104.
468 *Ibidem*, paras. 70 and 73–75.
469 *Case of Furlan et al. v. Argentina*, para. 72.

compensation for damages following his son's accident, which resulted in him becoming mentally disabled.[470] During this trial, the Juvenile Defender's Office did not participate, which was a legal rule in Argentina.[471] The Court found that the lack of representation was a violation of the child's right to access to justice.[472] When Salvador Furlán reached adulthood, he also had a right to a defender as a mentally disabled person, since that was the law in Argentina, but he did not have this representation either.[473] Furthermore, in order to receive the compensation accorded to him after almost ten years, his father had to start an administrative procedure to have the judgment enforced, and that lasted around two years.[474] Following its case law, the Court found a violation of Article 25 in relation to the enforcement procedure instead of Article 8. This notwithstanding, it decided that the time spent in the proceedings for enforcement should be counted for the examination of the delay under Article 8, because it considered "that the main purpose for which the alleged victim filed a civil suit was to obtain compensation for damages; therefore, for the purposes of analyzing the reasonable term, said proceedings cannot be considered completed until that purpose is materialized". The enforcement procedure, in the Court's view, was thus "part of the proceedings".[475] Its length constituted a violation of Article 8.

In the case Mendoza *et al.*, several children were sentenced to life imprisonment or perpetual reclusion. The Court considered that "differences between children and adults, as regards both their physical and psychological development, and their emotional and educational needs, must be taken into account for the existence of a separate juvenile criminal justice system". The principle of specialization requires this, as well as specialized measures or punishments.[476] Not only is an appropriate legal framework necessary but so are public policies adapted to international standards.[477]

94. In August 2014, the Court issued an Advisory Opinion on the rights of migrant children. The Opinion borrows from its case law regarding migrants and children and from the Convention on the Rights of the Child and the interpretation of the Committee on the Rights of the Child.[478] One section is

470 *Ibidem*, para. 78.
471 *Ibidem*, paras. 237 and 240. Article 59 of the Argentine Civil Code establishes that "apart from the necessary representatives, minors are jointly represented by the Juvenile Defender's Office which shall be empowered in all types of proceedings, judicial or extrajudicial, in contentious and non-contentious proceedings, in which minors are defendants or respondents, or in proceedings concerning their property, under penalty of nullity of any act or proceeding which would be conducted without the minor's participation."
472 *Ibidem*, paras. 241–242.
473 *Ibidem*, para. 243.
474 *Ibidem*, para. 148.
475 *Ibidem*, paras. 149 and 151.
476 *Case of Mendoza et al. v. Argentina*, para. 146.
477 *Ibidem*, para. 151.
478 Advisory Opinion *OC-21/14* of August 19, 2014.

destined to examine the guarantees of due process applicable in immigration proceedings involving children. The Court examines the right to be notified of the existence of proceedings, and of the decision adopted herein, and stresses its importance when the migrant is a child, stating that the right "extends to every kind of procedure that involves them".[479] It also deems that children need trained personnel to communicate with them and those who handle the administrative procedures (a judge or a special official) must be qualified to operate having the best interest of the child in mind.[480] The Court also reiterates that children have the right to be heard in all parts of the proceedings, as established in General Comment No. 12 of the Committee on the Rights of the Child.[481] This is particularly important for unaccompanied child migrants. The State has to guarantee "that the proceedings are conducted in an environment that is not intimidating, hostile, insensitive, or inappropriate to the child's age, and that the staff responsible for receiving the declaration are appropriately trained so that the child feels respected and safe when expressing her or his views in an appropriate physical, mental, and emotional environment".[482] A translator or interpreter has to be provided to them free of charge.[483] They must have effective access to communicate with consular authorities and to consular assistance. In light of the Convention on the Rights of the Child, the consular official is under the obligation "to safeguard the interests of the child, in the sense of ensuring that any administrative or judicial decisions adopted by the receiving country has evaluated and taken into consideration the child's best interest".[484] States have to offer free specialized legal representation in all proceedings, both in the field of migrant law and in the special treatment of children regarding their age.[485] In the case of unaccompanied or separated children, States must appoint a guardian who is a specialist in childcare and maintain this guardianship, if necessary, until the child reaches the age of majority.[486] There must be special care not to appoint a guardian who might be in conflict with the interests of the child; in principle, an adult family member or non-primary caretaker, if the child is separated from the family. There must be review mechanisms to monitor the actions of the guardian.[487] All other requirements of Article 8 should be applied to the immigration procedure, with some nuances. For example, the right to appeal the decision will have to be carried out before a judge and the appeal must automatically suspend the effects of the decision that is being appealed.[488]

---

479 *Ibidem*, para. 117.
480 *Ibidem*, para. 121.
481 *Ibidem*, para. 122.
482 *Ibidem*, para. 123.
483 *Ibidem*, paras. 124 and 125.
484 *Ibidem*, para. 127.
485 *Ibidem*, para. 131.
486 *Ibidem*, paras. 132–134.
487 *Ibidem*, paras. 135 and 136.
488 *Ibidem*, paras. 140–142.

Because of the "particular degree of harm that this type of proceedings could have on a child", the requirement that the proceedings comply with the requirement of being carried out within a reasonable time is stressed. The Court adds that, this notwithstanding, the right of the child to be heard will prevail over the speed of the proceedings.[489]

95. In the case of the expulsion of persons of Haitian origin from the Dominican Republic, the Court applied Advisory Opinion 18 on Migrants and Advisory Opinion 21. There were a number of children among those expelled[490] and the Court equated the situation of those expelled with that of the migrants. The Court found a violation of Article 8 because the State had not presented any evidence of the application both of the internal rules for expulsion and the guarantees set forth in Article 8.[491]

---

489 *Ibidem*, para. 143.

490 *Case of Expelled Dominican and Haitian persons v. Dominican Republic.*

491 *Ibidem*, para. 393.

CHAPTER 7

PRINCIPLE OF LEGALITY, FREEDOM FROM *EX POST FACTO* LAWS, AND RIGHT TO COMPENSATION FOR MISCARRIAGE OF JUSTICE

Article 9

Freedom from Ex Post Facto Laws

> *No one shall be convicted of any act or omission that did not constitute a criminal offense, under the applicable law, at the time it was committed. A heavier penalty shall not be imposed than the one that was applicable at the time the criminal offense was committed. If subsequent to the commission of the offense the law provides for the imposition of a lighter punishment, the guilty person shall benefit therefrom.*

Article 10

Right to Compensation

> *Every person has the right to be compensated in accordance with the law in the event that he has been sentenced by a final judgment through a miscarriage of justice.*

1. THE PRINCIPLE OF LEGALITY: *NULLUM CRIMEN SINE LEGE*

1. Article 9 of the American Convention enshrines a basic principle of criminal law the Latin wording of which is *nullum crimen et nulla poena sine lege*. This constitutes "the principle of legality" explained by the Court in Berenson as follows: "The definition of an act as an unlawful act and the determination of its legal effects must precede the conduct of the individual who is alleged to have violated it; because, before a behavior is defined as a crime, it is not unlawful for penal effects".[1] It is a fundamentally important principle for the protection of several human rights, leading the Convention to establish it as an international

1 *Case of De la Cruz Flores v. Peru*, para. 104. See also *Case of J. v. Peru*, paras. 278–279.

State obligation that cannot be suspended, even in an emergency situation.[2] This provision also enshrines the principle that a convict must receive a lesser punishment when a lesser punishment is established by law after the commission of a crime.

Like Article 8, Article 9 of the Convention applies to all criminal convictions, regardless of significance or scope. However, it does not apply to procedural law, because that law applies at the moment a procedural act is carried out, independently of the date of the commission of the offense. In the case of Liakat Alit Alibut, the Court relied heavily on case law of Latin American States and of the European Court.[3] The Inter-American Court made an exception to the rule of immediate application of the new procedural norms: the principle could be applied if the procedure had "an impact on the classification of acts or omissions that at the time of commission were not criminal" or if it leads to "the imposition of a penalty that is more serious than the one in place at the time of the commission of the crime".[4] In the case itself, there had been no violation of Article 9.[5]

The Inter-American Court referred to the scope of Article 9 in the case of Baena Ricardo *et al.*, which addressed the application of judicial guarantees in the area of administrative sanctions. The Court found that administrative sanctions, "as well as penal sanctions, constitute an expression of the State's punitive power and that, on occasions, the nature of the former is similar to that of the latter".[6] It found that the principle of legality and freedom from *ex post facto* criminal laws "govern the actions of all bodies of the State in their respective fields of competence".[7] Referring then to the principle of legality, it added that the principle of legality was also applicable to these administrative sanctions.[8]

The law must be a law both formally and materially.[9] In civil law countries, it is easy to verify that a requirement for laws to be formally in place has been met, given that those countries have constitutions that precisely establish the steps that must be taken in order for a law to take effect. This ensures that the legislative organ, which represents the sovereign, who has the final power

---

2 ACHR, Article 27.

3 *Case of Liakat Ali Alibux v. Suriname*. See, for example, footnotes 80 and 81 and then 82–84 of the judgment.

4 *Ibidem*, paras. 69–70.

5 *Ibidem*, para. 75.

6 *Case of Baena Ricardo et al. v. Panama*, para. 106.

7 *Ibidem*, para. 107. See also *Case of Canese v. Paraguay*, para. 176.

8 *Case of Ricardo Baena v. Panama*, para. 106, quoted also in *López Mendoza v. Venezuela*, para. 183.

9 "Formal" refers to a law passed following the proceedings establish in the domestic legal system; "material" has to do with the content of the law, which must be general and thus not discriminatory. See Chapter 1, para. 40.

to make the law, makes the decision on what constitutes a criminal act.[10] In countries with a common law system, on the other hand, a law can be contained in a legal precedent that has emerged from practice. It would be the responsibility of the courts to apply it and often to develop the law through specific cases.

The requirement that a law should exist establishing an act as criminal has another purpose: that of informing people that the commission of a certain act would violate the country's criminal laws. From this, it follows that the definition of criminal conduct must contain all the elements necessary for a person to be able to know with precision what is prohibited; vague descriptions do not satisfy the requirements of Article 9 of the Convention. In defining prohibited conduct, the law must therefore consider this. The European Court of Human Rights has developed case law in this respect, indicating that the law must be accessible to individuals and must describe foreseeable conducts.[11] Under this line of thinking, the European Court used the so-called "foreseeability analysis", which takes into account three standards for determining whether a regulation is sufficiently foreseeable, namely: (i) the context of the regulation under review; (ii) the forum of application for which the regulation was created; and (iii) the status of the persons which the regulation addresses.[12] In contrast to a written law, the specific terms of a law established through precedent are harder to determine, as it is possible for such laws to develop gradually through case law. This can cause problems for the application of the principle in question. The European Court of Human Rights has placed a limit on this, on finding that the clarification by a judge of the existence and provisions of a law is permissible "provided that the resultant development is consistent with the essence of the offense and could reasonably be foreseen".[13]

Given that there can be no crime without a law specifically defining the conduct, it is clear that the law must be interpreted restrictively: there can be no crime by analogy. Consequently, international oversight can and should review the application of domestic law if an accusation of a violation of Article 9 invokes the application of a crime as defined by analogy.

Contrary to Article 15(1) of the International Covenant on Civil and Political Rights (ICCPR) and Article 7(1) of the European Convention, Article 9 of the Convention does not specify that actions or omissions can be classified as criminal by both domestic and international law. Rather, it uses the expression "according to applicable law". During the drafting of the Convention, the

---

10 In this sense, see *OC-6/86*, which interpreted the expression "laws" found in Article 30 of the Convention.

11 P. van Dijk *et al.* (eds.), *Theory and Practice of the European Convention on Human Rights*, 4th edition, Intersentia, Antwerp/Oxford, 2006, pp. 653–656.

12 *Case of López Mendoza v. Venezuela*, para. 199.

13 *Ibidem*, p. 482, citing the cases *S.W. v. United Kingdom* and *C.R. v. United Kingdom*, judgment of November 22, 1995 (A-355-B and A-335-C, respectively). See also, more recently, *Kononov v. Latvia* (Application 36376/04), judgment of May 17, 2010, para. 185.

delegate from Colombia, who proposed placing a reference to international law in the text, criticized this; the president of the Commission replied that the reference was not necessary given that the expression "applicable law" covered both domestic and international law. However, the delegate from Argentina argued that "the suggestion from the delegate from Colombia would be an interesting aspiration for the future, but the approval of a minimum number of acceptable articles must be achieved".[14] For this reason, one could assume that he felt that "applicable law" meant only domestic law. Colombia's suggestion was not voted upon, and there was no more debate on the subject. Given the prior examples of the ICCPR and the European Convention, as well as the wording of the provision itself, it seems reasonable to conclude that despite what the delegate from Argentina had said, the expression "applicable law" includes both domestic and international law. This interpretation raises the possibility that a crime not defined by domestic laws can be punished if it exists as a crime under international law, making use of universal jurisdiction.[15] However, I find it problematic that a State tries and convicts a person for having committed a crime on the sole definition in an international treaty; the foreseeability seems to prevent this. Of course, it is possible that a State be found responsible for not having provided in the domestic law a definition of an action that amounts to a crime in the treaty. For example, the Convention against Torture and Other Cruel, Inhuman, or Degrading Punishment mandates the State to typify torture in domestic law; if a State does not comply, it would be responsible for a violation of Article 4 of this Convention.

2. The Inter-American Court has addressed the requirement that criminal activity be specifically defined in judgments handed down in cases against Peru over the application of the Decrees Law on treason and terrorism. In the case of Loayza Tamayo, without alluding to Article 9, the Court criticized the fact that Peru's decree-laws 25.659 and 25.475 referred to conduct not strictly described, sufficiently unclear such that "they may be interpreted similarly within both crimes, in the view of the Ministry of the Interior and the corresponding judges and, as in the case under consideration, of the 'Police (DINCOTE) itself'", meaning that they could be understood just as easily to be part of one crime as of another.[16] In the case of Castillo Petruzzi *et al.*, the Court introduced on its own initiative an examination of a possible violation of Article 9 of the Convention. It indicated that the crime of treason was recognized by the parties as "aggravated terrorism", adding that in drafting definitions of crimes, strict and unambiguous terms must be used that clearly define criminal conduct, giving full range to

14 Inter-American Specialized Conference on Human Rights, San José, Costa Rica, November 7–22, 1969, *Minutes and Documents*, General Secretariat, OAS, Washington DC, 1979, p. 206.

15 See M. Nowak, *UN Covenant on Civil and Political Rights. CCPR Commentary,* N.P. Engel Publisher, Kehl/Strasbourg/Arlington, 1993, p. 276.

16 *Case of Loayza Tamayo v. Peru*, para. 68.

the principle of criminal legality. This means a clear definition of the conduct in question that establishes its elements and allows them to be differentiated from activity that is not punishable or from noncriminal illegal activity.[17] In the case of Cantoral Benavides, the Court reiterated this position, clarifying that Article 2 of Decree-Law 25.475 and Article 1(a) of Decree-Law 25.659 did contain definitions of the crimes of terrorism and of treason. However, the provisions "do not clearly describe the criminal acts in question, the elements used in their commission, the objects or assets against which they are directed, and the impact they have on society". The Court added that, even though with a different penalty, "the inclusion of such broad methods of participation in the commission of the corresponding crime [established in Article 2…] alters the definition of the perpetrator of treason against the fatherland, bringing this crime and the crime of terrorism so close together that they become one."[18] In De la Cruz Flores, the Court also found that the principle of legality had been infringed. There were several reasons, of which two appear to be more directly linked with Article 9. First, the national court had taken into account "as elements that gave rise to criminal liability, membership in a terrorist organization and failure to comply with the reporting obligation, but only applying an article that did not define these behaviors". Second, it had not specified "which of the behaviors established in Article 4 of Decree-Law No. 25,475 had been committed by the alleged victim in order to be found guilty of the crime".[19] In the case of García Asto and Urcesino Ramírez, the Court found that two criminal offenses in Peru, "collaboration with terrorism and membership in and affiliation with terrorist organizations", were "mutually exclusive and incompatible" and yet had been applied to the same conduct. This was found incompatible with Article 9.[20] In the case of J. v. Peru, the Court distinguished between the ambiguity of the law and the conduct of a trial, where J. had been accused of the crime of terrorism, aggravated terrorism and advocacy on the basis of various legal norms. The Court emphasized that the description of criminal offenses required the use of strict and univocal terms. It added that "[a]ny ambiguity in the wording of the definition of offenses gives rise to doubts and opens the way to the discretion of the authorities".[21] In the case, J. had been subject to the lack of specificity and vagueness of the conduct attributed to her during the trial. The court's demeanor had affected the capacity of J. to a proper defense, but surprisingly did not constitute a violation of Article 9. Ms. J. was rather a victim of the violation of Article 8.[22]

---

17 *Case of Castillo Petruzzi et al. v. Peru*, paras. 118 and 121. See also *Case of Pacheco Teruel et al. v. Honduras*, para. 105.

18 *Case of Cantoral Benavides v. Peru*, paras. 155, 157–158.

19 *Case of De la Cruz Flores v. Peru*, para. 102.

20 *Case of García Asto and Urcesino Ramírez v. Peru*, paras. 199–200.

21 *Case of J. v. Peru*, para. 287.

22 *Case of J. v Peru*, paras. 278, 284, 289 and 295.

There was a different decision in the case of Lori Berenson. Lori Berenson was tried twice in Peru, the first time by a military court, and the second time by an ordinary court. The second time, she was charged with the commission of "collaboration with terrorism". The Court had found in an earlier case, Castillo Petruzzi, that terrorism and aggravated terrorism or treason were incompatible with Article 9. In this case, it found that the crime of "collaboration with terrorism" is an autonomous crime, different to terrorism and sufficiently precise in terms of its definition; therefore, it was compatible with Article 9. This decision was taken in spite of the Court having recognized that "[e]vidently the assessment of the existence, when applicable, of acts of collaboration, must be made in relation to the definition of terrorism".[23]

In the case of Norín *et al.* v. Chile, the Court returned to the matter of terrorism, insisting that there must be a necessary distinction between terrorist offenses and ordinary crimes. This is essential as terrorist offenses usually receive a higher penalty and sometimes fewer procedural guarantees that may affect the right to defense, as was the case in Chile.[24] The Court deemed it important for the anti-terrorist law to not be applied when the criminal offense could be tried as an ordinary one (in the case, arson).[25] Furthermore, although the intention to cause terror among the people was a decisive element of the crime, the Chilean anti-terrorist law "presumed the aim of producing terror to the people in general unless there is proof to the contrary when the offence is committed through certain means, among which explosives or firing devices". The Court found that this constituted a violation of the principle of legality and of the right to the presumption of innocence as well.[26]

In the case of Fermín Ramírez, the issue was that in Article 132 of the Criminal Code of Guatemala the crime of murder is punished with imprisonment of 25–50 years or with the death penalty. The latter penalty will apply "'if a greater dangerousness of the agent is revealed', which will be determined according to 'the circumstances of the act and the occasion, the way in which it was carried out and the determining motives'".[27] The Court found that this assessment "implies the judge's appreciation with regard to the possibility that the defendant will commit criminal acts in the future, that is, it adds to the accusation for the acts committed, the prediction of future acts that will probably occur".[28] Consequently, the Court found that this subjective criterion is, among other violations, "not compatible with the freedom from ex post facto law and, therefore, contrary to the Convention".[29]

---

23 *Case of Lori Berenson v. Peru*, para. 127. See my dissenting opinion on Article 9 in that same judgment.

24 *Case of Norín et al. v. Chile*, para. 163.

25 *Ibidem*, para. 180.

26 *Ibidem*, paras. 170–174.

27 *Case of Fermín Ramirez v. Guatemala*, para. 92.

28 *Ibidem*, para. 95.

29 *Ibidem*, paras. 95 and 98.

The Court has asserted that in cases of disappearance there is no violation of Article 9 if the author is tried according to a definition of disappearance legally formulated after the disappearance has begun. Since disappearances are a continuous violation, the crime is being committed until the person or the body is found.[30]

In the case of Mohamed, the Court examined the principle of legality with respect to an offense of negligence. Mr. Mohamed, a bus driver, had been convicted of manslaughter for having run over a person who died as a consequence of this action.[31] The Court considered that such an act was of minor unlawfulness as its typical elements are "defined in a generic manner" what requires from the judge to identify the corresponding duty of care "infringed by the defendant's active behavior (imprudence) or omission (negligence), as a determining factor in bringing about the harmful result of the juridical right protected".[32] However, after these considerations, the Court did not deem it appropriate to decide whether there had been a violation of Article 9, because there were criminal issues that had to be examined by a higher court, since the Inter-American Court had declared that Mr. Mohamed had the right to appeal.[33]

A different situation obtained in the case of Argüelles *et al.* The issue in that case was the refusal to apply a statute of limitation to members of the Armed Forces who had committed fraud and forgery for their personal financial gain. The trial had been first conducted by the military courts and, after a change of law, by the ordinary courts. The alleged victims argued that the statute of limitations had to be applied, since the apparent continuation of the trial in an ordinary court was not accepted in the military criminal procedure as an action to interrupt the term to apply that statute. This would constitute a violation of Article 9. The State considered that the term had not passed because the change of court was part of the sequel to the trial. Another argument of the alleged victims was that the decision not to accept the statute of limitations resulted in a more repressive punishment. The Court did not agree with either argument and found no violation of Article 9.[34]

3. Article 9 also prohibits the application of a law *post facto*. In the case of Baena Ricardo *et al.*, in the view of the State a non-criminal case, the Court also found that a violation of the principle of legality had taken place, first, because characterizing a crime as "participation in acts contrary to democracy and the constitutional order", as Law 25 did, was "a very broad and imprecise concept of

---

30 *Case of Tiu Tojin v. Guatemala*, para. 87 and *Case of Gómez Lund et al. (Guerrilla de Araguaia) v. Brazil*, para. 177.

31 *Case of Mohamed v. Argentina*, para. 39.

32 *Ibidem*, paras. 134 and 137.

33 *Ibidem*, para. 140.

34 *Case of Argüelles et al. v. Argentina*, paras. 205–214.

possible unlawful conduct".[35] Article 2 of that law established that the executive, via the Cabinet Counsel, would be the one to determine "which actions would be considered attacks on democracy and constitutional order for the purposes of 'applying the administrative punishments of dismissal'". The Inter-American Court did not comment on the fact that the law would allow a non-legislative body to define the criminality of an act. Rather, it found a violation of the principle of non-retroactivity. The ruling finding that the abrupt collective public labor strikes was an attack on the aforementioned values was made long after the facts that were punished had taken place.[36] In addition, Law 25 itself had entered into force on December 14, 1990, although the facts took place on the fourth of that month, and established that it would apply not only to "those who *participate* in 'actions against Democracy and the Constitutional Order,' but also to those who *participated* in those actions",[37] thus clearly making it retroactive. The Court found a violation of Article 9.

2. *NULLUM POENA SINE LEGE*

4. A punishment cannot exist without a law that establishes it. In the European system, Van Dijk and Van Hoof argue that it is not necessary for a law to define a punishment with exactitude. Rather, they argue that it is enough for it to indicate, for example, a maximum punishment, or the nature of the punishment without specifying a maximum. If there is no maximum punishment, in order to prohibit the application of a sentence that is stricter than the punishment allowed for at the time a crime is committed, it should be understood that what must be applied "is the penalty which is usually inflicted within the legal system concerned, or which in any event was reasonable to be expected for the offender".[38] The Inter-American Court addressed punishment in the case of Baena Ricardo *et al.*, in which it said that "the categorization of an act as unlawful and the establishment of the subsequent juridical consequences must pre-date the conduct of the individual considered to be in violation".[39] This is then stricter than the European interpretation. There is still no case law on whether a law must establish something beyond the mere nature of the punishment.[40]

---

35 *Case of Baena Ricardo et al. v. Panama*, para. 108.
36 *Ibidem*, para. 114.
37 *Ibidem*, paras. 109–110.
38 P. van Dijk *et al.*, *supra* n. 11, pp. 656–657.
39 *Case of Baena Ricardo et al. v. Panama*, para. 106.
40 On this, see J. Mera, "Adecuación del Derecho Penal chileno a las exigencias de los derechos humanos", in C. Medina and J. Mera (eds.), *Sistema jurídico y derechos humanos. El derecho nacional y las obligaciones internacionales de Chile en materia de derechos humanos*, Universidad Diego Portales, special publications series No. L, Santiago, Chile, 1996, pp. 343–475 (389).

5. International law establishes certain rules with regard to the establishment of punishments. To start with, it bans cruel, inhuman or degrading punishments[41] and imprisonment due to debts.[42] In addition, a punishment always constitutes a restriction of a human right, normally, the right to personal freedom, or the right to property if fines are applied. The State does not have absolute discretion to establish a punishment, as it must abide by the requirement of proportionality.[43] Article 4 of the Convention is in this sense clear for the application of the death penalty, which requires that a crime be among "the most serious of crimes". Although strictly speaking this is not yet reality, the existing limitations on restrictions on human rights must apply to the regulation of punishments. It must be determined, for example, whether the punishment is appropriate for achieving its objective. In the case of deprivation of liberty, this objective includes not only the protection of the rights of victims but also the "reform and social readaptation of the prisoners".[44] One could expect this to develop further in the future. Research into the effects of punishments on criminals, especially imprisonment, could lead to a change in culture and legal perspective.

6. In the case of Vélez Loor, a migrant in Panama, the Court found a violation of Article 9 because the victim had been imposed a penalty that was different to that contained in the law. He had re-entered Panama after a deportation order and the penalty for that conduct was two years of agricultural work in the Penal Colony of Coiba. However, Mr. Vélez Loor was given a two-year prison sentence in an ordinary jail. The Court found "that the application of an administrative penalty or sanction, materially different to the one provided in the law, is in breach of the principle *of freedom from ex post facto laws*, given that it is based on extensive interpretations of criminal law".[45]

The foreseeability of the penalty set forth by the law was examined specifically in the case of López Mendoza related to some of certain political rights. Venezuela had barred Mr. López Mendoza from holding public office and prevented him from participating in regional elections, all this in violation of his judicial guarantees.[46] The issue of interest here was whether the sanction of disqualification imposed on Mr. López Mendoza by a decision of an administrative body and the subsequent failure to register his candidacy for an elective office was compatible with the American Convention. The national court had imposed a fine at the end of the proceedings, but after that, the victim had been disqualified by the comptroller from holding public office for a set period. The victim alleged that there had been no set date in the law to decide on an

41 ACHR, Article 5(2). On this point, see Chapter 3, section 2.
42 ACHR, Article 7(7).
43 On proportionality of punishments, see J. Mera, *supra* n. 40, p. 394.
44 ACHR, Article 5(6).
45 *Case of Vélez Loor v. Panama*, paras. 85 and 187.
46 *Case of López Mendoza v. Venezuela*, para. 2.

addition to the fine; that constituted an uncertainty for the person, because there was no foreseeability in the penalty to be imposed. The Court considered that granting some form of discretion with regard to the penalty is not inconsistent with the degree of foreseeability that the regulation should bear. This required that "the scope of discretion and the manner in which it should be exercised is indicated with sufficient clarity so as to provide adequate protection from arbitrary interference." In the case, there were standards, so the discretion had sufficient limits.[47] However, the Court found a lack in the domestic law in that after the declaration of responsibility there was no set date within which the Comptroller General had to exercise his powers to apply a sanction. There had been a decision of the Political-Administrative Chamber in which it attempted to fill this regulatory gap with the statute of limitations of administrative actions, finding that the power would cease after the time set for the statute of limitations elapsed; this was five years. The Court found that this was not an appropriate solution because of the lack of foreseeability, adding that a period of five years was too long for a person to wait for the application of the penalty. The Court thus found this "incompatible with the requirement that a sanctioning proceeding be concluded at the time the corresponding responsibility is determined, in such a way that the accused does not wait for a period that is too broad to determine the type of sanction that will be imposed for responsibility that has already been determined".[48]

3. THE MOST FAVORABLE LAW

7. In the case of Canese, the Court dealt with the most favorable law to be applied. Canese had been convicted and penalized and he had requested for four years the application of a new Penal Code containing more favorable norms that those that had been applied to him.[49] The Court understood that most favorable norms would be those that "decriminalize a behavior which was previously considered an offense, or create a new motive for justification or innocence, or an impediment to the effectiveness of a penalty". It clarified that this was not an exhaustive list. In addition, it emphasized that "the principle of retroactivity is applicable to laws enacted before the judgment was delivered and also during its execution, because the Convention does not establish a limit in this respect."[50] In addition to prohibiting the imposition of a punishment that is more serious than the one allowed at the time a crime is committed, the American Convention also establishes that "[i]f subsequent to the commission of the offense the law provides

---

47 *Ibidem*, para. 202.
48 *Ibidem*, para. 205.
49 *Case of Canese v. Paraguay*, para. 186.
50 *Ibidem*, para. 179.

for the imposition of a lighter punishment, the guilty person shall benefit therefrom". When the change in the punishment is one not only of severity but also of nature, such as for example from deprivation of liberty to a fine, the problem arises of deciding which punishment is harsher. The Court decided that the national courts "should have compared the most favorable aspects of the new Code applicable to the specific case and determined whether the sanctions imposed on Mr. Canese should be reduced, or whether only the sanction of a fine should be imposed".[51] At this point, with the advanced development of the idea that certain punishments can replace deprivation of liberty, the problem can take on new dimensions. The Inter-American Court has not yet had any opportunity to rule on this.

4. RIGHT TO COMPENSATION FOR MISCARRIAGE OF JUSTICE

8. Article 10 of the Convention presents us with problems of interpretation, as it is particularly cryptic. The *travaux préparatoires* could be useful for clarifying the meaning of the provision. In reality, however, it does not contribute much. Originally, the wording of Article 10 was very confusing, as it stated that:

> All persons who have been deprived of liberty illegally or due to a miscarriage of justice will receive indemnity for the losses suffered as a result of the conviction and the deprivation of liberty except in the cases in which the convicted individual contributed to making the miscarriage of justice possible.[52]

In its comments on the draft, the Argentine government did not criticize the wording but rather recommended that it should be eliminated, arguing that the provision represented "an aspiration for the future".[53] The comments of the Dominican Republic focused more on the content, indicating that it would agree "with this type of liability as long as it is understood that the error must be equivalent to an abusive application of the law, gross error, or an act of authority exercised in bad faith or with reprehensible negligence". It added that "the term 'miscarriage of justice' could include any case overturned on appeal, including cases in which the guilt of the accused is overturned for procedural or technical reasons".[54] For its part, Ecuador suggested replacing the text with the text found

51 *Ibidem*, para. 186.

52 Specialized Conference, *supra* n. 14, p. 17.

53 *Ibidem*, p. 46.

54 *Ibidem*, p. 50. In the comments, it also proposed an alternative text: "All persons who have been unjustly convicted and imprisoned will have the right to appeal to a court and another authority and to receive an indemnity as long as their convictions have been annulled and none of the actions for which they were effectively accused were committed, or the actions related to the accusation did not constitute a criminal offense and the individual in question did not cause or contribute to making the prosecution possible due to misconduct or negligence." (*Ibidem*, p. 60).

in Article 14(6) of the ICCPR,[55] which would have broken the link that existed up to that point between miscarriage of justice and deprivation of liberty. During the discussion of the text, the Venezuelan delegate stated that his country would not accept granting an indemnity for miscarriages of justice, while the delegates from Honduras, Argentina, Nicaragua, Mexico and Chile opposed the approval of the text on indemnities. The delegate from the United States also expressed concern at the wording of the provision, concern which Guatemala shared. The discussion ended by appointing a working group to study the article.[56] That working group later submitted a new text, which was itself replaced during the discussion (the content of which was not placed on the record) by another text submitted by Mexico. In the end, that was the text that was approved.[57]

In sum, one can conclude from the debate that the majority of the delegates who took part in drawing up Article 10 of the draft Convention sought to limit indemnity requirements in order to prevent abuse and an enormous financial cost to the State. However, they did not make this sufficiently clear.

9. In order to aid in the interpretation of the provision, it is also useful to take into consideration the fact that similar rules can be found in Article 14(6) of the ICCPR[58] and in Article 3 of Protocol 7 of the European Convention.[59] Both are drawn up in more detail; the text from the European system is also accompanied by an explanatory memorandum to help resolve possible problems of interpretation. For example, the memorandum indicates that Article 3 does not apply when an accusation has been dismissed or when the accused has been declared innocent, whether by a first instance court or an appeals court; the

55 *Ibidem*, p. 105. The text is as follows: "When a final judgment to convict has been subsequently overturned or when the convicted individual has been pardoned based on the production or discovery of evidence demonstrating a miscarriage of justice, the person who has suffered from a punishment as a result of the judgment shall be indemnified in keeping with the law unless it is demonstrated that the failure to reveal the unknown fact was in whole or in part attributable to that person."

56 The discussion indicates that the United States submitted written comments on the provision, but those comments are not included in the Specialized Conference, *supra* n. 14, pp. 207–209.

57 *Ibidem*, p. 250.

58 The text is as follows: "When a final judgment to convict has been subsequently overturned or when the convicted individual has been pardoned based on the production or discovery of evidence demonstrating a miscarriage of justice, the person who has suffered from a punishment as a result of the judgment shall be indemnified in keeping with the law unless it is demonstrated that the failure to reveal the unknown fact was in whole or in part attributable to that person".

59 The text of Article 3 reads as follows: "When a person has by a final decision been convicted of a criminal offence and when subsequently his conviction has been reversed, or he has been pardoned, on the ground that a new or a newly discovered fact shows conclusively that there has been a miscarriage of justice, the person who has suffered punishment as a result of such conviction shall be compensated according to the law or the practice of the state concerned, unless it proved that the non-disclosure of the unknown fact in time is wholly or partly attributable to him."

provision only applies when the conviction has been overturned or a pardon has been granted because *new or recently discovered facts* demonstrate conclusively that a miscarriage of justice has taken place, meaning "some serious failure in the judicial process involving grave prejudice to the convicted person". Domestic law is responsible for establishing the proceedings for determining whether a miscarriage of justice has taken place.[60]

10. The first requirement for applying Article 10 is that a final judgment to convict must have been issued, meaning a sentence has been handed down with regard to which no recourse remains for the convicted individual.[61] However, the provision says nothing about how an individual convicted in a final judgment can make use of Article 10 and before which authorities when seeking a decision as to whether the conviction was the result of a "miscarriage of justice". The discussion and the precedent of the similar provision found in the ICCPR lead to the conclusion that the "judicial error" must have been made in an authorized State ruling. Thus in order for the right enshrined in Article 10 of the Convention to function, national legal systems must establish the right to a remedy that allows for the individual convicted due to an error to file a related claim. This is the first State obligation arising from the article.

The ICCPR and the European Convention provide that the error may also be identified as such in a pardon, a power that always falls to the executive branch. A pardon, however, is an act of grace that does not revoke the ruling to convict. Should there have been an error in a ruling on the guilt of a person, it does not seem appropriate for the ruling to maintain any sort of validity. It therefore seems more appropriate to require a remedy that allows for the erroneous judgment to be revoked.

11. Article 10 of the Convention appears to be broader than Article 14(6) of the ICCPR and Article 3 of Protocol 7 of the European Convention. This because it does not establish that in order for an indemnity to be required, the revocation of a judgment or the pardon must have been based on new facts or facts that were discovered after the judgment. It is likely, however, that this is how the article would be interpreted should it be raised for the Court's consideration, as it seems to be the most reasonable interpretation. As already mentioned, it is the responsibility of the domestic legal system to decide how the right is to function. In many legal systems, there is a judicial review remedy that establishes

60 The Memorandum (Doc. H(84)5) is cited in D.J. Harris, M. O'Boyle and C. Warbrick, *Law of the European Convention on Human Rights*, Butterworths, London/Dublin/ Edinburgh, 1995, p. 568.

61 This coincides with the European system's provision. The European system's Protocol 7 explanatory memorandum indicates that the judgment must be irrevocable, that is, there must not be any ordinary remedy available, whether because the party has exhausted all remedies or because the time period for accessing the remedies has expired (see *ibidem*).

the circumstances that can be invoked in order to access it. The circumstances generally follow the provisions of the ICCPR and the European Convention, as they refer to the existence of a fact that is decisive for proving the error and that has taken place or come to light following the conviction.[62]

Finally, the second obligation that arises from Article 10 of the Convention is the obligation to establish laws setting forth the right to an indemnity once it has been determined that a miscarriage of justice has taken place.

12. As can be noted, space for interpreting and clarifying the provisions contained in Article 10 is vast and the work of the body that applies it will have to make use of international case law in order to give it content that is reasonable and favorable to persons. The Inter-American Court has not so far had any case on this provision.

62 The remedy of review is obviously compatible with the provisions of Article 8(4) (enshrining the principle of *non bis in idem*) given that its purpose is to correct a situation to the benefit of the convicted individual.

CHAPTER 8
RIGHT TO JUDICIAL PROTECTION

Article 25

1. *Everyone has the right to simple and prompt recourse, or any other effective recourse, to a competent court or tribunal for protection against acts that violate his fundamental rights recognized by the constitution or laws of the state concerned or by this Convention, even though such violation may have been committed by persons acting in the course of their official duties.*
2. *The States Parties undertake:*
   a. *to ensure that any person claiming such remedy shall have his rights determined by the competent authority provided for by the legal system of the state;*
   b. *to develop the possibilities of judicial remedy; and*
   c. *to ensure that the competent authorities shall enforce such remedies when granted.*

1. INTRODUCTION

1. The existence of human rights enshrined in the American Convention, constituting a minimum standard that State Parties must respect and ensure, requires the establishment of mechanisms for the supervision and protection of those rights. It is primarily the State that must establish effective domestic remedies for protecting rights, without prejudice to the existence of subsidiary international supervisory mechanisms. Human rights are to be enjoyed and respected at all times and in all places, and in the event they are violated, there must be a rapid response to re-establish their protection. This response can only come from the State in question, given that international monitoring is by necessity slow and late, and it would be completely impossible for such monitoring to replace domestic protection with any sort of efficiency. All this is, in principle, reflected in Article 8, which states from the beginning, "[e]very person has the right to a hearing". The European Convention sets forth in Article 6 that "everyone is entitled to a fair and public hearing". The International Covenant on Civil and Political Rights (ICCPR) states in Article 14 that "everyone shall be entitled to a fair and public hearing".[1] The European Court and the Human Rights Committee that supervises compliance with the ICCPR derive from these provisions all that is needed in order to ensure the judicial protection of human rights at the domestic level. In Latin America, however, the drafters of the Convention wished to add a specific remedy called the right to *amparo* – not because Article 8 would not be enough to judicially protect human rights, but in the interest of enriching the remedies with a Latin American construction.

Article 25 of the American Convention purported to be based on these fundamentals. This article would enshrine the individual's right – in certain situations – to have his or her human rights protected effectively, simply and promptly by domestic authorities via a judicial remedy. The importance of this remedy is evident and has been recognized by the Inter-American Court, which has found that Article 25 "is one of the fundamental pillars not only of the American Convention, but of the very rule of law in a democratic society in the terms of the Convention."[2]

The writ of *amparo* has its origins in Latin America. It was born with the Mexican Constitution of 1857 and from there spread to other countries in the region from early on.[3] The Court has recognized this origin, indicating that Article 25(1) is "a general provision that gives expression to the procedural institution known as *amparo*, which is a simple and prompt remedy designed for the protection of all of the rights recognized by the constitutions and laws of the States Parties and by the Convention".[4]

The writ of *amparo* ensures protection when there is a violation of or threat to a fundamental right and the situation must be resolved quickly without using the ordinary actions that are usually long and more complicated. It can be compared to *habeas corpus* or *habeas data* and its difference is that it protects in principle all other constitutional rights; that is why it is considered the generic concept. Although Latin American countries have sometimes deviated from the original idea, there are certain elements that characterize it. It requires that the right violated or threatened be certain, not doubtful; *amparo* will not discuss the existence of the right. The violation or threat must be manifest. Its purpose is to allow the victim to regain the enjoyment of the right affected in a very brief procedure, sometimes not longer than three days.

---

1 International Covenant on Civil and Political Rights, adopted by General Assembly Resolution 2200A (XXI) of December 16, 1966; entry into force March 23, 1976.

2 *Case of Castillo Páez v. Peru*, para. 82; *Case of Suárez Rosero v. Ecuador*, para. 65; and *Case of Blake v. Guatemala*, para. 102.

3 See C.M. Ayala, "Del amparo constitucional al amparo interamericano como institutos para la protección de los derechos humanos," in Inter-American Court, *Liber Amicorum Héctor Fix-Zamudio*, Vol. I, San Jose, Costa Rica, 1998, pp. 341–373 (342–344).

4 *OC-8/87*, para. 32.

2. This clear endeavor was muddled during the drafting of Article 25. The original wording read: "Every person has the right to an effective, simple, and prompt remedy".[5] In its comments on the draft, the Government of the Dominican Republic stated that cases may arise in which protection was "effective" even when it was not "simple and prompt", and argued that the only criteria necessary for a remedy to be legitimate was that it be "effective". It then proposed a new text in which this part is identical to that of the final version.[6] During discussion of the article, the Mexican delegate asked that the text be amended, again suggesting the original wording of a "simple, prompt and effective remedy". The American delegate had a different proposal – a return to the Dominican Republic's text without stating as much. With that exchange, discussion on this particular subject concluded.[7] The Report from the Rapporteur of Commission I clarified that the article contains the right to "a simple, prompt and effective remedy" without clarifying the implications of the new formulation.[8] There is no other background information in the preparatory work.

The change of the wording left Article 25 containing not only the *amparo* remedy, but all other judicial actions that can be exercised by an individual. I believe that the States did not wish to do away with *amparo* proper; they just did not realize what the change of the wording meant. The Court has accepted the article as it stands and treats Article 25 accordingly. The inclusion of all actions possible to exercise before a court dims the essential role that *amparo* has on a continent where authorities and also private individuals are sometimes prone to ignore the Constitution and violate or threaten constitutional rights, perhaps in the hope that a long, ordinary procedure to complain against these actions will deter those affected by these actions from initiating a judicial procedure.

A new addition caused a second problem, which luckily was solved through the Court's interpretations. The original text established the right to an "effective, simple, and prompt remedy before competent domestic judges and courts that protects against acts that violate fundamental rights recognized by the Constitution or by law".[9] This wording was rejected because it did not refer to the human rights set forth in the Convention. In order to fix this omission, two governments proposed inserting a provision similar to Article 2(3) of the ICCPR.[10] They suggested inserting this provision in the text presented as it

5 See text of Article 23 in Inter-American Specialized Conference on Human Rights, San Jose, Costa Rica, November 7–22, 1969, *Minutes and Documents* (OEA/Ser.K/XVI/1.2), p. 22.

6 *Ibidem*, p. 66.

7 *Ibidem*, pp. 261–263.

8 *Ibidem*, pp. 302–303.

9 *Ibidem*, p. 22.

10 Article 2(3) of the ICCPR sets forth three undertakings for States parties: "(a) To ensure that any person whose rights or freedoms as herein recognized are violated shall have an effective remedy, notwithstanding that the violation has been committed by persons acting in an official capacity; (b) To ensure that any person claiming such a remedy shall have his right

was.[11] Article 2(3)'s logic was impeccable, but it had to be taken up in its entirety in order to avoid contradictions. The suggestion, however, was to add it to the original text, where the right to a "judicial" remedy had already been established. Noting this, the Colombian delegate objected to the proposal, stating that the commitment to adjust the domestic legal system to the Convention was already enshrined in Article 1. For this reason, he suggested what seemed to be the obvious solution: simply add a reference to the Convention's rights to the text under discussion. Following a short debate in which Chile explained that the purpose of its proposal was "to establish clearly that the Governments were committed to adopting the proper measures for making the rights effective", the suggestion to reproduce Article 2(3) of ICCPR was passed.[12] This amendment of the original text could have left the idea that the protection in Article 25 was not immediately a judicial one and that there was just a commitment of the States to develop the possibilities to establish it. From a technical legal point of view, the passage of the proposal was a mistake. However, it is clear that the purpose of the change was to emphasize and reinforce the State's obligation to adjust its legal system to the treaty's obligations, as had been done with the addition of Article 2 to the American Convention. The intention was never to change the State obligation set forth in paragraph 1 and this has always been the Court's interpretation.

With these explanations, I will now examine Article 25.

2. ARTICLE 25 AND ITS CONNECTION WITH OTHER PROVISIONS OF THE CONVENTION

3. In order to examine article 25, it is necessary to have regard to the connections this provision has with other rights of the Convention (Articles 7(6), 1(1) and 8), and to the fact that Article 25 covers all the remedies that can operate in any trial.

Article 25 is not the only one that enshrines the right to *amparo* proper for the protection of human rights. The Court has stated that Article 25 has the same purpose as Article 7(6). Article 7(6) of the Convention establishes a specific remedy of *amparo* for the protection of the right to personal freedom – *habeas corpus* – with its own requirements, and that remedy takes priority over the general remedy found in Article 25. In an Advisory Opinion, the Court clarified

thereto determined by competent judicial, administrative or legislative authorities, or by any other competent authority provided for by the legal system of the State, and to develop the possibilities of judicial remedy; (c) To ensure that the competent authorities shall enforce such remedies when granted".

11 Specialized Conference, *supra* n. 5, p. 41 (comments from the government of Chile) and pp. 55–56 (comments from the government of the Dominican Republic).

12 *Ibidem*, pp. 261–263.

that the relationship between the two was one of genus to species,[13] with *habeas corpus* as established in Article 7(6) being the species. Without prejudice to this, the Court often finds that a fact has caused a violation of Article 7(6) and Article 25 at the same time. For example, this happened in the cases of Caballero Delgado and Santana,[14] Suárez Rosero,[15] and Castillo Páez.[16] In the case of Blake, it found that Article 25 "is an important means of determining the whereabouts of persons deprived of their liberty and of preventing forced disappearance in any circumstances".[17] It seemed curious that the Court would find it necessary to consider a fact as simultaneously violating the genus (Article 25) and the species (Article 7(6)); it was more appropriate to rule simply that there has been a violation of the species. In addition, it should be noted that the wording of these two remedies is different: Article 7(6) establishes that the remedy must be resolved "without delay", while Article 25 requires the remedy be "prompt". The difference in wording means that we must decide whether the two provisions differ, and if so, in what way. For example, one could reasonably lean toward an interpretation according to which the time period granted by Article 7(6) is shorter than the one allowed for by Article 25, or lean toward exactly the opposite interpretation. If the concepts are different, it is even more reasonable to draw a distinction between them when making a ruling. It would therefore be extremely useful if the Inter-American Court were to begin to differentiate between the different elements it takes into consideration in deciding whether a violation has taken place, as this would help develop the scope and content of each right more clearly. After many years, this is actually happening. In the case Anzualdo Castro, the victim's representatives requested the Court to declare a violation of Articles 7(6) and 25. The Court recalled that "Articles 7(6), 8(2)(h), and 25 of the Convention relates to different aspects of protection". Then it continued to consider that Article 7(6) had its own "legal content and that the principle of effectiveness (*effet utile*) is interrelated to the duly protection of all the rights enshrined in the treaty", so it found it "unnecessary to analyze such provision in connection with Article 25 of the Convention".[18]

4. There is also an intimate connection between the right to judicial protection and Article 1(1) of the Convention. The existence of a protective remedy is one means to comply with the obligation to guarantee derived from Article 1(1) of

13 On this point, see *OC-8/87*, paras. 33–34.
14 *Case of Caballero Delgado and Santana v. Colombia*, para. 66.
15 *Case of Suárez Rosero v. Ecuador*, paras. 64–66.
16 *Case of Castillo Páez v. Peru*, paras. 81–84.
17 *Case of Blake v. Guatemala*, para. 103. In the same sense, see the *Case of Bámaca Velásquez v. Guatemala*, para. 192.
18 *Case of Anzualdo Castro v. Peru*, para. 77. The same consideration is found in *Vélez Loor v. Panama*, para. 123 and *Contreras et al. v. El Salvador*, para. 157.

the Convention. The majority of the case law on Article 25 of the Convention was already analyzed in the examination of Article 1(1) and Article 8.[19] As far as the connection between Article 25 and Article 1(1) is concerned, for the purposes of this chapter, it is sufficient to cite what seems to be the most suitable interpretation given by the Court:

> This Court has established that "Article 25 is closely linked to the general obligation in Article 1.1 of the American Convention, in that it assigns duties of protection to the States Parties through their domestic legislation" […], from which it is clear that the State has the obligation to design and embody in legislation an effective recourse, and also to ensure the due application of the said recourse by its judicial authorities.[20]

Given the settled case law of the Court to the effect that the violation of any right in the Convention leads automatically to a violation of Article 1(1),[21] it is no surprise that when the Court finds a violation of Article 25, it also finds a violation of Article 1(1). Curiously enough, sometimes a violation of Article 1 is found due to the absence of remedies, yet no violation of Article 25 is declared. This was the case, for example, in the Court's first judgment on preliminary objections in the case of Velásquez Rodríguez, in which Honduras alleged the lack of exhaustion of domestic remedies. There, the Court recalls Article 25 and holds:

> When certain exceptions to the rule of non-exhaustion of domestic remedies are invoked, such as the ineffectiveness of such remedies or the lack of due process of law, not only is it contended that the victim is under no obligation to pursue such remedies, but, indirectly, the State in question is also charged with a new violation of the obligations assumed under the Convention.[22]

The reasoning appears to anticipate a final ruling of a violation of Article 25 should the ineffectiveness or nonexistence of remedies be proven. However, in the judgment on the merits, although the Court finds that the inefficiency of the remedies has been proven, it limits itself to rejecting the preliminary objection, which it had left pending resolution,[23] and declares a violation of Article 1 of the Convention. Perhaps this could be explained if the Court was in reality not examining the Article 25 *amparo* remedy, but rather other domestic remedies according to admissibility rules. However, that explanation does not appear in the text of the judgment. Also, in the case of Neira Alegría, although the

---

19 In the chapters on the right to life and the right to humane treatment, see the corresponding sections on the duty to investigate. See also the chapter on due process, principally the section on the right to a hearing.

20 *Case of the Street Children (Villagran Morales et al.) v. Guatemala*, para. 232.

21 This position was objected, with some justification, in a dissenting vote in the *case of Cantos v. Argentina*. See separate opinion of Judge Julio Barberis.

22 *Case of Velásquez Rodríguez v. Honduras*, para. 91.

23 *Ibidem*, para. 81.

Commission alleged a violation of Articles 1(1) and 25,[24] and the State made reference to the same articles,[25] the Court refrained from ruling on Article 25 and ruled that only Article 1(1) had been violated.[26] These are rather old cases and the position has been different in newer ones. As said above, the writ of *amparo* found in Article 25 is not the only remedy that States' domestic legal systems must establish. In contrast to the remedy found in Article 25 of the Convention, the domestic remedies that must be exhausted can require longer proceedings and may be various in nature. They run the gamut from providing for an action to put a judicial proceeding in motion to remedies that normally form part of a proceeding itself, such as appeal, for example. Naturally, all the remedies would be required to be effective and adequate, with effectiveness including that they do not take longer than necessary to reach a solution.[27]

5. With regard to its relationship with Article 8, the Inter-American Court takes a straightforward approach to the issue in Advisory Opinion 9, contradicted however by subsequent interpretations. The Court indicates that Article 25 enshrines the right to certain remedies – *amparo* and *habeas corpus* – while Article 8 enshrines the way in which they should be made effective, as the remedies are judicial and thus must be processed in accordance with "due process".[28] This position is reiterated in the judgment of Hilaire, Constantine and Benjamín *et al.*, in which the Court stated that:

> In order to protect the right to effective recourse, established in Article 25 of the Convention, it is crucial that the recourse be exercised in conformity with the rules of due process, protected in Article 8 of the Convention, which include access to legal aid.[29]

Without prejudice to this assertion, the dividing line drawn by the Court's case law between Article 25 and Article 8 is often tenuous or, in certain cases, invisible. For example, the Court often finds that the absence of remedies or their lack of effectiveness leads to a violation of Article 8 of the Convention. In addition, it finds that the absence of one of the elements of due process indicated in Article 8 leads to a violation of Article 25 of the Convention. Normally, the Court examines the violation of both articles in the same section of the judgment and combines them, like in the judgment handed down in the Cantos case: "Article 25 of the Convention also upholds the right of access to the courts".[30] This point is illustrated in the case of Ivcher Bronstein; there the Court found

24 *Case of Neira Alegría v. Peru*, paras. 2, 8, 58 and 73.
25 *Ibidem*, para. 59.
26 *Ibidem*, paras. 85 and 91.
27 *Case of Velásquez Rodríguez v. Honduras*, paras. 64, 66–68.
28 *OC-9/87*, para. 24.
29 *Case of Hilaire, Constantine and Benjamin et al. v. Trinidad and Tobago*, para. 148.
30 *Case of Cantos v. Argentina*, para. 52.

that because the requirements that the court be independent and impartial as established in Article 8(1) of the Convention had not been met in the domestic proceedings, the remedies available to the petitioner had not been effective.[31] The Court ruled likewise in the case of Durand and Ugarte. There it examined the problem of bias and lack of independence of military courts and the absence of an effective remedy for investigating the facts and trying and punishing those responsible, as well as failure to provide reparations for the damages, all according to the provisions of Articles 25 and 8(1). It reached the conclusion that both articles had been violated.[32] Here once again one notes the broadness of the interpretation, as it makes Articles 25 and 8 almost indistinguishable.

If we take the judgment in the Mack case as an example, one notes the symbiosis resulting from the simultaneous application of both articles. In that judgment, the Court ruled:

> In view of what the Court has deemed proven with respect to the right to fair trial and judicial protection, the analysis of Articles 8 and 25 will address the following topics: a) gathering of evidence at the scene of the crime; b) alteration and concealment of the report on the police investigation; c) manipulation of the evidence supplied by the Presidential General Staff and the Ministry of National Defense; d) official secret; e) murder of a police investigator; harassment and threats against legal operators, police investigators, members of the Myrna Mack Foundation and of AVANCSO and the next of kin of Myrna Mack Chang; f) lack of diligence of the judges in the criminal proceeding; and g) reasonable term.[33]

The quote shows that everything related to the due process requirements will be examined to decide on the violation of Article 25 and of course Article 8. A mixing of the two articles also happens in the opinion of Judge *Ad Hoc* Ricardo Gil in the Bulacio case, in which he expressed that judges

> must ensure compliance with the rules of due process, enabling unrestricted exercise of the guarantees set forth in Article 8 of the American Convention, but on the other hand they must protect the victim's right to justice (Article 25 of the Convention), the concrete expression of which is delivery of a judgment on the facts and responsibilities.[34]

In the Massacres of El Mozote, the Court found a violation of Articles 8 and 25 because the survivors and the next of kin of those who had died were prevented from being heard by a judge.[35]

This method of applying Article 25 is different from what the Court expressed in Advisory Opinion 9, as in the latter the relationship between the articles allowed for their differentiation. With this interpretation, both Article 8

---

31 *Case of Ivcher Bronstein v. Peru*, para. 139.
32 *Case of Durand and Ugarte v. Peru*, judgment on the merits, paras. 125–127 and 130.
33 *Case of Myrna Mack Chang v. Guatemala*, para. 164.
34 *Case of Bulacio v. Argentina*, separate opinion of Judge Ricardo Gil Lavedra.
35 *Case of the Massacres of El Mozote and Nearby Places v. El Salvador*, para. 295.

and Article 25 enshrine the "right to a hearing"; this does not contribute to the development and expansion of human rights through interpretation. Rather, it leads to a confusing situation, as will be seen in detail below. The interpretation just noted parallels the Court's position addressed during the examination of the issue of the "right to the truth"[36] and responds to the faulty formulation of Article 25 and the Court's interpretation thereof.

6. I think this is a crucial point in the interpretation of this provision. From its formulation, one can conclude that Article 25 indeed contains various remedies. The way the Court has applied it, however, distorts its original purpose of establishing the right to a fast and simple remedy and this is detrimental to the victims. The Court's case law has not developed the scope and content of this right to include the Latin American remedy of *amparo*, thus depriving *amparo* of the prominent position that it should hold. I would argue that beginning the task of identifying which particular prompt, simple and effective remedies must be included in the legal systems of States Parties in order to be in compliance with the obligations of this provision would represent a great step forward for the interpretation of the Convention.

3. CHARACTERISTICS OF THE REMEDY

3.1. JUDICIAL REMEDY

7. Article 25 is innovative with regard to the international law in existence prior to the adoption of the American Convention in the sense that it establishes a remedy that must be judicial. This is in contrast with the provisions of Article 2(3) of the ICCPR and Article 13 of the European Convention, which only require the State to provide an effective remedy.

Like all remedies in the Convention, the remedy in Article 25 exists for all human rights. In a case over a matter of electoral law, Mr. Castañeda, the alleged victim, wished to become a candidate in a presidential election, but was not eligible since the Mexican law required that he be appointed as such by a political party. If that had been the case and the Electoral Office had rejected him, he could have had a remedy to complain against that rejection. As the situation was, no remedy existed.[37] The Court found a violation of Article 25 since "there was no effective remedy in Mexico enabling an individual to question the legal regulation of the political right to be elected established in the Constitution and in the American Convention".[38] In addition, in the case of Abril Alosilla, the violation of Article 25 consisted in not having an appropriate remedy to

36 See Chapter 6.

37 *Case of Castañeda Guzmán v, Mexico*, para. 114.

38 *Ibidem*, para. 131. See also *Case of Yatama v. Nicaragua*, para. 172.

challenge the retroactive application of a labor law to 233 members of a labor union.[39] In the cases of Quintana Coello *et al.* and the case of Camba Campos *et al.*, both versus Ecuador, the Court found a violation of Article 25.[40] In the former, judges of the Supreme Court had ceased in their function by a decision of the National Congress, and they had not had a judicial remedy to complain of this decision.[41] In the latter, members of the Constitutional Court were dismissed and impeached and no remedy could be invoked against Congress. Again, a violation of Article 25 was found.[42] In the case of García Lucero, the Court decided that the existence of an administrative reparation program that had favored the victim could not obstruct the exercise of the right to judicial guarantees and protection to claim further reparations.[43] Finally, in the case of the Pacheco Tineo family, expelled from Bolivia in a swift action that lasted hours, the family had a right to a judicial remedy to contest both their expulsion and possible violations committed when their status as refugees was denied, a right they could not exercise because of their expulsion.[44]

3.2. SIMPLE AND PROMPT REMEDY

8. The Convention establishes the right to a "simple and prompt" remedy, adding "or any other effective recourse". The first question is whether the qualification of "simple and prompt" should be applied to all remedies or only to the *amparo* remedy. The formulation of Article 25 would point toward finding that these adjectives are to be applied only to the *amparo* remedy. Therefore, for example, in Advisory Opinion 9/87, the Court states that Article 25(1) "gives expression to the procedural institution known as *amparo*, which is a simple and prompt remedy designed for the protection of all the fundamental rights." The Opinion adds that "[t]his article also establishes in broad terms the obligation of the States to provide an effective judicial remedy to violations of fundamental rights to all persons within their jurisdiction." The Court's conclusion appears to favor the application of one common characteristic, "effectiveness", to all remedies and the other two, "simple and prompt", only to *amparo*. The difference between remedies is reiterated in the Apitz *et al.* case, where the Court reflects on the dissimilarity between the duration of *amparo* and that of an appeal for annulment. The judgment concedes, "the *amparo* should be a 'simple and prompt recourse,' pursuant to the terms of Article 25(1) of the Convention, while the annulment should be decided 'within a reasonable time,' in accordance with

39 *Case of Abril Alosilla et al. v. Peru*, para. 2.
40 These facts were also examined with respect to Article 8, since the Court found a violation of both Articles 25 and 8.
41 *Case of the Supreme Court of Justice (Quintana Coello et al.) v. Ecuador*, paras. 189–194.
42 *Case of the Constitutional Tribunal (Camba Campos et al.) v. Ecuador*, para. 238.
43 *Case of García Lucero v. Chile*, para. 190.
44 *Case of Familia Pacheco Tineo v. Estado Plurinacional de Bolivia*, paras. 192 and 195.

Article 8(1) thereof".[45] The position seems a sensible one, but it is not what the Court normally does by using the three requirements together for every type of procedure.[46]

9. The Court's case law still does not provide a guide for deciding when the remedy enshrined in Article 25 is "simple and prompt". As far as simplicity is concerned, there has been no ruling describing it in the terms of Article 25. Regarding the promptness of the remedy, the Court frequently analyzes it in connection with the parameters of reasonable time as established in Article 8 of the Convention contrary to what it did in Apitz. In the case of Ivcher Bronstein, it addressed the subject by stating that:

> Likewise, the general circumstances of this case indicate that the judicial recourses filed by Mr. Ivcher to defend his shareholder's rights were not simple and prompt; to the contrary, as the witness Emilio Rodríguez Larraín declared during the public hearing, "they were only resolved after a long time", which contrasts with the process given to the actions filed by the minority shareholders of the Company, which were resolved promptly.[47]

In the case of Cantos, the Court found that:

> [C]onsidering [...] the complexity of the case and the plaintiff's failure to take action to move the case forward, the overall duration of the litigious proceedings would not be significant enough for a finding that the articles that protect access to the courts and judicial guarantees have been violated.[48]

It does not seem possible to argue that the simplicity and promptness of an *amparo* remedy can be measured with the same standard as that of a reasonable time for concluding the trial. Furthermore, one clearly cannot argue that a ruling on such a remedy can last many years, even if there has been a "lack of interest on the part of the plaintiff".

In the case of Suárez Rosero, the Court connected the right to a writ of *habeas corpus* as established in Article 7(6) of the Convention with the rights established in Article 25. The Court found that 14 months was an excessive delay for ruling on the request for a remedy, and that therefore Articles 7(6) and 25 of the Convention had been violated.[49] In the case of the Constitutional Court, the Court based its ruling in part on the period given in Peru's own legal system for processing *amparo* remedies. It found that a remedy that had been ruled on more than six months after it was invoked, while Peruvian law gave a maximum and

45 *Case of Apitz v. Venezuela*, para. 170.

46 As examples, see *Case of Suárez Rosero v. Ecuador*, para. 66 and *Case of Yatama v. Nicaragua*, para. 254.

47 *Case of Ivcher Bronstein v. Peru*, para. 140.

48 *Ibidem*, para. 57. This decision was already criticized for other reasons in Chapter 6 on Article 8 of the Convention.

49 *Case of Suárez Rosero v. Ecuador*, paras. 64–66.

final deadline of twenty days, violated Article 25 of the American Convention.[50] In the case of Apitz, the Court found that three years to decide a precautionary *amparo* was contrary to the notion of "prompt".[51]

From another angle, in the case of Myrna Mack Chang, the Court used the delay the processing of *amparos* brought by the plaintiff as a basis for finding a violation of Articles 8 and 25 to the detriment of the relatives of the victim. If affirmed that in Guatemala *amparo* remedies could be ruled on in up to four different instances, paralyzing the main criminal trial where the facts of a violation of human rights were being investigated. Therefore, they were remedies that delayed the proceedings,[52] not to the detriment of the individual submitting them, but to the detriment of those who sought to hold the perpetrators of human rights violations criminally responsibility for their actions.[53]

3.3. EFFECTIVE REMEDY

10. The Court's case law on the requirement of the existence of an "effective" remedy is abundant.[54] In the judgment on the merits in the case of Velásquez Rodríguez, the Court explained the meaning of the word "effective," indicating that the remedy must be "capable of producing the result for which it was designed".[55] It added that this did not mean that all remedies must necessarily be granted, but rather that there must be at least a serious possibility that they will be.[56] Advisory Opinion 9/87 expanded on this argument, finding that a remedy that was "illusory because of the general conditions prevailing in the country, or even in the particular circumstances of a given case, cannot be considered effective". This would be the case, for example, where the judiciary lacks independence or has no means to enforce its judgments.[57]

Often, the Court associates the meaning of effective with the possibility of an individual to use it or describes it in quite a different manner. In the case of Tibi,

50 *Case of the Constitutional Court v. Peru*, para. 91.

51 *Case of Apitz v. Venezuela*, para. 171.

52 *Case of Myrna Mack Chang v. Guatemala*, paras. 204–205.

53 On this point, I would refer to the discussion of the role of the victim in a criminal proceeding. See Chapter 6.

54 I would add the caveat that much of this case law involves rulings on Article 7(6) and Article 8.

55 *Case of Velásquez Rodríguez v. Honduras*, para. 66.

56 *Ibidem*, paras. 67 and 68. Also see, *inter alia*, *OC-9/87*, para. 24; *Case of the Mayagna (Sumo) Awas Tingni Community v. Nicaragua*, paras. 111–113; *Case of the Constitutional Court v. Peru*, para. 90; *Case of Bámaca Velásquez v. Guatemala*, para. 191; *Case of Cesti Hurtado v. Peru*, para. 125; *Case of Paniagua et al. v. Guatemala*, para. 164; and *Case of Suárez Rosero v. Ecuador*, para. 63.

57 *OC-9/87*, para. 24. Also see, *inter alia*, *Case of Paniagua Morales et al. v. Guatemala*, para. 164; *Case of Suárez Rosero v. Ecuador*, para. 63; *Case of Ivcher Bronstein v. Peru*, paras. 136–137; *Case of Cantos v. Argentina*, para. 52; and *Abril Alosilla v. Peru*, para. 75.

effective was explained in the sense that "the individual must have an effective possibility of filing a simple and prompt remedy that enables attainment, if appropriate, of the judicial protection requested".[58] The same was said in Acosta Calderón[59] and in Palamara.[60] In Reverón Trujillo, the domestic remedy employed by the victim was not effective because it did not offer the adequate reparations.[61] In the López Mendoza case the Court recalled that the remedy had to be "truly effective". In it the Court examined "whether the decisions taken there contributed effectively to end the violation of rights, to ensure the non-repetition of the wrongful acts, and to ensure the free and full exercise of rights protected by the Convention".[62] The judgment found a violation of Article 25 because the judicial appeals filed by the victim were not effective in providing protection of his right to be elected and his right to have a cause established for his disqualification.[63]

In consonance to the interpretation that Article 25 contains all possible remedies within a trial, the Court measures effectiveness by the remedy's potential capacity to achieve the whole spectrum of results expected from a full compliance with the obligation to ensure.

11. The lack of effectiveness of remedies is often the result of a situation and not of the facts of a specific case, and that has a bearing on the rules of evidence. As a rule, the Court considers that States in situations of massive and systematic violations fail to provide effective remedies, because the ineffectiveness of the remedies is in reality an aspect of the situation.[64] In the case of Bámaca Velásquez, who disappeared after his apprehension by State agents, the Court found that the lack of effectiveness of *habeas corpus* in Guatemala had been proven as there was in the State an intense internal conflict.[65] The Court has also found remedies to be ineffective because the individuals affected were prevented from exercising the remedies in practice. This is the case when individuals are secretly detained, secret detention being common in situations of massive and systematic violations. The Court's case law on this issue has not been consistent. In the case of the Street Children, in which the victims were detained for several hours before being executed, the Court ruled that Article 25 had been violated

58 *Case of Tibi v. Ecuador*, para. 114.
59 *Case of Acosta Calderón v. Peru*, para. 93.
60 *Case of Palamara v. Chile*, para. 184.
61 *Case of Reverón Trujillo v. Venezuela*, para. 127.
62 *Case of López Mendoza v. Venezuela*, para. 184.
63 *Ibidem*, para. 185.
64 On this point, see C. Medina, *The Battle of Human Rights. Gross, Systematic Violations and the Inter-American System*, Martinus Nijhoff, Dordrecht/Boston/London, 1988, pp. 15–16.
65 *Case of Bámaca Velásquez v. Guatemala*, para. 193. In addition, the Court considered the statements of the president of the Guatemalan Supreme Court himself to the effect that the "mechanisms that currently exist for habeas corpus procedures are inadequate to carry out an effective investigation under petitions for habeas corpus."

because the victims – both adults and minors – and third parties representing them were prevented from exercising the right to seek an effective remedy, *habeas corpus*, before domestic courts.[66] In contrast, in the case of Caballero Delgado and Santana, the Court did not find that Article 8 of the Convention – which, as mentioned above, the Court often applies jointly with Article 25 – had been violated. The reason given was "the short time that transpired between the capture of the persons [...] and their presumed death[s]"[67] under circumstances in which the victims would not have been able to make use of the remedy. In both cases, the relatives would have been able to request a remedy, but only the mother of the victim in the second case had done so, to no avail. In the case of Paniagua Morales, the basis of the violation with regard to several of the murder victims was that prior to their deaths, they had been in the hands of State agents and there was no evidence that while in that situation they had had access in any way "to the judicial remedy that would have guaranteed both their freedom and their lives".[68] With regard to Ms. Paniagua Morales, the writ of *habeas corpus* sought by the relatives was not successful "because from the time she was detained by members of the Treasury Police her whereabouts were unknown and she was subsequently found dead", thus proving "the ineffectiveness of the remedy of *habeas corpus*".[69] However, as explained above, in the case of Caballero Delgado and Santana similar circumstances led to a different ruling. In that case, the writ of *habeas corpus* sought by the relatives brought no results either due to the denial of the facts by the respective State agents. The Court found that this did not constitute a violation of Article 25 of the Convention.[70]

12. In some cases, the basis of a violation of Article 25 has been that State agents blocked the processing of a writ of habeas corpus, for example in the case of Castillo Páez. In that judgment, the Court found "that the remedy filed by Mr. Castillo-Páez' next-of-kin against his detention (*habeas corpus*) was obstructed by State agents through the adulteration of the logs of entry of detainees, which made it impossible to locate the victim." For this reason, the writ of *habeas corpus* was ineffective and Article 25 of the Convention had been violated.[71] However, in the case of Genie Lacayo, in which the Commission argued for violations of Articles 8, 25 and 24, and in which the Court found that Nicaragua's military authorities' obstruction or failure to collaborate adequately in the proceedings were proved, the Court decided differently. It only found a violation of Article 8 but not Article 25, because "the Commission has indicated

66 *Case of Villagrán Morales et al. v. Guatemala*, para. 236.
67 *Case of Caballero Delgado and Santana v. Colombia*, para. 64.
68 *Case of Paniagua Morales et al. v. Guatemala* para. 167.
69 *Ibidem*, para. 166.
70 *Case of Caballero Delgado and Santana v. Colombia*, para. 66.
71 *Case of Castillo Páez v. Peru*, paras. 81–83. In the same sense, see *Case of Suárez Rosero v. Ecuador*, para. 65.

the possible violation of [...] procedural rights protected under Article 8(1) of the Convention".[72] It seems that the Court found that the obstruction was not enough to rule that Article 25 had been violated because the father of the victim had been able to take part in the military proceeding, offer evidence, execute the corresponding remedies, and bring a cassation appeal before the Supreme Court.[73] Blake is a similar case. Therein, the Court ruled that Article 25 had not been violated because the father of Blake, whose body had been missing for several years, had not specifically sought a writ of *habeas corpus*. This in spite of one of Blake's relatives stating in the hearing before the Court that they had not pursued a judicial action because "the State alleged that the area in question was controlled by the army and that it was better to deal directly with the military officials".[74] The obstruction by State agents of the criminal proceeding opened in this case was not enough for the Court to find that Article 25 of the American Convention had been violated.[75]

13. Of course, the lack of effectiveness can also be specific to a single case. The Court has found that when a court sets court or legal fees that are unreasonably high, this is "an obstruction to effective administration of justice" and a violation of Articles 25 and 8 of the Convention.[76] In the case of the Constitutional Court, the lack of impartiality of the members of the Constitutional Court was enough to find a violation of Article 25.[77] In addition, if the law itself does not grant the remedy, the violation is a general one and clear. In two cases against Peru in which the victims were individuals being tried for terrorism, the Court ruled that the fact that Peruvian law did not admit the remedy of *habeas corpus* for the plaintiffs constituted a violation of Article 25 of the American Convention.[78] The Court has also connected the application of the statute of limitations to a pending trial with the right set forth in Article 25, indicating that:

> the general obligations enshrined in Articles 1(1) and 2 of the American Convention require that the States Party adopt timely provisions of all types for no one to be denied the right to judicial protection, enshrined in Article 25 of the American Convention.[79]

14. From all of this case law one can see that the Court does not distinguish *amparo* from other remedies and does not differentiate between *amparo* and

72 *Case of Genie Lacayo v. Nicaragua*, paras. 68, 76 and 89.
73 *Ibidem*, para. 85.
74 *Case of Blake v. Guatemala*, paras. 100 and 104.
75 *Ibidem*, paras. 89, 92 and 93.
76 *Case of Cantos v. Argentina*, para. 54–56.
77 *Case of the Constitutional Court v. Peru*, para. 96.
78 *Case of Loayza Tamayo v. Peru*, paras. 52–55; *Case of Castillo Petruzzi et al. v. Peru*, paras. 180–181.
79 *Case of Bulacio v. Argentina*, para. 116.

habeas corpus. These two confusions have prevented a development of the remedy that the States wished to set forth when the idea of Article 25 emerged and which, as noted earlier, constituted an important instrument to protect individuals mainly from abuses by State organs.

4. STATE OBLIGATIONS

15. Paragraph 1 of Article 25 sets forth the right of every individual to a simple, prompt remedy or to other remedies that prove effective. From this prescription, one can deduce the State's obligations in their regard. According to paragraph 1, States must set forth in their legal orders one remedy – *amparo* – which has to be simple and prompt, and other remedies, the characteristics of which are not determined except for the requirement of being effective. The remedies must be heard by a competent court or tribunal and protect the rights in the Convention and those in the Constitution and laws of the State. Since they are judicial remedies, the decisions on the remedies must be enforced. Despite this, paragraph 2 of the provision sets forth other obligations of States, in my view unnecessary and confusing. Had Article 25 remained as it was when first drafted, with the addition that it would also protect the human rights of the Convention, much uncertainty would have been avoided. Uncertainty would also have been less if the Court had interpreted the provision uniformly in the sense that paragraph 2 was unnecessary and that paragraph 1 established different types of remedies with different characteristics that should be treated accordingly. In this section, I will deal with paragraph 2(c), which establishes the obligation of local authorities to ensure enforcement of such remedies when granted. I think it is important not to read that paragraph 2(c) to the detriment of Article 8 on a fair trial.

16. Strangely enough, the idea that the enforcement of a judicial decision was "one of the elements that comprises jurisdiction" appears early in the Court with regard to its own jurisdiction to monitor compliance with its judgments. In the case Baena *et al.*, where this idea was expressed, the Court states that otherwise "the judgments delivered by the Court are merely declaratory and not effective". Stronger yet is its consideration that "[c]ompliance with the reparations ordered by the Court in its decisions is the materialization of justice for the specific case and, ultimately, of jurisdiction; to the contrary, the *raison d'être* for the functioning of the Court would be imperiled".[80] This notwithstanding, the Court added cryptically that this compliance was "strongly related to the right to access to justice, which is embodied in Articles 8 [...] and 25 [...] of the American Convention".[81]

---

80 *Case of Baena et al. v. Panama*, judgment on competence, para 72.

81 *Ibidem*, para. 74.

The treatment of Articles 25 and 8, however, has not been consistent with this approach. For example, the Court took a somewhat bizarre position in the case of Acevedo Buendía *et al.* (discharged and retired employees of the Office of the Comptroller), where it dealt with the lack of enforcement of certain judgments of the Constitutional Court of Peru. It started with a consideration based on cases of the European Court. The European Convention contained no equivalent to Article 25 but that Court had found the right to a fair trial "would be illusory if a Contracting State's domestic legal system allowed a final, binding judicial decision to remain inoperative to the detriment of one party [to the case]". Consequently, the European Court had decided that "[e]xecution of a judgment given by any court must therefore be regarded as an integral part of the 'trial' for the purposes of Article 6".[82] This was the Court's position in the case of Baena *et al.* mentioned above. Nevertheless, in Acevedo Buendía the Court found a violation of Article 25, not of Article 8, because of the failure of the State to comply with these final judgments and because it failed to carry out the proper execution of an order of habeas corpus.[83] The lack of consistency is found again in the case of Operation Genesis. There the Court attributes solely to Article 25 the State's obligation to have judicial decisions enforced, although it had stated that "a judgment that is *res judicata* grants certainty in relation to the right or dispute examined in the specific case and, consequently, one of its effects is the obligation or need to comply with it",[84] adding that a judgment not executed supposes the denial of the right involved.[85]

17. On examination of the case law,[86] one can conclude that the interpretation of Article 25 considers this provision as the sole rule to set forth the obligation of States to see to it that a judgment is executed. With this interpretation, one should conclude that Article 8 – which sets forth the right to a fair trial – protects access to justice and regulates the requirements that will make a trial fair but stops short of protecting the judgment's execution. This sounds odd. What would happen if a State were to make a reservation on Article 25? How would the European Court, which does not have an equivalent to Article 25, find a violation of Article 6 when a judicial decision has not been executed? Again, this is a diminution of the concept of due process. The Court should revise and interpret these provisions in a manner that gives both Articles 8 and 25 their rightful autonomy.

---

82 *Ibidem*, para. 71, quoting *Case of Hornsby v. Greece*, Judgment of March 19, 1997, para. 40; *Case of Popov v. Moldova*, Judgment of January 18, 2005, no. 74153/01, para. 40; *Case of Assanidze v. Georgia*, Judgment of April 8, 2004, no. 71503/01, para. 182; *Case of Jasiúniene v. Lithuania*, Judgment of March 6, 2003, no. 41510/98, para. 27, and *Case of Burdov v. Russia*, Judgment of May 7, 2002, no. 59498/00, para. 34.

83 *Case of Acevedo Buendía v. Peru*, para. 73.

84 *Case of Camba Campo et al. v. Ecuador*, para. 229.

85 *Case of the Afro-Descendant communities displaced from the Cacarica River Basin (Operation Genesis) v. Colombia*, para. 405.

86 This examination can be seen in Chapter 6, section 4.5.

5. THE RIGHT TO A REMEDY AND STATES OF EMERGENCY

18. Article 27 of the Convention, which limits the way in which States can suspend the obligations implicit in the Convention in an emergency situation, includes among its limitations a list of rights whose obligations may never be suspended. That list concludes with a ban on the suspension of the judicial guarantees that are indispensable for protecting the rights contained in the Convention.[87]

As Article 27(2) does not link the guarantees to any specific provision of the Convention, it is the responsibility of the body applying the Convention to decide to which provisions the article applies. The Court moved to interpret the wording in two Advisory Opinions. In the first, at the request of the Inter-American Commission, it addressed the situation of *habeas corpus* in the case of an emergency situation, a remedy provided for in Article 7(6) of the Convention, and on the right to a simple and prompt remedy for preventing human rights violations, as established in Article 25.[88] In the second Advisory Opinion, this time requested by the government of Uruguay, it interpreted Articles 8 and 25.[89]

19. Regarding Article 25(1), the Court based its opinion on two basic suppositions: firstly, the need to examine which proceedings will effectively guarantee the full exercise of the rights and freedoms protected by Article 27, in order to advise or give an opinion on which guarantees may not be suspended;[90] and secondly, the need to be aware that the non-derogable guarantees are different depending on the rights affected. As examples, the Court pointed to the guarantees of the rights protecting personal integrity and name.[91]

The Court began its analysis of the suspension of guarantees regime in general terms, indicating that the abuses that could arise from the State authority to suspend obligations as set forth in the Convention could not be ignored or left aside. Consequently, "the Court must emphasize that the suspension of guarantees cannot be disassociated from the 'effective exercise of representative democracy' referred to in Article 3 of the OAS Charter".[92] Thus, it establishes as the condition for the regulation of suspensions of guarantees that they may not affect representative democracy. Next, it states that the suspension of guarantees does not entail "a temporary suspension of the rule of law", nor does it authorize a government "to act in disregard of the principle of legality by which they are

---

87 While the subject of states of emergency was already discussed in Chapter 1, this is a more appropriate place to develop this aspect of it.

88 *OC-8/87.*

89 *OC-9/87.*

90 *OC-8/87*, paras. 27 and 29.

91 *Ibidem*, para. 28.

92 *Ibidem*, para. 20.

bound at all times", as "the principle of legality, democratic institutions and the rule of law" are inseparable.[93] The Court structures its opinion based on this, placing special emphasis on the fact that the guarantees referred to in Article 27 are "judicial," stating that:

> The expression "judicial" can only refer to those judicial remedies that are truly capable of protecting these rights. Implicit in this conception is the active involvement of an *independent and impartial* judicial body having the power to pass on the lawfulness of measures adopted in a state of emergency.[94]

This statement is important if one considers that in the countries on this continent, authority in a state of emergency is often given to military courts that do not meet the required conditions of independence and impartiality.

Using these ideas as a basis, the Court found first that with regard to the rights set forth in Article 27(2), both Article 25(1) – genus – and Article 7(6) – species – represent judicial guarantees that cannot be suspended, arguing additionally that they also serve "to preserve legality in a democratic society".[95] Second, legal provisions authorizing, expressly or by implication, the suspension of *habeas corpus* or of *amparo* in states of emergency are incompatible with the Convention.[96] Of course, remedies that protect rights which are not suspended during a state of emergency cannot be suspended either.[97] The second Advisory Opinion repeats these arguments with regard to Article 25(1) and examines Article 8 in detail, concluding that, as examined previously, Article 8 contains the requirements necessary to give substance to the remedies set forth in Article 25(1).

20. The Court has applied this interpretation in several contentious cases. In the case of Durand and Ugarte, the problem arose of ruling on the limitations that the application of certain decrees declaring an emergency in Peru had imposed on judges hearing *amparo* pleas. Those limitations prevented judges from entering the prisons because they were located in restricted military zones. Therein, the Court considered that in a state of emergency there was a general requirement to have appropriate means to control measures taken, to verify they are proportionate and within the limits imposed by the Convention.[98] Taking that into consideration, this limitation on the judges made the writ of *habeas corpus* – the appropriate remedy for establishing the whereabouts of victims – useless, and therefore the limitations were not permissible during a state of

93 *Ibidem*, para. 24.
94 *Ibidem*, para. 30 (emphasis added).
95 *Ibidem*, paras. 44 and 42.
96 *Ibidem*, para. 43.
97 *OC-9/87*, para. 46.
98 *Case of Durand and Ugarte v. Peru*, para. 99.

emergency.[99] Similar arguments and conclusions can be found in the judgment in the case of Cantoral Benavides.[100] The case law of the Court on this point is of great value and has undoubtedly served as inspiration for other international supervisory bodies for the broadening of their interpretations of the rules they apply toward consolidating the need for the right to a simple, prompt and effective remedy to remain in force during periods of emergency.

99 *Ibidem*, paras. 100, 103, 108 and 109.

100 *Case of Cantoral Benavides v. Peru*, paras. 165–166.

INDEX*

* The numbers refer to the page numbering.

www.ingramcontent.com/pod-product-compliance
Ingram Content Group UK Ltd.
Pitfield, Milton Keynes, MK11 3LW, UK
UKHW051919100926
8556IPUK00021B/1267

9 781780 683218